The Destruction and Heroism of the Town of Markuszow
(Markuszów, Poland)

Translation of
Hurbana u-gevurata shel ha-ayara Markuszow

Original Book Edited by: David Shtokfish

Originally published in Tel Aviv, 1955

A Publication of JewishGen
Edmond J. Safra Plaza, 36 Battery Place, New York, NY 10280
646.494.2972 | info@JewishGen.org | www.jewishgen.org

©JewishGen 2025. All Rights Reserved.
JewishGen is the Genealogical Research Division of the
Museum of Jewish Heritage – A Living Memorial to the Holocaust

The Destruction and Heroism of the Town of Markuszow (Markuszów, Poland)
Translation of *Hurbana u-gevurata shel ha-ayara Markuszow*

Copyright © 2025 by JewishGen. All rights reserved.
First Printing: April 2025, Nissan, 5785
Original Yizkor Book Edited By: David Shtokfish
Project Coordinator and translator: Moses Milstein
Cover Design: Rachel Kolokoff Hopper
Layout, formatting and indexing: Jonathan Wind

This book may not be reproduced, in whole or in part, including illustrations in any form (beyond that copying permitted by Sections 107 and 108 of the U.S. Copyright Law and except by reviewers for public press), without written permission from the publisher.

JewishGen Press is not responsible for inaccuracies or omissions in the original work and makes no representations regarding the accuracy of this translation. Digital images of the original book's contents can be seen online at the New York Public Library website or the Yiddish Book Center website.

Library of Congress Control Number (LCCN): 2025932224

ISBN: 978-1-962054-24-9 (hard cover: 344 pages, alk. paper)

About JewishGen.org

JewishGen, is a Genealogical Research Division of the Museum of Jewish Heritage - A Living Memorial to the Holocaust, serves as the global home for Jewish genealogy.

Featuring unparalleled access to 30+ million records, it offers unique search tools, along with opportunities for researchers to connect with others who share similar interests. Award winning resources such as the Family Finder, Discussion Groups, and ViewMate, are relied upon by thousands each day.

In addition, JewishGen's extensive informational, educational and historical offerings, such as the Jewish Communities Database, Yizkor Book translations, InfoFiles, Family Tree of the Jewish People, and KehilaLinks, provide critical insights, first-hand accounts, and context about Jewish communal and familial life throughout the world.

Offered as a free resource, JewishGen.org has facilitated thousands of family connections and success stories, and is currently engaged in an intensive expansion effort that will bring many more records, tools, and resources to its collections.

Please visit https://www.jewishgen.org/ to learn more.

Vice President for JewishGen: Avraham Groll

About the JewishGen Yizkor Book Project

Yizkor Books (Memorial Books) were traditionally written to memorialize the names of departed family and martyrs during holiday services in the synagogue (a practice that still exists in many synagogues today).

Over the centuries, as a result of countless persecutions and horrific atrocities committed against the Jews, Yizkor Books (Sefer Zikaron in Hebrew) were expanded to include more historical information, such as biographical sketches of famous personalities and descriptions of daily town life.

Following the Holocaust, the idea of remembrance and learning took on an urgent and crucial importance. Survivors of the Holocaust sought out other surviving residents of their former towns to memorialize and document the names and way of life of those who were ruthlessly murdered by the Nazis. These remembrances were documented in Yizkor Books, hundreds of which were published in the first decades after the Holocaust.

Most of these books were published privately, or through *Landsmanshaftn* (social organizations comprised of members originating from the same European town or region) that still existed, and were often distributed free of charge. The languages used to document these crucial histories and links to our past were mostly Yiddish and Hebrew. JewishGen has undertaken the sacred responsibility of translating these books into English so that the culture and way of life of these communities will be preserved and transmitted to future generations.

In 1986, a group of farsighted JewishGenners started a project to pool their efforts together in groups based upon their ancestors' towns and donate funds to translate the Yizkor books of their ancestral towns into English. As the translated material became available, it was made accessible for free at https://www.JewishGen.org/Yizkor . Hardcover copies can be purchased by visiting https://www.jewishgen.org/Yizkor/ybip.html (see section below).

It is our hope that the translation of these books into English (and other languages) will assist the countless Jewish family researchers who are so desperately seeking to forge a connection with their heritage.

Director of JewishGen Yizkor Book Project: Lance Ackerfeld

About JewishGen Press

JewishGen Press (formerly the Yizkor Books-in-Print Project) is the publishing division of JewishGen.org, and provides a venue for the publication of non-fiction books pertaining to Jewish genealogy, history, culture, and heritage.

In addition to the Yizkor Book category, publications in the Other Non-Fiction category include Shoah memoirs and research, genealogical research, collections of genealogical and historical materials, biographies, diaries and letters, studies of Jewish experience and cultural life in the past, academic theses, and other books of interest to the Jewish community.

Please visit https://www.jewishgen.org/Yizkor/ybip.html to learn more.

Director of JewishGen Press: Joel Alpert
Managing Editor – Peter Harris
Publications Manager - Susan Rosin

Notes to the Reader

The images in the original book were reproduced from photographs from the time of the first edition. These reproductions were already of poor quality, most being pre-war and others at least 60 or more years old. As a result, the images in the book are the best achievable.
A reader can view the original scans of the book on the websites listed below.

The original book can be seen online at the Yiddish Book Center website:

https://www.yiddishbookcenter.org/collections/yizkor-books/yzk-nybc313881/sztokfisz-david-hurbn-un-gvure-fun-shtetl-markushov-hurbanah-ve-gevuratah

OR

at the New York Public Library Digital Collections website:

https://digitalcollections.nypl.org/search/index?keywords=markuszow

To obtain a list of Shoah victims from **Markuszow (Markuszów, Poland),** the reader should access the Yad Vashem web site listed below; one can also search for specific family names using family name option. These lists are continually updated by Yad Vashem, so it is worthwhile to periodically search them.

There is more valuable information (including the Pages of Testimony, etc.) available on this website: https://yvng.yadvashem.org/

A list of all books available from JewishGen Press along with prices is available at:
https://www.jewishgen.org/Yizkor/ybip.html

Cover Photo Credits

Front and Back Cover Background Cover and Texture: Rachel Kolokoff Hopper

Front Cover and Illustration and the Background:

At the shtetl's entrance stood broadly growing Linden trees on both sides of the road—a sort of natural entry gate to Markuszow. The leaves of the trees served as important remedies. Using steeped "Linden tea" we treated stomachaches, various kinds of pain and diseases. But more than anything, they provided shade for the passerby, cooled his heat, and drove away fatigue. Every wanderer wanted to have the satisfaction of having a nap under the Linden trees. The oldsters would tell of how a Markuszow nobleman, a good-hearted man, ordered the planting of these trees in 1815 on both sides of the road, so that tired travelers could benefit from the shade and rest. Later, another nobleman from Garbow planted cherry trees the length of the road with the same good intent so that the lone traveler could refresh himself. [Page 14]. By Rachel Kolokoff Hopper

Back Cover Photos:

Top Left:
Chanaleh Grossman, the rescued child—now in Israel. [Page 344]
Top Right:
From left to right: Esther Grossman-Kitenkorn, her rescued little daughter, the farmer lady, Shikora. Standing center: Levi Grossman. [Page 343]
Bottom Left:
Kalman and Malkeh Gothelf. [Page 404]
Bottom Right:
Markuszow besmedreshniks. Seated left to right: Aryeh Weinriber, Avraham Rothstein, (future Krasnystow rabbi). Standing from left to right: Shmuel Goldstein, Chaim Wiener. [Page 136]

Geopolitical Information

Map of Poland showing the location of **Markuszów**

Markuszów

Markuszów, Poland is located at 51°22' N 22°16' E and 82 miles SE of Warszawa

	Town	District	Province	Country
Before WWI (c. 1900):	Markuszów	Puławy	Lublin	Russian Empire
Between the wars (c. 1930):	Markuszów	Puławy	Lublin	Poland
After WWII (c. 1950):	Markuszów			Poland
Today (c. 2000):	Markuszów			Poland

Alternate Names for the Town:

Markuszów [Pol], Markushov [Yid], Markushuv [Rus], Markushev

Nearby Jewish Communities:

Kurów 3 miles WNW
Wąwolnica 8 miles SW
Końskowola 9 miles WNW
Michów 10 miles N
Kamionka 11 miles NE
Bełżyce 13 miles S
Puławy 13 miles WNW
Kazimierz Dolny 14 miles WSW
Baranów 15 miles NNW
Lublin 15 miles ESE
Wieniawa 15 miles ESE
Jeziorzany 16 miles N
Firlej 17 miles NE
Janowiec 17 miles W
Majdanek 17 miles ESE
Lubartów 17 miles ENE
Chodel 18 miles SSW
Głusk 19 miles SE
Opole Lubelskie 20 miles SW
Bobrowniki 20 miles NW

Kock 20 miles NNE
Granica 21 miles WNW
Gniewoszów 21 miles WNW
Irena 22 miles NW
Serokomla 23 miles N
Dęblin 23 miles NW
Ryki 23 miles NW
Adamów 25 miles N
Sieciechów 26 miles WNW
Stężyca 26 miles NW
Łęczna 27 miles ESE
Czemierniki 27 miles NE
Ostrów Lubelski 27 miles ENE
Bychawa 27 miles SSE
Urzędów 27 miles S
Solec 27 miles SW
Józefów nad Wisłą 28 miles SW
Garbatka 28 miles WNW
Zwoleń 29 miles W
Zakrzówek 29 miles SSE
Lipsko 30 miles WSW

JewishPoulation in 1897: 1,123

Project Coordinator Introduction

The contributors to the Markuszow yizkor book describe their town as having been much the same as every one of the thousand shtetls in Poland before the Second World War. And in most respects, this was true. There were the same nascent, vibrant youth organizations, filled with starry-eyed young people looking to Zionism for a better future, the same local welfare institutions trying to ameliorate the poverty and discrimination that characterized generations of Jewish life in the shtetl, the same conflicts between the old religious order and the secular movements of the twentieth century, and the same tragic end as all the rest.

The Markuszow yizkor book, however, distinguishes itself from many of the other yizkor books by its testimonies of the partisan movement. Although the existence of Jewish partisan groups was not unique to Markuszow, in most cases, tragically, there were very few survivors to tell the tale. This yizkor book contains documentation of the heroic resistance mounted by the youth of Markuszow, and the pride of the survivors in their struggle.

Among the testimonies there is the heart-rending story of a mother forced to make the impossible decision whether to try to survive with her infant daughter, or to abandon the child to the mercy of fate. Stories like hers, and the others in this book, must not be forgotten.

Moses Milstein
February, 2025

Acknowledgments

I would like to thank Lance Ackerfeld, Director of the JewishGen Yizkor Book Project for his dedication to making all yizkor books available in translation, and the JewishGen press team: Susan Rosin, publications manager; Jonathan Wind, formatting, layout and indexing; and Rachel Kolokoff Hopper, cover design.

Moses Milstein
February 2025

Table of Contents

Introduction — 3

First Part - This is How the Shtetl Looked
Several Historical-Statistical facts about Markuszow Jews — Dr. Rafael Mahler — 6
Some Historical Dates and Figures about Markuszow — 10
A Stroll Through Markuszow — Dvoireh Chapnik-Fishman — 11

Memories of the Past — Sholem Wasserstrom
Introduction — 13
1) Markuszow Piety: — 14
  Fisheleh Melamed
  The "Silken" Shtetl
  The "Shokl"
  The Draftees
  The Upside Down One
  R' Hersheleh the Shamess
  The Veker
  Gepslt the Shoichet
  The chalatl
  A Story of a Bride and Groom
  Markuszow Had No Luck
  The Well
  The Ya'in Nesech
  Siyem hasefer
  Two Houses
2) Guests in the Shtetl: — 26
  The Russo-Japanese War
  The Revolution of the Fifth Year in... Markuszow
  The Natchalnik is Here!
  Stolen Cholent
  A Disturbed Purim
  The Gramophone
  The Goblet
3) Types and Figures: — 31
  Avrum-Ber the Maskil
  Berish Lehrer
  Pinchas Kandel
  The Lamed Vovnik
  Kiss-Kiss

The Shabbes Goy
The Tall Itzchak
The Sportsman
The Composer
Zelig Gutbasitser
The Explainer
Avrum-Dovid Kapitkpo
Markuszow Coachmen

Religious, Political, and Cultural Life

The Chasidic War Between Radzin and Markuszow	M. Nachshon (Capa)	44
The Community and its Dozors	Aryeh Weinriber	49
Sholem Asch and I. M. Weissenberg in Markuszow	Chayah Hertz Loterstein	54
Kadima–First Zionist Organization	Moshe Nachshon (Capa)	57
Memories of Kadima	Chayeh Hertz Loterstein	60
Zionist Organization	Aryeh Weinriber	61
Plans for a Markuszow colony in Israel		63
Chasidism and Zionism		63
Off to the Revisionists		64
Without an esrog		64
Another schism		65
Difficulties in the Zionist Work	Sarah Fianka (Weinriber)	65
Revisionists and Betar	Moshe Nachshon (Capa)	66
The Left Poalei-Zion	Dovid Brenner (Tevl)	74
Recollections	Tzipora Fedberg (Beigelman)	82
The Trade Union	L. Kandel, Dovid Brenner	85

Jewish Income

The Monday Market	Moshe Nachshon (Capa)	91
Sadovnikes [orchard renters]	David Brenner (Tevl)	95
Young Housewives	Pese Wasserstrom	97
Merchants and Artisans	Sholem Wasserstrom	98

Aid Organizations

Markuszow Philanthropy	Sholem Wasserstrom	101
Banks	Aryeh Weinriber	102

To the Memory of Our Personalities

Reb Yosef Ze'ev Ashkenazi Idlish (Rabbi in Markuszow)	Avraham Yuri	106
Reb Yosef Ben Ze'ev Idlish z"l	Sholem Wasserstrom	107
R' Avraham-Moishe of Markuszow	N. Shomen	108
The Rebbe R' Avraham Moishe	Sholem Wasserstrom	109
In Memory of Itzchak Wasserstrum	M. Nachshon (Capa)	111
The Four Maskilim	M. Nachshon (Capa)	112

Builders and Fighters: In Memory of a Comrade	Aryeh Weinriber	114
Israel-Itcheh Roguski	Sarah Fianka Weinriber	116
Moishe Eidelstein–the Heroic Sheliach Tsibur	Sholem Wasserstrom	117

Second Part - Death and Resistance

A Yorzeit Light for the Fallen		121
With Partisans, Among Farmers, in Bunkers	Dina Gothelf	122

   The shtetl up to the churban
   Markuszow is bombed
   The first days of the occupation
   The deportation actions
   We acquire weapons
   In Wole forest
   Back to the bunker
   Partisan stories

In Battle with the Nazi Enemy	Moishe Pelz	143
With Markuszow Partisans	Nathan Westelschneider	164
My Experiences During the German Occupation	Eidl Fishbein	173
Memories of Nazi Hell	Esther Fishbein-Friedman	183
The Hero of Majdanek	Rivkeh Nachshon (Capa)	193
Two-Week Period of Partisan Life	Shmuel Rubinstein	195
Jewish Partisans in the Armia Ludowa	Michal Loterstein	202
A Group of Partisans at Plouszowice	Alter Rasset	213
My Child Wanted to Live	Esther Zilbering	215
Two Sisters Speak	Fradl Zilberman-Oshenked and Rivkeh Zilberman-Kesselbrenner	218
My Experiences During the Occupation	Esther Kitenkaren-Grossman	221
Miriam Loterstein		247
In the Partisan Movement	Shmuel Laks	248
List of Jews Who Perished during the Occupation		272
Obituaries		298
Markuszowers in Israel		321

Last Name Index

325

The Destruction and Heroism of the Town of Markuszow
(Markuszów, Poland)

51°22' / 22°16'

Translation of
Hurbana u-gevurata shel ha-ayara Markuszow

Editor: David Stockfish

Published in Tel Aviv 1955

**Our sincere appreciation to Yad Vashem
for the submission of the necrology for placement on the JewishGen web site.**

This is a translation of: *Hurbana u-gevurata shel ha-ayara Markuszow* (The destruction and heroism of the town of Markuszow),
Editor: David Stockfish, Former Residents of Markuszow in Israel, Published: Tel Aviv 1955 (Y 436 pages)

Note: The original book can be seen online at the NY Public Library site: Markuszow

This material is made available by JewishGen, Inc. and the Yizkor Book Project for the purpose of fulfilling our mission of disseminating information about the Holocaust and destroyed Jewish communities. This material may not be copied, sold or bartered without JewishGen, Inc.'s permission. Rights may be reserved by the copyright holder.

JewishGen, Inc. makes no representations regarding the accuracy of the translation. The reader may wish to refer to the original material for verification.
JewishGen is not responsible for inaccuracies or omissions in the original work and cannot rewrite or edit the text to correct inaccuracies and/or omissions.
Our mission is to produce a translation of the original work and we cannot verify the accuracy of statements or alter facts cited.

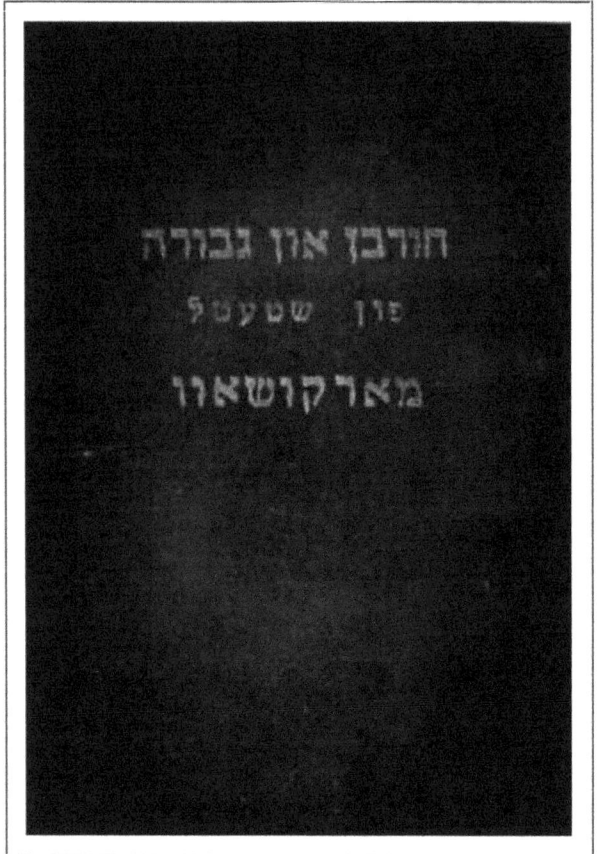

חורבן און גבורה
פון שטעטל
מארקושאװ
●
חורבנה וגבורתה
של העיירה
מרקושב

פאריין פון מארקושאװער לאנדסלײט אין ישראל • ארגון יוצאי מרקשב בישראל
תל־אביב
1955

[Page 7 - Yiddish] [Page 5 - Hebrew]

Introduction

Translated by Moses Milstein

Jewish Markuszow doesn't exist anymore, annihilated like all the Jewish communities of Poland.

This particular settlement was small, not even marked on some maps, but it too shared the same fate of millions of Jewish lives, killed for being Jewish during the great destruction.

But today, we, the remnants of Markuszow, are oppressed by a grief deeper and more painful because of the prematurely extinguished lives of those who do not even have a grave. And this knowledge was painful: how to perpetuate their memory? How to describe the noble images of our religious parents, the beloved brothers and sisters, and charming little children? How not to allow the ebullient and creative lives of an entire Jewish community to be forgotten, and the lives martyred under the occupier, and their brutal deaths?

As soon as the news of the destruction of Polish Jewry, which also included Markuszow, came to Israel, the thought of a perpetual spiritual monument to the memory of the murdered shtetl Jews was constantly on our minds. The will to produce such a book grew stronger when the surviving Jewish youth of Markuszow, who thanks to their determined, organized and heroic resistance in the partisan *otriads*, they were able to survive the hell–alive, proud, with the knowledge and satisfaction that with weapons in hand they had fought against the German murderers, taken revenge for the shedding of innocent blood, rescued the honor of the Jewish people, and made an important contribution to the Jewish resistance in occupied Poland.

Sorrow over the destruction, and the pride in the bravery were the two most important stimuli

[Page 8]

to putting out this yizkor book, although we realized that for the 50 Markuszow families in Israel, and a few others outside Israel, it was a Herculean task–and who knew if we would be successful with a memorial book about Markuszow. The difficulties were enormous, really not realizable: Where do you get the intellectual power to bring out Jewish life in the shtetl in the 19th century, to describe their struggles and their spiritual world of dreams and aspirations, messianic ideas, and secular thought? Who could evoke on paper the sorrows and pain of a Jewish community condemned to death, and who could be capable of recording the countless facts about Markuszow bravery in the resistance? And to this was added a difficult, prosaic question: how can such a small collective, like the association of Markuszow landsleit in Israel, find the necessary money for such an enterprise?

Nevertheless, we undertook the burden as a holy mission, and overcame all the difficulties. The book produced, a product of two years of work, was put together on the basis of personal recollections and memories which bind Markuszowers to their shtetl still to this day, no matter where they find themselves. Because of the absolute lack of historical materials and documents, which we couldn't acquire, in spite of strenuous efforts in that direction, almost all the material was put together from memory–something which does not always correspond with the historical, statistical, and factual situation, for which we apologize to the reader. These and other gaps in the book can be justified by the singular goal of lighting a yorzeit candle, a *ner tamid* over the unknown grave of the Markuszow Jews known so well to us, and to tell future generations about the heroic deeds of a group of young Jewish people in a small settlement in Poland during the worst era of the Jewish people.

* * *

The yizkor book, "Destruction and Bravery of the Shtetl Markuszow" is divided into two parts: The first part, "This is How the Shtetl Looked" consists of memories and descriptions that give an overview of the political, social, religious and cultural life of the shtetl for the last 50 years. The second part, "Destruction and Resistance" is dedicated

[Page 9]

to the martyr journey and the martyr deaths of Markuszow Jews, and contains articles by survivors of the resistance, partisans and fighters from their lives in the forests, in bunkers, and farm hideouts–a tragic and heroic chapter in the Jewish destruction and heroism during Hitler's occupation.

Finally, we would like to extend a heartfelt thanks to all those who helped materially and spiritually to bring out this book about Markuszow, a severed Jewish community in Poland.

[Page 10] Blank [Page 11]

First Part

This is How the Shtetl Looked

[Page I]

Several Historical-Statistical facts about Markuszow Jews

Dr. R Mahler

Translated by Moses Milstein

In 1686 Markuszow received the privilege of a city (municipal self-governance) from king Jan Sobieski. Three years later, guild privileges were established by the same king. There is little doubt that Jews were already living in Markuszow in unknown numbers. That means that after the first half of the 18th century the community was not completely independent. In the lists of Jewish head taxes of the time, Markuszow was not counted among the communities of the Lublin voivodeship. One theory, in any case, regarding the Jewish head tax, is that Markuszow was dependent on a neighboring larger community, probably that of Korew which is not far away to the northwest. Yet Markuszow was in size already a typical Jewish shtetl like the many hundreds of other shtetls in the Poland of the day. This is seen in the census of 1764.

At the end of that year, a census of Jews in all of Poland took place under the orders of the Sejm. The Sejm kept that revenue from the Jewish head tax, which used to go into the state coffers through the Council of the Four Lands.[1] (in Poland; in Lithuania through the *Vaad Medinat Liteh*) The total amount came to a lot less than if it were based on a census of Jews. The Sejm, therefor, decided to terminate the Council of the Four Lands

[Page II]

whose main function as regards the state was the distribution of the income from the head tax on the communities, the carrying out of the census, and the placing the responsibility on each community directly for the amount based on the number of Jewish souls. The head tax levied was above 2 Polish Guilders for every Jew, man and woman, and infants under a year of age.

The results of the census showed that the Sejm had calculated well: Up to 1764 the Jewish head tax sum, according to a 1717 law, was 220,00 guilders for Poland and 60,000 guilders for Lithuania. After the census, the tax reached 859,312 guilders, and in Lithuania, 315,297 guilders. And all of this even though the count was not exact, and the number of Jews was in reality significantly higher than the official one.

The manner of the counting itself lent itself to inaccuracy by its primitiveness and crudeness. In those days the counting did not take place on the same day everywhere in the country, but stretched on for months. The count in each community, according to the law, had to be carried out by a commission of four composed of a rabbi, a *parness*,[2] and a *shamess*[3] and a *shliachtshitz*[4], an "inspector." They were required to go from house to house and record the heads of the family with their names and nicknames and their wives, children and servants with their names. The village Jews were obliged (under a ban) to come to town for the census.

Obviously, under this system there was an opportunity to hide from the census. Another way to circumvent the census was to represent children over a year old, as infants. The main thing was that the community itself was interested in keeping the count lower than it was in reality especially when it concerned the poor and indigent, because the community was responsible for the tax for all the families, and was obligated to cover the tax for those who were unable to pay. The results of this count

[Page III]

of 1764 should therefore be increased not just for the unrecorded percentage of nursing children, but also through the addition of the probable number of "unregistered inhabitants." According to an analysis of the census in all of the kingdom of Poland, it seems that the number of uncounted people (except for infants) at any rate, amounted to less than a fifth of those recorded.

According to the census register the number of Jews in Markuszow in 1764 was 237 souls, and in the villages of the area that were included in the Markuszow community, 119 souls. Adding the infants (about 7% of the souls older than a year) the approximate number in the shtetl was 255 and close to 130 in the area villages. Including the unregistered, the real number of Jews in the city was probably greater than 300, and village Jews, 150-155 people.

But even the official numbers from the register, although not comprehensive, reveal interesting aspects of the demographic composition, and the social-economic structure of the Markuszow community in the 18th century. The 237 registered Jews in shtetl were divided according to sex and age:

Total 237 people:	**Men**	**Women**
	100	127
Great grandfathers and great grandmothers		1
Grandfathers and grandmothers	4	10
Parents	58	59
Widows and widowers of undetermined age	2	6
Sons and daughters	36	43
Servants	10	8

While there were only two widowers, the number of widows was 7 times higher and reached 14. It is characteristic that the two widowers were both beggars, and of the 6 widows of unknown age, five lived in rented houses as "lodgers," i.e. "occupants."

[Page IV]

It appears that widows and widowers of a poorer class had fewer opportunities to get married again than those of a wealthier class. A light is thrown on the social composition of the community by the housing data. Of the 63 heads of families in the shtetl, 29 lived in their own homes, and 34 lived with others as "lodgers." Among the 29 houses there were 7 where 2 lodgers lived, and in one, three lodgers together. Also recorded were three Jewish heads of family living as lodgers in non-Jewish homes. Only 8 of the 29 Jewish houses were inhabited by the owners alone without lodgers.

Against the backdrop of poverty, and lack of opportunity, there was a group from a richer class. Well-to-do were doubtless the bosses who hosted sons-in-law, and married sons: one son-in-law is supported by two families, and another two have two married children being supported. A more certain sign of wealth was the number having servants. In truth, servant girls, mostly cooks, were also found in those days in families that were not very well-off: with the minimal wages paid, cooks could be found in the homes of not only storekeepers and tavern keepers, but also a shoichet, a melamed, and a well-established artisan. But *"parobkes"*, that is, boy servants, were only found in homes of wealthy store owners, especially merchants, innkeepers and landholders.

The 10 Jewish *parobkes* in the shtetl were recorded for 9 business owners, 5 employing one each without a servant girl, two employing both a servant boy and servant girl, and one had two *parobkes* and a servant girl. That was the rich man of the shtetl, Kalman ben-Yekutiel. He was recorded as the "*arendar*[5] of Markuszow." That means he was the head *arendar* who leases from the nobleman all his income from the shtetl. The brew house: the distillery, the market dues, the scale dues, the city gate, etc. He also had living with him a married wine merchant, a distiller. He probably also rented the *rathouse* of the shtetl from the nobleman because he alone and his household and servants and two lodgers lived there.

[Page V]

Unfortunately, contrary to other shtetls in the Lublin voivodeship, the vocations of the family heads were not recorded except for some: the aforementioned head *arendar*, a vintner working for him, another vintner who lived separately as a lodger, and a tavern keeper, one of the businessmen who employed a single boy servant. With the example of neighboring Jewish shtetls of about the same size (Kuzmir), or smaller (Baranow) we can assume with the greatest plausibility that the professional structure was the same: Except for a few *arendars*, tavern keepers and distillers, the community was divided half and half between storekeepers and merchants on one side, and tradesmen on the other, with the addition of several melameds and religious functionaries.

In contrast to the shtetl, the village Jews of the Markuszow community were mostly recorded by their vocation.

Of the 119 recorded village Jews, 62 were men and 57 were women in 30 families. They were spread over 19 villages, mostly 2 families per village, and 10 were the only Jewish families in their village. Just as the settlements were spread out, so were the professions characteristic of those times: nine of the family heads were *arendars*, 13 tavern keepers, one dairy worker (milker), and 7 only "lodgers," who probably made a living as distillers, village cobblers, home tutors. A social gradation from rich to poor also existed, although not as marked as in the shtetl: The *arendars* were richer than the tavern keepers, and the poorest were the "lodgers." Of the nine *arendars*, 2 employ one Jewish "parobkeh," one employs a Jewish servant girl, and one has three Jewish servants, two *parobkes* and a servant girl. Of the 13 tavern keepers, only two keep Jewish servants, namely a single servant girl, while the lodgers and the milker, as expected, generally didn't have servants. Not recorded are the non-Jewish *parobkes* and servant girls who were doubtless employed by the *arendars* and the tavern keepers.

The signatories of the census register of the community were

[Page VI]

Avraham ben-Itzchak Isaac and Shia (Yehoshua) Bchh"R Binyomin. One can be sure that one of them signed as rabbi and one as *parness*. It was also possible, however, that both were just well regarded businessmen in the shtetl. According to the law, if there was no rabbi or *parness* in the shtetl, the census had to be carried out by the two "finest Jews" in the shtetl.

What proportion the approximately 60 Jewish families constituted in Markuszow itself in the year of the census, 1764, in relation to the rest of the population, can be calculated with the information of that time: in 1788 the German statistician, Bishing, estimated the number of chimneys in Markuszow to be 120. If a chimney represented a whole house, the Jews in any event constituted a lot more than a quarter of the population of the shtetl, because the 30 Jewish houses (including the *rathouse*) were more densely inhabited than the houses of the neighbors, due to the large numbers of Jewish lodgers. The number of chimneys given by Bishing is a complete exaggeration, because even in 1827 the official census showed no more than 78 chimneys in Markuszow. The actual importance of the Jews in the shtetl was much bigger than their absolute and relative number. Like all shtetls in old Poland, the Polish population was primarily occupied with agriculture, except for some smiths, shoemakers, etc., whereas the town element in the economic sense, merchants and businessmen, and in the cultural aspect, were exclusively the Jews. The non-Jewish town dwellers were farmers not just by profession, but also with respect to illiteracy.

The Jewish population in Markuszow continued to grow both in absolute numbers, and in proportion to the general population of the shtetl until the 10th (sic) century, while in the 20th century a decrease is seen, both relative and absolute.

Year	Total population	Jews	Percent
1764	—	300 (approx.)	
1827	808	343	42.5
1857	892	368	41.3

[Page VII]

Year	Total population	Jews	Percent
1861	826	387	47
1885	1256	672	53.5
1897	1732	1123	64.8
1921	1848	1001	54.2

Sources and bibliography:

Archivum Glowne, Akta b. Skarbu Koronnego, oddz. 65 B.nr. 22
Slownik Geograficzny Krolestwa Polskiego.
B. Wasiutynski, Ludnosc zydowska w Polsce w wiekach XIX Warszawa, 1930, str. 63
Jewreskaya Entziklopedia, Tom X, str. 635
R. Mahler, Statistics for Jews in Lublin Voivodeship, Yunger Historiker, vol 2, Warsaw, 1929, 67-108

Editor's note: After this book was printed, we received the above-mentioned work of Dr. Rafael Mahler that we happily inserted in the book, but without the usual numeration. That is why these pages are listed in Roman numerals.

Translator's Footnotes:

1. Autonomous body regulating communal life in Kingdom of Poland-Lithuania from the 16th to the 18th century
2. Elected member of Jewish community council
3. Beadle
4. Polish nobleman
5. An arendar was a tenant farmer

[Page 13]

Some Historical Dates and Figures about Markuszow

Translated by Moses Milstein

Markuszow–in the republican epoch–a shtetl in the Lublin voivodeship, belonged to the places where Jews had no obstacles to settlement in 1765–365 Jewish taxpayers (head tax) according to the data of 1856–514 Christians, 368 Jews. According to the census of 1897–1732 residents, of whom 1123 Jews.[a]

Markuszow a shtetl between Lublin and Pulawy, three and a half miles away, an ancient property in the name of the Markuszewskis, Lewart[b] coat of arms, died out in the 17th century. At the beginning of the 18th century Markuszow belonged to the Firlejs. In 1608 a cloister called Holy Spirit was built. The second cloister was erected in 1668 by Jan Czebicki, Kracow bishop. In 1780 the shtetl had 120 houses.[c]

In the Jewish Historical Institute's in Poland quarterly, "Historical Pages," (January–June 1950, volume 3, journal 1-2) a major work by T. Brustin-Bernstein titled "Expulsion as a Phase of German Annihilation Policy." In table no. 9 (in the tables provided in the previously mentioned work), it is recorded that Markuszow belonged to the Pulawy powiat that, before the war, counted 1250 Jews. The seventh month of 1940 there were 1320 Jews, in March 1941–1643 Jews (1510 local Jews, 133 exiles and refugees). The final expulsion and extermination of Markuszow Jewry occurred May 9, 1942. They were taken to the Sobibor extermination camp.[d]

Original Footnotes:

1. Jevreskaya Entziklopedia, center volume, S. Feterberg, 1913, p. 635
2. Families that descended from the original medieval clan
3. M. Balinsky and Sh. Lipinsky, Ancient Poland, second edition, Warsaw 1885, vol. 3
4. The above facts and dates were provided by the historians, Dr. Rafael Mahler (Jerusalem), Yosef Milner (Paris), Dr. Philip Freedman (New York)

[Page 14]

A Stroll Through Markuszow

Dvoireh Chapnik-Fishman, Tel Aviv

Translated by Moses Milstein

Because of the small size of our shtetl, I knew every corner, every little street and house, every store and workshop. Even now, after so many years, torn away from the old home, it is not hard to refresh the memory of the entire panorama of Markuszow–from the first building on the Lublin side to the last house on the Warsaw road.

At the shtetl's entrance stood broadly growing Linden trees on both sides of the road–a sort of natural entry gate to Markuszow. The leaves of the trees served as important remedies. Using steeped "Linden tea" we treated stomachaches, various kinds of pain and diseases. But more than anything, they provided shade for the passerby, cooled his heat, and drove away fatigue. Every wanderer wanted to have the satisfaction of having a nap under the Linden trees. The oldsters would tell of how a Markuszow nobleman, a good-hearted man, ordered the planting of these trees in 1815 on both sides of the road, so that tired travelers could benefit from the shade and rest. Later, another nobleman from Garbow planted cherry trees the length of the road with the same good intent so that the lone traveler could refresh himself.

The Lublin-Warsaw road intersected the shtetl from one end to the other. This was the main street, Lubelska, treed on both sides, and covered with small houses, divided with narrow entryways–the Markuszow streets.

The first building of the shtetl, beginning on the Lublin side, was a {unclear word} stall, the property of the Garbow nobleman, where Jews kept their horses and cows for a price. A little further, to the left, were three kasha mills, one next to the other, and a quiet noise issued from them constantly, a sign that something was being milled there.

[Page 15]

Markuszow business (aside from the weekly market) took place in various stores and shops which were found in every second or third house. Products sold there included fish, meat, wine, manufactured goods, shoes, kitchen utensils, writing materials, and everything that a small town business needs to provide for its customers.

In the center of the shtetl, on the right side of the road, stood a modest sized cloister around which stood the houses of the Christian population. Also there was the fire hall known as the "*shopeh*" where all the cultural events and theatrical performances of local or outside artists, Jewish and Polish and sometimes also Ukrainian took place.

On the same Lublin street, also in the middle of the shtetl, was the besmedresh, the jewel of Markuszow Jewry, in Gothic style, the broad stairs at the entry for men and to the women's shul. The tall perimeter wall and the taller trees around it clearly separated it from its surroundings. On the wide entry stairs leading to the besmedresh stood four columns, nicely painted, under which all the shtetl's *chupah's* took place. Left of the besmedresh, a wide street cut through that led to the "*lachess*"–a grass-covered lawn, low trees and bushes that have many secrets to tell. There was found the "*hoif*"[1] where the shtetl young people would spend their free time. Songs sung by the youth, and the sad singing of the shepherds grazing their sheep and goats issued from there. Sometimes these shepherds would pelt us with stones, or throw our clothing in the small river nearby while we swam on a hot day.

After the "*lachess*" at the edge of the shtetl–the cemetery with its eternal silence that was rent with cries during funerals from orphaned relatives. The cemetery at the very edge of town symbolized the end of life.

Back at the Lublin road, right from the Warsaw side, were several houses after the besmedresh, and among them–the public school (*powszechne*) and the *gmineh*[2] with a large free square, allocated to the weekly market,

[Page 16]

from which shtetl Jews drew their livelihood. Next to the *gmineh* were the police post and the jail ("*kozeh*").

Right of the town hall, the wide avenue led to the non-Jewish cemetery street bejeweled with tall trees on both sides. This street, which began with an empty place where a shul building had been built, had many orchards flanking it on both sides with various fruits, and ended at the Christian cemetery. Left again, because of the trees on both sides, you could see the Koscielna street, a nice avenue, ending at the palace of the nobleman's court, where there were many trees and fish ponds. We swam there in the summers, and skated in the winter.

Next to the nobleman's small courtyard stretched meadows that had a special attraction because of the hay sheaves. Young people spent the beautiful summer nights at the feet of the sheaves singing folk songs and popular songs, carried on with conspiratorial meetings and whispered declarations of love. In one word–the court and the nearby meadows were the nightclubs (in the better sense of the word!) for our youth. There was also a big place there where on a Sunday or Christian holiday dances took place (*zabawas, tancowkas*) for the Polish youth of the shtetl, and from the surrounding villages. More than one Jewish mother went there to look for her daughter out of fear that, God forbid, she was dancing with a non-Jew…and it used to happen that such a rebellious Jewish girl would be slapped in front of everyone.

Both streets–the cemetery and the Koscielna–led to the Warsaw highway lined by tall Linden trees on both sides. That very spot served many purposes for the Markuszow and the Korew youth in a social as well as a romantic sense. These trees absorbed the stories of a previous generation concerning demons, spirits, monsters, and the evil. The next generation passionately discussed Herzl, Eretz-Israel, Karl Marx, and Russia. And all of this woven through with youthful passion and faith in a better tomorrow.

The shtetl ended at the little bridge. That was the border, but not for our youthful thoughts and dreams which carried far and wide over the shtetl, over the borders of Poland and other lands, and primarily–to Eretz Israel.

Translator's Footnotes:

1. Literally "courtyard"
2. Municipal hall

[Page 17]

Memories of the Past

Sholem Wasserstrom

Translated by Moses Milstein

Introduction

The description of Markuszow's earliest days, I leave for others better qualified. Historians would certainly have more to tell about its establishment and development. I, as one of the oldest residents, will relate my recollections and descriptions from memory alone. They entail facts and events that played out in Markuszow 40-60 years ago.

None of us could have imagined that it would come to such a destruction of the Jewish presence in Europe, to the annihilation of Polish Jewry, and among them–our Markuszow Jews. And none of us certainly dreamed that we, the people, would have to write about the destruction of cities, shtetls, and settlements that once seethed and bubbled with Jewish life. I take pen in hand with a heavy heart and bowed head in order to describe pictures from the true reality of the shtetl, the dark and bright sides of a Jewish community, its way of life.

The following recollections are divided into three parts: a) Markuszow piety; b) guests in shtetl; and c) personalities and images. Staying true to small town customs, I will not mention any family names, just the two or three names with which every Markuszower was familiar. By bringing out certain negative events or personages, I do not intend to hurt anyone, the proof–in this case I did not spare myself either. I wanted to describe Markuszow as it was 50 years ago, and how it has remained engraved in my heart and mind.

[Page 18]

a) Markuszow Piety

Fisheleh Melamed

Fifty years ago, if you had asked in Markuszow who Fishl Melamed was, few would know what to say about him, even though he was renowned in the shtetl because of his cheder where Jewish children got their education. Fisheleh Melamed was known everywhere under his nickname, "*kaller*." Woe to the Jewish child who fell into his hands. He would hit without mercy (*kaln*) and hence his nickname. Our parents, however, (with all due respect!) maintained that there was no better educational institution than the cheder. That's why we darkened our childhood days in such cheders. Especially at Fisheleh's. Parents trusted him for the very reason that he had a reputation as a hitter. The shtetl convinced itself that Fisheleh Kaller taught respect. It was enough to tell the child that we were going to tell Fisheleh the rabbi–and the child would freeze in fear. And the worse Fisheleh treated his students, the happier the parents were. They often blessed his hands–and that hurt more than the rebbe's blows.

Fisheleh excelled in another thing as well: he gave every kid a nickname–I am embarrassed to repeat them, much less write them down. He had a special "weakness" for a poor kid, Velveleh, with the nickname *mazek*.[1] He would spank his rear end so much that Velveleh's eyes were always red from crying. At home Velveleh cried because he didn't want to go to the cheder–and at the cheder, he cried from the rebbe's smacks. Every morning, when Fisheleh Kaller saw his least favorite student, Velveleh, he would say to him, " Nu, Velveleh Mazek with the creepy eyes. Come over here!" And hit him mercilessly. Maybe it was because Velveleh's father was not a rich man. A pauper, as is well known, doesn't like a pauper.

But telling tales on the cheder is not done. So why tell so much? Better to talk about the rebbe himself. Fisheleh was known in the shtetl for something else:

An order had come down from the czarist government that every Jewish child had to attend school. And if not a school, then a cheder,

[Page 19]

but a "*prawne*" with rights, something modern, meaning two separate rooms for teaching (it was not permitted to live in them), with all the installations. Aside from that, there had to be a teacher of Russian come in to teach the children "grammar." Not one melamed in the shtetl obeyed the new rules. In the room we were taught in, lived the rebbe and his large household. And about learning Russian in the cheder, there could be no discussion even. Nevertheless, inspectors would come down from the powiat from time to time, to see how the orders were being carried out from the higher "*natcholstwe*.[2]" At these visits, a new talent of Fisheleh Kaller's was revealed.

The melamdim in shtetl used to put in several rubles, and give them over to Fisheleh. He would take them to the police, and "grease" whoever was necessary. Then the police would lead the inspector around all the places in town: in the shul, in the besmedresh, even to the bathhouse, but not in the cheders. That this was possible was not just the effect of the few rubles, but because of Fisheleh's black *kapoteh*, which he used to wear only to simchas, and his knowledge of the Russian language, since he had served in the czar's army. On the day of an inspection, Fisheleh would put on his holiday *kapoteh* and with majestic strides go to the police station. On that day, of course, he let the kids go home. In such a moment, we forgot all about the blows that Fisheleh would mete out to us so generously, and at the words, "Go home!" everyone wished him long life. And when Fisheleh Kaller went out on Markuszow's main street dressed in his black *kapoteh*, the women who sold apples, pears, beans, vegetables, in the market, would know what it signified and wished him success in his mission.

Fisheleh Melamed was successful with the police, but even more, with our parents who entrusted him with their children.

He carried out his duty with passion and faith.

The "Silken" Shtetl

That was how Markuszow was known. An uninformed person might wonder what kind of silk factory existed in the shtetl, or what sort of business goes on here with that delicate fabric. In truth our town did not have the least connection with the manufacture or sales of silk.

[Page 20]

The name came from the fact that Markuszow's professional matchmaker, Moishele Israel's (Srolieh), used to travel to Tomaszow-Lubelski to look for matches for the shtetl's boys and girls. He used to say in Tomaszow that "his" groom comes from a silken shtetl. The future in-law was not so inclined to hear the matchmaker's opinion of the whole shtetl, because he was foremost concerned with the proposed groom. At this point, R' Moishe Srolis proposed to him a silken young man, that exactly like all the besmedresh young men in shtetl, is clothed in silk, satin and velvet. His matchmaking spiel painted a picture of a Torah scholar, who put on a silken *kapoteh* with a velvet hat on Shabbes. In the same way, the matchmaker described the girls of Markuszow, who used to go to shul on Saturdays and holidays with silk shawls on their heads, and their mothers–silk caps over their wigs and silk shawls on their shoulders. Yes a "silk" shtetl for outsiders, for export, while we Markuszowers, born and raised there, knew that this "silk" included most of the boys who, after finishing cheder, went on to the besmedresh, studied there day and night, deep into the Gemara, debated Talmud, and hoped for better times.

The "*Shokl*"[3]

There was a tradition from ancient times for besmedreshniks to buy a "*shokl*" from a *sadovnik*.[4] So a group of them would collect a few kopeks, pay the *sadovnik* and one of them, the strongest, would shake the tree. Any fruit that landed on the ground belonged to the boys. The *sadovnik*,of course, gave us all a good lookover first, assessing the strength of each one of us, and agreed on the condition that the we*akest* of us should be the shaker. In truth, all the besmedreshniks, due to their always studying, looked pale and emaciated, and it took the *sadovnik* a long time before he determined who to give the *shokl* to, and not lose too much thereby. More than once he rejected a Torah student–and a bargaining ensued either about the shaker, or about a few more kopeks. It must be noted that aside from besmedreshniks, no one else could buy a *shokl*, because the *sadovniks* hoped that they would buy a little in the afterlife by virtue of this good deed.

[Page 21]

There was a woman called Leah-Etteh who lived in the shtetl. A true *eyshes chayel*,[5] a merchant, a letter courier (if she was paid for the trip), a matchmaker, and anything the shtetl of Markuszow could require of her. We just wondered how such a small, skinny, and weak woman could accomplish so much.

Aside from her two names, she was called "*Der Kurtzer Freitik*,[6]" because of her small stature. She moved with the speed of quicksilver, but for all her good qualities and jobs, she and her husband could not make a living–and like the majority of the shtetl Jews, had an orchard not far from Markuszow. In one of the hot summer evenings in 1911, the besmedreshniks went off to Leah-Etteh's orchard to buy a *shokl*. Since she was not there, the gang paid her husband the 10 kopeks.

"Have pity," the *sadovnik* pleaded. "Just one of you should do the shaking."

"You insult us," the boys answered. "It has been many years that we have been keeping the tradition of a *shokl*, and only one of us does the shaking, as much as he can."

R' Moishe, calmer now, looked at the pale faces of the besmedreshniks and it did not occur to him that the skinny boy with three names–Yomi (from Binyomin) Itche Meir's could have strong arms. The boys gave him a wink to get him to do the shaking. He quickly evaluated the trees, stopped at a one that was covered with ripe fruit, stretched his arms as high as he could, grabbed the branch and gave it a shake. The tree almost bent over as the fruit fell with an extraordinary noise. The *shokl* was successful, and they bent down to the ground to begin to gather the fruit. At that moment Leah-Etteh came into the orchard, and by the echo of the falling fruit she immediately got the picture. In an instant she lay spread out on the ground, managing to cry out, "I'm done for!"

The besmedreshniks quickly ran to the woman on the ground, one ran to get water, another went off to the *feldsher*[7], while the rest occupied themselves with cheering her up, pressed her temple, and massaged her forehead. The husband, however, did not busy himself with his fainted wife, and he quickly gathered up the fruit that the besmedreshniks

[Page 22]

had shaken off the tree. And when he had almost completely gathered them up, Leah-Etteh got up off the ground, and with a whining voice thanked the boys for their goodness. Then they realized what fools they had been, and had let themselves be conned by a phony fainting woman. They returned to the besmedresh in shame and related the event. One of the listeners, Pinchas Tovieh's, chimed in that it was a great pity that he hadn't been there, because he would have advised the guys to pick up the fruit first, and then look after the fainted woman. In his time, when he was studying in the besmedresh, it often happened that after the *shokl* the *sadovnik* or his wife fell down in a faint. The trick only worked once, because the second time the boys knew how to conduct themselves.

The Draftees

When the time came for the draft, the 21 year old besmedreshniks, little beards sprouting already, had to present themselves to the Tsarist draft board. Understandably, those who studied Torah day and night were not very enthusiastic about the perspective of changing their smocks for the uniform of a Russian soldier; changing the besmedresh for the barracks, or the Gemara for the military "*ostov*." The boys used to march around day and night in order to lose more weight from their already meager bodies, and demonstrate to the commissions that they were weaklings who had to be rejected for the army. But even the short summer nights were boring, and you had to find something to do that was either useful or fun. In this case as well they remained true to tradition that the draftees instituted in the shtetl: Collecting money from the merchants and putting on banquets. Woe to the person who refused to give the draftees the agreed-upon "contribution."

There was a storekeeper in town, Shmuel-Leib, a rich man and an extraordinary miser with the name, "Toitl, because of his yellow, elongated face. Toitl declined to contribute the few kopeks. Since people knew that this Toitl was a big miser, they decided to teach him a lesson about proper behavior. A bunch of them went into his store,

[Page 23]

asked him to weigh and package various bits of merchandise, and while he was occupied with the "customers," other draftees took the door of the shop off, and put it next to the store. The ostensible customers left the packaged merchandise, and said they would return with the money. After they left, the merchant waited until late in the evening, and not seeing anyone, he went out to close up his shop. Now, he finally noticed the dismantled

Yehuda-Dov Rosenberg-
the Nicolaievsker[8] soldier

door, and immediately knew whose work it had been. By himself, he couldn't put the door back on, and he went out to look for the draftees around the shtetl, apologized for refusing to contribute money, and quickly brought the requested sum.

[Page 24]

In the meantime, he had to guard his shop all night, because the boys didn't reinstall the door until the morning.

A similar thing happened with the naphtha seller, "the Red David," Toitl's brother-in-law. He too refused to give a penny to the draftees. So he too was "kept busy" with a conversation while other boys stole a keg of naphtha from the shop and hid it so cleverly, near the shop, that the owner was later astonished when the spot was revealed to him, after he brought the sum requested.

The Upside Down One

There was a tradition on the night of Shavuot, not to go to sleep. They used to recite *Tikun Shavuot*, and sing new melodies heard from the chasidim, and go visit the Markuszow rebbe. Of course, on such a night the opportunity to drink a little liquor and make merry was not missed.

There was a young man among the besmedreshniks by the name of Israel-Meir Motele's. He was not well liked because of his excessive nosiness, although he himself never joined the discussion during debates. That's why he was anointed with the name "*Shatkan*," (The Silent One). There was a suspicion that he reported on everything that happened with the besmedreshniks. As there was no evidence of this, he was not boycotted. Nevertheless each one of us was tempted to do something to him, and then the opportunity arose.

For all his good qualities, Israel-Meir, had a weakness for napping. On that Shevuot night, when the boys were partying in the besmedresh, The Silent One felt like having a nap. He stretched out on a long bench and began to snore. The guys were waiting for that. Some of them took off their waist sashes, tied him to the bench, and then stood it up so that Israel-Meir was hanging with his feet up and his head down. Disregarding the fact that it was forbidden on such a holy night to turn down the naphtha lamps, they still did it in order to put the besmedresh in darkness. One of the boys covered himself in his taliss, approached the sleeper, and began to speak in a changed voice.

"Israel-Meir Motele's, you should know that you are called to the *beis-din shel myleh*[9],

[Page 25]

and just as you see me here in a taliss, there are thousands behind me with talissim, to accompany you to heaven."

The Silent One let out a fearful cry, and fainted. They turned the light back on, righted the bench, and poured water on him until he regained consciousness. After this event, Israel-Meir took sick and was bedridden for several weeks. It wouldn't have taken much for him to really go to the *beis din shel myleh*.

When Israel-Meir regained his health, he returned to the besmedresh, took part in all the debates, and even became a partner in all the pranks that the besmedreshniks did. It seems that turning him upside down worked. As the saying goes, "*Er hot sich in gantzen ibergedreit.*"[10]

R' Hersheleh the *Shamess*[11]

At the end of the last century, there was a shamess in the shtetl who demonstrated extraordinary loyalty and dedication to the besmedresh. This loyalty expressed itself in the following way:

When he was asked to take away the used up *hoyshaynes*[12] from the ark that had been thrown there, he replied that these worn out willow twigs made the besmedresh more holy. When the spreading cobwebs in every corner were pointed out to him, he would shout back, "Who ever heard of a holy place being cleaned?" And he would say it with such innocence, and with such a tone that no one suspected that he was wrong. He didn't mean the besmedresh should be dirtier, but he was just afraid to diminish its holiness. He got really worked up when he learned that they were preparing to whitewash the besmedresh. He shouted loudly that we were dishonoring and insulting a house of prayer, and such a sin would not be forgiven. "If so," he said, "you can take down all the *sheymess's*[13] from the besmedresh attic and do what you want with them."

One day, a fire did break out in the attic and the burned *sheymess's* were carried away by the wind. Our shamess was actually happy about this, because now they had become a *tikun* and were flying straight up to heaven.

[Page 26]

There was a dozor in the shtetl, R' Lozer, a Radziner chasid. When the painter was whitewashing the besmedresh, several boys, the constant Torah students, asked him to paint a Star of David on the ceiling. The painter agreed and painted a big Star of David on the white ceiling. When R' Lozer saw the painting, he started such an uproar that the shtetl Jews came running. The dozor warned, "You want to bring a plague on the shtetl?"

All the explanations and arguments from the religious besmedreshniks did not change the stubborn man's opinion. One boy tried to show R' Lozer that the coverlets of the holy Torah sported a Star of David, so why could this Jewish symbol not be painted in a besmedresh? But try talking to an obstinate and fanatic man. He had to be assuaged, and the Star of David covered over.

Most of the besmedreshniks, preoccupied with studying, but still dreaming of a Jewish land (symbolized by the Star of David) gnashed their teeth, kept silent, and submitted to the will of the dozor.

The *Veker*[14]

Every young man in Markuszow that studied in the besmedresh (and who did not?) was occupied from 4:00 am to 11 at night, with an intermission of three hours–from 12:00 to 3:00, in order to daven and eat. It wasn't easy on a winter's dawn to get up to worship God. Outside the frost reigned. The besmedresh was not yet warmed up. That's why religious parents provided a waker who would knock on doors and windows and remind the sleepy youngsters of the holy debt of the student.

There were two night watchmen in the shtetl who guarded against misfortune: a Pole and a Jew. It's understood that the job of waking the Torah students could not be entrusted to a goy. This holy mission was entrusted to the night watchman, Itzchak-Eli. He was not one of the big geniuses, but also not one of the small fools. In addition, he stammered. He used to brag, "I boss Mashov" (I am the boss of Markuszow).

During the night hours, police patrols used to come to the shtetl,

[Page 27]

and ask Itzchak-Eli if everything was in order. After such a visit our night watchman bragged, "I'm guard one!"

At around 4:00 am Itzchak-Eli would knock on the shutters loud enough that a corpse in the grave could hear him. With the knocking he would cry out, "Get up, *Yiddelach, titgaver kari*, to the worship of God!"

True, he did stammer, but his voice was nevertheless cleaner, clearer and sharper. Everyone wondered how the stammerer, Itzchak-Eli, spoke so clearly when he was waking up the people. It turned out that he would put his hand over his ear and sway, an indication that this movement and the singsong nature of his voice led to his clear expression.

If Itzchak –Eli entered a house during the day, and he was offered something, he would not accept it under any circumstances. But the moment the man or woman of the house turned their backs, the proffered item or food quickly disappeared. Itzchak-Eli would quickly grab it and hide it.

With his complete innocence, Itzchak-Eli honestly believed that by waking the besmedreshniks to the holy work, he was buying himself a big share in the afterlife. In this case also he had an opportunity to brag that thanks to him Jewish boys wouldn't be late for their studies.

Gepslt the *Shoichet*[15]

A neighboring shtetl decided it wanted to take for itself our Markuszow shoichet, Chaim-Yehoshua, a Kotzker chasid. We called him "Cham-Shieh." After he left, Markuszow had to hire a new shoichet, and fortunately one was found right away, actually right in town, a pious young man with all the certification for slaughter. For some it was, however, enough that the candidate, Chaim-Mendele Binyomin's was one of ours, a shtetl resident, that made him undesirable. A stranger impresses more. One of ours, we won't look at. There were two camps in the shtetl. The majority, the common people, actually favored the Markuszow shoichet, who was incidentally ready to bring money to the community, a kind of "*shlisl gelt*.[16]" The other side, the minority, almost all Radziner chasidim, found a flaw in the shoichet candidate: he didn't wear a *techeilis*.[17] The shoichet, a Lubliner, did not hold with

[Page 28]

the notion that a blue thread must be woven into the *taliss katan*. Nu, so began a dispute in the shtetl, a real uproar. At the end, the majority won, and Markuszow finally had its own shoichet from the shtetl.

The Radziner chasidim did not give up so easily. One of them, Lozer Yankl's, claimed that the slaughter was not being done according to the law, and he did not consume any of it.

The *chalatl*[18]

The shtetl, with its blessed rich, black soil that after every rain greened and freshened, is etched deep in my memory. Such a rain is always a blessing for the residents, a promise of a good harvest. Rain in winter, however, used to transform into a curse for us chasidim (and who in our little shtetl was not a chasid?) And all because of the long clothing, the robes that were worn in every city and shtetl in Poland not excluding Markuszow. We never parted from the *chalatl*, not during the week, not Shabbes, not the holidays.

As soon as any rain fell, the *chalatl*s would become splashed with mud that then dried on the bottom. But in wintertime, if the weather was freezing after a rain, the mud on the *chalatl* would freeze, and the coattails would rub against each other making all kinds of noises. The frozen part of the *chalatl* became as stiff as a sheet of tin. Woe to the garment if you tried to clean it. Pieces would come off the cloth, holes would appear, and goodbye *chalatl*.

I remember one incident: A Jewish merchant from Markuszow traveled one day to a village to collect a debt, something he rarely did. As usual he was wearing a *chalatl* with a lot of mud on the bottom. When he was traveling to the farmer, two forces of nature were warring: the sun had warmed what the frost had penetrated, and as the merchant was returning home in the evening, it turned cold, and the mud on the *chalatl* stiffened. The two hardened coattails rubbed against each other, creating strange sounds, and it seemed to the chasid that demons, or other evil forces, were following him.

[Page 29]

Aside from that, the frozen *chalatl* was banging against his boots creating new sounds that could really instill fear. Not far from the shtetl, the chasid fell down in a faint. Unconscious, he lay stretched out on the snow. Passersby lifted him up, and with great difficulty revived him, and when he regained consciousness, he was certain that evil forces had met him on his way home. Nevertheless, he was able to prove the blame fell on his own *chalatl* and the evening frost.

After this story, some began to talk in the shtetl about the need for shorter clothing. The religious folk, however, accused such a person of being an *apikoiris*[19]. "What, it is explicitly written, 'You shall not walk in their ways,' or, 'This is his way,' because that is the way of *yetzer horeh*[20] " Today we are told to wear short clothes, and tomorrow–who knows what he will tempt us with."

A Story of a Bride and Groom

At the end of the 19th century, Markuszow was a small shtetl. There were about 150 Jewish families living there (a few years later the number doubled). The old synagogue stood in the center of town separated from the besmedresh, and maybe connected through the old small cemetery. The old cemetery was not used by the community in those days, because there was another one, far outside town, where Markuszow Jews were buried.

There were no monuments to be seen in the old cemetery. Only two stones remained to remind everyone of the old cemetery. They were not two ordinary stones, but tomb stones for a bride and groom whose story was the following: As the old timers tell it, years ago a couple was led to the *chupah*.[21] At the words "*harei et*"[22] the couple felt ill, and fell down in a faint–never to rise again. The next day, the rabbi reasoned that they should be buried together, the bride in her wedding dress. So it was done as the rebbe ordered, the couple was buried, and two tombstones erected in the memory of the sad event. The words on the tombstone were illegible due to their age. Green moss covered the stones,

[Page 30]

and we youngsters strained to read the words, at least one letter, but without success.

There is another interesting story about the old cemetery that caused a commotion not just in Markuszow but on the whole surrounding neighborhood.

The Czarist government had decided to construct the Lublin-Warsaw highway. Since the shtetl lies on the route, engineers were sent down. They measured, evaluated, calculated, and finally discovered that the route passes right through the old cemetery. This created an uproar in the shtetl. Jews cried and complained that a holy place would be desecrated. Many prominent Jews sent delegations, drafted requests to the Powiat–to no avail, however. So the shtetl took to the old Jewish way that if you can't succeed, at least don't make it worse–and had the rabbinical authority issue a decree ordering an extraordinary fast for the community. They begged God to avert the decree.

After this, an order suddenly came down to change the plan, and to have the road detour around the cemetery which moved the road a few dozen meters away from the old cemetery. The community was astonished. Up to the complaints, nothing helped, even a promised bribe for the {smudged print} was not able to cancel the decree. And here, such a change for the good. The eyes of the religious Jews gleamed as they told the Markuszow Jews that the inhabitants of the old cemetery had warned the *nachalnik*[23] and the engineer that if they disturbed their rest, they would be each be strangled. The authorities had to change the plan. That night–the religious said–both the engineers and the *nachalnik* from the powiat awoke with fearful cries and soaked with the fear of death, and decided to change the plan, and to let everyone in the shtetl know about it.

The question of how the religious knew so precisely about the annulled decree did not occur to anyone. For a long time the shtetl told and retold the story of how the old cemetery did not allow itself to be desecrated. Slowly the story lost currency, and new events took place of which there was no lack in the shtetl.

Markuszow Had No Luck

It was said of Napoleon that he was born with two teeth.

[Page 31]

Well, Corsica was a lucky island, and the ready teeth with which the future military leader was born, heralded a lucky person whose name would ring throughout the world. Markuszow, however, was different. It was not Corsica. It so happened that a child with two teeth in its mouth was born to the shoemaker, Itzchak Fingerhut (Hershele Batche's) and his wife, Rivkeh. So they went straight to the rebbe to ask how it could be, as if it were a religious matter he had to decide on. The rebbe was no slouch, and he came to see the living creature with two erupted teeth. The rebbe put his glasses on his nose, and looked in the baby's mouth for a long time, gave it serious thought, and spat three times so as not to hurt the parents, and, God forbid, the child. Next he wrapped himself in his taliss, and recited some prayers and exorcisms. On leaving, he gave instructions on how to behave with the child.

Meanwhile the city was in a tizzy; there was something to talk about. They were also afraid of a tragedy. Markuszow Jews did not yet know about Napoleon's two little teeth. They were afraid both because of the child, and because of the fate of the shtetl. It's quite possible that the little soul felt the unrest and trembling of the congregation of Jews, and in time passed on to the other world.

Markuszow had no luck with its Napoleon.

The Well

In the very center of the shtetl there was a very deep well with a story about it. The well was circular, with a round cover, and its whole appearance resembled a monument. Two large buckets hung from an iron chain, one of which was let down into the well, while the other, a full one, rose to the top. Not everyone had the strength to pull up such a heavy bucket.

The biggest attraction of the well was its salty water. It was said in town that the salty water was good for wisdom. Because of that, a saying used to go around Markuszow, "He's a salty one," meaning a smart one.

When a Markuszow Jew married off a daughter, and the groom was from another shtetl or city, the groom would have to ride around the well on the eve of the wedding several times. It was a custom that was ancient. They used to say, however,

[Page 32]

that this could be a way to get a groom to forget claiming the promised gifts from the bride, and the remaining part of the dowry not yet bestowed. They believed that traveling around the well, the groom would get dizzy and he would no longer demand what was promised. Apikorsim however said that the story of driving around the well was a joke by a rich bride, a progressive girl, who wanted to take revenge on all grooms (except her own). First of all, she tried to make it so that she wouldn't have to walk in a circle around the groom during the chupeh, and when she was told that she must do so, she bribed the carriage driver, who was to bring the groom to the chupeh, with a few rubles to make a few circuits around the well. Her reasoning was simple: If you want to make circuits, then so be it! Then let the groom go too! And so the custom remained of driving around the well.

The *Ya'in Nesech*[24]

1908. The revolution of 1905 has long ago been suppressed. But Czarist police search and snoop everywhere for rebels, especially in the small shtetls. We remember well how on a Shabbes or holiday the gendarmes would suddenly fall into the besmedresh, and begin to inspect the faces of the praying. If they didn't like the look of someone, they would ask for his passport. The more suspicious ones were immediately arrested causing no end of trouble for that person. Only the compassion of the *soltis* or the *gmineh* secretary could allow such a captured man to get out of further entanglements.

In their zeal the gendarmes not only paid visits to the besmedresh, but in all the suspicious places.

Markuszow Jews were sitting around in good holiday spirits in the sukkah, and with song, food, and communal joy enjoying the holiday. Suddenly the curtain at the entrance moved. First a shiny, black cap from a hat appeared followed by two thick, long, mustaches. They gave a quick shake and the excited Jews heard the question, "*Kakoyeh sobrani*?!" (What kind of meeting?)

The gendarme appeared. He fell in as it is said, "Like an Ivan in a sukkah." Now the Jews were really scared. Shimeleh *Diener* was there (The nickname, *Diener*, was given to him by a relative, Chaneh

[Page 33]

Mahler from Lublin who had come from America on a visit and remarked that in the Golden Land "*badinen dieners*.[25]" R' Shimeleh didn't have the patience to listen to all the talk about *dieners*, and interrupted him, "What's all this "*diener*" talk. I know without you that it thunders in America. It's the same sky, the same God. And so the nickname, "*Diener*," stayed with him[26]), his 14 year old son, Isroolik, Pinchas-Yekil's and his boy, Velvl, and some other men. They were afraid not so much of the gendarmes but of their presence in a holy place. It is notable that the gendarme's first glance was at the wine. According to Jewish law, such wine is no longer fit for making kiddush. And in general, a goy showing up in a kosher sukkah is likely to spoil the whole holiday.

But there was little time to deliberate. It was necessary to invite the gendarme to the table, give him some good schnapps, the beverage loosened his tongue, and he himself declared that there were certainly no rebels in Markuszow. Obviously the Jews agreed with him–and poured another glass.

That Sukkot was somewhat spoiled, because we had to make kiddush over the *challes*. There was satisfaction, however, that the gendarme's visit ended peacefully.

Siyem hasefer[27]

"*Me sheh lo ra'ah simchat beit hasho'evah, lo ra'ah simcha byamo.*"[28] (He who has not seen the joy of Sukkot in the times of the Beit HaMikdash during the drawing and pouring out of the water {ceremony}, has never seen joy in his life).

"He who has not seen such a simcha, has never in his life experienced a decent simcha." So said the Markuszow Jews after celebrating the big simcha for the end of the writing of a Torah scroll. And such celebrations were not rare, simply because Jews in the trades and business were always collecting money for a new Torah. And when the Torah scribe was finishing the last letters, which were sold to the Jews in the shtetl, the joy was unbounded. No small thing–to live to see the Siyem Hasefer.

Young and old prepared for the event of carrying the Torah under

[Page 34]

a *chupah* canopy to the shul with an orchestra and the biggest parade Markuzow was capable of. The people keeping things in order (although every Jew at such a simcha kept himself in order) were: Shloimeleh Golde's, Mordechai Dovid Yankel's, and Mordechai Golde's–the "triplets" that were also actually the head committee in charge of the celebration. These three used to ride on horses at the front of the line of dancing and enthusiastic Jews, and poured naphtha into the torches that the besmedresh boys were carrying. Every time they poured the naphtha there was an explosion of flame and sparks that resembled the biggest fireworks that could be seen kilometers away. More than one coat or shirt ended up with holes from the sparks. But who was concerned with such foolishness on such a joyful night. The crowd was drunk with joy, ecstatic, and with song and dance and shouts, and an overall celebratory atmosphere, marched through the shtetl. The chasidic dances, their passion and zeal affected everyone, and Markuszowers old and young were up until dawn.

In czarist times, we had to get a special permit to play in the street. The "triplets," however, never bothered to get such permission from the authorities that were located in Pulawy, and always relied on the fact that the police rarely showed up in the shtetl. This time, however, at the very height of the celebration, several policemen showed up, and undertook to arrest the rabbi, who was carrying the Torah, and the musicians. Since the police were not particularly sober, the arrest did not go so smoothly. Meanwhile, Shloime Golde's, who spoke Russian and knew all the agents, went up to the police, began to negotiate with them, and gave a wink to the secretary of the *gmineh* who helped convince the police they should mount the horses of the parade organizers, lead them to the *gmineh* building where the jail was– and locked them up there overnight. It was done of course with their agreement and a bribe.

After that, the Jews really got going and celebrated the seym hasefer the likes of which Markuszow had not yet seen.

Two Houses

On a height, on the west side of the shtetl, stood two houses that were distinguished, one from the other, by their size and color.

[Page 35]

On the front of one of them hung a sign with the word "*piwiarnia*" (beer house), owned by the pole, Trembicki. There was always a great din coming from there, shouts from not sober farmers, and shtetl residents. This particular house also had a revolutionary past. In 1905, during the first Russian revolution, two Russian gendarmes were disarmed there by Polish revolutionaries: Stankewicz, a bricklayer, and Boczkowski, farmer.

Standing opposite Stempicki's house was the house of R' Baruch Eidelstein, or as he was called, Baruch Pietrowizer. From this house too there issued a din and a racket, but it came from the people in the house: the sons, daughters, daughters-in-law, sons-in-law, grandchildren, and other relatives who all lived there together. It was especially raucous on Shabbes in Baruch Pietrowizer's estate. The *zmires*[29] on Friday evening and Saturday morning blasted out from the house to the shtetl even with the windows closed, and caused consternation in the shtetl about this family. Notwithstanding the traditional Jewish religiosity that was strictly observed there, the children, especially the sons, benefited from an unusual freedom to read secular books, become familiar with books about science, technology and medicine. One of the grandchildren, Yoseleh, was a frequent besmedresh attendant, but with his stories, he was always revealing new worlds to the Torah students and fanatically religious besmedreshniks. Those who didn't dare to lift their eyes from the Gemara, would swallow with open mouths his words, and more than one envied Yoseleh who had the freedom to learn the worldly pearls of wisdom.

It was, therefore, said in the shtetl that Baruch Pietrowizer's house distinguished itself from its neighbor's house not just by its tavern, but also from all the other Jewish houses and homes of the shtetl where piety and religiosity was guarded with the utmost strictness, while there, in the house on the hill, worldliness went along with the Torah.

b) Guests in the *Shtetl*

The shtetl did not live on piety alone. Time did its thing–wars and revolutions, new inventions and new ideas.

[Page 36]

Shtetl youth, mostly besmedreshniks, became the carriers of the new thinking. They gradually disturbed the established way of life of strict Jewish tradition and religiosity. Guests in the shtetl brought various news from which Markuszow drew its own conclusions.

The Russo-Japanese War

Much blood had already been shed on the battlefields of the Far East when Markuszow received the news about the war in Russia with the Japanese. It happened like this:

As on every Thursday, the provider of yeast, Hershl Rapaport, came from Korew. He declared that this was the last time he would be bringing this particular merchandise, because the Russian train was busy transporting troops and ammunition to Vladivostok, and was not available to bring yeast from Poland. This created an uproar in the shtetl: What–leave a shtetl without yeast? How can a Jewish home give up the mitzvah of eating challah?

Still not having made peace with the idea of having no yeast, further news arrived hat there would be no raisins to make wine for kiddush, and no candles from Russia would be coming (Niewski's candles), which also jeopardized the mitzvah of blessing the candles. Pious people (and who then was not pious?) went around worrying about this sad news that in their eyes appeared more tragic than the defeats of the czarist army. And who knows how long this unrest would last if not for the happier news that the Korew Jew brought that, God willing, there would soon be yeast, and raisins, and candles, and Jews could perform the most important mitzvahs undisturbed. And in reality, the holiness of making kiddush, blessing candles and challah eating were not disturbed.

Who knows how Markuszow would have learned about such an event as the Russo-Japanese war if not for the importation of the three most important articles, because no newspapers reached the shtetl in those days.

The Revolution of the Fifth Year in… Markuszow

That is why the shtetl, in its way, took part in the revolutionary uprising in 1905. New Year's Eve, when merchants had to

[Page 37]

buy the business licenses to be able to carry on their businesses, several "strikers" (that's what revolutionaries were called in the shtetl) agitated strongly against buying the certificates. The frightened storekeepers didn't want to antagonize the Russian officials, but also were afraid to go against the will of the revolutionaries. So they decided to send a delegate to the" strikers", and get them to annul the decree. As emissary of the storekeepers, they chose the Kotzker chasid, Itche-Meir Capa, a shopkeeper himself. The following dialogue took place between him and the most prominent revolutionary, Hersh-Feivl:

"Itche-Meir: What's going to happen? We still have an emperor, and for not buying the licenses, we could be punished.

Hersh-Fevl: Listen, R' Itche-Meir. What to tell you, I still don't know, because I have to receive a directive. But you have to wait, and not be afraid that you will be punished. The emperor won't be coming to Markuszow. The punisher here is the policeman. Before he walked around with his head down and bayonet low. Today when the revolution has broken out the police walk around with lowered heads and raised bayonets, and as long as they find themselves in this situation, there is no reason to be afraid. No one will punish you.

Itche-Meir was astonished at these words. Surprised and upset he asked, "What do you mean not to be afraid of kings? For the czar himself?"

* * *

Itzchak'l Schneider (Lame Itzchak) embarked on a daring step in that revolutionary year. In a packed besmedresh, he mounted the *belemer* and shouted, "Nikolai has been Kaiser long enough!"

Pointing to his black shirt, although the only one he possessed, he called out with pathos, "May this shirt be my only one–and Kaiser Nikolai must abandon the throne!"

The crowd was beside itself: how can you allow such words to be expressed, especially in the besmedresh where every Shabess and holiday they invoked a "*me shebarach*"[30] for "*yewo Wielichestwo*"[31] the czar-imperator? But even greater was the fear of telling the authorities about the lame Itzchak's outburst against the czar.

[Page 38]

While some of the attendees praying there had quiet satisfaction from the rebellion against the monarchy, others regretted his words, and still others simply thought he was crazy.

When the news that the revolution had been suppressed came to the shtetl, the chasidim decided to take revenge on the strikers: At a gathering in the besmedresh, after drinking a glass of whiskey, they embarked on a little dance, singing a song of their own creation:

> See here Moishe Ber,
> Come now over here,
> You will have fun,
> And I will tell you,
> That the Kaiser has already,
> Arrested the last striker!

The chasidim had another reason for being happy. The ban on wearing the long chasidic clothing was repealed. They had even stopped cutting off beards and side locks. Because he who wore short clothing was regarded not only as an *apikoires*, but really as a revolutionary.

The *Natchalnik*[32] is Here!

At the beginning of 1905, a new natchalnik was sent down to Nova Alexandria (later Pulawy). Since Markuszow belonged to the Pulawy area, the new high authority came to visit the shtetl. The Christians and the Jews had the duty of receiving the guest with bread and salt and other honors as was suitable for a representative of the government. At the head of the Jewish delegation was the then Markuszow rabbi, Moishe Eliyahi, z"l. The guest arrived in the shtetl, the rabbi presented him with the tray of bread and salt. The natchalnik did not take his eyes off the Jewish delegation which consisted of just pious Jews in their traditional clothing, with beards, payess and the round, black hats on their heads. The tall Russian looked with special curiosity at the face of the fifty year old Yechezkel-Aharon Shaul's, and pointing out his gloomy red eyes asked him, "Shouldn't this Jew present himself for conscription?"

Most of the onlookers quickly understood the meaning of the question

[Page 39]

that the natchalnik meant to apply to the entire Jewish population with the clear insinuation that they were damaging their eyes in order to avoid military service.

After a short painful period of silence, the Pole, Adash Sobinski, a fighter of the *fifth year* who was also in the delegation, spoke up: "This Jew was exempted from military service by virtue of a bribe."

It was not hard to guess what the Pole intended with his pointed answer.

The Russian continued to receive his refreshments and honors from the residents. He did not, however, forget the big insult from Adash Sabinski, ordered the capture of the courageous revolutionary, and put him in jail. Later he was shot in Pulawy and artillery drove over his grave in order to wipe out any trace of his existence.

Stolen Cholent

Among the infrequent but interesting guests to a shtetl like Markuszow were the army. Soldiers coming to town brought business to the stores, bakeries, sold merchandise from the wider world, and brought good cheer and greetings from far away unknown places.

One day on a Saturday before noon (summer 1906) a military detachment stopped outside Markuszow and right away individual soldiers began to show up in the shtetl, looking for, as was their habit, whiskey. Others went to the bakery looking for bread, but instead of that they found full earthen pots, still hot, wrapped in cloth or paper, on the floor. One of the soldiers didn't ruminate long, grabbed a pot, put it under his arm, and left. It is possible that in another shtetl, where Jews suffered from excesses, especially from the army, such a theft would not have made much of a commotion, and everything would have proceeded quietly. But in Markuszow, where we didn't have many antisemitic acts, even in the most turbulent of times, the idea of a stolen cholent could not go by unpunished. The community did not want to take it quietly. A delegation immediately went off to the officer and told him about the theft. They searched all the solders–to no avail. In the meantime, another report came in that in another Jewish

[Page 40]

bakery, a cholent had been stolen. The officer realized that just by searching, he wouldn't accomplish anything, so he brought out the whole company and solemnly promised no one would be punished if the theft was revealed. One of the soldiers got out of line, went over to the drum, opened it up, and took the pot out. They took the top off, and a delicious aroma was emitted of a true Shabbes cholent. The Jews told the officer that the soldiers should eat the cholent with pleasure.

The other cholent was found the next day hidden in the baker's bed, because the soldier committing the theft got interrupted in the middle, and frightened he hid it under the mattress and alone, barely alive, escaped.

The shtetl had fodder for talk about the stolen cholent for a long time.

A Disturbed Purim

Once upon a time in Purim, more than fifty years ago, some Purim *shpielers*[33] came to us from Korew. Among them was a musician with his own violin. The troupe went to Noach Glazschneider (Noach Zalman's) directly. He was a simple man, a tailor by trade, (now in Israel). They spent the whole day there, singing folk songs, playing the fiddle, and truly celebrated the holiday. Thus, Noach Zalman's understood better than anyone in the shtetl how to really celebrate this happiest of all the holidays.

When the shtetl youngsters heard about the arrival of the Purim *shpielers*, they went off to Noach Glazschneider, stood under his windows, and with bated breath listened to the singing and playing of the guests. We stayed there for hours amazed, carried away with the playing, and entirely oblivious to who we were and where we were. The yearning sounds of Zion coming from Noach Zalman's house rooted us to the spot, not to be torn away. And the fiddle? It was the first time we had heard such sweet, heartfelt tones and we were enchanted. A small thing–to hear a fiddle in the shtetl. We didn't even feel the biting cold that ate into our bones, but we stood and listened and dreamed, and in reality begged that it would never end.

Meanwhile the worried parents were looking for their children and learned where we were. They came up to Noach Zalman's window and

[Page 41]

led us home with the actual orchestra, accompanied by a drum. But the drum was us. It drummed into us how right it was to listen to songs that elicited so many dreams and yearnings in us whose significance we as children could not exactly understand.

Our Purim was disturbed–our parents tore us away from the windows. They did not, however, tear us away from our yearning for Zion.

The Gramophone

In 1906 the shtetl received a surprise: a man appeared with a music box that they called a *katarinkeh*. A monkey did tricks to the rhythm of the melodies played. Markuszow still hadn't finished talking about this event, when an opportunity arrived to gape at and be astonished by, a box with a big trumpet from which a chazan sang out beautiful prayers and various Jewish melodies. We happily paid the three kopeks to hear the touching Jewish music again and again. The curious wanted to look into the box to see the chazzan who must have been very tiny, if not a child with a heavenly voice. The cantorial pieces carried throughout the shtetl, and much later were sung in Markuszow homes after the wandering gramophone had left the shtetl.

The appearance of the gramophone was a message that even here the penetration, the events, and achievements of the wider world were beginning, and that we are not backward but are making progress albeit belatedly.

The Goblet

In Markuszow, exactly like in the other small shtetls in Poland, there was no lack of vagabonds, professional beggars who used to wander over the land, and also stopped in our shtetl. If they stayed for one or several nights, they would sty in the besmedresh. Many of them felt like our own, so often did they visit Markuszow. These gentlemen got insulted if you gave them a half groshen. In their eyes it looked like too little a donation, which they returned angrily. Their demand

[Page 42]

was–minimum two groshen. There was one wandering pauper who, when he was invited to someone's home for a meal, was always accompanied by another, who slipped into the house with him as soon as the door was opened. To the question by the host of who the other one was, the invited guest replied, "This is my son-in-law. I promised him *kest*."[34]

One *motzi-Shabbes*, when several Markuszowers got together at Tuvieh Ettinger's house in order to conduct a traditional *melaveh malkeh*,[35] the beggars quickly sniffed out the news that there was a feast being prepared, and hurried over there. They ate and drank, and there was a glass of schnapps too as is the custom among Markuszow chasidim. The crowd sang zmiress and partied until late in the evening. Suddenly someone called out, "Rabbotai, we sincerely beg whoever took the silver goblet and put it in his bag to immediately put it back, otherwise we will be forced to search every one of those present, no matter who."

Of course, with these words the whole party was interrupted, and since no one offered up the goblet, they began the search. First they emptied the bags of the local Markuszowers, and after that they turned to the guests. One of them began to plead not to be searched. He was ready to pay for the value of the goblet, even more than its price, as long as he was left alone. The crowd, however, did not want to enter into any negotiation, and decided to carry out the search anyway. The pleading, weeping, and groveling words from the beggar could have touched a stone, but it became a matter of stubbornness, even though the beggar offered the sum of 50 rubles, which in those days was a legendary amount. They were even more stunned when he offered 150 rubles, as long as they would not search him (The goblet was only worth a few rubles). "You will be killing me if you search me," he whimpered. It was no use, and the crowd looked first in his bags, then began to look under his clothes. On his neck they found a little bag in which there were five hundred rubles.

Markuszow Jews were not envious types. The millionaire pauper was that same night taken to the nearest train station, 18 kilometers away, accompanied by a dozen of ours so that nothing bad should happen to him along the way. As a result, however, night time attacks took place often on

[Page 43]

guests who slept in the besmedresh. They were looking for hidden fortunes.

c) Types and Figures

Avrum-Ber the *Maskil*[36]

The first maskil in Markuszow as I recall was the *derdeki melamed*,[37] Avrum-Ber–a short, fat little Jew who used to beat the alef-bet into his 4 year old pupils. Since that was far from being a good livelihood, he used to also make a kind of alcoholic drink that was called "kvass" or "lemonade." Every Markuszow Jew knew that after Saturday's fatty cholent, you could get a bottle of kvass at Avrum-Ber's. Even this production was insufficiently profitable. So Avrum-Ber began dealing with "spiritual" food. At his house, you could get *bencherlach*,[38] a "God of Abraham," *Shir Hamayles*[39] for pregnant women, *mezuzes*, and the like.

He was an enlightened man, and had knowledge of various things that Jews of his class had no inkling of. Fifty years earlier, however, an epidemic broke out in Markuszow and grew significantly during the hot months (Tamuz, Av, Elul) because of the consumption of a lot of fruit with which they drank a lot of water. Somewhere in one of the newspapers that had now begun to reach Markuszow, it was written that fruit had to be washed before eating, to drink only boiled water, and to wash hands with carbol. All these notices only came to Avrum-Ber and through mysterious means. Our hero used o come to the besmedresh with his hands washed in carbol, and because of the strong odor people shied away from him, especially since he explained the reasons for sickness were due to tiny invisible creatures found in the air, and they, the microbes are responsible for various sicknesses in the world, even epidemics like cholera that pious Jews thought were God's punishment,

[Page 44]

whereas Avrum-Ber blamed it on microbes. He recounted so many illnesses that the crowd thought he probably suffered from them all.

Avrum-Ber, the owner of a goat, used to say that when you milked into a vessel, it lost much of its nutrition. It would be better to milk it straight into your mouth. Shtetl wags later said that they themselves had seen Avram-Ber's goat standing on the table while he milked it straight into his mouth.

Berish Lehrer

He was not a native Markuszower. He appeared in the shtetl in 1906 when the czarist government took to persecuting the revolutionaries of 1905. Such suspicious and persecuted Jews would move to other places, mix in with the local population, and in this way got away from czarist persecutions.

He came from Korew as a teacher, and got settled in Markuszow, because the police rarely looked into the shtetl. He was never without two things: sugar in his mouth, and a siddur in his bag. His broad beard (which grew earlier) belied his revolutionary exterior, while inside him there always burned the revolutionary fire of a rebel and fighter. True to his revolutionary nature, to always be active, organizing, he quickly organized a "circle" which every Saturday night after cholent met in the women's shul. He would explain the meaning of the workers' struggle, and taught them to sing worker songs.

There were three of them, the first of Berish's listeners: Eli Roizes, and Nathan and Abish Yomaleh's. At first it was hard for them to accept Berishe's ideas, but he ignored everything and delivered a chapter on socialism with no less vigor than a rabbi with a page of Gemara. When an uninvited guest showed up in the women's shul during his "circle," R' Berish did not panic, took out his little siddur that was always with him, and began to chant psalms, and translated the chapter for his listeners.

Pinchas Kandel

No one could explain how the first secular book wound up in the besmedresh, but everyone read it, practically swallowed it,

[Page 45]

and having tasted the forbidden fruit, came the desire to read more and more books. But where to get them?

Here, unexpectedly, a young man from Markuszow, Pinchas Kandel, or as he was called (exactly like everyone in the shtetl) Pinchas-Moishe Shaul-Zelig's, came to the rescue. It was said that when it was his Bar Mitzvah, his father, as was the custom then, traveled with him to the rebbe who began to moralize, and wanted to plant a spark of Chassidism in him. The whole time the rebbe went on with his lengthy sermon, the bar mitzvah boy stood straight, earnest, hearing every word. The rebbe was happy thinking that his work was not wasted, but as soon as he ended, Pinchas asked," Rebbe, how much money did you get for this spiel?"

The rebbe sat stunned at such insolent words, as if he had lost the ability to speak. When he revived he shouted in a voice not his own," Take this scoundrel away, drive out this unclean wretch!"

You can imagine that Pinchas was not inclined to follow the footsteps of his religious parents. He was the first in the shtetl who subscribed to the Hebrew {newspaper} "*Hatzfira*," and saw to it that the newspaper went to the besmedreshniks. He used to explain articles, arranged for readings of the paper, and helped explain difficult problems. But there was one thing he couldn't help: convincing our parents to give us a little free time and freedom.

It was only thanks to such Pinchases that, in time, we succeeded in convincing our parents.

The *Lamed Vovnik*[40]

In his youth, he worked at tailoring. Later he wandered around the Polish villages repairing the farmer's fur pelts. He was called by two names–(like all the Jews in Markuszow)–Meir'leh Itzikl's. Why Meir'leh? Because he was short, deformed on both sides which made him bend over and appear even shorter.

It was whispered in the shtetl that he was one of the *lamed vov* saints, in whose righteousness the world exists. He always carried a book of psalms with him, and it was said that Saturday at dawn, while it was till dark outside, R' Meir'leh sat

[Page 46]

in the besmedresh and read psalms. An ordinary person could not see in such darkness, and he can? He must be a holy man. The storytellers added that one could see that a brightness hovered over each page while he held the book of psalms in his hands. Because of his modesty and honesty, everyone in the shtetl cherished him, and was always concerned about him.

Once, late in the evening, the shtetl found out that Meir'l had still not returned from the village. A large number of men went outside the town to look for the *lamed vovnik*, or to find out what had happened to him. Although the weather was cold and raining, they still went out calling his name along the way. Suddenly a prayer was heard coming from a field just as if it were coming from the heavens. The crowd was frozen with fear. Some of them wanted to retreat, but the more courageous ones approached the spot the voice was coming from. And here a crazy picture was revealed to them:

R'meir'l was sitting in a tree reciting psalms. When the crowd saw him in such a situation, no one doubted in that moment that R' Meir'l was a real *tzaddik*[41] in whose merits the shtetl lives.

But there wasn't a lot of time to spend thinking. The bad weather and the enveloping darkness sobered up the men who took Meir'l down from the tree, and listened to what had happened to him. They learned this:

When R' Meirl had found himself not far from the shtetl, a strong wind began to blow. And night fell. Two forms approached him, the wind disheveling their clothing, and they looked malevolent. R' Meir'l got scared, and began to climb up the nearest tree. Because of his small size and handicaps. He couldn't get up the tree. Suddenly he felt four hands lifting him up and helping him get onto a branch where he settled in until the arrival of the Markuszow Jews. In the meantime, he recited psalms, and begged God not to abandon him in the field, because alone he wasn't able to get down.

From the further questions that he was asked by the curious crowd, it turned out that the forms were two women farmers who were going home to the village from the shtetl, and their shawls were so blown around by the wind that R' Meir'l thought that evil people were coming toward him.

[Page 47]

When the women farmers neared the tree, and saw how someone was trying to climb up, they helped him.

And that's how it seemed the psalm was coming down from the sky.

They led R' Meir'l back to the shtetl in a big parade. His renown as a pious honest man grew even larger. The eyes in pious faces glistened, and they whispered that he was certainly one of the thirty-six.

Kiss-Kiss

It's hard to imagine Markuszow without Berl Wassertreger who used to provide water for every house from the city pump. Everyone knew this man who, except for Shabbes and holidays, was always behung with two big buckets that dangled from his shoulder yoke. He worked hard, loyally, and honestly, and displayed an extraordinary concern for the water. There were times when he was left with a bucketful or half a bucketful of water. He would carry it back to the well, and pour it back in, even when the well was far from where he was. That was his habit even on the coldest days when slippery ice and cold were life threatening. On the many occasions when he was questioned about his devotion to the water, his only answer was, "You must not waste water, it's a crime to spill it on the ground."

Although he was known as Berl Wassertreger, he was stuck with the nickname, Kiss-Kiss which happened like this:

Our fellow townsman, Zeligl, had several goats. Once he called to his goats in the street, "Kiss–kiss–kiss–kiss !

Berl Wassertreger happened to be passing by and hearing the kiss-kiss, he dropped his two buckets of water and with the freed yoke, he started to hit R' Zeligl, screaming with one breath, "See here, he's calling me kiss-kiss. I am smarter than you. You can go all over Markuszow, and you won't find a genius like me!"

There was a time when the watchman, Itzchak-Eli and Berl Wassertreger were inseparable. They used to walk together through the shtetl, even though they were markedly different one from the other. The former used to

[Page 48]

show great concern and respect for the dozor of the shtetl, Lozer Brandeleh's, while the latter used to stick up for the same dozor but with the name reversed, Brandeleh's Lozer having in mind his wife, Brandeleh.

If someone in the shtetl got sick, or someone suffered a misfortune, Itzchak Eli used to say, "May it be a torment for Lozer Brandeleh's!"

May it be a torment for Brandeleh Lozer's, Berl Wasserteger would instantly chime in.

One cold winter, when it was really slippery in the shtetl, Berl Wassertreger fell down with his buckets. He lay injured for a long time on the snow. As soon as he revived, and got up from the ground, he said right away, "Oi, may it not harm Brandeleh Lozer!"

"May it be a torment for Lozer Brandeleh's," Itzchak Eli who just happened to be coming by with two buckets of water (with all his other jobs, he carried water as well), replied.

The Shabbes Goy

Wladek, who Markuszow Christians used to say was more Jew than Pole, was the city Shabbess goy. The Polish residents of the shtetl used to warn Wladek that when he died, he wouldn't be buried in a Christian cemetery. In reality, Wladek, if not for his black mustache and his short jacket, could, with his back hair and dark eyes, especially with his speaking Yiddish, pass for a one hundred percent Jew. (Markuszow Christians threatening Wladek with burial in a Jewish cemetery was not done out of antisemitism. In this area, Markuszow had nothing to complain about, because the relations between the Christian and Jewish population was quite a friendly one. The following facts can serve as proof: At that time–1908–several Cossacks that were carrying out maneuvers not far from the shtetl, attacked the Markuszow resident, Kalman-Itzik, and beat him up. In the process, he lost his documents and 50 rubles which were found by a poor Pole who carried it all to the priest who then called Kalman-Itzik and returned the money to him, and his passport).

[Page 49]

Wladek Shabbess goy was employed every Erev Pesach to whitewash the Jewish houses in Markuszow. When a child entered the house where Wladek was whitewashing, the goy would immediately begin reciting *modeh ani*[42] with the child. If the mother heard this she would let out a groan, and say to the child, "Woe is me. The goy has to remind you of the *modeh ani*."

Wladek felt hurt by these remarks and said, "I not goy."

Most of the Jewish children in the shtetl were suspicious of Wladek that while lighting the candles for *Neileh* on Yom Kippur, he was stealing the wax from the burned-out candles, and they, the children, had nothing to play with. Consequently, they would look at his hands when he went around lighting the candles in shul the eve of the prayer.

As per usual, they sold all the *chometz* to Wladek Erev Pesach. He would brag to the town Poles, "Look at how rich I suddenly became. All of Markuszow's riches lie in my hands!"

The Tall Itzchak

A strictly religious Jew, tall and strong as an oak–such was the Markuszow Jew, R' Itzchak. Because of his height he was given the nickname, *Der Langer Itzchak*–and everyone trembled before his courage. If some Poles arrived for the weekly market, and wanted to let loose on the Jews, *Der Langer Itzchak* would kill their appetite for that kind of adventure. These farmers were later careful not to start up with Markuszow Jews as long as *Der Langer Itzchak* would stick up for them.

Once the Markuszow rebbe, with a group of chasidim, went off to the field that they had bought from a farmer in order to sow and harvest the wheat for *Matzeh Shmureh*. When the shepherds saw the rebbe and a number of Jews working in the field, they at first made fun of them, then hurled insults, and finally started throwing stones. Who knows how the matter would have ended, if not for the instant participation of *Der Langer Itzchak* who with his strong arms taught the antisemitic shepherds that it wasn't always a good idea to start up with Jews.

[Page 50]

The Sportsman

There was a boy in town with Jethro's names: Sholem-Wolf, Sholem-Zev, Zev Shalom. Mostly he was called Velvl. His father was not one of the great rich, but also not one of the lowly poor. He was little bothered by the many names of his son. But he was very upset by one of Velvl's weaknesses that the child could not overcome by any means: As Velvl walked through the streets of Markuszow, and saw something lying on the ground–a stone, a piece of carrot, the remains of a fruit, and anything he encountered along the way–it was immediately either kicked or thrown. He most liked to tie a string to a stone, then throw the stone in the air so high you could barely see it anymore. Since the string often tore, the stone would go straight into a window and the pane would explode in pieces. Even the stones he threw without a string often wandered into a window pane. And his father, Pinchas-Yankl's, who didn't have the means to replace a window pane, also had to bear the guilt and shame because of his child. The blows and entreaties only increased Velvl's passion for throwing stones, a sport that had, like narcotics, poisoned the young organism, and drove it to a mania. The blows and gentle words of his father, just like the savage fists of his melamed, Fisheleh Kaller, did not change a hair of Velveleh. As soon as he saw a stone, he became spellbound. He did not own more than one hat or cap, because as soon as one of his stones shattered a pane, his hat was immediately grabbed from his head–let his father come and ransom it back. But Velveleh did not give in. He would cover his bare head with his *chalatl*, and a stone seen along the way was flying again. More than once it happened that the *chalatl* was also torn from his young body. Then he wept bitter tears over why there was nothing to cover his head with. He was still nevertheless a cheder boy!

His father finally concluded that this could not go on. There were often scandals at home, because his mother, Sureh, from despair would wring her hands and shout as if she was in pain when father would hit Velveleh with a thick rope. The boy would lie in bed for several days afterward until he came to and– further continued his vocation

[Page 51]

of stone throwing. The father understood that perhaps with a positive approach the boy could be cured of his sickness. Consequently, Velvl was surprised when his father asked him, "What do you like?"

"Throwing stones!"

His father wasn't enthusiastic about this answer and said, "Good, I haven't yet seen how you throw. *Tishe Bov*, God willing, when I'm free and you don't have to go to cheder, and we don't have to study Torah, we'll go outside town and you can throw stones to your heart's content.

At the time they were repairing the road, and on both sides lay heaps of stones in the form of sloped roofs. They brought Velvl to one of those mounds, and his father said in a cheerful tone, "Throw, as much as your heart desires."

The boys eyes actually lit up. He did not expect such good naturedness. With one hand he picked up a handful of stone, and with the other began to throw them into the empty field, his heart bursting with joy. The father smiled along with pleasure.

After slaking his appetite after the first stone throwing, the boy wanted to take a breather, and rest in order to gather renewed strength to go on with his sport. But the watchful eye of the father paid close attention so that the boy would not lose heart. Velveleh didn't have a choice. (A father must be obeyed!), and threw stones left and right. The pretty pyramid of stones disappeared. The boy was exhausted, he couldn't catch his breath, and his hands pricked and hurt. When he complained about the pain, his father didn't give in, and told him to continue.

Again stones flew up in the air, over the road and into the field–again Velvl begged mercy from his father, he should allow him to stop this work.

"*Tateh*, I can't anymore."

"What, you're crying? And did you ever think of your father, when his heart was weeping with the shame you brought him every day. Now you should be happy that I'm ordering you to do a thing you love so much."

[Page 52]

And who knows how long this stone throwing would have gone on when behind the father's back they suddenly heard the popular Russian curses from the road watchman, angry as to why the mound of stones was messed up. Now the father realized what his son had done. In order to avoid paying a big fine, both of them, father and son, had to harness themselves to the job of gathering the stones and arranging them back into a nice pile.

From then on Velveleh stopped engaging in his sport.

The Composer

He was more of a scholar than others, and weighed more than others. While praying, he used to drag out the prayer so long, that you thought he was loathe to let a word out of his mouth, recited over and over. As a rabbi for girls, he used to give his pupils entire pages of siddur to copy out, and in the meantime, sneak into the besmedresh around 11:00 am, when there were no longer any minyans, go up to the *shtender* and favore the besmedresh students with a *broche* or a *kdushe* as if they were starving for it…nevertheless they were thankful for it. Because of one of his "*nikdishcha*," they had a chance to stand up and straighten their backs from their constant studying.

He was called Yoziv. He also distinguished himself with his love of singing. It was said that he once had a beautiful alto when he was young, but it was lost after an illness. When he began to sing, the wags would say to him that he once had an "alt"[43] which had become "alt," but after comes a tenor. The tenor never arrived, and Yozib strained his voice trying to bring out the sounds. He was often asked why, with such a voice, he had not gone to study music or begun to write it. For an answer, Yozib took a pencil and paper, and began to write notes, humming the melody with his erstwhile alto, and future tenor…two times: lam-tara-ra; three times: lamto-ro-ro; five times: bim-bom boom.

"Why do I need to travel to study, when I write the notes for myself, and sing them," was the answer Yozib gave.

[Page 53]

Zelig *Gutbasitser*[44]

In our shtetl, where every law was strictly observed, we used to go bathing in the little lake only after Lag B'Omer. The lake was the property of the Jewish landowner, R' Zeligl. Another in his position would certainly have enriched himself from the fields, meadows, fish ponds, and other assets which in those years (1903-1904) were worth a lot of money. But he was either unaware, or he didn't want to exploit these riches, and he remained a simple Jew, a pauper. His real occupation was carpentry, and he was at the top of the profession. But if you wanted to get something made by him, you had to order it at least six months in advance, but not because he was overwhelmed with carpentry work. He also had to look after and work his hay fields, his wheat fields, and keep an eye on his two fishponds. True, he did sell his fish several times a year, but the profits went back into the fishponds, enlarging them, deepening them. He worked like this every day, and remained a pauper. His conduct was unlike a landowner, because dozens of youngsters would bathe in the ponds where he raised his fish, and he was happy that on hot summer days, Jewish children could take advantage of his ponds. People told him that the soap could poison the fish in the ponds, but he good-naturedly waved them off, as was his wont. He also used to say that when he saw besmedreshniks bathing, it warmed his heart. (It was quietly whispered that since his wife, Malkeh, only bore him daughters, he was hoping to find them a suitable match).

R' Zeligl had a special satisfaction on Rosh Hashanah when the whole shtetl descended on his ponds where a whole year's worth of sins by the community were cast into the water. But our Markuszow Jews, exactly like R' Zeligl, had, because of their piety, very little to in their purses to shake into the water. They really hadn't sinned. That's why they went to *tashlich*[45] accompanied by all the children, with song and dance. The music for the dancing and singing was done by Yoske Soifer who called out, "*Tson kdoshim*!"[46] and the bunch of kids would answer with a drawn out, meh-h-h-!

[Page 54]

The Explainer

With that name (or nickname) the Markuszow Jew, Moishe-Yosl, was crowned, primarily because of his proficiency in military strategy. He never missed the opportunity to explain how wars are conducted, talking about tactics, and especially military conduct, and revealing to his listeners other pearls of wisdom from the art of war, as if he had graduated from a military academy.

Where did this weakness come from in the pious Moishe-Yosl? It can only be explained by the fact that he lived next door to Mechl Ettinger where the general staff could always be found, that practically every summer conducted maneuvers in the Markuszow neighborhood. At those times, Moishe-Yosl would live it up, his mouth never shutting for a second. He would constantly reveal and explain where the staff was coming from, what it was doing now, what plans were being made, and where they were going after the maneuvers. He would relate this with such cleverness, that you could think that the general staff consulted with Moishe-Yosl in all his matters.

Moishe-Yosl bragged that he knew the Russian language, but he often stumbled when he had to speak the language. When a military company of Cossacks came to town, he was especially exhilarated by the red stripes on their Cossack pants. It was a weakness for him, and he abandoned all his other jobs in order to hang around the house where the general staff was staying, and gazed to his fill at the red stripes. More than once he was in danger of being accused of being a spy, but who can resist their weaknesses, especially a man like Moishe-Yosl–the "strategist," and "explainer" of the shtetl?

Avrum-Dovid Kapitko

He was the butcher in the shtetl, but that was not the source of his status. Markuszow knew him for his bizarre stories that he would tell in his butcher shop, and that's why it was always full–not so much with customers, but listeners. And above all–his exorcism of the "evil eye" almost transformed him into a shtetl doctor.

With respect to his stories, most of them didn't have a particle of truth in them, but the more fantastic and exaggerated they were, the more

[Page 55]

they excited the curiosity of the listeners. When he was asked, how is this possible, he would answer, "That's how it is!" He was exactly as strange in exorcising the evil eye; everyone thought him an expert in that area. If a despairing mother brought him her sick child, he immediately demanded that they bring an item of the child's clothing, examined it in his hands, stood in a corner, his eyes beginning to glisten, then casting glances in all four directions. When he was done with all that, he would shut his eyes, and turn the child's thing seven times over his left foot, and then give a big yawn. Both he, and the astonished child's mother believed that the child would be helped.

And if it did not help, nobody blamed him, especially since he didn't take any money for exorcising an evil eye. A true idealist.

Markuszow Coachmen

The oldest of them–Israel-Zalman and Dovid-Yankl, as I remember them, began their employment in 1880 before the Lublin-Warsaw road was built, and when a train was still not even dreamed of. They were pioneers in the area of establishing links with the neighboring shtetls and cities. They were so embedded in the life of Markuszow, that even when the train arrived years later, and was actually quite far from the shtetl, they still used the homegrown carriage drivers, as an expression of loyalty for their life-saving work.

Israel-Zalman was distinguished by his majestic appearance, especially when seated on the coachman's seat, and urging the horses on. He held the reins and the whip in one hand–and in the other, the long pipe stem without which it was impossible to imagine this illustrious coachman. The two of them–Israel-Zalman and the pipe were like conjoined twins, one always with the other, only separated on the Saturdays and holidays. He was a serious man, although he was not lacking in joy. Every time he shouted "giddy-up" to his horses, he never forgot to add the word, "crow!" This began with him from the days when he used to carry sacs of wheat, and to drive off the crows who chased after the seeds, he yelled, "crow!" at them which meant they had to get away.

[Page 56]

From that "giddy-up crow" became a lexicon that Israel-Zalman used.

Our coachmen, among whom there was also a certain R' Pinchas, had a common language, understandable only to them especially when they found a little hay in the fields passing by. Traveling in single file, the leader would shout, "*Kdoshim*!" On this, the other would reply, "*Hazinu*!"

In plain language this meant: kdoshim– *heilik*, which the coachmen interpreted somewhat differently, *hay ligt*.[47] The reply was, *hazinu*–taken. And if there was no one in the field, our coachmen would take the hay lying there and feed it to their horses.

The pride of the Markuszow coachmen was their horses, so, for example, one of them would brag, "I have two bays that before I shout hey giddy-up, they tear themselves from the spot with the speed of flying birds."

Moishele Shustak (a nickname because of the six fingers in his hand) would reply to the boaster that his chestnuts were the best in the shtetl. Yechezkel Balagoleh vied with them that his "*gniades*"[48] could be a part of a king's team.

There was another coachman in later times who was called Areleh-Shieh's. He himself, exactly like his horse and wagon were renowned in the shtetl. First, because of his piety, no small thing a Radziner chasid. Second, his connection to the wider world, which meant the neighboring Jewish shtetls with which he maintained constant contact bringing and taking away passengers, merchandise, letters and everything required for the mutual commercial relations between Markuszow and its surroundings. He would have had more renown and importance in the shtetl if not for his great nosiness, especially regarding the behavior of the shtetl youth.

Driving home in the evening, he would get off his wagon not far from the shtetl and watch the strolling young people. When it became darker, he would light a match in order to see who had come out for a stroll. The following day, Markuszow already knew who in the preceding evening had been outside town, and who their accompanier (male or female) had been. Our parents

[Page 57]

therefore blessed him, while the youth gnashed their teeth over the uninvited informant. Incidentally, his surveillance of the strolling boys did not prevent him from looking for a husband among them for his then, only daughter.

The guys decided to teach the nosy coachman a lesson. One summer evening in 1909, when they heard his wagon coming, they left the main road

Sholem Wasserstrom, author of "Memories of the Past"–as besmedreshnik

and began to walk in the fields. Some of them hid in a nearby ditch, and when Areleh-Shieh's, driven by his strong curiosity, went into the field to see the walkers, the hidden youth went over to his wagon, unharnessed the horses, and left them standing like that. When the coachman had gotten the names of the strolling boys, he went back to his wagon, got up, grabbed the reins, and as soon as the horses moved, Areleh-Shieh's was thrown and lay stretched out on the ground. He didn't know the horses were unharnessed, and when he commanded them to move, holding the reins, they pulled him off the wagon.

The guys went over, helped him up, harnessed back the horses, and wished him a happy voyage. That night, he told no one about the strolling boys, and also kept silent about his falling off the wagon.

[Page 58]

Grandmother, Peseh, with her two grandchildren

Translator's Footnotes:

1. Scamp, demon
2. Authority
3. The "shake"
4. People that leased orchards
5. An exemplary wife
6. The Short Friday
7. Folk doctor
8. Jewish soldier in the army of Tsar Nicholas I

9. Court of the afterlife
10. "He turned himself around completely"
11. Shamess is the synagogue beadle
12. Willow twigs that are beaten during the hymns of the seventh day of Sukkot
13. Detached leaf from a prayer book. Stored in attic because they cannot be desecrated.
14. The Waker, someone who wakes people up
15. Ritual slaughterer
16. Literally "key money", buying the position
17. A blue thread in his fringes not worn by most Jews at the time because knowledge of the source of the blue dye had been lost. The Radziner rebbe claimed to have found the snail said to produce the dye.
18. A little smock
19. A heretic, freethinker
20. The evil inclination
21. Wedding canopy
22. The first words of the marriage ceremony
23. Russian high official
24. Wine forbidden to Jews because it may have been consecrated for another religion
25. Servants serve
26. The joke is a pun on the word thunder, *diner*, and servant, *diener*. Although it may be a pun on the American English "diner."
27. Ceremony on the completion of the writing of a Torah.
28. Mishnah Sukka 5:1 Celebration held during the intermediate days of Sukkot harking back to the celebrations in temple times.
29. Religious songs
30. Prayer for the health of
31. His majesty
32. Russian authority, sometimes humorously
33. Participants in the tradition of dressing in costumes and putting on plays in Purim
34. *Kest* was the custom of providing food and shelter for students
35. Evening meal marking the end of Sabbath
36. An adherent of the *Haskallah*, the Jewish enlightenment
37. Teacher of the youngest children
38. Booklet with the text of grace after a meal
39. Piece of paper with the text of psalm 121 meant to dispel evil spirits during childbirth
40. One of the 36 righteous men who roam the world unknown to anyone including themselves
41. A saintly man
42. *Modeh Ani* is a Jewish prayer that observant Jews recite daily upon waking, while still in bed.
43. Pun on alt=alto, and alt=old in Yiddish
44. Landowner
45. Ceremony on first day Rosh Hashanah where clothes are emptied out, and/or crumbs thrown into a body of water, representing casting away sins.
46. Holy sheep and goats
47. Pun on *heilik* (holy) and *hay ligt* (hay is lying)
48. Roan

[Page 59]

Religious, Political and Cultural Life

The Chasidic War Between Radzin and Markuszow

M. Nachshon (Capa)

Translated by Moses Milstein

-1-

"*Hakol talui al hamazal*," (everything depends on luck)–stated the *Chazal*.[1]

"*Afilu sefer Torah shebaheichal*"[2]… Luck was also on our shtetl's side, because to whom would it have occurred that Markuszow would rise to greatness, that the shtetl would be put back on its feet.

It was an ordinary Friday, when most of the Jews were getting ready to greet the Sabbath queen. In the mikvah, filled with boiling hot water and steaming Jews, the holy tzaddik immersed himself three times. He left the mikvah with his eyes fixed on heaven–and firmly decided: this very shtetl would be his residence.

A new life began in Markuszow.

Every Friday night, the rebbe's *tish*[3] was attended by the shtetl men and their sons. Pious women stood on tiptoes outside the rebbe's window, stretching to catch a glimpse inside, or to hear some holy words from the Torah that poured like olive oil from the rebbe's lips. During the day on Saturday, the rebbe began to preside at the tish that lasted through *shalosh seudes*, and *melaveh malkeh*, and went on till past *chtsos*.[4] Piety spread through the shtetl as if the *shechina* were resting over Markuszow.

On the eve of the Days of Awe, heavy wagons carrying Chasidim appeared in the shtetl, coming to see the rebbe for the holidays. Many young men from all parts of the land streamed to the Markuszow rebbe for the holidays, dressed in low shoes with white socks in which they stuffed their pants. On their bodies,

[Page 60]

long, satin *kapotehs*[5] that reached to their ankles, sashes over their hips, and tall *shtreimls*[6] covering their close-cropped hair. And on either side of their youthful faces stretched long *payess*[7] that were always dangling, as if they were helping their owner to serve the Creator. A red kerchief in the back pocket of their satin kapoteh was always peeking out. The young people ran around the shtetl as if there was someone chasing them. Someone's coming from the mikvah, someone's going to the mikvah, to the rebbe's little besmedresh, to his hostel. The older chasidim lead their ten-twelve-year-old children around with the intent of acquainting their children from the very beginning with chasidic passion and faith. They walk through the shtetl somewhat slower than the youngsters, stroking their long beards, and chatting about half-chasidic, half-business subjects.

On such days, Markuszow women were greatly affected by the grace that came to the shtetl. They could be seen running to the bakery, roasting ducks and geese for the guests, baking challehs and bread to make the visitors staying with them happy. The *dorfgeyers*[8] bring all manner of goods to the shtetl. Good cheer reigns, excitement, truly a "prosperity."

-2-

The Markuszow rebbe had an only daughter, a "gentle-hearted child." They called her Menuchaleh. She was betrothed to an only son of a rich Radziner chasid who lived in another shtetl. Ozer'l (that was his name) attained a prominent position in his younger days, and was one of the closest tish participants of the Radziner rebbe. It seems that this time the "heaven criers" had not looked for the presence of a *techeilis*[9] thread in the *tzitzis*,[10] and betrothed Menuchah and Ozer. Markuszow celebrated for seven days and nights because of the wedding. The *Karahod*[11] saw a mixture of chasidic shtreimels and women's hats, burning torches and extinguished candles, old and young, big and small, all seized by such rapture, with such fire, that many thought: Whoever has not seen the wedding of Menucheleh and Ozer'l, has never seen a real wedding." Joy reigned in the rebbe's court, in the shtetl, among all the Jews. But happier than everyone was the lucky couple.

-3-

At the entrance to the shtetl on the Warsaw side, on the left side, there stood a house long as a Russian barrack, with a name also

[Page 61]

a long one: "Grandfather's House." No strangers lived there, just our own: the grandfather, his devoted sons, daughter, grandchildren–a big family. All the adult men in the court wore shtreimls, and all of them belonged to the Radziner "cheder." The Radziner *shtibl*[12] was also found there. In one word, a Radziner "republic" at the very entrance to Markuszow.

One Saturday evening, a meeting was held in the shtibl. The shtibl was packed, a needle couldn't have fit in. After a brief consultation with the "big shots," it was decided to send a delegation of four Radziner chasidim who then went off to Ozer, and without discussion delivered an ultimatum:

"Get a divorce!"

"How can it be?" asked Ozer'l.

"How can it be? It's making a whole commotion in heaven. How can a young man do such a terrible thing–you're disgracing the techeilis tradition. It's a sin the like of which the world has never seen.

"God forbid," answered an abashed Ozer'l. He showed the emissaries his talliss–real Jewish tzitzis., Kosher, but without a techeilis.

The delegation left with the determination to take revenge on the rebbe and his young son-in-law, who had so quickly converted, God help us, and stopped wearing techeilis. They returned to the court and loudly proclaimed: "It's a *milchumeh mitsveh!*"[13]

The big debate began in the court. Should war be declared on Ozer or not? If yes, should it be an open war, or an underground one. The grandfather's oldest grandson, a man in his thirties, got up on a chair and in a strange voice shouted:

"It is a desecration to insult our techeilis. We have to completely destroy the "yellow herring." (Meaning the rabbi).

He said this with such passion, shouting so that his shtreimls and his satin kapoteh danced with him as if they didn't belong to him.

The "*zayde's*"[14] son also got up on a chair and delivered these words:

"I wanna tell you, I do, that ya can't keep silent on this, ya can't. This Ozer, we gotta break his bones, we do, he should remember it forever, he should. And because he is a transgressor, he is, we have to stone him, we do, for insulting our techeilis. And this "skinny hook" (meaning the rebbe) we have to drive from our shtetl, we do. Let us show our strength, let us."

[Page 62]

The zayde himself chimed in:

"If I were your age," he began, "I would have, without hesitation or discussion, grabbed this little rebbe by his big rabbit ears, and dragged him out of here, he should never see the shtetl again. Such insolence and chutzpah–stealing from us such a jewel, a gem, among the nicest tish companions. This cannot be ignored!"

Among the court people there was a carriage driver, Israel, a Radziner chasid. He davened in their shtibl, and actually wore techeilis. Understandably, he was also present at such an important gathering. After the zayde's words, he didn't reflect long, but quickly jumped up on a chair, banged his big boots on the chair and said:

"Gentlemen! I don't understand what you want from the rebbe. Friday, I went to the mikveh and saw him there–he seemed a perfectly ordinary man. He may not wear a techeilis, and it's certainly a sin, but there are, *kaneinehoreh*, plenty more Jews who don't wear a techeilis. Do we have to, therefore, tear them limb from limb? I don't know why you have ganged up on him, he is a very ordinary boy."

The carriage driver's words were a slap in the face of the court folk. They did not expect such a blemish in their family. It was hard to make peace with the thought that in the presence of the whole gathering, the Radziner were contradicted, and by one of their own. But picking a quarrel with Israel no one wanted, because, boy, did he have a punch.

The zayde himself went over to R' Israel and explained to him the desecration of techeilis, and that a jewel was taken from the Radziner tish.

"Imagine," the zayde explained to the carriage driver," if they took away your best…horse, ha, what, would you be silent?"

After such an argument from the zayde, R' Israel lowered the brim over his good-natured eyes, and said, "Do what you want." And without a "good week" left the shtibl, where the passionate debate continued until they came to a decision–open warfare with the dissident. All methods are kosher.

-4-

For the rebbe's son-in-law it was hell on earth. The first salvo by the Radziners was to send the little scamps to throw rocks at him

[Page 63]

as soon as he went out on the street. They called him all kinds of names. The holy war went so far that they reported the rebbe to the czarist authorities. Since the products of the rebbe's slaughter were forbidden, the rebbe forbade the consumption of the Radziner's slaughterer. The shtetl was left with no meat, because not everyone wanted to eat meat from outside the system.

There were many Kotzker chasidim in the shtetl. A prominent businessman of theirs, Itche Mayer, respected by everyone, took upon himself the initiative

The residents of R' Baruch's "court"

to call a meeting. In a packed besmedresh, between Mincha and Maariv, R' Itche Mayer stood on the steps before the ark. The crowd waited to see what he would have to say, because he had never before spoken in front of the community in shul. This time he screwed up his courage and said, "I have never spoken in front of an audience before. It is certainly not my vocation, but I will nevertheless ask, my dear Jews, why should we be lower than the animals in the forest, or in the desert? It is well known that, before a storm,

[Page 64]

the animals gather together in one place, and yesterday's bloody enemies huddle together in order to collectively protect themselves from the approaching danger. Is the current antisemitism in Russia and Poland not a dark storm over our heads? How long has it been since the bloody pogrom in Kishinev? A shudder passes through us when we give a thought to all of that. And we must state, to our great pain, that the shoichet has not been neutralized yet. Because of the rebbe's son-in-law, who had previously worn tzitzes with techeilis and then took them off, a quarrel has flared up in the shtetl. As if there was nothing else to worry about. I have to say that the devil himself is leading you on. But this cannot continue. I stand now by the holy sefer-Torahs, and I call out to you, "*Shalom al Israel!*"

The crowd began to push toward the ark where R' Itche Meyer was standing in sorrow, but at the same time, exalted. The crowd lifted him up in their arms, and with shouts of, "Shalom al Israel," went off to the rebbe's court. There the peacemaker explained to the rebbe why he had come. Happy, the rebbe shouted, "*Shalom al Israel.*" That was a message that the war between Radzin and Markuszow was now over.

Translator's Footnotes:

1. Sages of Mishnah and Talmud.
2. Kabbalah reference, Sha'arei Orah, Spain c1300; "Even the sefer-Torah in the sanctuary is dependent on mazal"
3. Literally, "table," referring to the meal at which the rebbe presides, an important custom among chasidim.
4. *Chtsos*, custom of arising at midnight to pray
5. Coat-like garment
6. Round fur hats
7. Sidelocks
8. People who made their living trading in the villages
9. The Torah instructs that a blue thread (techelet) be added to the fringes of the tzitzit. The source of blue dye was a sea creature called the chilazon. The identity of the chilazon was lost long ago, and the blue thread was not worn. The Radziner rebbe, Gershon Henoch Leiner (1831-1891) believed the chilazon was the cuttlefish, and his followers wore the techeilis. He was known as the *Ba'al Techeilis*. Today, the marine snail, Murex trunculus, is favored as the source of the blue dye, and is used by many.
10. The tallis fringes
11. Circle dance
12. Shtibl is a small, informal house for praying.
13. War of duty, or holy war.
14. Grandfather

The Community and its Dozors[1]

Arieh Weinriber, Holon

Translated by Moses Milstein

The *kehileh*[2] in Markuszow, as in most shtetls in Poland, was dominated by religious interests for two reasons: a) The devout were actually the majority in the shtetl; b) Since the kehileh was only concerned with the elections of a rabbi, a shammes in the besmedresh, and other functionaries, the elections did not interest the less religious parties.

Nevertheless, every campaign was a passionate one. The different chasidic shtibls, and the community big-shots, competed against each other. The tradesmen were always represented by one dozor, almost always the same one–Hershl Wichter. He was a shoemaker by trade, but a man with a clever mind. For R' Hershl, the voting was a matter of personal prestige, whereas for the tradesmen, it was important to have their own representative to look after their interests and work on their behalf to avoid being

[Page 65]

saddled with high community taxes (*etat*). It has to be admitted that he carried out his duty honestly and resolutely so that "his" tradesmen were not abused. That was why he was always certain to be reelected.

An important person, and also secure in his reelection was R' Shloime Schwartz. A good Jew, a constant *ba'al Musaf* during the Days of Awe, he had the support of the Radziner chasidim, and Baruch Edelstein's court. Since he was well educated, he kept the kehileh books, and dealt with the state's representatives in determining the budget. His son, Gedalieh, who took the position of Jewish soltis in the gmineh, helped with this task, and thanks to this, had close relations with the state's representatives.

A third member of the kehileh was R' Mechl Weiner, the representative of the storekeepers and the Kotzk chasidim. Another member of the board of directors was Mordechai Morel, a rich Jew, but a simple man and a kehileh activist, a true *oysek betzorche tsiber bemuneh*[3]. This man could be trusted with the kehileh money knowing it would not be touched. There were times when he was asked to change money for smaller denominations of coins or bank notes, but he refused on the grounds that he must return exactly the money he was entrusted with.

There were other artisans elected in the kehileh: Yakov Yosef Gothelf, a smart man, who carried on big businesses, and even exported produce to Danzig, and another, R' Yankl Mayerl's who played a role only in the voting.

The whole work of the kehileh consisted of developing and deciding on the budget for the coming year, and taxing every Jew. Shloime Schwartz carried all that out, made sure that the budget was approved, and delivered to the gmineh (more accurately to the Jewish soltis, Gedalieh Schwartz), banked the taxes, and paid the rabbi and shoichet every month.

The shtetl population didn't know what was going on in the kehileh, relying completely on the elected dozors, while the other part, the non-religious, as mentioned above, displayed no interest in the elected Jewish representation. A change in

[Page 66]

this area was first brought about in 1932 when the Zionists in Markuszow decided to take part in the elections, and as their first candidate, put forward the well known Zionist activist, Pinchas Liebhober, who was actually elected. The various kehileh big shots couldn't bear this change in the composition of the kehileh, and R' Pinchas Liebhober was a thorn in their side, especially as, right away during the first meeting he attended as dozor, his proposal was to broaden the kehileh activities to the social domain, hold open meetings so that the shtetl residents could listen to the current kehileh concerns, and to give reports from time to time on general kehileh activities.

Such demands in those days meant an upset in the whole established order. It's worthwhile remembering that Pinchas Liebhober, in composing the budget, managed to pass a motion to donate 150 zlotys to *Keren Kayemet L'Israel*.[4] Those who know how "*treif*" Keren Kayemet was then in the eyes of the devout who had 90% of the seats, can imagine the effect of such a decision. On the other hand, it was the greatest satisfaction for the Markuszow Zionists.

Stormy sessions also took place on the question of hiring a shoichet. Some members would propose another candidate, or a second shoichet, advancing various reasons, like a shtetl could not remain with one shoichet only, because God forbid, he could get sick. And we also needed a reserve chazzan, and a reserve mohel, because the shtetl mohel, Yoel Ettinger, had had several incidents with children. All these problems could be solved, argued the proponents of a second shoichet, if we hired a shoichet-chazan-mohel in one person. And with two shoichets, there wouldn't be any funny business with the butchers who often slaughtered without a certificate of payment to the kehileh. The most important thing is that there would be new money coming from the new shoichet. The shtetl was excited, passionate debates took place in the besmedresh, and in the streets, where knots of debaters could be seen, all because of the shoichet. And the decision came down: to hire another shoichet!

A number of Yiddish newspapers carried the request from the Markuszow kehileh to find another shoichet. Young men

[Page 67]

began to appear in the shtetl, hale and hearty, who were ready to undertake the advertised position. First, they listened to their voices. Every Shabbes, one of them would daven Shacharit or Musaf, and in the end the community agreed on hiring a certain Chaim-Yosl–a truly decent young man with a good voice. The kehileh treasury received a big sum of "*shlisl gelt*," and– *shalom al Israel*.

The old shoichet, Chaim Goldstein, did not lose any of his salary, but he had to share in the *chalokim*[5] of the slaughter suffering a loss Erev Yom Kippur during the slaughtering of the *kapores*.[6]

The kehileh budget was increased by the addition of another position: salary for a second shoichet.

Our functionaries

Over 20 years ago, there was an old rabbi in Markuszow, R' Moishe-Eliyahu Goldwasser. Because of his age, it was hard for him to fulfill the duties of the head of a community. As a result, his son, Peretz, who had expectations of the rabbi's chair after his father's death, helped him out. He used to go with his father to the slaughterhouse, ruled on religious questions, helped with arbitrations, but still was not considered an authority by Markuszow Jews. Also the *Agudah* groups did not see in him someone who could attract the youth, and were doubtful of his ability to lead the religious life of the shtetl Jews. The chasidim also did not favor him, because he did not belong to any of their shtibls. The progressive circles saw in him a backward man who did not know the Polish language, and who would therefor not be able to represent the Jewish population before the Polish authorities. There were those who held that he did not even properly know the Yiddish language. His only employment was trading in dry goods at the market, and there was no lack of jokes in the shtetl about his expressing himself in Polish with his customers.

The first shoichet, Chaim Goldstein, a *batlan*,[7] recognized only two things in his life: study and slaughter. On the other hand, the other shoichet, Chaim Yosl, was an educated young man with a lot of intelligence and worldly views.

There were also two shammeses:[8] the red-headed shammes who knocked on the door shutters Friday evening announcing the coming of Shabbes, or called to Slichot

[Page 68]

Erev Rosh Hashanah. The other shammes, Mordechai Westelschneider, lived in the basement of the besmedresh.

The cantor, Moishe Weinriber, or as he was called, Moishe Beinish's, was a strictly observant man, but a little bit modern. His job was in general not an easy one, because aside from davening before the congregation every Shabbes, holidays, and especially during the Days of Awe, he was also *ba'al koreh*,[9] and *Ba'al tokeh*,[10] and kept a list of all the yorzeits of deceased relatives in order to remind people of the time to light the candle and say Kaddish. He also performed wedding ceremonies, and assisted the mohel. In this manner, he fulfilled the important religious functions in shtetl.

Moishe Weinriber z"l - shtetl cantor

Jewish Markuszow survivors describe his last moments: During the expulsion after Pesach, when hundreds of shtetl Jews were driven away by German soldiers from whence they had lived for dozens of years, he believed it was the end of the road for Markuszow Jewry. In the middle of the march, he stopped and declared that he would go no further. His example was followed by about ten Jews. They were killed on the spot by the German murderers.

Markuszow elects a rabbi

In 1930, the old rabbi died. After he was duly buried, eulogized and lamented, the real hullabaloo about electing another rabbi began.

The dead rabbi's son, Peretz, claimed his inheritance–the rabbinical chair. He brought many rabbis from the whole region to his father's funeral all of whom found it necessary to emphasize, during their eulogy, that according to the law, the son must be the heir. Peretz, in the meantime, had begun to assemble supporters. His nephew, a capable young man, understood how to carry out such a difficult job, because this Peretz had rather weak chances

[Page 69]

to be elected. but since the entire adult (25 years and up) Jewish population had the right to vote for a rabbi, Peretz initially campaigned among the tradesmen and the ordinary people who wanted to elect him out of pity. You can't let the rabbi's son go hungry, especially since he could still be elected rabbi among all the proposed candidates. He did make rulings while his father was still alive, after all. On the other hand, the more progressive circles in shtetl maintained that it was time to hire a modern rabbi, an intelligent one, educated, someone you could be proud of. The chasidic side wanted a rabbi–a *gaon*,[11] a chasid, and scholar.

In this vein, various gatherings, and meetings were organized; people ate drank and lobbied. Those who participated with passion in the campaigning neglected their businesses, preoccupied exclusively with the rebbe issue. There was an announcement in the press. Candidates began to appear in the shtetl and gave sermons. Whereas for the shoichet elections 5 votes (out of the 8 vote members) were enough, a rabbinical candidate had to get a majority out of all the Jewish voting population, and above all, have the support of a designated group of people who would agitate and work for him without which his chances were slim. Concerning the strictly orthodox circles which consisted of Radziner and Kotzker chasidim, if the former put forth a candidate, the latter immediately began to oppose him, and announced their own candidate, a certain R' Aharon Zelichower from Lublin, a man of advanced years but with a keen mind. True, he was not yet a rabbi, although he had one or more rabbinical diplomas, and was well known for arbitrating in important disputes.

But here an unanticipated development occurred: since the Kotzker chasidim were afraid that a Radziner chasid could be elected as rabbi in Markuszow, they decided that it was better for Peretz to become the rabbi rather than a Radziner. With chasidic passion they threw themselves into the election turmoil and battled for Peretz's candidacy. The opposing side was not silent either, and the shtetl was in an uproar. Election day was especially heated.

Late in the evening the results were announced: Peretz was elected as rabbi by one vote. But since the other side was in close contact with the powers-that-be, the *starosta*

[Page 70]

in Pulawy annulled the results and ordered a new election. In the meantime, the Radziners brought their candidate to Markuszow, and paid him a salary as rabbi. Now a dispute flared up. Other rabbis appeared in town, and mixed in, and ruled that R' Aharon Zelichower should remain rabbi in the shtetl, and receive 60% of the rabbi salary, while Peretz would be his successor and would get the remaining 40%. In order for neither of them to be officially elected as rabbi, it was decided that with regard to the authorities, to appoint a businessman of the shtetl. Yenkl Rubinstein, the son of Sholem Heshl's, was elected during the second vote, as the only candidate, as the putative rabbi. It is worth emphasizing that since the Zionists voted for Aharon Zelichower, they were pretty unhappy with this candidate.

Harav Weizman

In 1933 R' Aharon Zelichower suddenly died, and the question of electing a rabbi arose again. It was then that the Zionists, with Pinchas Liebhober and Gedalieh Schwartz at the head, took the matter into their own hands and brought their own candidate for rabbi, a member of Mizrachi, who had graduated from the "*Tachmoni*" school in Warsaw. He was called Elchanan Weizman. On November 11th, Poland's independence day, the representatives of the authorities, were invited to the besmedresh, and Weizman the candidate gave a speech in the Polish language that made a tremendous impression on all the listeners. It was felt that this man had the best chance to be elected, especially considering that a few days before the election a representative of the starosta came and clearly stated that if we elected a person like Peretz, they would annul the results again. The authorities' representative called for electing a man with a worldly education. The most surprising thing happened: Weizman received a resounding majority. The joy of the Zionists, like a minority in the shtetl, was great because of the voting success. Agudah and the other religious circles were outraged that the Zionist apostates were successful in electing one of theirs for rabbi. In their eyes it was a disaster.

-.-

Before I made aliyah to Israel in 1934, I went to say good-bye to the Markuszow rabbi, Weizman. With tears in his eyes,

[Page 71]

he gave me his blessing for the journey, and was truly envious that I could realize my dream. He wished that he would soon be there too where his heart was yearning, but this, unfortunately, did not come to pass. He was killed in a terrible way by the Nazi murderers sharing the fate of the other Markuszow Jews.

Honor to his memory!

Translator's Footnotes:

1. Member of the synagogue council
2. Jewish community organizations
3. One who does volunteer community work.
4. Fund for purchasing land in Israel
5. Bits of meat and offal the shoichet was allowed to take
6. Sacrificial chicken
7. Can refer to man who spends all his time in synagogue studying, or an idler, or unworldly person.
8. Sexton

9. Torah reader
10. Shofar blower
11. A brilliant scholar

Sholem Asch and I. M. Weissenberg in Markuszow

Chayah Hertz Loterstein (Buenos Aires)

Translated by Moses Milstein

Both masters of Yiddish literature, brilliant depicters of the Jewish shtetl–Sholem Asch and I. M. Weissenberg–visited our shtetl at various times and circumstances. These two visits emerge from my memory with the greatest detail.

It was deep in autumn. Rain mixed with snow hammered at the roofs and windows of Markuszow's houses without cease. The shtetl became smaller, shrunken. The weather outside was so awful, you didn't even want to look through the windows. And what could you see other than the soggy, muddy market. Everyone, therefore, sat indoors whether at work, or with a book, or religious work, or just doing nothing because of the foul weather.

I remember as if it were yesterday that an unexpected guest arrived that day. I was sitting in my room reading a book. My mother suddenly opened the door and said:

–Some *shlimazel* is asking for you. (That was how my mother referred to anyone she didn't know who came to visit me).

I went into the front room and saw a man of average size, wearing a *burkeh* (winter coat) from which rivulets of water ran, his face depressed, frozen, but very familiar. I looked closely at his face, recognized him at once and called out:

–Ah, Herr Weissenberg!

The writer seemed to change, his face happier. He straightened his somewhat rounded back, and with good humor asked:

–You, Fraulein, recognized me. From where and how?

–What do you mean how? I happily answered. After reading

[Page 72]

your book, *Shtetl*, I then looked for your picture. Both then became engraved in my memory and in my heart.

His face lit up. He pressed my hand warmly and asked if I had read any of his other creations. I naively cried out–What are you saying? If you like one of an author's work, you look for everything he has written. I have read everything you have written to date.

Excitedly, I began to list off a whole bunch of the stories I was referring to. In the middle of our discussion, Weissenberg takes the book I was reading, and catches a glimpse of the cover, A *Shtetl*, by Sholem Asch. His face becomes serious. He loses the previous cheerfulness and asks:

–Of the two *Shtetls*, which one do you like better? But answer honestly.

I panicked for a second, embarrassed, but my heart began to expand from joy that Weissenberg himself was asking my opinion. I thought for a while and answered timidly–It's possible that Asch's *Shtetl* is more beautifully written, but your *Shtetl* is more authentic, not invented.

I can't forget how Weissenberg's facial expression changed, and his mood. He said,

–Believe me, I am happier with your opinion than with the reviews of the greatest critics. And with enthusiasm he added–Because I have written for people like you.

I invited him to my room. It turned out that his visit to Markuszow was connected with getting subscriptions for the magazine he was preparing to publish. He was visiting a lot of shtetls for this reason, disregarding the bad weather and difficulties a trip like this entailed.

That same evening, in the locale of Kadima, an intimate meeting of lovers of the written Yiddish word took place. We spent several hours with Weissenberg in a warm, friendly environment. I had to read his *Kreindl*, which pleased him very much.

The shtetl talked about the visit of I.M. Weissenberg for a long time. The writer too left our shtetl with the best impressions.

Several years later, my husband, Leizer Loterstein, travelled to

[Page 73]

Warsaw in order to invite I. M. Weissenberg to a reading in Markuszow. The writer replied to the invitation:

–Markuszow?! You have dear, intelligent, young people there. Unfortunately, I can't accept your invitation because of my poor health.

We were very happy and proud with the great writer's opinion of our youth. On the other hand, we greatly regretted that I. M. Weissenberg could not come to Markuszow.

Monday–market day in the shtetl. One of those lovely summer days of which it is said–a God-blessed day. And even in Warsaw, they knew about Markuszow's market day. Merchants would come from Warsaw, and of course traders, storekeepers, tradesmen, and thousands of farmers from all over the surrounding area. The market was already underway Sunday evening when the booths and stalls were set up. Of course there were quarrels around choosing the spots over which some of the shtetl people had tenure.

It's also worth mentioning that, because of this weekly market, the neighboring shtetl of Korew, older and larger than Markuszow, held a grudge. And not without reason. For years a bitter battle had been fought between both shtetls over where the market was held. The Tsarist governor in Lublin ruled in favor of Markuszow. Our shtetl was lucky and honored that this big market would be held here. Korew did not readily give up. They tried to attract the farmers to their market through various means, but with little success. The farmer folks knew just one address where to buy and sell: Markuszow!

All week no farmers were seen in the shtetl, not even for medicine. But when Monday came, it was hard to move through the streets. A commotion, a hoo-ha, a rush–everybody did business that day. If someone did not own their own business, he was helping his father, his mother, a sister or a brother who had interests in the market. That day everybody was a merchant. Even *melamdim*[1] were transformed into storekeepers on Monday, although most of them did not know one word of Polish. I would like to tell the following story about this:

There was a melamed in the shtetl called R' Mendeleh. He dealt in clay pots but only on market day. However, he could only count up to twenty in Polish. If a pot cost 32 groshen, he would give the price

[Page 74]

like this: 20 groshen and 12 groshen. You can imagine how that was received when he expressed it in Polish. The farmers, however, understood him well, and the shtetl clowns had material to make fun of.

On one such market day, when I was also deeply involved in business, a relative of mine came running and told me I must go right away to our cousin, Tzipeh Halbershtat (the wife of the man of letters, and translator, Shloime Sheinberg of Pulawy). My mother, whom I was helping at the moment, became upset, and wringing her hands, she asked, "Precisely now? In the middle of the market? Thieves could rob us, and how will I cope now?"

But regardless, I ran quickly, and my mother did not protest much anymore because she liked Shloime Sheinberg, especially his wife, Tzipeh. She only asked that I come back quickly, even with the cousin in tow, because she needed our help.

I didn't really know how to reply to my mother, and I went off to my relative. I found her alone in the house. To my question of why she asked for me, and where her husband was, she hastily replied that I should hurry over to Shloime Schwartz's house where her husband and Sholem Asch were. If my memory does not mislead me, she also mentioned the name of Shloime Rosenberg who was supposed to have come to Markuszow with Sholem Asch. We immediately went to the residence of Sh. Schwartz, and we saw Sholem Asch standing at the window, captivated by the market then going on in the shtetl. The great writer was wearing a beautiful white summer suit that lay nicely on his figure. He had a full head of black hair; his eyes were focused on the market. He could not look away. Shloime Sheinberg introduced me to him, but I felt that Sholem Asch extended the tips of his fingers without enthusiasm. A little perplexed, timidly, I invited him to go down to the street, and visit the market full of Jews. He, however, declined the invitation, and declared, no, not now, perhaps another time.

With that, he left the house, quickly got into a carriage, and practically without a fare-thee-well, drove out of the shtetl.

Leaving my cousins, I could not hide my disappointment at the short visit of Sholem Asch in Markuszow. Shloime Sheinberg and his wife understood me well, and felt the same.

Translator's Footnote:

1. Teachers of the younger children

[Page 75]

Kadima–First Zionist Organization

Moshe Nachshon (Capa)

Translated by Moses Milstein

My recollections of the first Zionistic cultural organization are closely bound up with the years of WWI.

A Saturday in August 1914. The shtetl was covered with large posters. At first, we thought a travelling troupe was coming to perform in Markuszow, something that had never yet happened in Markuszow. The men going to shul very early to daven could not ignore the colorful posters on which was written in large letters the terrible news: "War!"

All men under the age of 45 had to report to the conscription centers. The bad news quickly spread, and elicited fear and consternation in everyone. Women and children wailed and lamented, and men felt the Angel of Death was about to begin his bloody harvest. Before noon, over 100 farmer wagons were gathered at the *gmineh*[1], and the *soltis*[2] with the policemen rounded up the arriving reservists. Everyone was out on the street. Even the besmedresh was empty of praying men and students. Wailing and lamentations carried through the shtetl.

Afterwards, the crowd re-assembled at the besmedresh. They did not begin davening, but stood around talking. The old rabbi, Rav Eliyahu Goldwasser, mounted the *belemer*, and with tears in his eyes, he begged them not to cry on the Sabbath. Whoever was destined to live would return home in peace. The crowd calmed down somewhat.

The next day, Sunday–back to normal life. Some went to their stores, some to their workshops. Jews returned to business, worked and earned more than ever. Entire regiments rolled through the shtetl, and the soldiers spent money. Various types of merchandise became scarce.

* * *

The Jewish youth, who used to study day and night in the *besmedresh*[3] began to stay away from the holy house. Individually and in groups they joined

[Page 76]

the newly created organization, Kadima," which was established in Markuszow in 1916 during the Austrian occupation. But before the Russians left Markuszow and the Lublin region, they set fire to the shtetl, and 80% of the buildings went up in smoke. It took a year before the shtetl was rebuilt a little. Jewish social life also began to be rebuilt. The leaders of Kadima campaigned for the establishment of a library. The youth zealously took to reading books by Mendeleh, Sholem Aleichem, D. Frishman, Sh. Asch, Sh. Anski, and others, Yesterday's Torah scholars saw a new world before them. The amateur drama group performed L. Tolstoy's, *Kreuzer Sonata*, to great success on Motzi-Pesach 1916. The successful performance encouraged the shtetl youth, and they began to get ready for a second performance on Shavuot. This time, with no less success, they put on "*Der Vilder Mench.*"

It would be a mistake to think that the activities of Kadima were limited to performances. They also carried on Zionist education work, although without a political party orientation. Lectures on Jewish history, *Altneuland*, and *Judenstat* by Theodore Herzl often took place. The speakers were: Itzchak Wasserstrom, and Hersh Loterstein. The members of Kadima had one idea, one goal: Eretz-Israel for all the Jewish people.

Kadima carried on its above-mentioned activity until 1919, after Poland achieved independence. This happy occurrence was however darkened by the antisemitic wave of pogroms in Lemberg and other Polish cities. There was a justified fear that Markuszow too would suffer antisemitic excesses.

Kehileh officials were always lobbying the authorities, knowing in advance that "*kesef yaaneh hakol*"[4] Every Sunday, when the farmers went to church, there was a threat of pogrom in the air. There was a similar feeling every Monday at the weekly market in Markuszow. Every Jew felt it was about to happen. There were actual cases of Jewish stores and stalls being robbed, but with Jewish money everything was "smeared over." The authorities were focused on the money, and did not allow harm to come to the Jews. In the meantime, the Poland-Russia war broke out, and Jewish youth were mobilized for the army. Since the shtetl was emptied of young men, Kadima stopped

[Page 77]

all its work. The library migrated over to Itzchak Ettinger's attic, and the cultural activities in the shtetl completely stopped.

It was not until a year and a half later, in July 1921, that a general meeting took place on the initiative of several young people in order to revive the Zionist work, rent a locale, and renew cultural activities. Itzchak Wasserstrom had died two years before, and the youth laid great hope at the feet of his right-hand man, Hersh Loterstein. But at the meeting, it was learned that Hersh Loterstein had been carrying on "secret work" among the youth, and had tried to bring them over to his side. It seems that the "Bolshevist invasion" had strongly influenced this erstwhile passionate Zionist. He had reversed himself. Loterstein demanded that the name Kadima be removed, that the commission for national funds be eliminated, and the union emptied of all Zionist content. Although he had the enlightened part of the shtetl youth on his side, he was unable to realize his plans at the meeting. The majority was Zionist–and the meeting blew up in scandal.

Nevertheless, negotiations continued between the two sides, because everyone regretted the absence of the organization. They came to an understanding with a compromise. *Chol-Hamoed* Sukkot the long awaited general meeting took place in a rented venue. According to the agreement reached, the Zionists relinquished the name Kadima. From now on the organization had to be called, "*Kultur*." The leftist opposition agreed that the commission for national funds within the board should be able to continue its work. But after reaching agreement, there were incidents that took place for a long time around the picture of Theodore Herzl that was hanging in the venue. The left argued that the library was an apolitical cultural institution where only pictures of poets and authors should be displayed. The Zionists argued that

Herzl was both. Nevertheless, broadly diverse Zionist and cultural activities were carried on. In 1924 the library contained about 700 books.

At that time, Zionism went through a serious crisis with the failure of the fourth aliyah. The communists established the left Poalei Zion and the trade union. New winds began to blow though Markuszow exactly as in other cities and shtetls of Poland where there was a Jewish population. The Kadima library

[Page 78]

was liquidated in order to later be divided among the three parties that had influence in the shtetl then: Zionists, Poalei Zion, and communists. Three libraries in such a small place all at once enriched Markuszow.

Board of the "Kultur" society

Seated from left to right: Kopl Kerschenblatt, Ita Goldwasser, Binyomin Kerschenblatt, Chaim-Mendl Goldwasser, Ita Loterstein, Pinchas Ettinger, Ita Schwartz, Beirech Weberman.

Translator's Footnotes:

1. Community center
2. Village magistrate
3. Study hall
4. Money solves everything.

Memories of Kadima

Chayeh Hertz Loterstein

Translated by Moses Milstein

In 1916 several boys and girls, practically children, got together with the goal of establishing an organization. The main initiator of the meeting was Itzchak Wasserstrom, in whose residence it was decided to found a "union." One can imagine the commotion in the shtetl and the upset among our parents. A real war flared up between us and our parents. They used to lock up our clothes, our shoes, and not let us leave the house. They often tried inducements–but this too did not help. Were we an exception? The drive for knowledge, culture and

[Page 79]

organization was a force of nature in all the cities and shtetls of Poland, and drew in large segments of Jewish youth. Our parents did not give in for a long time because they saw in it not only a meeting of boys and girls (which also used to occur in the union) but a weakening of their power over the children. That was what worried them most. But our will, our stubbornness, were the deciding factors. Even though our numbers were small, our parents finally gave in. What choice did they have? They made peace with fate.

With the pennies that some of the youth accumulated, we rented a room for the union. The founders were the "cream" of the shtetl. We threw ourselves into the work with all the passion of youth, and in a few months the organization counted about 100 members from various classes. The union was Zionist throughout, even by its name–Kadima. Right at the first meeting, it was decided to establish a library. Said and done! Time and energy were not lacking after all. We denied ourselves all other pleasures, and saved money for the organization. At the beginning, several hundred books were bought. What joy, what enthusiasm in bringing the books to the shtetl–the most beautiful and the best of literature of the time. And no wonder: the buyers were experienced scholars and readers. I am moved now in remembering those young people who showed themselves to be such excellent experts in leading a union, writing statutes–really a constitution with paragraphs and subsections. If our later meetings were pretty stormy, the early times were harmonious, simply an idyll. We soon established an amateur drama club and began to act in plays: pieces by Gordon, and later–Peretz Hirshbein, Sholem Aleichem, Nomberg, Asch. We also did not omit the world masters: Moliere and Ibsen. There was nothing to complain about in the artistic taste of both the actors and the audience. The artists were at the top of their work. Other than that, we used to put on literary-artistic evenings at which Ita Goldwasser (now in Paris) and the writer of these lines, used to recite poetry. The monologues of Sholem Aleichem that my brother, Israel, (perished during the Nazi occupation) used to present with such talent on the stage such that professional artists could learn from him, are firmly entrenched in my memory. Kadima also had its own choir.

[Page 80]

Such was our harmonious, active, and creative work until 1919-1920. Afterward, other winds began to blow. The horizon widened; it was after the October Revolution. The great need of the Jewish population, and the still rising antisemitism on one side, and the hope of seeing a free humanity, and consequently a free Jewish people on the other side–strongly influenced our spirit. The first Tarbut school was founded in Markuszow in that period, thanks to the initiative of Pinchas Liebhober, Eliezer Eidelstein, Yudl Schwartz, and Itzchak Rosenberg. Zimmerman, the Yiddish teacher, a leftist, had a huge influence on the youth. The young people were really devoted to this energetic, intelligent young man, fine speaker, singer and reciter of poetry. Two groups began to form, but it did not go so smoothly. The passionate discussions devolved into arguments. One side wanted to save all of humanity, the other side–only the Jewish people. They tried to change the name, change the union into a so-called apolitical library, but it did not help. Kadima was shut down, and the books stored in an attic.

The left Poalei-Zion arose in Markuszow in those days–later the trade union (communists). The library, and the Y.L. Peretz-union that had tried to open, breathed their last. The books were divided among the three parties of the time: Zionists, Poalei-Zion, and Communists. Of the first founders of Kadima, hardly any were left in the shtetl, many having gone away to other places.

Zionist Organization

Arye Weinriber

Translated by Moses Milstein

The Zionist movement in Markuszow dates from the moment when religious youth and *maskilim*[1] began to dream of the Zionist idea, came together in Noah Glazschneider's house, and sang Zionist songs. But the organizational framework of the movement only began with the founding of Kadima, where the more aware part of Markuszow youth came together. At the very beginning of Kadima, the work was solely cultural, whereas the ideological, political and organizational activities, as well as the money collections for the national funds did not begin until 1926.

[Page 81]

The first Zionist task consisted of teaching the Hebrew language. In 1918, right after the end of WWI, Pinchas Liebhober, Gedalieh Schwartz, and Moishe Breinsky founded a Tarbut school[2]. Several rooms were rented at Shlomo Schwartz's. Two teachers were brought in. One of them, Friedmacher, was supposed to teach Hebrew. The second teacher, Zimmerman–Polish and Yiddish. The Zionist-inclined parents saw the school as a major achievement, and tried to maintain it.

The very first founders were: Alter Kandel, Gedalieh Schwartz, Shmuel Avraham Marchewka, and Yosef Goldberg. They excelled at delivering experienced arguments in the street or besmedresh. However, they were weak in carrying on the day-to-day organizational work. In 1926, younger powers arrived, like: Israel-Itche Roguski, Avraham'tche Eidelstein, Pinchas Laks, and Pinchas Liebhober.

Thanks to their efforts, a venue was rented, and a new library was opened with the books passed on from the Peretz library, and newly purchased ones.

On Lag B'Omer 1921 a meeting took place with the students of the Korew Tarbut school, in the middle of the road that connected the two shtetls. This meeting evolved into a big Zionist demonstration. Hundreds of children with blue-white flags in their hands demonstrated under a large Jewish national flag that was carried at the front of the procession. Zionist songs echoed in the air. There were also a lot of parents taking part in the demonstration. Every flag and song evoked yearning and hope for our own land. The parents and children of both shtetls were astounded at the meeting. The history and meaning of Lag B'Omer were explained in a large field. The impressive day ended with singing, recreation and games.

After free obligatory education was instituted in Poland, and a government school was opened in Markuszow, where no fees were paid, the poorer parents took their children out of the Tarbut school, and registered them in the government school. As the number of parents that wanted to support the Tarbut school kept decreasing, the Tarbut school,

[Page 82]

Lag B'Omer celebration of Zionist youth in Markuszow

[Page 83]

after existing for several years, had to close. In 1926, another attempt was made to open a Jewish school. The teacher brought in, Yagoda, began to give classes in Hebrew, and in order for him to survive, efforts were made to have him teach Jewish religion in the Polish schools. But because there were few students in the Hebrew classes, they did not last long.

Plans for a Markuszow colony in Israel

In 1925, the whole shtetl was obsessed with a plan to travel to Eretz-Israel and settle on the land, which was to have been purchased beforehand for Markuszow Jews. They got ready to sell everything and move to Eretz-Israel to their own Markuszow colony. A committee was elected that began to register people for aliyah. Since many Jews saw the Balfour Declaration and the San Remo Act as truly a sign from God to fulfill the ancient dream of *shivat Zion*[3], the committee had a lot of work since about 80% of the Jews registered. Everyone "bought" dunams of land according to their material wealth. To this day, I can see my father's, z"l, sad face at not having the money to acquire a little inheritance in Eretz-Israel. He, along with several other Jewish families. had to remain in the diaspora, meaning, in Markuszow.

They chose two businessmen–Chaim-Yoineh Kitenkorn, a chasid, a rich man (as he was considered in the shtetl), and Pinchas Liebhober, a Maskil and Zionist, began to work on travel permits. But in the meantime, some unhappy news arrived from Eretz-Israel about fraudulent acquisitions, deceptive transactions, and land speculation that put to naught the Markuszow plans for their own colony. The enthusiasm was quickly extinguished especially since the chasidic circles in the shtetl took up the declaration of war against the Zionists on the side of the rabbis, and every pious Jew took it as his obligation, if not his *mitzvah*, to fight Zionist thought and everything that has to do with it, because in their eyes, it was simply heresy. But

[Page 84]

the upcoming youth rather saw a final solution to the Jewish question, and on this ground sharp conflicts between parents and children occurred in dozens of Jewish homes.

Chasidism and Zionism

While the working youth found its way in the left Poalei-Zion, or in the trade union (communist), the Zionist movement had to get its strength from chasidic circles. The religious parents did everything possible to keep their children from becoming infected with Zionist ideas. More than one parent fought an internal battle with himself. On one side, the nationalistic instinct dictated a positive attitude to the very idea of restoring the old-new homeland, while on the other hand, they had to deal with statements from prominent rabbis whose authority and importance they greatly respected. It was lucky that, among the rabbis, there was no consensus on'the matter, and the Zionism-inclined chasidic parents used to relax their strict orthodox attitudes in favor of Zionism, referring to the Zionist orientation of a number of prominent rabbis. I am reminded of when I found a letter from the Gerer rebbe, z"l, to his chasidim. The letter, in the form of a printed notice, called on the religious Jews to buy a plot of land and settle there, basing his call with citations from the Talmud and other holy books. "The last redemption will come via nature," the rebbe argued in his message, and "first you have to settle, then the Messiah will come." This letter was published after the rebbe's visit to Eretz-Israel in 1924 when he bought land himself in Jaffa. It seems that the pressure from the members of his entourage, and from the chasidic world in general, was strong on the Gerer rebbe, and a little while later a decree to hide the letter was issued. I personally carried the letter around for a long time as if it were a treasure. After my father confiscated it from me, the letter disappeared into thin air.

Had our chasidic parents more understanding of the dreams of their children, that Torah and religious tradition can go together with Zionism, many Jewish children would have remained religious Zionists. But the disputations between the parents and the children caused the latter to break the artfully erected barriers, and each one of them found his own way according to his intellect and aspirations. Zionist ideas

[Page 85]

continued to more forcefully affect the chasidic youth and influence the national liberation concept. The struggle between Zionism and Chasidism in Markuszow ended with the victory of Theodore Herzl's adherents.

Off to the Revisionists

In 1929 several activists of the Zionist organization–Abraham'tche Eidelstein, Pinchas Laks, and others, left the movement and established a Revisionist party in Markuszow (*Hatzohar*) and a youth organization–*Betar*. It didn't take long, and practically all the members of the Zionist party and its youth went over to the Revisionists. Only Pinchas Liebhober and Israel-Itche Roguski remained loyal. Both organizations, having no choice, found themselves in the same locale. At the evening meetings that took place very often, the Zionist representatives were inundated with questions that they always answered. Markuszow became a Revisionist fortress. The local activists allied themselves with the central in Warsaw, and speakers came down.

The very fact that uniformed Jewish young people were marching in military step down the main street singing Hebrew songs attracted the young people standing by the side. The simple person in the shtetl, to whom the idea of Eretz-Israel was not foreign, saw in this nationalistic youth both Jewish strength, and consolation and hope against the antisemitic hooliganism and boycott actions.

The *Betar* youth also often organized get-togethers with their brother organization in Korew, Wawolnica, and other shtetls around. *Betar* projects always attracted a lot of people whether it was a Herzl commemorative gathering, or the *yortog* of the hero of Tel Chai, Yosef Trumpledor, as well as literary readings, amateur plays, lectures and *kestl* evenings.[4]

Without an esrog

In those days, in Polish cities and shtetls, there was a strong drive on the part of the Zionist parties to buy products from Eretz-Israel. (*Totzeret Ha'aretz*" action). Markuszow stores began to display the first products from there: Halvah and candies. We, the Zionist youth

[Page 86]

in the shtetl, decided to fight to make sure that all the shtibls, the besmedreshes and certain individual Pious Jews should, for the coming Sukkot, obtain only etrogs and lulavs that come from Eretz-Israel. We openly warned that if any etrogs were brought in from another country, we would destroy them without mercy. We reasoned that an etrog from our land can also be beautiful, and in addition, we would fulfill the verse' *V'lakachat lecha–mishelcha*." The religious Jews, who were bitter opponents of Zionist thought, and held that everything that came from Eretz-Israel was *treif*, actually brought in foreign etrogs. When our youngsters went to shul the first day of sukkot to bless the etrogs, we bit the *pitems*[5] off. Now Markuszow was left with no etrogs.

The next year, our chasidim imported etrogs from Eretz-Israel.

Another schism

In 1931, a split occurred in the Revisionist movement. Such an event soon had an effect on Markuszow. Almost all the *Hatzohar* supporters went over to the A.G. Grossmanists (Jewish State party)[6]. Only *Betar* remained true to Jabotinsky.[7] But the frictions in the organization also led to personal fallings out. Friends of yesterday could not and would not work with opponents of today. The Grossman organization became smaller, especially after several activists made aliyah to Eretz-Israel. The parent Zionists and Revisionists let *Betar* have the locale, and it remained practically the only organization in the shtetl.

When it came to voting for the Sejm,[8] the gemineh or for other general political actions, the organization worked alongside the older Zionist and sympathizers. There were other separate committees active for *Keren Kayemet, Keren HaYesod, Keren Tel Chai*. Money for them was raised during every celebration or gathering of a large number of people.

Translator's Footnotes:

1. Followers of the secular Jewish movement, the Haskalah.
2. Secular Zionist educational institutions. Language of instruction was Hebrew.
3. Return to Zion
4. A kestl is a question box that was hung up prior to a meeting where answers were then discussed.
5. Protuberance on the blossom end
6. Meir Grossman (1888-1964) split from the Jabotinsky Revisionists and established his own party, the Jewish State Party.
7. Ze'ev Jabotinsky (1880-1940) eminent Zionist leader, writer, poet, and soldier.
8. Polish parliament

[Page 87]

Difficulties in the Zionist Work

Sarah Fianka (Weinriber), Holon

Translated by Moses Milstein

Our parents could not, under any circumstances, come to terms with the idea that their children, the apple of their eye, would join the Zionist organization in Markuszow. For them it was certain that the moment the child stepped into the "union", it departed from the path of righteousness, and no longer followed in the ways of the parents. The son stops being a *besmedreshnik*, and the daughter stops saying a *perek Shabbes* on waking. It was on this issue that conflict arose in almost all the Jewish homes in the shtetl, and more than one household had its peace disturbed. If the father were a real fanatic, he would sit shiva for a son or daughter who set foot in the organization, as if they were no more.

As if there were not enough troubles to endure as a Zionist, the opposing parties spared no effort to cause injury to each other with frequent attacks and condemnations.

The most active in fighting us were the left Poalei Zion. Whenever we held our discussion evenings or lectures, they would send their comrades outside our windows who would carry on "concerts" and interfere with the normal progress of the evening. But the following two events are etched in my memory:

Our drama club was getting ready for a performance on the 11th of Adar. The rehearsals, the procurement of decorations, and other jobs related to such an undertaking, were a great difficulty for us. It was decided that all the money from the performance would be given to Zionist causes. The big fireman's hall was rented, many tickets were sold in advance, and success was assured. But a group of supporters of the left Poalei-Zion showed up, led by a comrade who is in Israel today, and who is very dear to us (I don't want to give his name), and spread themselves out not far from the stage. As soon as the curtain was raised, and our performers began the play, a hail of rotten eggs and potatoes rained down on us. Understandably, we were not silent.

[Page 88]

They expected this as well. Chairs began to fly through the air, and a fight was underway, where there were, miraculously, no serious injuries. The police were alerted and mixed in and separated the fighting sides. The performance was however interrupted. We left for home, disappointed and embittered.

The second case as I recall, took place in the area in front of the besmedresh when we were assembled for the *yortog* of the Zionist leader, Theodore Herzl. The same hecklers, this time strengthened by a group of communists from the trade union, immediately provoked a fight, and blood flowed. Again the police intervened, and again it was a miracle that there were no serious incidents, because passion and party ambitions, especially in fighting, was not lacking in anyone.

It was under these difficult conditions that we had to conduct Zionist activities in Markuszow.

[Page 88]

Revisionists and Betar[1]

Moshe Nachshon (Capa)

Translated by Moses Milstein

The events of 1929 in Israel, when the shocking murders of the yeshiva boys in Hebron by Arab killers, as well as the attack in Motza, near Jerusalem where an unarmed Jewish family was slaughtered, shocked the Jewish world, especially its nationalistic youth. The need to accomplish a tangible act, to actively resist against this wave of murder and plunder, was embraced by large segments of Jewish youth all over the world, and even reached Markuszow.

Markuszow youth at that time belonged to the General Zionists organization (of Itzchak Greenboim), of which Pinchas Liebhober, and Israel-Itche Roguski were at the head. At the protest meeting held in 1929 in Markuszow, where harsh words of condemnation of the Arab pogromists were heard, and where Jewish youth were called on to join the battle, it was unanimously decided to approach Betar central in Warsaw to send an instructor to the shtetl immediately, in order to institute normal organizational activities of "*Brit Trumpeldor*."

[Page 89]

Two weeks after this request, two emissaries came from Lublin, dressed in brown uniforms with blue and white armbands, and military caps. That very evening, because of their initiative and energy, the two instructors–Yechiel Prachi (Rosenberg) and Abraham Tahori (Reinman), Betar was created in Markuszow.

On Lag B'Omer, 1930, dozens of Jewish youngsters dressed in military style, marched through the streets of Markuszow. Their external appearance, the uniforms, their military march, and the songs, left an extraordinary impression. The shtetl talked about it for a long time. Avrumtche Eidelstein was elected as commandant (*mfaked*) of Betar at that time.

Although the representative of the Zionist organization in Markuszow had belonged to the supporters of Itzchak Greenboim and his *Al Hamishmar* group it did not prevent him from evincing pride at the Jewish "militarists," not imagining that in time they would be transformed into his greatest political opponents.

Meanwhile the shtetl was in an uproar. Imagine, Jewish youth being schooled in military matters in order to make aliyah to Eretz-Israel, to fight with weapons in hand, liberating the land from foreign hands. Passionate discussions went on in the street, in homes, and in the besmedresh. Between Mincha and Maariv you could hear this kind of talk:

–What kind of a creature is this? Who could have predicted such an affliction? Soldiers of all things! What does this have to do with Jews? Putting on uniforms and marching along singing all over the shtetl– Like the goyim…Who is this person, their leader.

R' Pinchas Liebhober readily answered the last question and talked about the personality of Ze'ev Jabotinsky, the creator of the Jewish Legion in 1917, and who, four years later, risking his life, helped, along with others, to save Jerusalem from a pogrom.

The great *gaon*, Harav Kook, z"l, signed a petition on Shabbes asking the British for clemency in Jabotinsky's sentence of 15 years imprisonment. Subsequently, the British banished him from Eretz-Israel, and forbade him ever to return.

And in this way, discussions in the besmedresh would go on until late in the night about an important event like the recently established Betar organization in the shtetl. Unfortunately, the work of this new youth

[Page 90]

organization was focused exclusively on military drills and military knowledge, while the cultural and organizational activities were neglected. That approach came back to haunt them in 1932 when its senior part joined the newly established party of the "*Yudenstatler*."[2] under the leadership of Meir Grossman. Betar then also lost its leader, Avrumtche Eidelstein. He was replaced by the young Henoch Eidelstein (his younger brother) who, in the span of the 8 months he was in that position, failed to bring any order to the organization. Shaul Schwartz then took on the leadership of Betar.

The new leader took to his work with gusto. His first achievement was to get a new flag for the organization. According to the plan, it was supposed to be constructed with golden nails with broad heads. The members began to collect their few pennies for such an important goal. Everyone was getting ready for the unveiling of the flag which was to be carried out with great ceremony.

In 1933, on a beach in Tel Aviv, one of the representatives of the Israeli worker's party, Mapai, was murdered. A passionate debate about this political murder took place in all the Jewish papers. Mapai accused the Revisionists of being directly responsible for the murder of the young Arlozorov, while the Revisionists flung back that the accusation was groundless. Ze'ev Jabotinsky in particular, distinguished himself in this polemic with his passionate and convincing articles, and left a strong impression on the writer of these lines. That same year, I joined the Revisionist organization in Markuszow. Because of my active organizational work, especially in the area of political lectures, I was elected as chairman of Hatzohar (Zionist-Revisionist).

During a meeting at headquarters it was decided to establish a drama club with the goal of enriching the cultural work and strengthening the organization financially. The very capable Betarist Shaul Fierstein was chosen as director. After rehearsing for several weeks, they performed the play, "*Sureh-Sheindl the Rebbetsin*," which gave us moral as well as material success. The attitude to the organization changed completely; it now benefited from trust and recognition among broad classes.

[Page 91]

If until then, Betar members were considered as "boys playing with sticks," they were now treated with respect and admiration. The older youth began to register for the organization.

In 1934, Jabotinsky proclaimed a drive for a worldwide Jewish petition which was to be sent to three addresses: to the king of England; to the League of Nations in Geneva: and from every Jew to the leader of the country he was living in. As petition commissar in Markuszow, (appointed by the central office), I, along with two other Betarists from headquarters, visited every Jewish home in the shtetl, and campaigned for signing the three letters. The signatures also entailed contributing 90 groshen for postage stamps, so that the petition could be sent to the three addresses. The emissaries of the Revisionist organization

Pinchas Laks,
commander of Betar in Markuszow

were very warmly received by our shtetl Jews, and thereby validated the political action of the petition. Our reputation and importance grew significantly, and the sympathies of the population rose from day to day. And in order not to lose the moral credit that the Markuszow revisionists had recently acquired, it was necessary to cancel the previous agreement about the flag unveiling, so that the money could be used to create a library, and introduce political lectures and classes in Hebrew. The Betar commander, Shaul Schwartz, did not like such far-reaching

[Page 92]

proposals, arguing that they were not permissible in an organization like Betar, where the flag matter was definitely not a secondary matter. Incidentally, he really insisted on the previous agreement in the question. When I proposed asking the 90 Betar members about their position on the whole issue, the commandant was very insulted, and declared that only he, as commandant, had a right to decide. His deputy, Itzchak Fishbein, did not agree with such an approach, and accused Shaul Schwartz of committing a double disciplinary breach: a) the representative of Hatzohar has authority over the commandant of Betar, b) a commandant of Betar, also has to take into consideration the will of the members, because there was no room in the organization for dictatorship and personal ambition. This resulted in an uproar in the local. I managed to calm the heated mood a little, after I explained to the Betarists that a flag with golden nails was a very important thing. If we didn't want to learn the creed that the commandant of Betar, Ze'ev Jabotinsky, teaches us, or if we have no idea about the history of martyrdom of our people, would we then be capable and ready to sacrifice ourselves for the flag which symbolizes our people?

All the assembled members, with the exception of the commandant of course, agreed with such an approach, and the organization began to lead intensive culture activities. Shaul Schwartz left not only the locale then, but Betar in general.

The newly appointed commandant, Pinchas Laks, occupied himself with the necessary reorganization of Betar. Political lectures and classes on various themes took place three times a week. By the end of 1934, Markuszow Betar counted 105 uniformed youth, aside from a group of older youth who considered themselves belonging to Hatzohar.

In the latter half of 1936, Yerachmiel Rubinstein. was appointed Betar commandant. As a response to the events in Eretz-Israel that broke out again that year, Rubinstein and I undertook a trial to create in the shtetl, as was done in other places in Poland, a *"Brit Hachayal"*–a union of former Jewish soldiers and officers. An invitation from the new organization to a founding meeting was sent to all the former soldiers. Intense efforts were made to establish a *Brit Hachayal*–but without success. Very few ex-soldiers accepted our invitations and approaches.

In 1937, the famous royal commission, with Lord Peel at its head, came to Israel in order to, ostensibly, determine the reasons for the unrest.

[Page 93]

Lord Peel and his commissioners concluded that 4% of the land of Eretz-Israel should become a Jewish state, whereas the remaining 96% should become an Arab state. But before the World Zionist Organization could take a stand on the Peel plan, Jabotinsky issued a strong "no:" "The cripple will not be created!" A big education effort was necessary around the conclusions of the English commission. In a shtetl like Markuszow, the best place for this was the besmedresh. I actually exploited the opportunity: On Tisha B'Av,

Avrumtche Edelstein, first commandant of Betar

around 5 in the evening, when almost the whole shtetl was assembled there, I ascended the *belemer* and explained to the audience about the essence of the Peel plan, and the dangers associated with it for Judaism in general, and for Eretz-Israel in particular. Turns out that my words must have convinced even the very pious, the sharpest opponents of Zionist ideology, because after finishing my talk, two orthodox Jews–Yudl Mechl's and Mendl Moishe's–declared before the congregation:

–We want to help Jabotinsky's people!

These words were spoken in a time when the only obstacle to Revisionist work in Markuszow was actually the chasidim who used to revile us as "*Tzionim shkootzim*." But afterward, when the two

[Page 94]

chasidic authorities mentioned above declared themselves supporters of Revisionism, there were no particular obstacles to creating a religious group under the name of "*Achdut Israel*". It met in Itzchak Fingerhut's house. A sefer-Torah was placed there, and 4-5 minyans of religious Markuszow Jews were now loyal chasidim for Revisionism. Every Shabbes, before the reading of the Torah, it was already a custom to have a political lecture about the most important events of the week in and around Eretz-Israel. The supporters of Achdut Israel listened with great interest to the information about the battles being waged by Jewish heroes there.

As mentioned, most of the older Jews in the years 1937-1939 were Revisionist inclined, and that insured success in advance for every action that Hatzohar carried out in the shtetl. In 1938, an order came from central in Warsaw to set up the work necessary for the illegal aliyah, the so-called Aliyah Bet, in whose framework we had to get Betar members to make aliyah. In Markuszow, a "committee to support low income youths for aliyah" was created. The first work of the committee consisted of calling together a board of the most prominent social activists with the kehileh representative at the head. Moishe Ettinger, the president of the kehileh at the time, its dozors, and other important activists on the board, came to the conclusion that not only the well-to-do Jews should benefit from the right to make aliyah to E.I, but also poor youth who want to settle in the land of our fathers, and who don't have the material opportunities thereby, should receive the full support of Jewish society. Moishe Ettinger was ready to demonstrate the far-reaching support of the plan, with the proviso that the committee should be legalized by the authorities, and thus get official permission to solicit funds.

The day after the meeting, I went to se the *soltis*[3] authority in Pulawy, and got the permission necessary for our new initiative. The following Sunday we three–the kehileh representative, the Betar commandant, and I, went from house to house, explained the job of the committee, and everyone contributed a monthly fee. It was also decided that the revenue from the performances of the drama club be used to help the *olim* with fewer resources.

It is worthwhile to take the opportunity to relate the following characteristic case:

[Page 95]

A number of activists from the trade union, which was under the influence of the communists, approached Betar leadership in the shtetl with the request to be included in the organization with the reasoning that if Betar looks after the poor, the idea of belonging to such a movement is not a bad one.

The committee accomplished a lot both in the domain of education, and funding. It did not however manage to send any of the Markuszow youth on aliyah. World war II was approaching. The Nazi occupation destroyed all the beautiful plans of the Jewish youth, destroying the dreamers along with their dreams.

In August 1938, on the initiative of Markuszow Betar, a summer colony was set up in Bobowiska, a village about 4 km from Markuszow, for the Betarists from Lublin, Korew, and Markuszow. Two hundred and fifty Betar members from these places spent 6 weeks in 8 houses in a pine forest. A tradition was established that the "colonists" would come to daven in the shtetl on Saturday. Markuszow residents, Jews as well as non-Jewish Poles, were stunned to see, on a Saturday morning, the arrival of the Betarists in military uniforms, with a steady step and singing, marching into the shtetl and to the besmedresh just when the first minyan had ended their davening, and the second minyan was about to start. Our little Trumpeldorniks settled on the shul pews, took their little siddurs out of their bags, and davened. The congregants were full of pride at their "Jewish army," and were a topic of conversation that Shabbes day. After the davening, Rivkeh Capa distributed refreshments to the Betarists who left in the afternoon accompanied by practically all the Markuszow Jews. Young and old accompanied them all the way to the colony in Bobowiska.

I will end my recollections about Betar with the attempts to establish a division of the secret Jewish youth organization, "*Irgun Zvai Leumi*" (*Etzel*).[4] It happened like this:

While the Betarists were in the colony in Bobowiska, and I was strolling around on a Saturday afternoon with some young people from our shtetl, two young people dressed in civilian clothes called me aside, and after we had found a quiet place in the woods, they transmitted an order to me from the head of Etzel,

[Page 96]

that I was nominated to be their man in Markuszow, and that I would be sent the necessary materials, instructions, and written lectures for the new organization under the most strict rules of conspiracy. I accepted this nomination, and set up a connection with several young people from the shtetl. A few days later, the material for our work was sent to me. The daily newspaper, "*Die Tat*," was also published at the time, edited by Nathan Friedman (Yellin). As an Etzel publication, this particular organ, helped a lot for our education work, and had the largest circulation in Markuszow–50 copies a day, a number that far exceeded the circulation of "*Heint*," "*Moment*," "*Folkszeitung*," and all the other Jewish newspapers put together. The success of the spread of Die Tat, was helped in great measure by the 14-year-old Pinchas Capa.

The members of Etzel held frequent secret meetings in the fields or the forest. Everyone of them was filled with a blazing belief and enthusiasm for a Jewish land. They were registered for Aliyah Bet, and hoped to make aliyah to Eretz-Israel at any moment. They did not live to realize their dream, sharing the fate of the murdered Markuszow Jews.

Honor to their memory!

[Un-numbered next page]

Betar in Markuszow

[Page 97]

Betar and Hatzohar in Markuszow

Translator's Footnotes:

1. Betar is a Hebrew acronym of Brit Trumpeldor (Yosef Trumpeldor Covenant). It is also the name of the Jewish fort that survived during the Bar Kochba Revolt and the last to fall to the Romans (136 C.E.) Yosef Trumpeldor (1880-1920) was a heroic fighter who was killed at the Tel Chai massacre by Lebanese Shia.
2. Jewish State party
3. Village magistrate in Poland
4. National Military Organization

[Page 98]

The Left Poalei-Zion

Dovid Brenner (Tevl), Ramat Gan

Translated by Moses Milstein

Markuszow caught on late to the echoes reverberating from the turbulent Jewish life of Poland in the first years after WWI. A mere echo of the *"sturm und drang period"* reached the shtetl, broke into traditional Jewish homes, aroused and excited hearts, and implanted new beliefs and ideas.

News about the fruitful work of the proletarian-Zionist workers movement, Poalei-Zion, came to Markuszow from neighboring shtetls like Korew, Konskowola, and Pulawy, from nearby Lublin and from more distant Warsaw, with their comprehensive activities in the political, social, cultural, and Israeli realms. There were several supporters of Poale-Zion in the shtetl who determined to establish an organization and carry on party activities.

The origin of the left Poalei-Zion in Markuszow dates from the year 1923. At that time, *chaver*[1] Beinish was sent from Warsaw. First, he began to organize the youth. He was, however, impeded from doing this work when the police began mixing in.

A year later, (1924) *chaver* Yehoshua Tarchitz came down from Pulawy and with equal energy began to establish the Poale-Zion party, the first Zionist worker organization. The founding meeting took place in the residence of the Glazshneider brothers with the participation of about 30 people, among them: Shmuel-Yakov and Avraham-Lozer Wichter, Obadiah Glasman, Velvl Bratten, Mordechai Glasman, and others. The most important decisions of the founding meeting were: affiliating with the central committee in Warsaw, subscribing to the *"Arbeter Zeitung"* (central organ of the party), and legalizing a division of the "social evening classes for workers in Warsaw" with the authorities.

[Page 99]

Chaver Tarchitz used to come to us once a week from Pulawy, most of the time on foot, ignoring the rain, snow or the hottest days. With his help the first lectures on Marxism, Borochovism,[2] and actual political events, were held. From at the beginning, there was no fixed locale, the lectures, or as we called them–circles, were always held at a different comrade's house. The organization grew, however, and by 1925, the comrades had collected enough money to get their own locale. (In the Pole, Zurman's, house). During the house warming the red flag was hung up for the first time. Over 60 workers and other people came to the celebration. Motl Glazshneider chaired the event. The keynote speech, including well-wishes from the central committee, was given by Yehoshua Tarchitz. While delivering the greetings from the Peretz library, Binyomin Kerschenblatt, forgot his memorized speech, apologized, and had to read the written welcome. A different impression was made by Shmuel Nierenberg from the Konskowoler Poalei-Zion organization, but not especially by his words, but by his traditional chasidic garb.

The first board of directors of the evening class society (that was the official, legal name under which Poalei-Zion carried out its activities in Poland) was composed of: Chaim-Mendl Goldwasser, Motl Glazschneider, Israel Edelstein, Yakov Goldschlager, Abraham-Lozer Wichter.

Thanks to the locale, it was possible to carry out normal activities. Once a week a political discussion took place on the nature of Poalei-Zion related to the events in Eretz-Israel, in Poland, and across the world. Public readings on literarary or political themes were held quite often.

One such reading, I recall, was given by the writer, Yoel Mastboim, "On the Emancipation of Women." The speaker strongly criticized the use of powder and lipstick by women.

All these discussions and lectures were led by *chaver* Yosl Lerman (from Korew) and a *chaver* from Kuzmir whose name I can't remember, and other party comrades.

The designation, "evening classes," was not merely a notice of our activities. There were indeed courses in reading and writing Yiddish. Aside from those, Pinyeh Ettinger read interesting

[Page 100]

fragments of classical works every Saturday. Every Friday evening, "*kestle*"[3] discussions were held where various questions were addressed.

The chaverim were strongly dedicated to the organization. Over 40 members regularly attended all the party activities and paid the weekly fee of 25 groshen.

The decision to establish a library was rather quickly realized. We bought books from the representatives of the publishing houses in Warsaw and Vilna that used to visit Markuszow, levied fees, and in that manner, acquired the first hundred books. The librarian was Yankl Goldschlager.

--*--

May 1, 1925 was celebrated for the first time by Jewish Markuszowers. The red flag flew from the roof of the party clubhouse. Over 100 people attended the May meeting. Everyone wore a red symbol on their lapel. The audience listened to the speeches of Shmuel-Motl Glazshneider (chairman), and Yosl Lerman (Korew) with the greatest attentiveness. The specially prepared choir sang worker songs.

--*--

The ideological differences among Jews in Poland was reflected in Markuszow. At the end of 1926, a group of Poalei Zion members left he party and founded a trade union that in time became transformed into a branch of the local Communist party. (Reds) Because of the internal dissension, frequent discussions, and general turmoil, party work stopped almost completely. A lock was hung up in the locale–the sign of inactivity.

The trade union did not have its own locale. It seemed as if cultural life in the shtetl was finally halted.

At the time, a large number of Jews, Polish citizens, were expelled from Germany. One of them, Dovid'che Sandberg, an erstwhile Korew resident, settled in Markuszow along with his wife and three children. A member of Poalei Zion for years, he was not happy with the inactivity of the party. Even though he was not yet properly settled in, he threw himself into party work and carried it out prodigiously. He was helped by a group of activists: Israel Edelstein, (from the Peretz library) Pinyeh Ettinger, Chaim Mendl Goldwasser. This same Sandberg also formed a drama club

[Page 101]

that produced well-attended performances in the fire hall (*Shopeh*) and elsewhere. They put on: Andreyev's *The Seven Hanged*, Hirshbein's, *The Empty Tavern*, Sholem Aleichem's, *The Big Win*."

Political education was carried out regularly in clubs, discussions and lectures. This all took place in *chaver* Sandberg's house. Once we had a visit from Y. Petezeil (from Warsaw) who had just returned from visiting Eretz Israel. Then we learned that *chaver* Zerubabel was in Pulawy where the Jewish Workers' *pinkas* was being prepared for print under his direction. Zerubabel accepted our invitation to come to Markuszow and lecture on Peretz. The lecture took place on a cold winter evening. The room was so overfilled that many people had to stand outside, and the windows had to be opened so that the crowd could hear the lecture.

In 1925, the Peretz library stopped its activities. Most of the activists either got married or immigrated overseas, or to Warsaw, and there was no youthful energy to continue the cultural work. The 800 books found a place now in Pinyeh Ettinger's attic. But the youth of the shtetl began to protest over why we had liquidated such a library that was rotting in storage. After long negotiations, and passionate discussions, it was decided to divide the library into three equal parts among Poalei Zion, Zionists, and the trade union (Communists).

The difficult material circumstances of Dovid'che Sandberg forced him to relocate to Korew. After he left the shtetl, we aspired to continue the party work. Comrades donated small and larger sums and a locale was rented at the Pole, Opolski's, house. Rent was paid for a year in advance. The house worming for the second locale was celebrated with a magnificent banquet. Meyer Schildkraut came from Lublin to address us. A group of comrades from Korew also joined us in the celebration.

1927. The elections for the Sejm[4] were approaching. In Markuszow, as well as in the rest of the country, a passionate campaign for votes took place. Our party first of all carried out an assessment for the vote fund which brought in a significant sum. Comrades happily contributed to the vote campaign–not only with money but also with house calls. They visited every Jewish house in the shtetl, and campaigned for votes for the Poalei Zion list.

[Page 102]

Our voter meetings and gatherings met with great success. Speakers like Meyer Schildkraut and Sh. Mittleman from Lublin, and Itzchak Levi from Warsaw came to our meetings. Aside from them, *chaver* Yosl Lerman of Korew, Yehoshua Tarchitz from Pulawy, and a *chaver* from Kuzmir came to Markuszow to help us in our work.

Youth committee

Sitting from L to R: Chaneh Gothelf, Sureh Mast
Standing: Asher Holtzhendler, Moishe Wichter, and D. Brenner (Tevl)

At every one of our meetings we gave members of other parties the opportunity for rebuttal. We also instituted receptions in private houses, and came in contact with every Jewish

[Page 103]

voter. The results of such work was seen in the voting: Our list–number 5–received a large number of Jewish votes in the shtetl where also other lists ran: Agudah, Zionists, "Reds." We came out victorious in our first political campaign.

During Passover, 1927, the fifteenth year jubilee of the party's existence was celebrated in Konskowola. About 20 male and female comrades from Markuszow planned to take part in the celebrations. To do that they had to secretly gather outside the shtetl at a predetermined spot and then arrive in Konskowola in a rented wagon because it was Shabbes, and we didn't want to make trouble for our parents with *michalel Shabbes*[5] in public. It did not however help. There are no secrets in a small shtetl. Our parents found out about our *chilul Shabbes*, and the shtetl buzzed about it for a long time. I also wanted to hide my Saturday trip to Konskowola, but I was outed by the carriage driver, Borek's son, who came to our house to collect the fare for the trip. It went from bad to worse: my mother's first reaction was–a broom over the head.

In general there was no lack of interference in our party-social work, because of the frequent mixing-in of the shtetl religious bureaucracy, and our strongly religious parents. The party's drama circle was keen to put on performances in the shtetl. One time, we had prepared a Saturday night piece. Both the actors and the audience were looking forward to the "premiere." Saturday morning we learned that the fire hall (*shopeh*) had been reserved for a concert, and we would not be able to put on the play. We did not however want to cancel the performance, and we remembered that there was an unfinished building in town, around which there were lots of construction materials and boards. With little hesitation we went over there and built a stage and benches for the audience. Not far from there lived Chaneh the kasheh maker, a very pious woman, who heard the hammering and quickly went and told the shtetl rabbi. Shtetl Jews as well as the rabbi came to observe the curious sight of Jewish youths hammering, sawing, constructing a theater hall on Shabbes. They decreed that we must stop our work, but we did not obey, until they called the police. Nevertheless, the show took place that evening. The hall was packed. The play

[Page 104]

went on with no interruptions. The rabbi's granddaughter, Itteh Goldwasser (now in Paris) was among the "artists." Her mother could not forgive such a desecration, and she was always knocking on the window, calling, "Itteh, come home!" Her younger brother who was in the hall, chimed in, "Itteh, get down off the stage! Mother wants you!" We were helpless. We had to stop the performance. Our anger was great, and for revenge, we–girls and boys–marched through the shtetl crying, "Down with the clerics! Down with darkness!"

"Yugnt, "Yungbor," and sports

Thanks to the new location that we managed to acquire at the beginning of 1927, the Poalei Zionist youth organization, "Yugnt" was founded in the spring of that year, the first of its kind in the shtetl at that time. Soon after, the children's organization, "Yungbor" (young Borochowists) was founded.

Among the first founders of Yugnt were: the sisters Perl and Dvoireh Gothelf, Itteleh "Machornik," Chaim-Leib Fishbein, Israel Nadelman, and myself. Young workers, tradesmen, and students joined the organization. Political discussions took place every Saturday afternoon led by Avraham-Lozer Wichter[6], Pinyeh Ettinger, and others. Our comrades from Korew helped us in this activity: Aharon Akerman, *chaver* Leibl, and emissaries from Warsaw. An instructor specially sent from Central, initiated regular activities: kestl evenings, and regular discussion about Borochovism.[7] All these events were well attended, and the youth developed an active movement. In winter we would organize excursions on the ice–with skates and sleds. We were sometimes attacked on these excursions by Polish {Christian}young hooligans. We never retreated from these attacks, however, and we endured these wars and all their consequences even in the face of violence.

There was an unspoken agreement with the nearby shtetls of Korew and Konskowola that we would attend each other's party celebrations or social events. We would travel to the shtetls in sleighs and wagons, stuffed with a lot of straw, to help out our brother organizations achieve success in their undertakings.

Mechl Ettinger, a member of the sports club, Gwiazda (Star) returned from Warsaw. With his help,

[Page 105]

a sports club was established in Yugnt whose only activity was soccer. Aside from that, we used to organize excursions every Shabbes, far from the shtetl, in forests and villages. We really enjoyed those Saturdays, picking fruit from the trees, eating with the farmers, and free of the daily concerns. In the summer of 1927 we organized a get-together with the youth of Konskowola halfway between us–in the forest near Korew. After that first meeting, we continued such gatherings with other neighboring organizations.

Central in Warsaw would send us lectures and instructors from time to time whose visits we would often use as the occasion for public lectures like for example: M. Grob, Y. Miller, Burstin, Motl Knobowitz (from Pinsk) Meir'l Reich, Inzsh, Steinmetz. The latter reported on *"The Way to a Jewish Land."*

Even our youngsters–Yungbor–were not lagging in their activities. Children from school or the workshop belonged. Almost every Yungborist knew the life story of the great worker-thinker, Ber Borochov. The growth of Yungbor necessitated the installation of a special children's section in the library. The members who could not read or write were given courses by the organization. The children also had their own drama club, and with the participation of Shloime Mittleman from Lublin, they put on Y. L. Peretz's *"Die Din-Torah Mitn Vint."* The children waited impatiently for the publication of "Kindervelt" edited by *chaver* Yakov Kenner. The Markuszow Yungborists collected money so that everyone could get the special uniform (a navy blue blouse with a red tie) that could be purchased at Central in Warsaw. Our Yungborists used to greet each other enthusiastically with the password "Ready–always ready."

I was given the honor of representing Markuszow Yungbor at the first national conference of the Yungbor organization in Warsaw in 1928.

At the fifth anniversary of Yugnt in Markuszow, Yungbor brought the most valuable gift, 20 Yungborists graduated into Yugnt.

[Page 106]

Persecutions

On the eve of May 1st 1929, one of our most active comrades, Shmuel Yakov Wichter was arrested. He was accused of distributing illegal Communist literature. The arrest took place in the following circumstances:

There was a poor farmer in Markuszow who made a living from various jobs, from delivering a package to herding cattle. The communist activist, Feivl Wichter, hired him to go to the train station in Naleczow to receive a package. When he had retrieved the package, he was stopped by the police, and it turned out that the small package contained hundreds of leaflets for the May demonstrations from the then illegal KPP (Polish Communist Party). The farmer identified our comrade, Shmuel Yakov Wichter, as the person who hired him to go to the train at Naleczow to pick up the parcel. The farmer's mistake stemmed from the fact that both brothers resembled each other, and Feivl Wichter had also covered his face with a kerchief to prevent identification. Shmuel Yakov Wichter knew who had brought down the package of leaflets, but he decided to keep silent, even though during the investigation and in jail he endured much grief and persecution. He spent nine months in the Lublin *"zamek"*[8] before his trial. In the meantime, a hard battle was going on between the political prisoners and the prison administration connected to a 4-day hunger strike. After Shmuel Yakov Wichter was freed at the trial, we saw him in the shtetl with clear signs of beatings and exhaustion. This did not prevent him from continuing to advance his party work, undertaking the distinguished role of chairman of the left Poalei-Zion in Markuszow.

Big Yugnt celebration

Pesach, 1932, marked the fifth anniversary of the founding of the Yugnt organization in Markuszow. To mark this date, we undertook to organize a big celebration with the participation of bigger delegations from Lublin (15 comrades), Korew, Konskowola, and Miechow. Chairman of the event was Nachum Glasman. After his opening speech, various representatives delivered greetings from different areas.

[Page 107]

I reported on the five years of Markuszow Poalei-Zion youth. David Stockfish from Lublin gave a report titled, *The Duties of the Jewish Labor Movement*. Then a richly artistic event was put on: the choir sang the workers' hymns, the drama club put on various stage adaptations under the direction of A. Akerman. Then the sport group managed to successfully display some pyramids. The celebration ended with a comradely banquet the next day.

Decline and rise

During the Sejm elections of 1932, the party organization, along with Yugnt and Yungbor, were very active in education work and propaganda. There were a lot of competitors for the vote in the Jewish street.

However, after the voting came depression. Many members, especially the older ones, began to demonstrate apathy and indifference to the turbulent atmosphere. In truth, many were caught up in the emigration waves to larger cities or abroad. Some got married and it was difficult to be involved with worries about livelihood, especially for a family, along with party and social activities. These discouraged comrades were not disappointed in the party, in its ideology, but were simply tired. In such circumstances it was hard to hold onto the locale which was costing a lot of money. Fortunately, our youth did not participate in this atmosphere of apathy. Thanks to their personal experiences and the close relationships among them, they got together every evening in another house, entertaining themselves socially and politically, and continued to live in an atmosphere of collective thought and deeds. Thanks to these youths the authority and reputation of our organization in the shtetl did not diminish, and we continued to receive the credit and trust of the Markuszow Jews. We led political discussions, and shone a light on the events that were going on in the wider world, Eretz Israel, and Poland. The contacts with Central in Warsaw, and the regional committee in Lublin were not severed. On the contrary, instructors and lecturers were regularly coming to visit us, especially in relation to the debates in the party about the forms of active action on Zionist and Eretz Israel issues. The Markuszow organization remained true to the attitudes of the majority.

[Page 108]

We understood that it was difficult to go on with party work when there was no appropriate locale. It was actually the youth who came up with the idea of creating a party-club, and the first to donate their pennies to that goal. We managed to get a locale, renew the library, and continue the party work until 1935, when I immigrated to Eretz Israel.

That year, I took to getting ready to realize my longstanding dream about immigration. Contributing to this were the strong antisemitic winds that were

Poalei-Zion committee

Sitting from L to R: Nachum Glasman, Esther Friedman, David Brenner (Tevl), Chanah Rothstein, Moishe Wichter, Yechiel Gothelf

blowing through Poland, and the economic crisis which hit the Jewish population especially hard. I connected with comrade Itzchak Lev of Poalei-Zion who was involved with matter of immigration of the party. And I was lucky to get to the land under illegal auspices.

Even now, I can still see before me the dozens of comrades who affectionately bid me farewell on a special evening. It was hard to part from such

[Page 109]

close friends, friends I had lived with for years. The only consolation and hope was that we would all meet in the Jewish state. Who could then have predicted the tragic fate of our brothers?

To the memory of friends

From the countless letters I received from Markuszow while in the land, I was kept informed abut the Poalei-Zion work in the shtetl which continued until the catastrophe of 1939. I want to mention several names of the loyal guard Poalei-Zion who in really difficult conditions continued the beautiful traditions of our party.

Nachum Glasman, a carpenter-worker, took my place in the party. He distinguished himself with his earnest comportment and responsibility to party work. At the age of ten, he had to begin work and could not finish even the *folks-shule*. He managed to flee to Russia during the war, and as a soldier in the Red Army, he took part in almost all the major battles and fell at the start of 1945 when Berlin was being stormed.

Hershl Nadleman was a child of poor parents who distinguished himself especially by his energetic youth work. On his own, he went over to Borochivism, and led Yungbor for a while.

The brothers, Moishe and Shaul Wichter were among the most loyal comrades in the party. Unfortunately, I don't know of their tragic end. There was news about Moishe Wichter who was believed to have been seen in Italy after liberation.

The energetic and youthful Rochl-Leah Wichter distinguished herself with her devotion and activity. She shared the tragic fate of the Markuszow Jews.

Honor to their memory!

Translator's Footnotes:

1. Comrade
2. Ber Borochov, 1881-1917, Marxist-Zionist, founding member of the Labour Zionists, and important contributor to Yiddish language studies.
3. Kestle means "box." Questions were submitted to a designated box and addressed during the meeting.
4. Polish parliament
5. Desecration of the Sabbath
6. Name unclear
7. One of the founders of Labor or Marxist Zionism.
8. Polish: lock, castle, fortress

[Page 110]

Recollections

Tzipora Fedberg (Beigelman) Tel Aviv

Translated by Moses Milstein

We put on plays

If a resident of a big city has an inclination to see a play, he just has to consult a billboard or a newspaper in order to decide how to spend an evening. He picks a play that appeals to him, buys a ticket, takes his designated place in the theater, and enjoys himself for a few hours. But acting or seeing a play was an entirely different experience in Markuszow, because Markuszow Jews, especially the young, had to provide the theater for themselves. They were the artists, the organizers, and the audience. I, as one of the Markuszow public, empathized and sympathized with all the worries over the success of the spectacle which at bottom was just amateur performances. But for this very reason, the responsibility fell on the entire youth collective, and not only on the actors.

I remember this: the drama club of Poalei-Zion Yugnt (where I was a member) decided to put on a well-known piece. The comrades began to prepare the performance with great enthusiasm, and the parts were handed out and quickly learned. As usual, the leading role was given to our "star," Ruchl Leah Wichter, an energetic young girl. She always came to rehearsals cheerful, bringing the whole street of neighbors along. The happy gang filled the little room where the rehearsal was held. A little stove was burning red hot because it was cold winter outside. The room was warm due to its closeness. You couldn't fit a pin in. Hearts were light, young people bubbling with energy and enthusiasm.

So the rehearsals continued on in the long winter nights. Almost every member of the organization who was not acting, considered it his holy duty to attend one or more rehearsals, and took part enthusiastically in the preparations for the performance scheduled for Pesach.

[Page 111]

The day of the performance approaches. The roles have been well studied. The last details of the decorations and the costumes are finished. The hall has been rented from the firemen. Everyone lends a hand to the spectacle which must–has to–succeed, because the performance represents not only a moral victory for the actors themselves, but above all, a major political win for the organization, a success for the party, which is after all the point.

The other parties in the shtetl know this as well. They will certainly also come to the presentation. What an effort it is to get everything ready! And we stayed on guard…Every opponent from another party was "covered" by one of our own. We kept our eyes on everyone. Anything could happen…My heart had one wish: "*Gotenyu*, may nothing spoil this!" -----And nothing spoiled it. The performance went on brilliantly. To the chagrin of our enemies, everything transpired smoothly. The actors acted well, the piece was a big hit, the hall was in order. The party scored an important success!

Today, I remember with love and respect not only my party comrades with whom I shared a common language, ideal, and goals, but also our ideological opponents who later met a beastly fate.

Fooled father

Winter with its deep frosts passed, and the warm winds of spring blew over the shtetl beginning to dry up the mud. Markuszow came alive freed from winter's vice, and the gentle sun warmed the earth. Fields and gardens greened and bloomed. Everyone was enveloped by freshness and longing.

On such days, the shtetl youth organized excursions to the fields and forests. Once (I don't remember the year exactly), the Poalei-Zion organization decided to plan a trip to the forest at Poczeche[1], 14 km from Markuszow, and to meet up with Lublin comrades there. Being a young girl, I had never yet stepped out of the house on such a long trip. Perhaps that's why the whole plan with the trip appealed to me so much, even though there was no small danger associated with it. The trip was to take place on a Saturday, and it was hard to imagine my religious parents allowing me to leave the house. But I was so obsessed with the thought of getting out of the shtetl for a few hours, that it was clear to me that I had to take part in the Saturday trip. Of course, I kept the whole thing a secret from my parents so that they couldn't, God forbid, interfere with my plans. But as the saying goes, "Man proposes and God disposes." That very Saturday when the trip was to take place, my father left quite early for the besmedresh (that was his habit every Shabbes) and no sooner had he crossed the threshold of the holy place, than he was accosted by his fellow Jews with a broad "Gut Shabbes" accompanied by a pained expression: "Nice, R' Asher. Very nice! What can you say…Asher Beigelman's daughter goes to Lublin on Shabbes, along with all the goyim. A fine *naches* you lived to see…"

At first my father refused to believe it. He even laughed at the idea. He was sure they were kidding him. But a thought slowly crept in: Who knows? Today's times… He quickly took off his *taliss*, ran home, burst thorough the door, and instead of the usual "Gut Shabbes," he asked loudly, " Chaneh, where is the girl?" (Meaning me).

The people in the house were shocked at the question. My mother, who had no idea of what was going on here, first shot a glance at me, and was going to answer my father that I was home. My father saw me, made a gesture that ignored my mother's answer, and explained in minute detail what they sere saying in the besmedresh. He complained at what a disgrace it was to have lived to see this–an obvious *chilul haShabbes*.[2] He angrily hit the table with his fist and said, " I will not allow this girl to leave this house. She will be confined to the house the whole Shabbes! I am not going to daven today. We will all sit here. It will be *Tisha B'Av*[3] here! The girl needs to be torn limb from limb."

Afterward, my father took out a *chumash*, sat down near the door, and began to study the sedreh.

It meant that I was now imprisoned like in a jail. There could be no talk of leaving the house, and time was passing by. I sat with a broken heart by the window and cried. I saw boys and girls from the shtetl assembling outside. Everyone was happy and cheerful. No small thing–going off to the forest on foot. There they would meet the Lublin comrades and enjoy a Saturday morning.

[Page 112]

Some of the girls approached my window, called to me–but I could not respond to them at all. An oppressive mood reigned in the house. Father had finished his davening. (I think it was the first time he davened alone on a Shabbes). At frequent intervals, he would look at me to see if I was still there. Clearly, he was happy to have managed to prevent his daughter from committing a *chilul Shabbes*. Now he was certain that I would not be going to the Paczecher forest. The gang had probably already left. He didn't need to watch me anymore.

Mother prepared the Shabbes table, and we began to eat. I did not hurry, so as not to arouse suspicion. Mother apparently wanted to placate me and served me first the sooner to be free of house arrest. After eating, I slowly left the house. My father even warned my mother to keep an eye on me. I headed intentionally for the center of town, and my parents were now happy and certain that I was not going to meet with the Lubliners.

Yes, dear father, please forgive me for fooling you then. From the house, I went to my friend Leah Rottenberg where my clothing was waiting for me. From there, via a side street, I ran towards the Lublin road where my friends were waiting for me.

That day we walked more than a *tchum Shabbes*…[4]

Translator's Footnotes:

1. The closest approximation to the Polish name I could find is the forest at Parchatka, about 17 km from Markuszow
2. Desecration of the Sabbath
3. Day of mourning for the destruction of the temple, the 9th of Av
4. The distance permissible to walk outside town on Saturday

[Page 113]

The Trade Union

(According to the testimony of Leibish Kandel and Dovid Brenner)

Translated by Moses Milstein

L. Kandel reports:

In 1924, as a 14-year-old child, I began to work for R' Nafatli who made clothes for farmers. There was no question of actually learning the trade at that age. First you had to do housework, look after the babies, and whatever else had to be done that had little to do with tailoring. For the first six months you were a messenger boy and a servant girl. Then after that time, you were worthy enough to pick up a needle.

After working for a year with no wages, Shmuel Bratten and I went to work for the tailor Benyomin-Shloime. R' Naftali begged us to stay with him promising us a salary. But we had had enough of his little house, and aside form the housework, there were also four little children,

[Page 114]

a goat, and we had to work from dark to dark. In winter we sat and sewed even until midnight. We knew, however, that Naftali earned nothing from this hard work.

In 1926 I returned to the shtetl after having been in Lodz for a year working for my brother-in-law, a tailor. I went to work for Benyomin-Shloime where there also worked Gershon Glazschneider, Shmuel Bratten, and the Pole, Janek. Binyomin-Shloime's was one of the better class of tailors, making clothes for the shtetl Jews, but the work day was very long. Thursdays, we would work all night so that we could stop work on Friday. The weekly wage was from 3 to 5 zlotys. But Binyomin-Shloime invited all his workers to a restaurant on Saturday, provided enough liquor to get drunk, so that we would have the courage to work the coming week.

I did not work long for this master either. After working there for a few months, we "loaned" ourselves out to Lame Itzchak, the tailor to the gentry who served the surrounding landowners, police and officials. The workday here was no shorter than by the previous masters. He was a keen disciple of the "bitter grape," and he would tipple from his flask during work. He was an angry man who, if you dared to talk back to him, would smack you, and throw you out.

In our shtetl, where most of the residents were tradesmen, similar conditions obtained between workers and businessmen. If memory serves, there were about 15 carpenter workshops, 20 shoemaker workshops, several boot makers, tailors and others. With the carpenters, a very different situation existed. During the last 4 days of the week (Tuesday, Wednesday, Thursday, Friday) the carpenter masters and their apprentices would travel to the nearby villages and work for the farmers. Saturday evening, Sunday and Monday they would work in the shtetl workshops making cupboards, beds, tables and chairs for the market. This was of course principally low quality work. Monday evening, after the receipts were received, the workers came to get their share. The master always tried to get away with paying half only. This arrangement always led to quarrels. A different situation existed with the shoemaker workers. They did get their wages regularly, but the work hours were in dispute. There were cases where in certain workshops

[Page 115]

the workers fell asleep on the ground bending down over their lasts. This mostly happened in Hersh Karliner's workshop.

The boot makers earnings were not bad. The few workers in this trade worked under more humane conditions.

The notion of an eight-hour workday came late to Markuszow. It wasn't until 1927 that most of Markuszow's wage workers, who toiled in the workshops for 16-20 hours a day, began to develop a greater interest in their conditions, and set their goals on an organized defense. The first meeting took place on a sunny Saturday morning in the Kaliner mountains. The initiators of the meeting were: Shmuel Glazschneider, Hersh Leib Lomberg, Mordechai Fishman, Yankl Glazschneider, Israel Eidelstein, Dina Kerschenblatt, and Laizer Loterstein (the latter two live in Argentina). Since most of the attendants were communists, the chairmanship was given to Mordechai Fishman, and at all the sessions, the complaints over the harsh conditions of the Markuszow Jewish worker were articulated. The majority opinion was that we needed to institute a trade union in the shtetl and create regulations in working conditions, hours, and wages. As was customary, we passed an appropriate resolution and sent it to Warsaw, to the trade union central. We waited for over half a year to get the legalization, and finally received it. But before the document arrived, we had slowly begun to get Markuszow masters used to an eight-hour workday. The temporary commission dealing with trade union issues consisted of the workers, Hersh Leib Lomberg, Mordechai Fishman, Feivl Wichter, and others. Inspections were carried out in the workshops, and working more than 8 hours was not allowed. The entrepreneurs began to understand that the exploitation was coming to an end. If you worked more-you had to be paid. And here tough conflicts arose which ended more than once in physical fights. If the commission so much as showed up, the bosses would accost them right away with questions: "How dare you? Who gives you the right to come and dictate to me? I will do what I want here."

The more excitable ones raised their fists, but at the end the most antagonistic had to give in and we lived to see the institution of a legal 8-hour workday.

[Page 116]

We received the certification in the winter of 1927 when the majority of the workers had returned from the orchards and had a little money. We collected a sum of money and rented a locale. The representatives to the authorities (Pulawy *staraste*) were: Motl Glazschneider, Mordechai Fishman, and Hersh Leib Lomberg. The opening of the trade union was celebrated in an unimposing manner. Noach Tarchitz from Pulawy gave the political speech, and many greetings from related Markuszow organizations were read out. The union immediately became popular in the shtetl, and at the beginning of 1928 almost all the members of the Y.L. Peretz library became members of the union, which in essence meant membership in the communist party.

With the institution of normal trade union activities, the masters had to reckon with the new situation, paid the salaries on time, and no longer demanded overtime. The bosses understood that they could not enter into conflict with the union, because otherwise they risked the danger of not having any workers. Taking a worker or firing one had to be done through the union. Workers were also insured in a health plan, not because of respect for workers, but because of the frequent inspections from the state workers inspectors. In time, the union also managed to bring the youth under their aegis.

Culture work

The trade union work was carried on at the same time as the cultural activities. Reading events were held every Friday evening. Binyomin Loterstein, Kopl Kerschenblatt, and Itta Loterstein read out excerpts from books, especially about worker life. These reading evenings were well attended. On almost every Saturday evening, speakers from Warsaw or neighboring Korew came and lectured on political or literary topics. Aside from that, there was an active drama club in the union in which the following participated: Yankl Roguski, Tzadok Goldstein, Mordechai Fishman, Machle Kerschenblatt, and others. The performances, taking place in the firemen's hall, were on a high literary level, because they presented pieces from the best Jewish writers.

The union also celebrated worker holidays and

[Page 117]

kept the tradition of annual memorials to the memory of worthy labor activists. In 1928 I recall, we carried out the first demonstration in Korew together with the local trade union activists. A year later we celebrated the workers' holiday with the surrounding farmer population at the sugar factory in Garbow. The speaker was to have been a well-known Communist activist from Warsaw. As the crowd arrived in Garbow, they were met by a large contingent of police who prevented them from getting to the factory, and who tried to disperse the crowd. It would certainly have resulted in a blood bath if not for the intervention of the Pulawy starosta who had given permission for the meeting to be held, on condition that it not be used to agitate against the government. After the meeting, the crowd gathered there dispersed peacefully.

In the evening, at the trade union locale in Markuszow, a May academy took place with the same speaker from Warsaw who spoke at the meeting in Garbow. Also speaking were Feivl Wachenheiser (Ox), from Korew, and our Motl Glazschneider.

Since I left Markuszow in 1930, I have nothing more to add about the further activities of the union.

Dovid Brenner reports:

Persecutions

The police in Markuszow knew that the then banned communist party was operating within the union. They kept an eye on the union itself as well as on the active members. In 1929 the first big arrests of activists took place: Rochl Loterstein, Hersh Leib Lomberg, Mordechai Fishman, and a shoemaker-worker whose name I can't remember. They found an encoded list with names of the whole network in

Lomberg's possession on his arrest. He was severely beaten and tortured by the investigating authorities in order to get him to reveal the code, and hand over the rest of the comrades. Hersh-Leib Lomberg did not break, and thanks to his resistance, the survival of the union was maintained and dozens of members were kept out of jail. Because of that, the remaining four were freed at trial, but Lomberg himself was sentenced to five years which he served in the Lublin "*Zamek.*"[1]

[Page 118]

The active work of the union, carried out by its Jewish workers, had a big influence on the Polish street. Many Polish[2] workers, farmers, and youth joined the communist party, and because of that, the region became known as a stronghold of communist influences. A large number of workers from the Garbow sugar factory considered themselves ideologically close, and organizationally connected to the KPP.[3]

This, of course, gave rise to many persecutions and chicanery on the part of the Polish administrative authorities.

In the thirties, when the emigration wave among Jews increased, and the activists from the leadership left the shtetl either because of the danger of going to jail, or because of the need to escape to another place, the decline of the union began. In 1935, when I was getting ready to emigrate to Eretz Israel, the union had lost a lot of its dynamism.

[Page 119] ## Jewish Occupations in Shtetl

In 1939 there were 373 Jewish families in Markuszow. The adult and working population were employed in the following vocations:

Merchants and dealers	197
Shoemakers	42
Tailors	25
Carpenters	17
Butchers	13
Carriage drivers	12
Kasha makers	11
Bakers	7
Teachers	7
Glaziers	4
Rabbis	2
Slaughterers	2
Shammeses[4]	2
Porters	2
Water carriers	2
Hat makers	1
Smiths	1
Barbers	1

Watchmakers	1
No profession	25

This list was prepared by the book committee on the basis of the general list of Jewish residents of Markuszow.

Translator's Footnotes:

1. Lockup
2. It is characteristic of the times that the attribution "Polish" meant Christian Pole, whereas Jewish Poles are referred to simply as "Jews."
3. Polish Communist Party: *Komunistyczna Partia Polski*
4. Beadle of the synagogue

[Page 120]

Jewish Income

The Monday Market

Moshe Nachshon (Capa)

Translated by Moses Milstein

Every locality has its noteworthy things, its monuments, its ancient history, its trade or industry, that are renowned among other peoples or countries. And with what could Markuszow become famous, if not in all Poland, at least in the surrounding area? Nevertheless, our shtetl was worthy of something. In 1912, the czarist governing authority in Lublin decreed that there should be a market day on every Monday in Markuszow. Thanks to this, thousands of farmers from near and far, merchants, retailers, tradesmen from large and small cities, commissioners, brokers, and customers from the shtetl itself, and from the surrounding areas, flooded into Markuszow on that day. They filled the shtetl with the usual commercial clamor, and aided not just in making money but also in making a "name."

It is hard to imagine the economic life of Markuszow, especially the livelihoods of the local Jews, without the Monday market. It's quite likely that this market-day had no smaller (if not bigger!) significance than the textile factories of Lodz and Bialystok for the economy of these two cities, or the brush industry of Mezrich.[1] The significance of the market for Markuszow was also important in that around the weekly market day there simmered a bitter quarrel between our shtetl and neighboring Korew– a quarrel that was longstanding and was pursued with legitimate and illegitimate means. Markuszow won. Korew's complaint was that they were more entitled to have a market because they had a larger population, a larger area, and most importantly–production in Korew was more developed than in Markuszow, and suited markets well. For example, furs for farmers clothing, clothing, harnesses, and other things. Countless delegations from Korew travelled to the governor in Lublin to beg them, demand from them, calling for intervention. But it was all like a voice in the desert. The delegates from Korew returned home in shame and disappointment. In 1912 the decree was issued that the weekly

[Page 121]

market was to be held in Markuszow every Monday. The joy in Markuszow was boundless, as if they had won the greatest prize.

But with this satisfaction also came problems. While the shtetl waited a whole week to make up for the empty days preceding, various animal diseases appeared affecting the cattle and pigs, and other livestock, and the governor could close the market. We knew that Korew residents had immediately spread the word about the diseases in order to hinder Markuszow. The Korewers complained that the diseases were infectious, and the market must be closed–but how can you not let a group of people have a market day? Consequently, it would be only fair to transfer it to Korew. This time the governor gave a categorical refusal to the lobbyists from Korew, and after a four week interruption, the Markuszow market was revived, and in order for that to happen it was enough for the governor to receive a visit from the Markuszow elite only once. On the fifth week, the market took place with such volume that everyone really felt as if the earth was going to cave in under the weight of all the people and merchandise arriving.

Korew still wouldn't give up. When Poland became independent, they tried again with the {new}leadership. Since that didn't help, they tried to win over the farmers. Korew declared Thursday a market day, put up placards in all the surrounding places, advertised in the newspapers, and promised every farmer that came to Korew on Thursday, a kilo of salt, and a half liter of naphtha for free. But this didn't help either. In truth small fairs were held, but they came to nothing.

As a result, the market in Markuszow became a household word in the nearby, and even farther away, circles. Whoever occupied themselves with markets, did not let the opportunity go by to nip down to Markuszow on Mondays. There were things to see on such a day: a captivating picture of thousands and thousands of people all concerned with business.

As soon as day broke, you could see Jews milling around at the entrance to the shtetl –buyers. They were strolling along the entire roadway, or waiting for the oncoming farmers. In the meantime, they discussed the prices of fowl, eggs, butter, cheese. One Jew tells about how yesterday in Warsaw prices were deplorable. "Poultry–a steal, but good only for throwing into the Vistula."

[Page 122]

To that comes a question from another Jew. "Why then did you come to buy today?" "We have to do business, after all," comes an answer. Discussions such as this, and similar ones, could be heard from very early on, before the market even started. In another hour or two, there wouldn't be any time to talk, because everyone is dragged with enthusiasm into the seething market, and it becomes impossible to see anything even a footstep away.

The majority of the farmers arrive from the Lublin side. The fields are green on both sides of the road. The birds in the trees promise a day of abundance. But you really have to earn something in today's market. It's Erev-Pesach, and the holiday costs a lot of money. At eight in the morning, you can count just a few farmers' wagons nearing the shtetl, but in an hour from now, they will be spread across the entire breadth of the road–four or five wagons wide.

A middle-aged farmer sits on one wagon, next to him, his wife. A large basket of butter and cheese sits on her lap. Next to her, an even bigger basket of eggs. In addition, four sacs of wheat are lying in the wagon, and at the very bottom a big pig is tied, surely 300 kilo in weight. The farmer drives the two nice horses. The wagon approaches the first houses in the shtetl. Leibl Wallach runs out of the granary and approaches the farmer.

"*Gospododzu*, drive in here."

"What are you paying for wheat," the farmer asks, without slowing down.

"Thirty-three fifty."

"Will you give forty-four?"

"Another ten groshen," shouts Leibl Wallach. "In the city, you won't get more than thirty-three twenty-five. Stay here, right here, drive in!"

But the farmer is not impressed by R' Leibl's bid. He flicks his whip at the horses, and shouts," Vio,o,o, I'm driving to Simcha, my Jewish friend."

He can, however, drive no further. His wagon is surrounded by the category of traders called "*Vos es lozt sich*."[2] They examine the butter, the cheese, the eggs, ask her about the prices, bargain, make a racket, clamber over the merchandise. The farmer cracks the whip over the horse, and the wagon moves off. But the buyers do not desist. They hang from the shaft of the wagon, the ladders, the rungs. Several have jumped on the wheel axels while in motion. The wagon lurches, the farmer lady hits at the hands

[Page 123]

of the insistent buyers, but it doesn't help. Like skilled acrobats they hand over money in the air, carry on the business airborne, probably likely they spend their lives in the air.

Similar scenes can be seen with the *"feesgeyers"*[3]. This means that the poor men and women farmers are literally beleaguered by the yet poorer Jews. Here poultry transactions are taking place. The buyers catch the hens by the wings, palpate the bones on the underside, blow into the down. Feathers begin to fly. The farmer women grab their chickens back. They don't like the prices offered. They will look around the market to judge the way the prices are going.

The large livestock market has filled with horses, cows, oxen, sheep, goats, and pigs. The clamor of the animals melds with the commotion among the farmers who have come to buy and sell the four-legged creatures. A farmer leads a young, shiny horse by the bridle. Someone smacks it, the horse shies, and the farmer has to chase it. He will not let such a fortune escape. The crowd looks on at the gait of the horse, smack their lips with approval. The owner smiles happily. A customer sidles up, calls out a price. A middleman springs out, and they begin to slap hands.[4] For 2 zlotys, 2 slaps. For 5 zlotys, 5 slaps. The middleman mixes in with a compromise. "You go down 10 zlotys, and you go up 10 zlotys–and make it final." The slapping begins again, and the horse passes to a new owner. The same business goes on with the buying and selling of a pig, a cow, a sheep. Hands are well slapped before the transaction is completed. The middleman gets his.

You have to know how to navigate the Lublin road, the main artery in Markuszow, on market day. The side streets too are filled with wagons, horses and people. All the stores, warehouses, shops, including the covered wagons, are filled with customers. Farmer men and women spend the money they have just earned today in the market. And there is no lack of what to buy–as long as the money holds out to buy everything. A farmer lady remembers she has to buy seed. You don't have to go far. Here they are in a separate place, grain of varying sizes and colors peering out of their sacs.

On the Warsaw side, the places and passageways are filled with wagons carrying everything: potatoes, tomatoes, all kinds of greens, young radishes, and young onions, fruit–dried and those left over from the winter cellars. A little further off, but quite close to the road, the clang of metal is heard.

[Page 124]

Iron mongers display their goods here: scythes, shovels, axes, hammers, saws, and assorted ironwork. Farmers try out the scythes, listen to the reverberations issuing from the metal, and begin to bargain. Without this, even the smallest transaction doesn't get done. Bargaining occurs with small and large things. The business goes on for long minutes, tiring out both the customer and the merchant. One of them or both lower the price, and a deal is finally completed.

The same happens in the pot market. But everything is called a pot: big, small, midsized, earthen, crockery, metallic, aluminum and tin, copper saucepans, and steel frying pans, teapots, and food containers. Every pot purchased or about to be is tapped with a little stick, or the fingers, examined for a hidden defect, and after–the bargaining.

In another location, the harness makers have hung their ware on tall poles: reins, saddles, harnesses, belts, whip handles, and leather whips. Their brown hands and faces with spots bear witness to the trade they practice. Many farmers come to examine the merchandise, but not all can afford to buy an entire harness even though they would have loved to get it for their horse and wagon.

At the very end of the street that leads to the big cloister, the renowned furriers of Korew display their goods. They are known in the whole region for their double pelts for farmers. Now the merchandise lies on display in stalls, and even though it is Erev-Pesach, a long time before furs and pelts will be needed, farmers and wives stand around the fur wares, pick through the merchandise, ask about prices, and again–bargaining until a sale, or leaving with empty hands.

On the place near city hall, in the market itself, about one hundred bigger and smaller stalls are arrayed with finished goods, suits, farmer *sukmane*, hooded fur capes with "cheese sacs" on the shoulders, ready-to wear pants, undershirts, cotton jackets and all kinds of other clothing. In this place, money spent is mostly from what was earned that day at the market. Closer to the road–street stalls with haberdashery and confections, and what not? Any food you could want is supplied with the greatest courtesy and zeal. There is a big "universal" store, with everything, but of more doubtful quality.

At one stall–a big crowd: and the bigger the assemblage gets–the stronger the curiosity and crowding.

[Page 125]

A tall goy gets up on a chair, and his black curly locks, which peek out from under his garnet hat, fancy with colored feathers, makes an impression on the farmers. He lets out wild shouts and screams continuously, "*Zarraz, panowie, zarraz!*" He holds combs, mirrors, and other "bargains" between his fingers. Farmer hands with money stretch out to the junk. Everyone wants to do business with the "foreigner."

The market is nearing its close. Few farmers are left walking around the market looking for something to buy. They can choose not only the merchandise, but also the merchants. Competition among the Jews is great. It is no wonder–most of them have, as a result of this market day, earned money for taxes, private debts, paid off the Gemilut Chesed.[5] Yes, Pesach is coming fast, and the tax authority is waiting for the installments on business tax, income tax and other taxes.

There is a large assortment of boots and shoes for farmers at the market. Heavy boots hang on long poles, used and new shoes that farmers tried on their feet, and did not always fit. For these items, as for all merchandise sold at the market, bargaining went on without end.

On the "Eastern wall" of old Baruch's house, from ages ago, nails and hooks were hammered in that stared nakedly from the wall all week. Now, however, on market day, thousands of hats are displayed on boards, or hung on nails. Here, the hat makers from Korew, Miechow, Wawolnica, and Opole hang their products for sale. These Jewish businessmen are, because of competition (or without it), eternal paupers. They want to make money–yet not one of them advertises his merchandise, or calls out to the farmers to buy their hats.

The sun descends in the west, ready to disappear. The day is nearing an end, and so is the market. The Lublin road becomes more sparsely filled with merchants, farmers, and shtetl residents. The horses and wagons stand mostly alone, without their owners. What happened? Nothing bad. The farmer folk have filled all the restaurants, beer halls, various taverns, and every corner of the shtetl where you could get a drink. They eat, drink and get drunk–without end, without limit. Dozens of farmers in various unseemly poses wallow in the ditches and on the roads. Many are asleep

[Page 126]

having been beaten up badly, because that is the way of every market: fights to the blood by the drunk farmers, bottles flying over heads, and more than once with knives. The police would always mix in, but could never prevent the fights, the bloodletting, and the heavy wounds. Many farmers were arrested, and their abandoned wives had to drive the horses home alone.

The market day has ended. But not for long, because on the following Monday, the same thing will be repeated. Jewish livelihood in Markuszow was based on it.

Translator's Footnotes:

1. Yiddish version of Miedzyrzec, Lublin province.
2. Yiddish, rough meaning, "Whatever it takes."
3. Those arriving on foot.
4. Horse trading transactions traditionally involved slapping hands on every offer and counteroffer.
5. Community no-interest loan society

Sadovnikes

David Brenner (Tevl)

Translated by Moses Milstein

Jewish ways of earning a living in Markuszow cannot be described without a mention of the orchard leasing business. The orchard market began right after Erev-Pesach. As soon as the first blossoms appeared on the trees, people set off for the villages to examine the blooming trees like a doctor examining a patient. They visually appraised the bounty, listened to the asking price, negotiated sometimes for an hour or two, sometimes for several weeks, until the transaction was concluded. Then the Jew would put down a big deposit for leasing the orchard, accept the best wishes of the farmer, and travel back to the shtetl with a prayer on his lips that a windstorm, or strong rains, or thunder shouldn't harm the blossoming, that the orchard should be abundant, because his livelihood depended on it. It meant survival itself for dozens of Jewish families in Markuszow.

If the orchard had cherry trees or sour cherries (Morellos), then the orchard leaser, or sadovnik as he was called, swiftly moved himself and his family to the orchard, and there, they established themselves for the weeks it took until the last fruits were taken from the trees. The new dwelling consisted of a tent or hut, covered with woven straw where they kept their meager possessions, and laid their weary bones at night. Food was cooked outdoors. A pot was hung on a tripod over a fire of twigs. The main job of such a family of sadovnikes

[Page 127]

consisted of guarding the fruit against theft, picking the fruit, packing it in crates, and transporting it to Lublin, to the surrounding shtetls, or to the Markuszow market. If he was a wealthier sadovnik, he would send his merchandise to Warsaw.

The life of a sadovnik was hard enough. It was also a supplemental form of income to the existing jobs which were a means of support for only one or two days a week, whereas you needed to eat seven days a week. Where do you get the rest from? So, turning to this source was the city melamed or shoemaker, the storekeeper or carpenter, the pious scholar or the market wholesaler. In general, coming up with a few zlotys to pay the farmer was for these Jews a Herculean effort. They ended up investing in a thing that did not always return the amount invested. Sometimes damage occurred during the blossoming. Natural catastrophes made a mockery of the optimistic projections and hopes of a little income.

The real hard life began with the moving over to the orchard. As mentioned, such a family lived in their tent and always had to protect the trees from bird pecking, passersby or the village boys who considered it a righteous thing to eat their fill of Jewish fruit, even when the trees in their own orchards were sagging from the abundance of fruit. And if you made it to see a harvest, then the work began of climbing the trees, with a ladder or without, to collect the fruit. The work was associated with the danger of falling from the tree when the wind made it sway strongly, or when a branch broke. More than once, news reached the shtetl of a tragedy affecting a sadovnik.

The picked fruit was packed in crates, and around three in the morning, the sadovnik would harness the borrowed horses and wagon (if the farmer entrusted him with one) and ride off to the city, or the shtetls to sell the merchandise. Happy was the sadovnik who collected on his first sale. Then he forgot all the troubles and vexations he had had to endure. Happy, full of confidence, he travelled back to the orchard, told his wife the great news, passed out candies he had bought in the shtetl to his children, ate the prepared snack, had a little nap–and back again to the boring work.

[Page 128]

Sadovnik families in apple or pear orchards had to be there during the holidays.[1] The days grew shorter, the nights longer, but above all, the cold and rain of autumn ate into the bones. It was hard to get up at dawn, and crawl into your winter clothes, and transport the produce to the buyers. But they forgot about all these hardships if the season was a successful one, and the merchandise was sold without damages. Then you could prepare for winter with the hope that some zlotys would be left for after Pesach in order to rent an orchard again.

There were several categories of sadovnikes connected to the produce business, but about 90 percent of them were shtetl businessmen. Exporting produce to the big cities like Danzig, and especially Warsaw was the business of the Gothelf brothers, Yechiel Fishbein, and Itzchak Teitelbaum.

The fact that dozens of Jewish families spent long months in the orchards, carried on their family life and religious observance, helped more than a little to break down the artificially erected barrier of racial separation and hatred between two peoples. The farmer saw that the life of the sadovnik was exactly as hardworking, stressful, and all-consuming as his life. There were many cases where they would help each other out. When it was time to cut the wheat in the fields, the sadovnikes helped with the cutting from dawn to dusk, lived alongside the farmer, ate out of one bowl (if he was not so strongly observant of the commands of the Shulchan Aruch), and spoke the same farmer's language. The farmer knew how to value such contributions, and tried to help out the sadovnikes. The Jewish tenant farmers did not complain about antisemitic manifestations from the older generation of farmers. On the contrary, healthy, friendly relations existed (with certain small exceptions) between the Jewish population and the Polish population, both in the shtetl and in the surrounding villages. It did not seem strange in the eyes of the farmer, to see one of our sadovnikes, stand by his tent in his tallis, saying his prayers, and carrying out the rituals of a Shabbes meal. He did not make fun of the *zmiress*[2] which later carried from the tents, just as he had respect for all the religious behavior of his, now very near, Jewish neighbor.

Translator's Footnotes:

1. Presumably the High Holidays in the fall.
2. Religious festive songs

[Page 129]

Young Housewives

Pese Wasserstrom (Tel Aviv)

Translated by Moses Milstein

A saying about Markuszow used to go around: "When a wagon arrives there, the head of the horse is in one end of the shtetl, and the back wheels are at the other end." But as small as the shtetl was, it was nevertheless famous for its girls and their industriousness. They were called, "*Yunge balebustes*," and it could not be otherwise. Their mothers were always occupied with worries about a livelihood, with pregnancy, birth, and the raising of children. As a result, the whole burden of the household chores fell on the young daughters who never took their aprons off all day, occupied continuously primarily with peeling potatoes, the most popular, famous, and cheapest meal of the folk. They would sit for hours around the bowl and joke that potatoes grew so that paupers would also have the opportunity to skin someone.

A real trial for our young balebustes was cleaning and washing the pots. They would scrape the dirt with their fingernails and curse their lives while doing this kind of work. Although washing clothes was much harder and took longer than cleaning pots, they were happy when they went to the little river outside the shtetl, and rinsed and pounded the clothes. This was an opportunity to get out of the house, spend a few hours in the fresh air, and gossip about news in the shtetl, or the world.

In general, Markuszow girls had to obey their parents in everything, be quiet and obedient, give respect to the parents, and follow the commandments. As a result, after Shabbes, they had the right to read the *Tseneh Reneh*.[1] Our shtetl daughters were renowned for their beauty as well, especially for the rosiness of their complexions. The sun in Markuszow was not prevented by tall buildings from reaching everyone's face and tanning it brown or red. Since people used wood for cooking, which was wet most of the time, the young girls would spend a lot of time at the stove blowing

[Page 130]

on the fire with all their strength. The husband who had a sense of humor would joke, "Thanks to the wet wood, my food gets cooked, the wood is not all consumed, and my wife is always pretty, because of her rosy cheeks."

This was not the end of the entire hard burden of the Markuszow balebustes. As soon as a daughter was born, the parents began to think about a trousseau, and a dowry. As soon as she was a little older, she would have to pluck feathers for her own bedding, as if the groom was already at the door, and was only waiting for the bedspread. Twelve and thirteen year old girls would sit around until late at night until they were almost transformed into a bunch of feathers themselves. And if one of them were tempted to go outside, or to a friend, her mother would remonstrate that she had to help get her ready to become a bride.

This is how our girls lived in the shtetl. It's true that their hard work did not bring any money into the house, but their work was no less stressful and exhausting than the jobs of their husbands or fathers.

Translator's Footnote:

1. A Yiddish collection of stories from the bible ostensibly written for women who generally did not study Hebrew.

Merchants and Artisans

Sholem Wasserstrom

Translated by Moses Milstein

Before the outbreak of WWI, the social composition of the Jews in the shtetl was as follows:

Trade (stores, market buyers, middlemen, and others)–40 percent; artisans–30 percent; village traders–20 percent; employed in the larger cities–5 percent; religious functionaries and others–5 percent.

I can't provide an exact number of Jews in that period, but at the beginning of this century their number was estimated at around 700-800. How did they earn a living?

The first thing you saw in Markuszow were the two rows of stores which stretched along both sides of the main road to Lublin, a sign that small business was one of the most important sources of livelihood in the shtetl. What else could a just-married

[Page 131]

young man do than invest his dowry in a small shop that was managed by his young wife, while he studied day and night, and remained a stranger to money matters. When children were born, the good student had to become a storekeeper, even though he didn't know any Polish, and understood little about business. (A lot of curious stories were told about this). Nevertheless, such a young man slowly grew to learn about business, and began to care for himself, his wife, and the growing children. So you could see the freshly minted merchants in the stores, selling herring or a piece of cake for a groshen to a mother who would first chew it herself before giving it to the child.

As small and pitiful as these stores were, as poor a businessman as he was, they nevertheless drew a living from it, and married off their children (in whom they wanted to see the same merchants).

There was another category of merchants–the market sellers (women) who sold produce in summer, and hot beans or pickled apples in winter.

The shtetl also had various tradesmen such as shoemakers, tailors, hat makers, harness makers, boot makers, carpenters, cabinetmakers, locksmiths and all the rest of the trades for Markuszow itself and the surrounding area. I can recall several Jewish *podriatchikes* (purveyors) who supplied meat for the czarist military that was stationed in the Markuszow area, Nowa Alexandria (Pulawy), Ivangrod Fortress

(Deblin), Lublin and Lodz. About 60 animals a week were slaughtered in Markuszow, and many Jewish families made a living from it. The main purveyors were: Michale Heshil's, Shloime Heshil's, Yomi Yankl's, and Pinchas and Kalman-Itzik.

The Jewish carriage drivers bringing in and taking out the merchandise played an especially important role in the economic development of the shtetl. They would be on the road from early in the morning until late at night, and struggled mightily to help push the loaded wagons up every hill, and had the onerous responsibility to ensure that the merchandise arrived on time, and undamaged. They also used to bring the newcomers who wanted to settle in the shtetl, and transport the youth who went off to the wider world in search of good fortune and a better livelihood.

[Page 132]

Aid Organizations

Markuszow Philanthropy

Sholem Wasserstrom

Translated by Moses Milstein

In the realm of good deeds, Markuszow was no less invested than bigger cities. Jewish welfare bound to faith gave rise to the fact that there were several active philanthropic institutions dating back fifty years. I would like to report on some:

The mitzvah of *hachnosses kalah* is sacred among Jews. A small thing–helping impecunious brides to avoid the danger of remaining unmarried. Every Markuszow resident was committed to this institution with the greatest reverence.

Interestingly, hachnosses kalah in Markuszow was instituted thanks to a simple coincidence. Blind Yoineh needed to marry off his young daughter. Since there was no money, the poor father approached the wealthy Binyomin-Yankle for help. That person knew that no matter how much he gave it would not be enough, so he made an agreement with other people to create an institution to help poor brides. The idea pleased everyone. Soon several couples went out to the shtetl and began to collect money for Blind Yoineh. This was the beginning of hachnosses kalah for us. The first founders were: Binyomin, Itzchak-Hersh, Feivel-Yankl's, Mordechai-Yosef, Kalman-Itzchak. The system was organized in the following way: Every Friday, two men voluntarily visited each home, and collected small and large coins in a tin box for the organization. The collecting pair was called the "*tzedakah pushke*." The collected sums were given to the gabai of the hachnosses kalah, because in those days Markuszow did not distinguish itself with social organizational work. There were no elected committees, and all important functions were fulfilled by the gabai of the organization

[Page 133]

who was elected in the besmedresh every Simchat Torah with a glass of liquor. As the years went by, the same person was elected every year–R' Binyomin-Yankle's.

When R' Binyomin was asked for money for the marriage of a Jewish girl, he would answer, "What do you mean, give money? Did anyone ask me if I agreed to the match?"

Nevertheless, he would give the required amount generously and with a warm heart. If money were lacking, he would contribute from his own pocket no matter the amount. He never asked to be repaid. In time, the organization grew, attracted more members, and the custom of collecting assessments at every wedding was instituted. It was carried out by two members of the company dressed in colorful clothing with a round hat encircled by a piece of tin on which the letters of hachnosses kalah were cut out. The collectors also wore masks on their faces. In such attire they would also dress on Purim to collect for hachnosses kalah.

To help the poor sick, *Bikur Cholim* was founded in the shtetl. The gabai was R' Pinchas-Yankl's. When he was asked at the time to take over as gabai of hachnosses kalah, he declined on the basis that there would be no lack of candidates for that institution, because marrying Jewish girls was associated with *simchas*. Providing help for the sick is not such a happy matter, and few volunteers would be ready to undertake this kind of work. So he voluntarily undertook the onerous burden of providing a doctor for a sick pauper that then cost a heavy toll of 25 rubles. Amassing such a fortune was not an easy task, and in many cases the gabai made up the missing amount from his own pocket. Furthermore, the doctor had to come on a Shabbes which created a rush to the rabbi for a *heter*[1] which was achieved with some difficulty.

More than once the gabai was asked why he saddled himself with such a bunch of worry and responsibility. He would answer, "Whoever sustains one soul in Israel, is as if he sustains the whole."

It is possible that the secret of Markuszow Jewish good-heartedness and readiness to help its suffering and needy brothers lies in the meaning of that quotation.

[Page 134]

In my time there was another institution that had little to do with philanthropy, but was mostly concerned with mitzvahs and the hereafter. I'm referring to the *Tikun Sforim* group whose mandate was to buy new [religious] books for the besmedresh, and to mend the damaged books. In this case, the collectors were exclusively young bachelors who sat and studied day and night. They did their collections with great love and dedication, because it gave them the opportunity to leave the besmedresh every Friday for several hours, walk around he shtetl, take a look into all the Jewish houses, and in the process actually perform a mitzvah. Walking around town with the donation box gave them a chance to straighten their hunched-over backs. Wicked tongues gossiped that these visits also served a romantic purpose. In every house containing one or more Jewish girls, the collectors from the besmedresh were examined as potential candidates for a match…The boys themselves, even though they dared not raise their eyes while in a Jewish house, still had thoughts concerning this eternal problem. It's quite possible that something was achieved in this domain.

Translator's Footnote:

1. Rabbinical authorization

Banks

Arieh Weinriber

Translated by Moses Milstein

One of the nicest and useful achievements for hundreds of Markuszow Jews was our banks. "The bank for merchants and artisans" was founded in 1928. In the span of a very short time, 80% of Markuszow Jews became members. The managers of the bank were: Isaac Migdal (chairman) Meir Laks (vice-chairman), Pinchas Liebhober, Mordechai Morel, Hershl Wichter, Simcha Ettinger, and Chaim-Yoineh Kitenkorn. The founding capital was put together by the founders themselves. Later many residents began to deposit their savings, parents saved dowries for their daughters, and thanks to this their own and others' capital grew. Opportunities to help out the needy, and provide more credit, especially to the *sadovniks* who for the most part, had to pay for the orchards leased in the spring from farmers or the gentry, arose. We mustn't forget that about 40%

[Page 135]

of Markuszow Jews were involved in the orchard business. On those days, the bank had to provide a lot of ready cash, because every sadovnik needed at least several hundred zlotys to pay for one or two seasons. Before the bank's establishment, the sadovniks went through hell before they managed to accumulate the required sums of money. Thanks to the bank, dozens of Jewish families were able to get back on their feet in getting the needed help in a respectful manner. They, just like the Markuszow Jewish tradesmen–the tailor, shoemaker, carpenter, and hat maker who derived income from the weekly market, also had to be given credit from time to time in order to allow them to buy merchandise for the Monday. The bank was a savior for these artisans in hard times.

In 1931, at a general meeting of the bank, the vice-chairman, Meir Laks was strongly criticized and he was not elected in future elections. His son-in-law, Gershon Ettinger, a wealthy man, decided to take part but without the grievance of his father-in-law, and founded a second bank. Almost all the members of the old bank, took part in the founding meeting of the new bank. Gershon Ettinger provided a room in his own house, for no rent, to house the bank, and deposited his own money there, and the new institution began to carry on normal bank activities. The board of directors of the new "credit bank" consisted of the following people: Meir Laks (chairman), Yoel Ettinger (vice-chairman), and Dovid Schildkraut. This bank, although it was founded on the basis of personal ambition, brought many benefits to our shtetl Jews. This same Gershon Ettinger, a rich man, never helped anyone out before the establishment of the bank. But after the founding, his capital was used for short and long term loans for needy Jews. Incidentally, he worked as a cashier[1] at the bank with no salary. The value of the outstanding loans was in the range of several thousand zlotys.

We have to admit that while the first bank had an avowed social character, the second bank was more of a private credit institution, and that led to its demise after 3 to 4 years.

[Page 136]

Markuszow besmedreshniks

Seated left to right: Aryeh Weinriber, Avraham Rothstein,
(future Krasnystow rabbi)
Standing from left to right: Shmuel Goldstein, Chaim Wiener

Translator's Footnote:

1. The Yiddish word "*kassir*" could be teller, cashier, or treasurer

[Page 137]

To the Memory of Our Personalities

Reb Yosef Ze'ev Ashkenazi Idlish
(Rabbi in Markuszow)

Avraham Yuri (Jerusalem)

Translated by Moses Milstein

In 1825 R' Yosef Ze'ev Ashkenazi Idlish was sent to Italy and Turkey from Tsfat from the chasidim community (*kahal hachasidim*) and from the community of *Prushim*[1] (*kahal hapirushim*) jointly. In his letter to the philanthropists (Shpender) about his mission he said, "*The news of your good name and virtues have come to our ears…supporting souls…poor people…now, forced by great need in our holy community of ashkenazis, God safeguard and protect them. The two holy communities here in the holy city shall be rebuilt and restored. The mitzvah of pidyen shvuim (ransoming of hostages) we were forced to send to our brothers, the children of Israel…in the country of Italy may God strengthen them, where you will be…in this general letter in the possession of our dear shaliach derabeinu…great in nigle*[2] *and nister*[3] *…Maharar Yosef the son of Ze'ev Ashkenazi, the Av Bet Din*[4] *and Rosh Yeshiva*[5] *from the holy community of Markuszow, God strengthen her, and grandson of the gaon Rabeinu Maharasha ZTVK"L, crowned with virtues…with the holy writings of the Sephardic sages…and the rabbis of Jerusalem…Constantinople…Izmir…Smyrna…Baghdad God keep her…their letters…compassionate people, let your mercy awake for the sake of the holy congregation of Ashkenaz…so say they who beg in the name of the holy land and the holy yeshivas of the Ashkenazim, may God preserve and protect them and the holy congregations of Ashkenazim and Prushim.*"

The letter was signed by the chasidim: R' Gershon Margalit, R' Amram B"R Moishe Nechami, R' Moishe Shimon Wolf Bachar"yl, R' Nachmi Dinar, R' Meir from Zwet: From the Pirushim: R' Chaim Cohen, who was *av bet din* from Pinsk, R' Israel from Shklav, R' Yeshia B"R Yissachar Ber (Brdki) from Pinsk, R' Yechiel B"R Yehuda Leib.

On his journey as emissary he detoured to Padua and there in 1928 gave the rabbinical *smicha*[6] to the honorable Mordechai Shmuel Gerondi, and also wrote a forward to his book, *Kvutzat Kesef*. Gerondi wrote about him:

[Page 138]

"*Kmoharar Yosef Idlish Ashkenazi was av bet din in the city of Markuszow, and God awakened his spirit to go and live in the holy land in order to add holiness to his holiness, and afterward he went abroad in a mission of mitzvah, and I was worthy enough to have the pleasure of listening to his Torah knowledge for a long time here in Padua like a pomegranate, versed in negila and nister, and heard a lot of insights from him, they are written in my Chibur L'koti Shoshanim, first part, and he wrote a lot of books on Tanach and on Gemara Poskim Tosafot and on Kabbalah,and it is not printed…only the book Brachot Yosef…and may there be serenity and honor in the holy city, Tsfat, may it be rebuilt and restored soon in our days amen. May his merit sustain us.*"

From Italy he went to Turkey, and in 1831 his book, "*Birkat Yosef*," was published in Salonika, a pirush on the book Yetzira. To the book, there was a commentary, *Lev Yehoshua*, by R' Yehoshua B"R Chaim Itzchk Mousssafia added. The commentary (page *kof nun dalet, second side*) said:

"*And from that you will understand how great are the virtues of tzadikim and therefore they are worthy of every honor and to all the worldly satisfactions, especially if they are emissaries from Eretz*

Israel, as everywhere where an emissary comes to them from Eretz Israel, all of Israel is obliged to do what they can for the pleasure and favor of Eretz Israel, because from there comes the survival of the entire world and even the angels are ready to serve the sons of Eretz Israel."

(We further present the letter and opinions of the Markuszow rabbi R' Yosef Idlish as it was published in the original in Avraham Yaari's book).[7]

Translator's Footnotes:

1. Reclusive men who devote all their time to study
2. Body of Jewish text
3. Kabbalah lore
4. Head of the Jewish court
5. Head of a yeshiva
6. Rabbinical ordination
7. With the permission of the author translated from the book, "*Shluchi Eretz Israel*" The History of the Mission from Israel to the Diaspora from the Destruction of the Second Temple to the Nineteenth Century by Avraham Yaari, Jerusalem, 1971, published by the Rabbi Kook Institute, affiliated with World Mizrachi, 948 pages.

[Pages 138-139]

Reb Yosef Ze'ev Ashkenazi Idlish

Hebrew translation of the previous article.

[Page 140]

Reb Yosef Ben Ze'ev Idlish z"l

Sholem Wasserstrom

Translated by Moses Milstein

Markuszow could allow itself to be proud of its rabbis. One of them–R' Yosef Ze'ev Idlish, z"l, was a dear man, a *yachsan*[1], a descendant of the Marasha (a commentary on the Talmud Gemara). It is told that when he wanted to leave Markuszow, he asked that the money he had given to the shtetl when he took over the chair of the rabbinate be returned to him. Seeing that Markuszow was in financial straits at the time, and couldn't pay the requested amount–a thing they really wanted to do out of love and care for the rabbi–he called together the congregation and said to them in theses words. "Remember, if you would return my money to me, it would be fine"

The crowd was stunned, afraid that the rebbe, God forbid, would speak ill of the shtetl, because exactly as they believed in the steadfastness of his positive words, they were also fearful of his anger, because he was considered a holy man. But long they could not deliberate on the matter, because the rebbe continued, "And if not–it's lost! Be strong and healthy…"

The Jews gathered there breathed a sigh of relief, and wished him much success. He then left for Eretz Israel.

In prior years, he was considered a religious dreamer, due to his modesty and honesty. Soon after his wedding, while he was still being supported by his father-in-law, he was getting ready to go to the baths on a Friday, but didn't have the courage to ask his father-in-law for a tenner to pay. So he stood by the window talking to himself out loud while tapping on the window with his finger. "A shirt, a tenner *in bod arein*! A shirt, a tenner *in bod arein*."

He stood there like this for a long time. When the people in the house understood what he meant, it was already too late. The time for bathing was over.

His good friends used to allow themselves to joke, and remind him about "A shirt, a tenner *in bod arein*," but the rebbe did not show any resentment and just smiled along.

This so-called ineptitude did not hamper his wit. He would readily answer the most complicate questions. It was said of him that in the shtetl where he was rabbi before coming

[Page 141]

to Markuszow, a rich Jew had died, a great miser who never gave anything to the community while alive. The community, therefore, demanded a larger sum of money from his relatives for his cemetery lot. His rich sons did not intend to pay the requested amount and the deceased lay for days before burial. At the end, the deceased's children submitted, but at the same time, they took the community to court. The tsarist supervisor over the community knew that the community's behavior merited a heavy punishment for delaying the burial of a dead person. He called for the rabbi, and asked if the complaint was valid. Not wanting to deny the very fact of taking money the rabbi answered, "Yes, the community requested money from the rich man's family. We Jews believe that the Messiah will come, and then the dead will rise. That is why while still alive, we negotiate over a piece of earth for a grave for a certain amount of time only, and it costs very little. But the community behaves differently, however, towards those who don't believe in the Messiah. That kind of person buys a plot for eternity which amounts to the sum the deceased's children have paid. Since their father did not believe in the coming of the messiah, they had to pay this."

The supervisor really liked this response, and he dismissed the claim against the community.

Translator's Footnote:

1. Term for a descendant of a prominent religious figure

R' Avraham-Moishe of Markuszow[1]

N. Shomen (Canada)

Translated by Moses Milstein

A Lubliner Chasidism researcher once wrote about the Markuszow rabbi:

I remember when I was studying at the "*chozeh*"[2] besmedresh in Lublin.

R' Moishe Markuszow came in very early on one of the *Tamuz* days. He was running back and forth over the entire length of the besmedresh.

After I finished my studying, I went to eat lunch. I came back, and finished the next lesson. He was still running around from place to place, tirelessly, engrossed, not even having finished davening *Shachris*. When the evening shadows began to appear, he suddenly awoke from his

[Page 142]

holy thoughts and ran to the "Cohen's" besmedresh to daven *tefilles Shachris*.

When the holy rebbe and gaon, the "Cohen," passed away, he became rabbi and settled in Markuszow. He once came to Lublin and stayed in a Lublin suburb called "the sands." Saturday, I attended his table. He began with great humility, "a painter once painted a picture of a lion on canvas." One of the gathered saw the artistic work, and cried out, "It's not a real living lion." The crowd replied, "True, it's not a living lion–but the picture of a lion."

R' Avraham Moishe Markuszower, the follower of the Cohen's way and creator of a new branch, died in Warsaw 8th of Shevat 1918.

Translator's Footnotes:

1. Reprinted from the book, "Lublin" by N. Shemen (pp. 469-470) with the generous permission of the author.
2. Rebbe Yaakov Yitzchak Halevi Horowitz, known as the *Chozeh* of Lublin

The Rebbe R' Avraham Moishe

Sholem Wasserstrom

Translated by Moses Milstein

In the year 1900, the rebbe R' Tzadok Hacohen, z'tzl, of Lublin, died. Right after his passing, the chasidim assembled, the usual *tish*[1] attenders, and entourage members, and their eyes immediately fell on R' Avraham Moishe, and gave him a mazel tov. He was then middle-aged and considered himself one of the most loyal adherents of the dead rabbi. His imposing figure gave him the appearance of a holy man, and his face expressed only spirituality. He would sit and study for days on end. His daily food consisted of two pieces of challah and milk that he would eat only in the evening. Friday evening he celebrated the first meal in the besmedresh at exactly 11 o'clock so that his chasidim could first celebrate the Sabbath at home, get rested and develop an appetite for the rebbe's leftovers.[2] He conducted the tish like this until 4 a.m., eating little himself, studying Torah the whole time. We used to wonder where this weak person got so much strength, because he would study Torah at the tish with extraordinary passion. Wisdom and enlightenment shone from his eyes, and everyone who spoke with the rebbe was overcome by his sharp intellect and wisdom. He was not boastful or secret, but he lived with the people, understood their suffering and pain, and always encouraged and consoled them. When it was proposed to him that he behave like other rabbis, receiving petitions, he would reply,

[Page 143]

"I'm not a storekeeper."

His entourage never mentioned that again knowing in advance that the rabbi would not allow himself to be persuaded.

It is told that when the rabbi had only just arrived in Markuszow, R' Moishe Dovid Soifer and his boy, Yoskeh, approached him to welcome him.

"What are you called, young boy?"

I am called "ben yachid!"[3] he answered.

The rabbi then said as if to himself, " Woe to the parents when a child knows he is a ben yachid."

Once, Erev Yom Kippur, just before *Kol Nidrei*, the rabbi's son, Yehoshua, (Shieleh the Rabbi's) and some other chasidim began to sing and dance. So the rebbe was approached with a question, "Is now the time for such things?" The rebbe answered, " Yes, because with singing and dancing the prayers to God go faster than through sorrow and tears."

His adherents and opponents knew that the rebbe cared more for his chasidim than for himself. Once a Tsarist gendarme showed up unexpectedly in his home, and insisted that he needed to see the rebbe. But the rebbe managed to go somewhere else after he heard that a man in uniform was looking for him. He was asked after why he didn't want to be seen by the gendarme. He replied, " The gendarme would certainly have spoken to me in Russian and I would not have understood a word, because I don't know the language. How would I have looked in his eyes? And what would he have thought of the rebbe and his chasidim?"

The rebbe lived not far from the besmedresh, and the melody of his studying mixed in with the voices of the besmedresh boys who studied energetically. The shtetl was unable to hear the studying on just one day of the week, every Monday, because the noise from the market was greater and louder especially since the whole shtetl of Jews was occupied with the market.

We had the honor of having the rebbe, R' Avraham Moishe Markuszower for a short time, and benefited from it spiritually, and economically, because of the

[Page 144]

arrival of so many chasidim. He left Markuszow at the end of 1912, and settled in Otwock near Warsaw. The shtetl lost a source of income, and the besmedreshniks, a treasury of melodies that the visiting chasidim used to sing with the rabbi.

Translator's Footnotes:

1. A rabbi's tish (table) is where a chasidic rabbi eats and holds court.
2. It is considered an honor to eat food that was on the rebbe's plate
3. *Ben yachid* means "only child."

In Memory of Itzchak Wasserstrom

M. Nachshon (Capa)

Translated by Moses Milstein

Itzchak Wasserstrom, who at the age of 18 was sitting in the besmedresh studying, had managed, with the help of another young man, Hersh Loterstein, to establish the Zionist organization, *Kadimah*, in Markuszow, in a short time. In all, only two years had passed since this daring step, and the organization already had 80 members. And the library was filled with 300 books. And all thanks to this idealistic dreamer who possessed a heap of energy and initiative–Itzchak Wasserstrom. He was the first who breathed the vitality of Zionism and culture into the sleepy shtetl. He fought like a lion for these two principles, and at every opportunity, emphasized that Zionism was his most beautiful dream. He did not stop weaving his dream even when a united, hostile front against him began by all those who were always disunited, and quarreling amongst themselves, with various rationalizations: Lubliner, Kotzker, Radziner, Gerer, and Markuszower chasidim. They all declared a holy war against the 20 year old young man. But Itzchak Wasserstrom did not allow himself to be intimidated. He stayed firm to his principles: for the rebirth of Eretz-Israel and the Jewish people, it was worthwhile not just to suffer, but even to die. He pursued his struggle with courage and stubbornness.

He came often to the besmedresh where dozens of dreamy and fanatical believers sat over Gemaras, and holy books, and studied. He would call aside one of those young men deep in study, take him to the women's besmedresh, and begin a conversation with him.

"How can you justify to yourself doing nothing in today's times? Let's say that you will continue to study like this for another ten years, and really know your *Abbaye and Rava*.[1] Would that be of use to anyone? Because as a person goes through life, he has to recognize reality. He has to know the history of his people and look for ways to return to its roots…Because "suffering mankind" in our version means both a suffering Jew and a suffering person. You need to be shown that in every world crisis the Jews bleed the most. This every young Jew must know, and throw himself into the struggle to free the unfortunate people that he himself is a part of. I know you have influence with your friends. You have to win them to our cause. Zionism needs new young energy."

Itzchak Wassertrum waited patiently for a response. He understood that his simple persuasive words were not immediately received favorably, because too many of his targets were too deeply involved with the besmedresh, the books, and the traditions of the old Jewish home to be suddenly won over to Zionism. The response from a besmedresh student was in most cases the same:

As I understand it, the rabbis are the ideological leaders of the people, and they are intelligent people…Why then do they not do anything to see that Jews return to their own land? They, the rabbis, would not have to deliver a great sermon. A simple hint to their chasidim about the Jewish settlement in Eretz-Israel would in a few years have transformed our land into a great Jewish power. So answer me that."

Itzchak Wasserstrom regards the earnest speaker's pale face intently. He finds the question was sincerely posed, and with his usual passion begins to explain to the young man the essence of Chassidism and rabbinical positions. He speaks about precarious Jewish occupations, about antisemitism, the Pale of Settlement, and ends with the eternal yearning for Zion of the Jewish people which has a chance to be realized, if Jews would take the matter into their own hands.

More than one Torah student was captivated by Itzchak's words. Under his directorship, they filled the ranks of the Zionist organization, *Kadimah*–the pioneer of Jewish social life in Markuszow.

Translator's Footnote:

1. Important innovators in the Talmud

[Page 145]

The Four Maskilim[1]

M. Nachshon (Capa)

Translated by Moses Milstein

You could see them almost every Saturday after the meal, strolling along the broad sidewalk with slow steps, hands crossed behind their backs, (only when they were not actually talking), marching through the shtetl constantly arguing and debating, explaining and demonstrating and contradicting what the previous speaker had said.

[Page 146]

"The matter can be explained in other ways, and the proof------"

And here would follow a whole series of demonstrations and arguments to justify what was said, and to demolish the words from a second or third participant. There were four of them–and all Markuszow knew them well: Yosef Goldberg, Shmuel-Avraham Marchewka, Pinchas Liebhober, and Moishe Breinsky.

Their piety did not prevent them from admiring that part of the shtetl youth who, after Poland's independence, broke away from the traditional life of *besmedreshniks*, and set out on the broad road of worldly Yiddishkeit, and demonstrated interest in culture and literary questions, and began to build the cultural-political life of the shtetl.

By chance, I had the opportunity to listen in on one of their discussions during a Shabbes stroll.

The small-statured Moishe Breinsky looks up at the tall Shmuel-Avraham Marchewka, and suddenly asks: " Is the land we call Poland, really Poland, or actually a Jewish country?"

And he tries to justify his opinion with the situation in Markuszow. The three Poles who live on the central Lubelska street, are hardly ever seen. The tone and appearance of the shtetl is determined by its Jewish population. Trade and business are in Jewish hands. It sometimes happens that a farmer from the village forgets when a Jewish holiday is happening, and he brings his few products to town. The Markuszow Poles laughingly mock such a farmer for not being alert to the Jewish calendar…and tell him to take his merchandise back and come back only when the Jews are free.

Pinchas Liebhober was not so enamored with the "Yiddishkeit" of Markuszow. According to him everything is "*Chayei Sha'ah*."[2] A people must think and worry about the future.

Moishe Breinsky, as per usual, must not be in agreement with Pinchas Liebhober. One example, when a Polish store opened in Markuszow, the Jews raised a ruckus. What! We're going to Polishify business? And he asks with irony," What do you say to that Pinchas the philosopher?"

Instead of Pinchas, the attackee, replying, Yosef Goldberg, a Zionist veteran, answered. He developed Pinchas Liebhober's theme about our own land, and demonstrated the tenuous existence of Polish Jews in general, and Markuszow in particular, even when they are the majority in the shtetl.

[Page 147]

Moishe Breinsky does not, however, concede. With facts from life, he showed how Poles, especially the farmers, respect, and had high opinions of the Jews in business and the trades.

Pinchas Liebhober already knew about the Balfour Declaration. He had read about the growth of the Zionist organization, and that gives him a good basis for his opinion that the Jewish situation world-wide is now much better–and most important–that we had to exploit the set of circumstances created and get more and more Jews to forsake Poland and travel to the promised land. Yosef Itchele's and Shmuel-Avaham have a counterargument for this: The Arabs in Eretz-Israel will not be better to the Jews than the Poles in Poland.

The Zionist debaters don't want to concede. Pinchas Liebhober speaks with pathos about burning all his bridges, going off to Eretz-Israel, in our own land–and finally living in his own home.

Moishe Breinsky's conclusion is entirely another one: He points out that in the big cities as well as in the little shtetls, Jews are building houses, erecting workshops, establishing stores and–dealing with several hundred markets in Poland. They rent orchards for several years in advance, they buy woodlots, get married, have children, signs that they are not so ready to accept R' Pinchas' theory about burning bridges…

The sun is setting. We have to go to *Shalosh Seudos*[3]. Our maskilim are heading to the besmedresh, the debate gets interrupted in order to be renewed at another time with more vigor and passion.

Translator's Footnotes:

1. Followers of the Haskala, the so-called Jewish Enlightenment
2. Living for the moment, transitory pleasure
3. Third Sabbath meal

Builders and Fighters
(F. Liebhober, I.A Roguski, A. Eidelstein)

Aryeh Weinriber

Translated by Moses Milstein

One of the most active and loyal comrades was Pinchas Liebhober. He was completely dedicated to the Zionist cause, and was always at the head of every action and undertaking. His passion was social work, and he demanded much of himself, and often, too much from others. The Zionist organization always trusted him with representing it on the boards of the Jewish community, or in other institutions and committees. His shoe store was transformed into an assembly point for Zionist and social activity.

[Page 148]

Israel-Itche Roguski, one of my best personal friends, was also one of those types of activists, without whom it was difficult to imagine anything happening in social and political work in the shtetl. He came from a poor home, but he found his way to the movement through his own efforts. He was admired by everyone, both by his own friends, and by his opponents. Although he was far from adopting Revisionist ideals, he, nevertheless, found

Pinchas Liebhober

The right approach and language to work together with the Revisionists. He had a good, gentle character, always happy to do a favor. With a pointed joke or witticism he used to calm a heated atmosphere or entertain the company.

Avromtche Eidelstein had fewer financial worries than the previous two. This allowed him to dedicate himself more to organization work. At all times, he carried the entire burden of the movement both when he was a General Zionist, and as leader of Betar. His conscientious activity was felt everywhere, and his boundless dedication to the cause he was fighting for.

All three shared the tragic fate of Markuszow's Jews. They were murdered by the Nazi savages.

Honor to their memory!

[Page 149]

In Memory of a Comrade

Markuszow with its significant Zionist youth did not manage to achieve a pioneer aliyah. There was just a Revisionist youth that did not attend any *hachshara*[1] kibbutz, and therefore did not get any certificates. The drive to go was however very strong. The youth waited for another way of getting to Eretz-Israel to present itself.

Menachem Goldberg

Menachem Goldberg, a son of the Zionist fighter Yosef Goldberg, an active member of Betar himself, went away to the *hachshara* kibbutz from *HaOved Zioni* in Kielce. There he worked in a sawmill, and died during a terrible work accident.

The grief in the shtetl was great. Menachem Goldberg, z"l, was known as a very quiet boy and a good person.

Translator's Footnote:

1. Zionist pioneer working camps

[Page 150]

Israel-Itcheh Roguski
(To the memory of a good friend and loyal Zionist)

Sureh Fianko Weinriber

Translated by Moses Milstein

It is hard to imagine Markuszow Jewish life without Israel-Itche Weinriber, the backbone of the Zionist organization. Although he was a few years older than me, we were bound by threads of true friendship. Every Shabbes after lunch, he would come to visit our home in order to learn from my father how to be a *ba'al koreh*.[1] At every visit, he would bring two red apples, joking that they were the same color as my cheeks. Most of the time, due to my age,

Israel-Itche Weinriber

I was asleep. So he would leave the two apples under my pillow.

In later years, when I began to attend the Zionist organization, I first became acquainted with Israel-Itcheh. He was full of knowledge. If the cultural and social activities of the organization were in the hands of Pinchas Liebhober, Avrumtche Eidelstein, and Pinyeh Ettinger (coming from the left Poalei-Zion, they reorganized the library, held literary readings, led a question and answer series every Saturday evening,

[Page 151]

brought speakers in, and the like), Israel-Itcheh distinguished himself by his gentle character, and loyal dedication and concern for each comrade, young or old, demonstrating a lot of patience. I don't recall him ever getting mad at anyone. Always with a smile, a joke, with a fitting example that immediately calmed the stormy atmosphere. He was compassionate and very devoted to people, especially to the needy.

I know of many cases where he was worried about the fate of a given family, and using various pretexts, immediately went over there to see what was really happening, and to bring help. In winter particularly, he would be a frequent guest in poor homes where there was always a lack of money for coal or firewood, or perhaps there was a greater need for money for food in such a house, or just as an act of kindness that would sustain the soul. In such cases Israel-Itcheh Roguski demonstrated a lot of compassion and tact in order not to offend the recipient.

Sometimes when they came for help from him, he did not have the means required to help. Without delay, he would borrow from someone else in order not to leave the outstretched hand hanging in the air...We learned about all these cases by chance, because he was not the sort of man to boast. Helping someone near to him was his reward and pleasure. As is usual with such people, he had no luck in his own life.

As related by the survivors of Markuszow Jewry, who lived through the Hitler occupation in the shtetl, Israel-Itche remained true until the end. When the criminal Nazis came first for his wife, leaving the extermination of the men for a later time, he went along with her in order to share her tragic fate.

Honor to his shining memory!

Translator's Footnote:

1. Reader of the Torah before the congregation

Moishe Eidelstein–the Heroic *Sheliach Tsibur*[1]

Sholem Wasserstrom

Translated by Moses Milstein

This was the fate of Jews in the lands in which they lived: Before the first shots of the parties in the war stopped echoing at the front, the bodies of Jews were already swaying on the gallows, accused of espionage. These gallows marked the route of the Czarist army during WWI.

[Page 152]

The more setbacks at the fronts, the greater the anger at the defenseless Jewish population. Russian officers, especially the Cossack units, distinguished themselves with their savagery and persecutions, and never missed an opportunity to create trouble for the innocent Jews.

The outbreak of the war in 1914 brought dangers associated with the event in Markuszow as well. The first victim from the shtetl on the sacrificial altar of the First World War fell far from Markuszow while he was loyally and honestly fulfilling his mission to a community of Jews condemned to death. It happened like this:

In the dense forests of Sandomierz there were several Jews engaged in forestry, among them Markuszow's Moishe Eidelstein who was a writer. He was very esteemed by all for his honesty and piety.

As soon as the war broke out, several Czarist military units came to these forests. It became dangerous for Jewish workers to even move around the forest, not to mention going to the city. As the day of Yom Kippur approached, the forest Jews decided not to go to Sandomierz for the holiday, because the roads were full of dangers, and instead to put together a minyan in the forest itself. There were about ten Jews there along with the Jews who lived in the surrounding villages. They came together for Kol Nidrei in a forest hut. Hot prayers and even hotter tears issued from their hearts and eyes to the heavens. There was plenty to plead with God for: removing the Cossack danger that lurked around every corner; ending the war that caused so much loss of Jewish life; livelihood, health, good matches for the children, and anything necessary for a little good fortune. Some prayed for themselves, that is, for most of Israel, and some for the collective–for all of Israel. But everyone had one desire: Yom Kipur should pass peacefully. It should not be disturbed by the enemies who were very close then, a stone's throw away.

The night passed quietly with no disturbances. The Yom Kippur prayers began in the morning. The pleading and the tears of the congregants issued through the open door and windows and carried through the forest. The Christian watchman was also affected by the prayers and wept along with the Jews. The day was coming to an end slowly, the sun beginning to set, its rays shining through the tops of the trees. The worshipers began *Neilah*[2]

[Page 153]

with the conviction that the holy day had been a lucky one this time, that the danger from the army stationed in the forest had passed. Prayers became more cheerful, although with tears, but with thanks to the Everlasting that this random Jewish congregation was given the opportunity to observe the holiest day of the year.

Their impassioned prayers were suddenly interrupted. Several Cossacks with an officer in the lead broke into the hut and demanded that prayers stop. Such an order was not necessary, because the trembling Jews had immediately become silent. The officer shouted that our cries were a signal to the enemy. In vain the Jews tried to explain that they were only praying to God, observing Yom Kippur, and had no thoughts of any armies, fronts, and certainly no thoughts of signaling the enemy.

The Cossack officer had his fixed views of Jews, however. He pretended to believe their words and demanded a bribe. The poor village Jews did not have the kind of money that the senior Cossack demanded. So he was promised that one of them would immediately go to Sandomierz to get money. That is how Moishe Eidelstein, a Markuszow resident, became the emissary for nine Jews. In their name, and with their blessing, he went off to the city to get the contribution demanded from the community.

Just as the Cossacks thirsted for Jewish money, they also yearned for Jewish blood. As soon as Moishe Eidelstein left on his mission, the nine Jews were hung. With "*Shema Israel*," on their lips, they breathed their last, as the rope put an end to their lives. Both the emissary and the Jews of Sandomierz suspected this, and they gave him the money but warned him not to return to the forest where certain death would await him. May at least one person remain alive. The Sandomierz Jews were ready to send someone else to hand over the bribe.

Moishe Eidelstein, however, wanted to complete his mission. He did not agree to sending someone else with the money–and returned to the forest. The moon had already crossed the sky when the emissary reached the place he had set out from. Over the heads of the waiting Cossacks nine Jews in their *tallises* were swinging from the trees. The wind shook the stiff bodies of a congregation of Jews killed for their religion. The gentle heart of R' Moishe Eidelstein cold not bear this. He fell to the earth, and his bright soul left his body. And the Cossacks,

[Page 154]

as was their habit, took the money and hung his corpse on a tree.

The news of the ten murdered martyrs in the Sandomierz forest spread across Poland with lightning speed. When Jewish Markuszow learned about the death of its martyr, everyone was filled with sorrow and pride, because the *sheliach tzibur* passed his test, fulfilled his mission until the end, and did not betray his holy duty.

Moishe Eidelstein was certainly the forerunner of the later emissaries during the Second World War, those Markuszow young people who fought against Hitler's beasts with weapons in their hands.

Water pump in the market

Translator's Footnotes:

1. Community spokesman
2. End of the Yom Kippur service

[Page 155]

Second Part

Death and Resistance

[Page 156] Blank [Page 157]

A Yorzeit Light for the Fallen
A Reminder to the Survivors

Translated by Moses Milstein

List of the Jewish partisans from Markuszow who, with weapons in their hands, fought against the Nazi murderers and their accomplices.

(In alphabetical order):

Iberkleid Yosef, "Yuzhek" (killed)
Iberkleid (His brother. Now in Israel)
Breinsky Simeh (killed)
Gothelf Yerocham (killed)
Gothelf Yakov (killed)
Gothelf Yechiel ("Heniek." Now in Australia)
Gothelf Chana (killed)
Wichter Shaul (killed)
Westelschneider Nathan (in Israel)
Teitelbaum Yehoshua (From Plouszowice, killed)
Loterstein Michal (Now in Paris)
Loterstein Manye (killed)
Laks Veveh ("Wladek," killed)
Laks Shmuel ("Dziad." Now in Israel)
Laks Shmuel (Ben Meir, killed)
Morel Shloime (Now in Poland)

[Page 158]

Morel Itzchak (killed)
Melhendler Chaim ("Heniek," killed)
Ettinger David ("Dodek," killed)
Pelz Moishe ("Martchin," Now in Israel)
Pelz Motl ("Michal," killed)
Fishbein Hershl ("Yuzhek," Now in Brazil)
Fishbein Itzchak (killed)
Fishbein Avrumtche ("Adash," Now in Israel)
"Kozak" Yosef (killed)
"Kozak" Lozer (killed)
"Kozak" (name unknown. Killed)
"Kozak" Itzchak ("Yuzhek" from Plouszowice. Killed after liberation)
Kerschenblatt Mordechai ("Martchinek." Now in Paris)
Kestelman Tenochem ("Todek," killed after liberation)
Kandel Tobeh (killed)
Kerschenblatt Moishe-Noach (Now in Australia)
Brother-in-law of Rosenstein (Now in Israel)
Rosenberg Isser (killed)
Rubinstein Yerachmiel (killed)
Rubinstein Dovid'tche ("Stach." Now in America)

Rubinstein Shmuel ("Sever." Now in America)
Rubinstein Blumeh (Now in America)
Reich Meir ("Andzei." Now in Israel)

[Page 159]

With Partisans, Among Farmers, in Bunkers
(Memories of the occupation years)

Dina Gothelf, Ramat Gan

Translated by Moses Milstein

About ten years have passed since my terrible experiences in Markuszow itself, and in various hidng places in villages and forests, ten years since the pain and suffering of a spectator in front of whose eyes one's nearest and dearest were killed–so everything is all still so fresh in my memory, every deathly fright and experience so deeply etched into my heart, so that it is not especially a struggle to remember in order to put everything down on paper. The hell of Hitler shook us to our very core, and brought us to the edge of the abyss. It seems to me that I should not be allowing myself to keep within me those nightmarish hours and minutes where I struggled for my life. Every Jew, no matter where he is must, and is required, to feel and experience all that we underwent. May my mind and hand guide the pen, may it tell of our pain and suffering for generations, our heroic battle and tragic destruction. May the following words also serve as a yorzeit candle for the unknown graves of my nearest ones, my flesh and blood, who died for *kiddush hashem*.[1]

The shtetl up to the *churban*[2]

It is hard for me to begin immediately from the days of the *churban*. I can still see before me our shtetl Markuszow, situated on the Lublin-Warsaw road. The main street, Lubelska, consisted of two rows of closely connected wooden houses along the length of the road. On one side of the street, the market separated itself off–a large four-cornered place with somewhat nicer houses. One of them housed the gemina[3] office. The main street was almost completely inhabited by Jews who also had their shops there.

[Page 160]

Markuszow Jews dealt in anything you could want, but making a living from it–that's another question.

A big market day took place every Monday in my hometown. Farmers from the surrounding area came with their products. Incoming merchants and storekeepers used to put up their stalls, topped with a canvas roof, and lay out all kinds of manufactured goods, haberdashery, clothing, boots, shoes, and knitwear. The other side of Lubelski Street, somewhat away from the road, a large paved area with a wide sidewalk, buzzed like a beehive. Here the Jewish storekeepers bought butter, cheeses, sour cream, and poultry from the women farmers. A little farther away from the main street was the horse market, known as "*targowice*[4]." Here they dealt with horses, cows, pigs and other livestock. Hard-working and sweaty Jews ran around trying to earn the little that they looked forward to all week. Really rich Jews did not exist in our town. Better situated–yes, but far from wealthy. How disappointed and bitter were the Jewish shopkeepers and dealers when it rained heavily on Mondays and crowds dwindled. All debts, expectations, and hopes for a good return were lost in the drops of rain that fell on that day…

After a market-day, the shtetl looked like an earthquake had struck. Street sweepers had to work long hours to return the shtetl to its normal appearance. And not only on the main street, but also in the side streets. Our backstreets were mud-filled all year-round. On one side almost only Poles lived along with a few Jewish families. On the other side, mostly Jewish families with a few Polish ones mixed in. Here in the side-streets lived mostly the tradesmen who worked hard and "earned little enough to be able to live, and too much to be able to die." No, life was not easy for the Jews of Markuszow. Nevertheless, no one complained. An old Jewish habit: better to live with faith rather than sin against God…

The youth of the shtetl–exactly like the youth of all the shtetls in Poland, had no future, struggled for their survival, and dreamed of aliyah and emigration. It was especially hard when the Sejm[5] tribunal frequently called for economic boycotts against Jews, which was commonly associated with antisemitic positions. Our parents clung to the pitiful existence that others wanted to take from them with force.

[Page 161]

The shtetl youth began to wander, some to Polish cities, mostly to Warsaw, some emigrating to other countries, and some to Eretz Israel, the land of hopes and dreams. Those remaining in the shtetl continued to live in the atmosphere and conditions described above.

There were three parties in the shtetl: 1) the trade union with a membership of only Jewish workers (other than a few organized Polish workers). Everyone knew that the trade union was actually the Communist party of Markuszow. 2) The left Poalei Zion–a worker's party that had a larger youth membership. 3) The Zionist organization that was, in my opinion, the largest in town. All the Zionist inclined Jews belonged to it. The parents were General Zionists. The youth belonged to Betar. When Jabotinsky[6] left the Zionist organization, Betar and the General Zionists could no longer exist in one locale, and the latter had to find a new location. When two youngsters from different parties got together, an acrimonious debate would often ensue that did not always end peacefully. When, for example, Betar would celebrate a national holiday and bring in speakers from the central organization, the proletarian conscience of both worker parties–communists and left Poale-Zion–could not rest and with united efforts they would interfere with the enterprise. Obviously, this took place with blows and scandals, and whoever had more strength and perseverance was victorious…

This is how Jewish Markuszow existed with its pain and joy, with its hopes and desires–until the outbreak of WWII that put an end to all the obligations we had to each other.

Markuszow is bombed

The first days of the war were immediately felt in the shtetl as refugees from western Poland began to arrive in their journey to the east. From them we learned that German airplanes were attacking civilians on the roads, and that thousands of fleeing men, women and children were being bombed and strafed. These reports put fear in everyone. Nevertheless, it didn't occur

[Page 162]

to anyone that a little shtetl like ours, with no war industry, nor military objectives, would be bombed by the enemy. We were all shocked that the neighboring town of Korew was bombed at the beginning of the second week of war, on Friday September 8 1939, and was practically destroyed. The air raid on Korew was a warning to leave Markuszow, that it would share the same fate. The Jews in town began to leave for the nearby villages with their most essential and valuable things.

This careful approach was later completely justified. On Monday, September 11, a squadron of airplanes appeared over Markuszow and began to drop bombs. The civilian population began to run in panic, and was pursued by the German pilots who shot at them with machine guns. More than half the shtetl was destroyed in that air raid. The following day, a large number of airplanes reappeared and finished their work of annihilation. After the two murderous air raids, over forty victims were counted, mostly Poles, because the Jews of Markuszow had fled the shtetl beforehand. It should be emphasized that the bombs were not directed only at the official structures, the mill, the shul, the church and other public buildings, but also at the houses around the market. Not long after, German tanks appeared in town. Markuszow was now in the grip of Hitler.

The first days of the occupation

As soon as the Nazis occupied Poland, Jewish life became chaotic, subject to the caprices of any SS officer or other German murderer. In some communities, they immediately began their murderous work among the Jewish population. Markuszow meanwhile endured Germans entertaining themselves with Jews, especially with the older ones they saw in the street. Our brothers went around beaten and full of fear for the immediate future. Young people, mostly men, were anxious that they would be grabbed for work at any moment where they would be beaten some more and humiliated. Many of them fled to the Soviet border that, at the beginning, was not hard to cross.

[Page 163]

Little by little the situation normalized, if one can use such a term. That means that we simply got used to the problems as the folk-saying goes: "*Baheet zol men veren tsu vos men ken zich tsugevoinen.*"[7] Jews returned to the burned-down shtetl. They do what they can to earn a living. Several families live together in one small room, and the better-off begin to rebuild their houses.

Just as in other cities and shtetls in Poland, a Judenrat and security service (police) was established. The German gendarmes appointed a Markushow Jew, Shloime (Shliamke) Goldwasser as the elder, against his will, and ordered him to put the Judenrat together. At first, there were no SS or Gestapo in the shtetl, and therefore, we experienced no special problems. From time to time German military units would stop in town, quartering there. There were cases where individual German soldiers would come into Jewish houses and enjoy some friendly time there. However, during market days (Monday) if German gendarmes showed up, the Jews would quickly pack up and leave, and with terror in their hearts, wait for the devils to go back to wherever they came from.

When it came to money, the Judenrat always strived to accommodate German demands. To the credit of the Markuszow Judenrat, it must be said that they always found the right approach to dealing with the German murderers, and for a while, they always managed to avert many decrees against Jews that other shtetls could not manage. During all this, everyone lived in fear, because any German ruled over any Jew's life. The first winter of war passed with constant visits by the Germans who used to come from the nearby sugar factory where they were stationed, and would drive out the youth to various jobs. Our young boys would often return beaten, humiliated, insulted by the supervisor, a savage sadist. At that time, we would hear of individual Jewish martyrs, but it was not yet on a mass scale. It was hoped that we would survive the enemy's efforts.

Life in the shtetl carried on. Jews continued business, and some did not bad. Our tradesmen worked, each at his trade. Many Jews rebuilt their dwellings, and there were even some Jewish weddings celebrated. Love affairs were carried on, and it was hoped that Hitler's defeat would occur.

[Page 164]

We would get together quite often in private houses, discussing everything and everybody, talk about the latest war news that Poles we knew passed on from the secret radio broadcasts they heard. The bizarre news was the theme of such get-togethers.

Persistent rumors circulated that the Germans were preparing camps for Jews where they would be forced to labor under the worst conditions. This scared everyone. By summer, 1940, it was officially known that in the larger cities raids were carried out on work-eligible men, or the Judenrat itself supplied the required contingent of Jews. It was hard to get anyone out of the camps, and they were rarely seen coming back again. We also heard in Markuszow that in Warsaw and Lodz ghettoes were set up where Jews lived in terrible hunger and privation. A little later we saw living proof from there–starving and exhausted Jews who in mid 1940 got out of the Warsaw ghetto and wandered all over Poland looking for food. Living skeletons appeared then in Markuszow. We received them with open arms, fed them well, found them a place to sleep. After eating well and resting, they continued their wandering. Some of them hired out to farmers, just to get enough food and a place to lay their heads. As mentioned, the little shtetls were not yet familiar with ghettos. For the moment, they left us alone–but for how long?

The deportation actions

In the spring of 1941, large formations of German military passed through Markuszow in the direction of Lublin. That Pesach we had our first Jewish victim. A seder was being celebrated in a house and it was lit up until late in the evening. A military unit happened to be passing through Markuszow, and they were suspicious of why there were still lights on in the house. The officer, a little drunk, entered. One of the young people present, Shloime Goldstein, the shoichet's[8] son, was so overwhelmed and confused by the unexpected visit, he hid in a cupboard. The officer found him and killed him on the spot. Everyone was petrified by the event.

With the outbreak of the Soviet-German war, our conditions became significantly worse. The Judenrat was forced to supply a number of young people

[Page 165]

for forced labor in a camp by the Vistula. The Judenrat was later successful in exchanging this group for another where my brother, a 17 year old boy, also ended up. After a certain amount of time spent regulating the flow of the river, both groups managed to return home. Afterward, one after the other began to issue anti-Jewish decrees. First an order was issued that all Jews must give all their furs to German soldiers who were freezing on the Eastern front. After–an order that no Jew could leave his present home and travel away from the shtetl on pain of death. Nevertheless, few Jews were very upset by the latest decree. At night, through byways, they went to nearby villages in order to earn a little living, but every one felt the danger in the air. Through various reports, it became known to us that the Germans made frequent attacks on the Jewish population in the shtetls, shooting and murdering without mercy, and that they led old people and children to unfamiliar places from which they never returned. We awaited horrible events that made our lives difficult and desperate.

We learned from Poles coming from Lublin that in this old Jewish city a deportation of thousands of Jews had taken place. German gendarmes, Gestapo, and Ukrainians entered Jewish houses, dragged out the men, women and children, not sparing the old, drove them to the train station, loaded them in freight trains like useless baggage that one wants to get rid of, and sent them to an unknown destination. The sick and weak were shot on the spot. Even the healthy, for the slightest suspicion, or merely on a German's or

Ukrainian's caprice, received a bullet in the head. The Poles further related that many dead Jewish bodies lay about in the streets, having been dragged out of their hiding places discovered by the Germans, their dogs and the Jewish police. The routing of the Jews in Lublin took two weeks. Very few were left. They were used for various tasks by the Germans. Even though the news seemed highly accurate, we were still reluctant to believe it; that you could kill masses of people. There was also a rumor that Lublin Jews were being sent to Holland, and that the Jews of Holland would be brought to Lublin. It didn't take long before we knew the terrible truth.

There was a feeling that we were on the brink of disappearing. There was no Messiah to challenge Hitler. Among the youth, the idea of resistance was beginning to ripen

[Page 166]

even though under the conditions in our shtetl this resistance could not take on any realistic form. After the liquidation of the Lublin Jews, they took to the shtetls in our powiat[9] and then we understood that the tragedy would not bypass us. Every day that passed was a victory for life–but what would tonight or the following day bring?

The horrible day arrived. It was the last day of Pesach in the year 1942. We knew that two days earlier the entire Jewish population of Kurow was liquidated. A day later, the Judenrat was notified that tomorrow, one o'clock, all the Jews in the shtetl had to assemble at the city hall. Everyone could bring a backpack with things and food. We already knew (and more so, felt) what that meant. Everyone was filled with despair, disappointment, resignation. Most made peace with their fate, and determined to show up. In the meantime, they tried to talk themselves out of the tragedy. An 18 year old girl, who had just matured during the occupation, explained: "Let me pretend that I had experienced everything already, I'm now 70 years old, and it's time to die."

This last night we spent in our homes, readying ourselves for the last journey. But not everyone obeyed the Germans and showed up at the assembly point. Many of the youth escaped from the shtetl. Entire families who had Polish acquaintances who promised to hide them, left for the villages. Everyone did what they thought was best, what they needed, and what opportunities they had to escape from the hands of the murderers. My two brothers (died with partisans) left for a nearby village. My sister and her husband (also died) went to a Polish acquaintance in the shtetl. My mother and I decided to present ourselves at the city hall, because I believed it made no sense to hide, especially since our Polish neighbors displayed no willingness to help. They had always hated us, and now there was no reason to hope they would help, especially since to do so meant the death penalty. The Germans not only threatened, but also carried out their verdict.

The following day at one o'clock, the Jews of Markuszow arrived at the city hall with their packs on their backs. There a band of German murderers awaited them under the leadership of the Nazi murderer notorious in our region, Gedde. I stood in the row near my mother. They quickly separated us.

[Page 167]

The Germans separated the young and the old. The young were allowed to go home, and the old, accompanied by Polish police, were sent to the shul building. Seeing that my mother was going along with the others to the shul, I stole into the row and took her away. My mother was very confused. I forcefully took her hand and led her out of the line. A Polish policeman saw it all, but turned his head away. I was lucky–my mother came home with me.

During the first deportation, the Germans demanded "only" 500 Jews promising thereby that they wouldn't bother the shtetl anymore. We believed them because we wanted to believe. What choice did we have? We told ourselves that if they got the number demanded, the rest would be saved.

The [older] Jews taken away spent the whole night in the shul building. Heart-rending scenes played out there. The children wanted to see their parents feeling that it would be the last time. Disregarding the danger, many children tried to get their parents out from the place you don't come back from. There was however the opposite case. Mendl Ettinger, a member of the Judenrat, took his mother out of a hiding place and brought her to the shul being deeply convinced that he was doing the right thing, because a younger person would not have to go in her place.

The following day, when the unfortunate ones were to be taken away, the remaining ones hid fearing that if there were not enough they would begin grabbing people in the street. But there was no need to be afraid. Our parents were taken to the train station from whence they never returned. The weak and sick were shot along the way. The Jews of Markuszow later went out to gather the dead bodies and bury them. Little by little the hidden Jews crept out of their hiding places and returned to their homes. There was not one Jewish house that was not missing people from its family.

After the first deportation, an order went out that all the Jews in the shtetl had to move to that part of Markuszow where the majority of Jews used to live before the war. There were also attempts

[Page 168]

to create a work office for the youth of Markuszow believing that its establishment would prevent a further deportation. Such a workplace was established in the village of Kloda, 5 km from Markuszow, where they dug stones in a quarry. But there was no calm to be had. Those who worked, as well as their wives and children, hoped every day that they would not take them from the work directly. For five weeks we lived between hope and despair until another order came requiring us to assemble at the city hall again. This time most of the residents left town. Only a few tens of Jews showed up. They were all taken to a work camp in Konskowola. A small number remained in the shtetl and some managed to escape back to Markuszow.

Our family was split up again. My mother and two brothers went away to a village at the second deportation, while my sister and brother-in-law and I went to a Pole they knew in town, because it was easier to hide in smaller groups. For two weeks we lay hidden in an attic and in a horse stable. But the SS realized that the number of Jews in the shtetl had greatly lessened, and the day after the second deportation, they began to search and spy along the roads that led to the surrounding villages, and whenever they encountered a Jew, they shot him on the spot. Not far from our hiding place, some Ukrainians found a sick Jewish girl who the parents either couldn't or didn't want to take with them. She too was shot on the spot. The shot echoed in our ears fearfully close. We were certain that someone had pointed to our attic, and we would be quickly killed. In the evening, the Ukrainians left the shtetl and it became a little quieter.

A little while later, Jews snuck into the shtetl in the nights, took care of various things, and did some business with the money they had acquired thanks to the dirt-cheap but worthwhile things they had sold, anything to survive the critical period. At the beginning, many Poles behaved favorably to the Jews, even warning them when the Germans were coming. The outspoken antisemitic position came later, dictated from above, that is from the Polish government in exile located in London.

[Page 169]

We acquire weapons

On the fifteenth day of hiding in the attic, my younger brother came and told us that there was a farm not far from Markuszow where they were taking on Jews for work in the fields under the supervision of Germans. We decided to abandon the horse stall and move over to the farm. There we found a great many Jews from our shtetl and from surrounding places. The mood among them was depressed, because they had a supervisor who used to afflict and persecute them with sadistic pleasure. This degenerate would beat them for the slightest thing. Along with this, there was the constant fear of being taken away from this place–because where else can one be sent from here other than into the arms of death. We realized this was a devil's game, because no matter how much zeal the Jews would demonstrate, they would receive the stick from the overseer. And not just this. We felt that, after doing our work, we would in any case be condemned to die. Everyone posed the question: why try hard, why use up all our strength when we are sentenced to death. We returned to our hiding place in the loft of the horse stable.

At night we used to steal into the shtetl, meet with Jews who had been in various hiding places, and get reports. One man told us (it was later confirmed by other Jews) that in certain shtetls in the Lublin powiat, Jews were living in their own houses, conducting business, and were not experiencing such calamities. We left our hiding place and went to those places where Jewish life was still carrying on. First we arrived at a village. After–in the little shtetl of Kamionka where my remaining family members arrived. We rented part of a small room from a poor childless family, and established ourselves there. We lived from what we sold, and what we could still sell: a suit, better underwear and things of value. We had little left at this point because we were impoverished by the war. During the deportations we were left with practically no means to live. We did not stay long in Kamionka. We left for another village in the hopes of a better economic solution. Also a village was safer than a shtetl. We believed that in the village,

[Page 170]

we could work with the farmers, eat well and earn some money for the future. We had forgotten, however, that the harvest was over, and that there was little work on the farm. My sister could sew a little, so she would earn a little from the women farmers. When the time came to dig potatoes, everyone had work, although it was exceedingly strenuous, because we were exhausted and spent after what we had endured, and from poor food. Only the thought that we would finally get something good to eat and maybe save a little for even worse times, gave us strength and endurance. We would return from work dead-tired and with callused hands. We worked like this for the whole potato season. But we did not succeed in benefiting from the accumulated potatoes with which we were partially paid for our work.

On October 11, 1942, a decree was issued that all the Jews from Lublin powiat should present themselves for Belzec. A day before, my two brothers, Yankl and Yerocham, received a guest–Mordechai Kerschenblatt (now in Paris). They began to talk secretively, and we understood very well what that meant. My brothers were always saying that in the event of a final deportation, we would take off to the forests with weapons in hand, and what would happen would happen. Mordechai already had a pistol that he had taken from a German whom he had lain in wait for behind some bushes, and taken his weapon after he killed him. He threw the dead body of the German into the river. Now the three young men went to the village where the family Kozak, an old acquaintance, lived. There they found two youths from Markuszow whom the farmers had promised weapons to. They succeeded in getting several rifles. One of my brothers went off with the armed group. My sister and her brother-in-law went off separately in order to hide in a different spot. My mother and I went to my oldest brother who was hiding not far from us in order to consult with him about what to do next. I was of the opinion that we should present ourselves to

Belzec like all the other Jews, because with the little money we had it was impossible to survive. My mother had a different opinion however. She argued that rather than being sent off to a concentration camp and dying a slow death there, it was better to be shot in the freedom of a field. We understood that there was no chance we would survive the war. There was only a question of what kind of death and when.

[Page 171]

We parted from my brother. It was pitch black outside. An autumn rain was pelting down, as if the weather were weeping for our fate. On the way, we encountered my father's brother and his wife and children, and a good friend of theirs. We all headed over to a farmer they knew, and stayed in his stable until morning. He came to tell us to leave as soon as possible, because he was afraid.

In the village of Bogucin we knew many farmers with whom we had done business for many years. But most of them refused to take us in declaring that they were afraid of the Germans. It wasn't until evening that we came to the house of a poor farmer that my mother had sold a kerchief to before the war. We sat there for a while and asked if we could spend the night for which we would pay him. He hesitated a bit but still agreed. We spent several days there. It turned out however that the farmer with whom we had stayed before had followed us and knew where we were staying, because my sister-in-law by chance had gone to see him and had asked if he knew where we were, and he told her–and she found us right away.

We were now three people in the hiding place. My brother tried to get weapons for himself. But our landlord, the farmer, got truly frightened that it was known in the village that he was hiding Jews. He told us to leave for a few days, until the suspicion disappeared, and after, we could return. Unfortunately, there was nowhere to go at that time. In a field, we came on a partially built barn, and stayed there for a few days. My mother would sneak out at night to a village to bring us food. Once she told us that a colonist from western Poland, a fanatic antisemite who used to persecute my mother in pre-war times when she was doing business in the village, had sniffed out that we were hiding in the area, and he was jumping out of his skin to find us. We immediately decided to leave the barn and go back to where we had previously lived. There we could not find a permanent place and for a week we trudged along–where we spent the day, we did not spend the night.

There was no choice but to return to the farmer who had promised he would take us back as soon as it quieted down.

[Page 172]

But we could not stay more than a few days with him. He forced us to leave saying he was afraid.

In Wole forest

Homeless again, alone again–without a goal, or a direction. One of us said: Go to Wole, there are forests there and a village as well. So we went to Wole, and to our great joy, we found many Markuszow Jews there who, exactly like us, did not want to present themselves for expulsion. Many Jewish families from the shtetl had made themselves accommodations in cunningly hidden bunkers hard to discover. The people felt so secure and free in the forest that they walked around freely during the day. It gave the impression of a free autonomous Jewish neighborhood, as if there were no Germans in Poland. At night they used to buy food and bring water from the surrounding Wole and Meszno villages.

Wole farmers used to come to the forest to chop wood and freely watched the Jews' movements. The residents of Wole village were always voting for the Left, and their behavior to Jews was much better than the farmers of the whole surrounding neighborhood. But in a time when their lives were endangered by the presence of hidden Jews, a few helped the Germans search for Jews. More about this later.

In the Woler forest we met my sister and her husband who was armed. Several men who had their own weapons used to go get food for themselves and their families. Some of the women supported themselves in the village, and my sister also had a promise from a farmer that he would prepare a bunker for her in his stable. Here we also learned about the death of my younger brother, Yerocham, and how he died.

He, my brother-in-law, and a few other Markuszow Jews left for the shtetl one night in order to get to the highway to Przybyslawska. Suddenly they encountered two armed Poles on the road who identified themselves as members of the Polish workers' party (P.P.R.) which helped Jews. A pleasant conversation ensued between the Jews and the two Poles. Suddenly one of them wrenched the rifle from my brother and shot him. The rest of the group was so stunned they ran away in great panic. It turned out that the two were actually

[Page 173]

a reactionary band of bandits that ambushed Jews. My mother was devastated by this sad news. She went into spasms of crying in that farmer's hut where we were hiding. Involuntarily, some bitter words slipped from my mouth that I regret to this very day.

"Your tears are useless, because the same fate awaits us all. It may come to pass, mother, that you will have to mourn all your children."

That is how the bitterness and despair of my younger brother's death spoke from me. There was a basis for skepticism with regard to the hiding, because the "Jewish autonomy" could not persist for long in the forest. The farmers from around there had begun to say that all the Markuszow Jews were in Wole, and that they, the farmers will end badly because of them. And they began to drive the Jews from their hiding places. Rumors spread that the Germans were preparing a big attack on the forest.

At the Kozaks in Wole there was a large group from Markuszow they called the "Kozaks" (because of the name of their landlord). My brother, Yankl, was among them. Because of some differences of opinion, he left the group, a group of ten that had hidden in the places in the Lubliner powiat they had come from. Among them there was also a girl, Tobe Kandel. Several weeks later they all met their doom in a tragic way. One of the Poles alerted the Germans that there were armed Jews there. They surrounded them and shot them all. The only one who was able to save himself was Mordechai Kerschenblatt.

At that time, Jewish prisoners-of-war appeared in our forest (we called them "Plenne"). They were Jewish soldiers from the Polish army who had fallen into German captivity in 1939. They had worked in Lublin, at Lipowa 7[10] in the workshops created for them. In the early years, they benefited from their status as prisoners-of-war and received certain rights. After the Jewish population was deported from Lublin, they were declared ordinary Jews, and they knew it meant their death. So the majority of them acquired weapons, escaped from the camp, and succeeded in getting to our forest. It was of course their boldness and courage that led to their escape from the camp.

[Page 174]

My brother, Yankl, after leaving the Kozak group, joined with other youth in Wole who had their own weapons. My brother-in-law was also in the group. We also heard that a certain Tolka, from the Red Army, and his companion, Alexei, had escaped from German imprisonment and were in the forest. Our armed youth from Markuszow congregated around Tolek, a non-commissioned officer of the Red Army, good-natured and sentimental, a truly Russian person. Even the Polish famers demonstrated sympathy for Tolek. The whole group, the Markuszow youth and the escaped prisoners from Lipowa, represented a certain organized strength that could not be denied. Our youth really began to idolize Tolek, saw in him an authority that had to be respected by all. He was chosen as commandant of the group, and my brother, Yankl, ("Ivan") became his representative. The PPR organization in the village recognized the partisan group as their comrades-in-arms. Now they began to talk about sabotage and diversion actions against the Germans. The farmers got more weapons. They also dragged in from somewhere an old, rusty machine gun, and when, one day, the 40 armed men marched by on the Garbow-Wole road, the farmers later told of a detachment of 400 partisans.

While I was hiding in the forest, I did not have the chance to see my brothers. The oldest, Yechiel, was traveling with another group of armed youth. Meanwhile the rumors of a big raid the Germans were preparing for us were getting stronger. Just at that time, I suffered from a really painful foot rubbed raw by the too-large boots I was wearing. My sister-in-law reported to me that a farmer in the village was ready to hide two people, and proposed we go over there because there was a separate room. Never mind about the painful foot, I never contemplated leaving my mother in the forest. My sister, however, convinced me that it would be dangerous to stay in the forest with a bad foot, especially as we were expecting the Germans. That same evening, my sister-in-law's brother led me to the village.

I later learned that after I left, my mother moved over to the bunker of the Goldschlager family. A division of German army surrounded the forest and shot every Jew they met.

[Page 175]

It should be noted that they didn't shoot women, and left them free in the forest. After the raid, my sister-in-law went to the forest, saw my mother and relatives, and brought back greetings from our near ones.

We had nothing to complain about with the farmer we hid with. In general, we sat in his house. If someone showed up, we quickly went into another room, which resembled more a closet.

After the first raid, we saw through the little window in our room a large number of German soldiers approaching the forest where our partisans were. They encircled the whole area with machine guns. Our hosts, a half-intelligent farmer couple that had fled from the Russian occupied eastern territories demanded that we leave the house, because the danger was closing in on them too. Seeing our despair and sorrow, he said to his wife, "Putting them out on the street is putting them into the enemy's hands. Maybe it would be an idea for them to go to the stable, but each one of them should dress in your clothes so as not to arouse any suspicion. Even if they were seen from a distance, they would think it was her going to the stable."

We did just this. We got into the farmer's clothing and one by one we went from the house to the stable and from there to the barn where we covered ourselves well with straw. We stayed there for a whole day. Throughout, we heard the sounds of machine gun fire and rifles echoing. We knew that there was a heavy battle for life going on among our dear partisans. They were fighting for their survival, for my mother, my near and dear ones, and townsfolk. Yes, our feelings did not fool us. When we returned to the farmer's house in the evening, he told us about the horrible slaughter the Germans perpetrated in the forest. We promised to pay the farmer if he would take us to the forest at dawn.

On the Meszno side, hard by the forest, a farmer hut stood. We went in there, and the Pole told us that yesterday the Germans had discovered all the bunkers, and many people were shot on the spot. Only the bunker from the Rubinstein family, and the Lubliners (the escaped prisoners-of-war) remained. The farmer also told us that we wouldn't meet up with anyone in the forest, because a commission was to come. I couldn't understand why a commission was necessary. But returning to the farmer in daytime

[Page 176]

made no sense. It meant risking your life. So we decided to wait here. Soon two youngsters appeared from Komienko who we knew well from the time we had been hiding in that shtetl. We began chatting with the boys, when suddenly, my sister appeared. She was dressed as a villager so as not to be recognized as a Jew. She told us that her husband had made arrangements with a farmer for a few days (well-paid, of course), and on the day of the raid, she was lying in bed wrapped in the bedcovers, and could not move, because on that day, the farmer's house happened to be full of people. Now she has nowhere to stay. A farmer in Wole promised her a bunker, but it came to nothing. While digging the hiding place some German had come along and asked the farmer what he was digging. He replied that he was preparing a potato cellar for the winter. The lie succeeded. The Germans left, but the farmer became too afraid to hide Jews. I related to my sister how it was going with us, that the farmer was not keen on letting us stay, not ruling out that if we suggested one bunker for us all in the barn, he might agree, if he was well-paid. In any case, I gave my sister my address. Suddenly, my brother, Yankl, came in the door accompanied by Tolek, the same one who in our imagination had acquired a legendary persona. I had not seen Tolek yet. Now this partisan commander renowned in the whole area was standing before me. Both were carrying small arms and were in a great hurry. Our happy reunion was short-lived. They left right away. They gave us to understand that it was not safe to be in the forest today. We learned where they and their group were to be found (among whom was my sister's husband). Nevertheless, we went to the forest hoping to find my mother, or at the least, learn of her fate. We believed that she had gone to the farmer, Boguczin, where we had previously stayed. In the forest we met my oldest brother with a few more partisans. We described the situation to him. My brother promised to take us back to the farmer, and see to arranging everything.

Suddenly two youngsters came running from the village, Staroscin, and breathlessly related how some farmers had captured about 30 Jews, and they were all being driven to Markuszow

[Page 177]

to be handed over to the Germans. They were begging for help to rescue the Jews and save them from certain death. My brother said that it was essential to get in touch with Tolek's group who were near Meszno, and it might be possible to free the Jews with our combined forces. Tolek was however against the action. The partisans themselves were also despairing and crushed by yesterday's German raid. Nevertheless, some of them went off to help the captured Jews, but found no one on the road.

The forests around Wole were too small to support a group of partisans for an extended time. The Germans had good information about our partisans, and we could expect a second, bigger attack to finally liquidate the partisans.

We all began to feel as of the earth was shifting beneath our feet. Remaining in the forest was risky. The tactic of changing to another house or hiding place every day stopped working, because in the groups there were a number of girls some of whom had weapons. But most importantly, most of the partisans fell in love with the girls, and separating now was not so easy. The young men and girls wanted to share their fate together. Even Tolek fell in love with a beautiful girl and did not want to be split up with her. We actually met Tolek's group in the forest. They were all tired, dejected and poorly armed. Not everyone had a rifle or an automatic pistol and ammunition belt. Outside, German murderers were prowling, armed to the teeth, and a not overly friendly Polish population, although on meeting with the partisans they adopted a comradely attitude. It was hard to distinguish friend from foe. We parted from Tolek's group and left with my older brother, Yechiel's group. We entered the forest again to go to the bunker my mother had been hiding in. There in the forest we met a small group of gloomy and despairing Jews who had succeeded in saving themselves during the attack. But they could not flee far, because no one would take them in anywhere. So they returned to the forest, and tried to reestablish themselves. We were cursed– because of our appearance and with bringing tragedy to the farmers' homes that served as a refuge for us. Hunted like dogs, we came again to the same place where so many of our own were killed just yesterday. We were all certain that

[Page 178]

the same fate awaited us the next day. But as long as we are able, we will continue the struggle for survival. So we were now standing by the fire, blackened by smoke, and cooked our food. In the bunker, we found mother's coat and basket. We were certain she had been killed in last night's slaughter. We learned, however, that during the attack, my mother had left her coat and basket behind and gone to the village of Tomaszowice where we used to live. She went off with another woman. There the farmers caught her and handed her over to the Polish police in Jastkow. At the time, a group of mostly Markuszow Jews was working in the Jastkow court. My uncle's fourteen-year-old nephew who worked for the landowner happened by chance to see my mother under arrest. She managed to give him the little bit of money she had on her, and said: "Take the money, my child. Because where I am being taken, money is of no value. It will be of use for you."

From Jastkow my mother was taken to Majdanek where she had to endure all kinds of torture before she breathed her last.

Back to the bunker

My sister said goodbye to us, and returned to her previous hiding place. That was what she agreed on with her husband. I, on the other hand, went back to my place in the company of my brother and his group. My brother gave the farmer a little money and promised to repay him better if he would agree to dig a bunker for us in his barn. As soon as the farmer gave his assent, my brother left to look for a temporary place for us until the hole was ready. Finally we moved into a bunker similar to a den. It was impossible to stand upright there for any length of time. We had to always be seated on a bit of straw. The hole was dug in the barn that bordered the stable. To get to it, you first had to go into the stable. The farmer himself, had to work hard to get to us to bring us some food before he could reach our hiding place.

A few days later, my brother-in-law came to the farmer, and it took a long time before he could convince him who he was. My brother-in-law

[Page 179]

pleaded with the farmer to allow my sister to come, paid him more, and one evening my sister came to our bunker. There was only place there for two people, and we explained to the farmer that he had to enlarge the bunker and fit it according to our instructions. Since it was the eve of an important Christian holiday there was no talk of the farmer carrying out the work. For the same reason, he didn't want to borrow a shovel from a neighbor so that we could dig it out ourselves because his shovel was broken. We had no choice, and we dug with the broken shovel all day and night until the hole was wider and deeper. Now we could make it a little more comfortable, although another person arrived. We constructed a bunk on which four people could lie, and if necessary, five.

Tolek and his group, not knowing where to put themselves, decided to make a bunker in the forest, store food for a longer time, and to be careful. In that bunker there were many young people from our shtetl, and the prisoners-of-war from the Lipowa camp, and Jewish youngsters from Lublin, who had no weapons. Those of us hiding in the farmer's stable did not approve of the flight to the bunker, because it was winter, and every step out of the forest would leave footprints in the snow and betray the spot. My sister argued however that we all have the same chances of dying, and since her husband was in the forest she wanted to share his fate. My sister was ready to move to the forest, but on New Year's Day, my brother-in-law, and my brother, Yankl arrived. They told us that there was a bunker for us in the neighborhood of Gutanow. Tolek's bunker was not suitable, because they were not careful there, people went in and out, and it was impossible to hide from strangers' eyes. My older brother proposed to the younger one that he leave the forest and come to him, but without his girlfriend, because the farmer did not want any women for any price. Obviously, it applied to my sister who my brother-in-law explained could not go back with him to the bunker, because they would all be in danger. My sister however had her back up, and no longer wanted to stay with us.

They were all together in the bunker for a week. Then my older brother went back to his place, the second brother and my sister and brother-in-law

[Page 180]

to the forest in Tolek's bunker. This time we parted from my sister and brother forever.

Sad days arrived. We spent 24 hours a day sitting in the bunker, almost without moving. Pictures of the recent and far past floated by: dear faces, which were tragically ripped away, revealed themselves with full effect. It is hard to come to terms with the fact it all really happened. Fear for the survivors stares from every corner.

Food is brought three times a day. We try to determine the mood of the farmer and his wife from their faces, because we always suspected them of hiding things from us. There was something unspoken in their few niggardly words. We were constantly asking for news of the outside world, whether they heard anything of Tolek's group. They tell us about the unlucky Jews betrayed by the farmers to the Germans; of desperate brothers of ours who have no place to go and who surrender themselves to the murderers. They often share political news, news from the front, and sometimes a newspaper to read. We begged the farmer to bring something to read, but he refused. He didn't want to borrow it from anyone, in order not to arouse suspicion. Early one morning, we heard too much activity in the barn. We quickly extinguished the lamp, and tried to remain quiet, and unmoving. We heard movement in and out of the barn. Since no one had brought us our midday meal yesterday, we did not know what was happening. It wasn't until evening that the woman brought us something to eat. With fear, she told us that somebody had revealed to the Germans that she was hiding Jews. She suspected her woman neighbor who was with her Christmas Eve just when my sister-in-law happened to be there. She had begged my sister-in-law to leave the bunker that very day and help her get ready for the holiday. My sister-in-law even made her aware of the danger of this help because on Christmas Eve no one comes to visit. Nevertheless, on that day a neighbor did show up, and saw my sister-in-law at the window, and she surely informed the Germans, because just as they arrived with Polish policemen from Kamionka, they immediately asked where there were Jews and began to look in the closet, among the clothes and in the attic. Then they took the farmer out of his house, and she was certain he was going to be shot. Fortunately,

[Page 181]

the oldest of the Polish police was a good acquaintance of her first husband, and seeing her in such fear, he promised her, as he is a Pole, that nothing bad would happen to her. They then went into the barn, searched, tried to push a bayonet into the earth, and even approached near the entrance of the bunker. We were in great fear of our hiding place being discovered if not for the Polish commandant succeeding in distracting the Germans. The unwanted guests finally departed, and the farmer's wife firmly decided that if any of our near ones showed up she would tell them to go back where they came from.

Several days later, the farmer's wife brought us food and the terrible news that the Germans had discovered Tolek's bunker. They could not take the bunker for a whole day because the partisans bravely defended themselves. The Germans then made holes in the bunker and poured in gas and smoke. No one knows exactly how they met their end, because no one survived. As the farmers related, after digging up the bunker, all were found dead. At the same time, the Germans shot the remaining Jews who were hiding in the forest on their own.

At that time there was a case where a Polish family in the area that was hiding a Jewish family was shot, and their household goods went up in smoke. All this kind of news devastated us completely. Now we knew that none of our nearest and dearest were alive. In our despair we agreed on the worst: If in the next little while no one from our family showed up, we would present ourselves to the nearest police station, and put an end to this kind of life. These sorts of thoughts we did not even hide from our landlords, even though lately they had behaved very favorably to us. As it later became clear, this change was the result of the Soviet victory at Stalingrad where the Germans experienced their first painful blows. Goebbels gave an alarmist speech and it seemed that the war was ending quickly. Our landlords, in their naivete, believed that after the victory over Germany, the Soviets would reward them for hiding Jews, and they tried to dissuade us from such an unjustified step.

Meanwhile a happy rumor was going around: In the Jastkow region,

[Page 182]

there was a group of armed Jews. We were gripped with the hope that one of our near ones was present there. We hoped and waited. One evening we heard sounds of someone trying to enter our bunker. By the noise, we figured it was one of ours. First a pair of boots appeared at the opening, then riding breeches, and I was sure that it was my older brother. I cried out, "Yankl," but when his whole body came into the bunker it turned out to be my brother-in-law, Isser Rosenberg. He looked really depressed. In a broken voice, he told us that Yankl and Chana were dead. They had died in Tolek's bunker. This news hit me like a thunderclap. I convulsed in tears and all the experiences of the last years issued from those cries. I don't know how long it lasted, but when I had calmed down, my brother-in-law began to tell us of how this tragedy had happened.

A group of five men, occupants of Tolek's bunker, were sent out by the commandant to go to the villages in order to find food for the forest dwellers. When the five did not return so quickly, Tolek sent out another five to find out what had happened to the first group. My brother-in-law was among the second group. Luckily, both groups met in the forest, and happily began to go back "home" to the bunker. They were all shaken seeing the bunker which now resembled a big grave, especially since it was there that they had hoped to survive the horrible times, and instead had met their death. In sorrow, the ten men threw away everything they had with them, and went off into the woods where many Markuszow Jews were still living. Now they chose another tactic. They organized another place in the forest, but did not leave it during the day. Not until night did they go out looking for food, but at a distance of 10-15 km from the hiding place. My brother-in-law further related that if someone did not return during the night, he remained in the house a whole day in order not to arouse the suspicion that there are strangers wandering around the neighborhood. He was now in a group of ten men, among them eight from Markuszow, one prisoner-of-war, and one Pole. All of them had by chance been saved from death because they had been sent out for food for the residents of Tolek's bunker. My brother-in-law also met my brother, Yechiel, who had gone out to find out what was happening. He had absolutely no idea that

[Page 183]

such fearful attacks took place in the area. My brother-in-law warned him not to dare to come here because of the serious danger. He must wait until things settled down a little. And they agreed on a place and time to meet again. My brother-in-law left us a little money and told us to give the larger part to the farmer. We, to the contrary, proposed that he should do it because it would make a greater impression on the farmer, and he wouldn't deny a partisan. He then went to the farmer's house, gave him the money and promised to reward him well if he kept us longer. Our landlords, understandably, readily agreed to let us stay.

A few days later, my brother, Yechiel, came with a friend from his group. Together we now mourned the death of our brother and sister and were convinced that if they had taken our suggestion to stay with us in our bunker, it was possible they would still be alive. Now all we had left was to mourn their young lives.

We transmitted to our brother the time and place where he could meet my brother-in-law's group in order to combine them into one unit which numbered up to eighteen men. And so it came to be. As commandant they elected a certain Yeager, one-time prisoner-of-war, and my brother-in-law as his deputy. Other than this group there was another Jewish group in the forest made up of only prisoners-of-war, and a few youngsters from Kamionka. At the time there was no Polish partisan movement of any significance. There was just an underground movement of the PPR (Polska Partia Robotnicza) (Polish Workers' Party) that called on the Polish people to revolt, and performed small diversion actions. There were reactionary groups that did not recognize the Jewish resistance organizations and in general held that Jews in Poland had no right to exist. In keeping with this position, they murdered every Jew they came across. They also wanted to destroy the Jewish resistance groups. The Polish population was divided into two camps: one–under the influence of the reactionary Polish government in London. It was their position that now was the right time to get rid of the Jews once and for all, and that not one of them should remain alive. Against this, the left wing socialists and

[Page 184]

the communist workers' movement took into their battle ranks all elements without exception that wanted to fight against the German occupier. They gave the Jewish fighting groups moral and practical help, although some of them were not able to free themselves of the prejudices against Jews–prejudices that had been rooted for generations. In many cases, they ruled too negatively on the actions of the Jewish group, not taking into consideration the special circumstances in which they found themselves. There were also cases when our Markuszow group lost the trust of those who were the only support in these savage times that called for heroism. Because on the one hand you had to show readiness and capability for friends and sympathizers in order to carry out courageous acts against the a German occupier and his authority, and the group really did carry out such bold attacks on German interests. So one evening they set fire to the big dairy in Garbow that was on the main highway not far from a German station. This dairy supplied butter for the Germans, but in the flames a lot of documents that detailed how much the surrounding farmers had to supply also burned. This fire not only brought real harm to the Germans, but it also helped the farmers of the area because for some time they were not forced to provide products for the enemy. From time to time raids also took place on German posts that always ended successfully. Our people did not usually suffer any losses. On the other hand, it was necessary to demonstrate a strong hand against the outlaw Poles who helped the Germans in their annihilation work, handed over individual Jews to the murderers' hands who actively participated in the deportation of the Jewish population. A merciless, forceful hand was necessary with regard to the German collaborators. We Jews had nothing to lose at that time, because all that was beloved and dear had vanished. Our closest ones were dead, our homes were destroyed. But the farmers still had something to lose, and they knew that you could not trifle with Jewish partisans, that there is a power that demands blood for blood. The Jews hidden in the villages felt somewhat more secure because the farmers knew that behind every hidden Jews lay a connection to the partisans. Our partisan group also had to have enough food and money because they had to pay the poorer farmers for hidden Jewish families.

[Page 185]

Our heroic fighters knew how to take care of themselves. They used to get food from the richer farmers, especially by confiscating pigs that were destined for the German contingent (those pigs had rings in their ears). A monthly contribution was levied on the landowner afraid to oppose the Jewish partisans' wishes. There was one landowner, the Leszic nobleman who refused to pay the sum allotted to him, and brought in Germans to guard his property. Our partisans did not count on this and organized an attack. Because of a premature shot, the undertaking failed. My cousin, Hershl Fishbein, was wounded in the stomach. The partisans retreated. But when the Germans left, the partisans constantly attacked his holdings. The nobleman and his son would hide.

PPR also used to order the Jewish partisans to liquidate individual Poles who served the occupier, that the party deemed harmful and awful. Although we were sitting in the bunker, we knew exactly about the slightest activities of our heroic guys, either via the reports that my brother-in-law and brother used to accurately pass on during every visit, or through our landlords, the only connection between us and the outside world. Sitting in the bunkers we followed our partisans, among whom were found our closest relations, with our minds

We sat in our bunker like this until summer. Meanwhile, the neighboring farmers began to gossip that partisans were coming to our landlord too often, and that he must certainly be hiding Jews. The suspicion among the farmers was so strong that it began to threaten serious danger for the farmer and us. One evening we left the bunker we had been living in for months. We went to the Tomaszow region in the company of my brother and brother-in-law to look for another hiding place. We went on foot, because we didn't want to take a carriage. Sitting so long in the bunker had produced an effect on our legs. We didn't have enough strength to go ten km, and my sister-in-law declared she could go no further. We met a Pole in the village of Wole who belonged to a Jewish partisan group. My brother decided to install us with the same Bogucin farmer we hid with after the first deportation. My brother, however, was not successful,

[Page 186]

and we went on further, even though I was very tired and footsore. We came near the village, Tomaszowice, going on footpaths through the wheat fields. Suddenly we saw two people coming toward us. My brother and brother-in-law got their weapons ready. As the people approached, one of them called out a password and my brother answered. It became clear to us that these were people from the same organisation. It turned out that they were members of the B.Ch. (Bataliony Chlopskie–Peasant Battalion) who had a favorable attitude to Jews and often helped. The four combatants talked and we entered the village of Tomaszowice.

Meanwhile, my brother-in-law got me to a farmer where Hershl Fishbein was also hidden. He had been wounded in the unsuccessful attack on the Leszic property. After spending a few days there, my brother-in-law, with the help of the partisan, Moishe Pelz, brought me over to a bunker where there were already two Jewish families, acquaintances of Pelz. They all survived the war.

It became apparent now that, after having been sitting so much in one spot, having to walk 50 km had significant effects on my health, especially my legs, which were as swollen as blocks of wood. With great effort and pain I dragged myself to the new bunker, which in the final analysis, was only 2 km from my previous spot. My legs hurt for a long time, and for the two weeks I was sitting in the new "home" they gave me much pain. Then I learned that several families had left the bunker my sister-in-law was in, and I decided to move over there. After having been in the new spot for a couple of months, two Jewish women came over: the sister and sister-in-law of Shmuel Rubinstein, who is now in America. These two women had been at the Jastkow property where dozens of Jews were slave laborers. When the Nazi annihilation actions reached there as well, the two women managed to escape. It had been planned in advance when they met with their partisan brother. The Jastkow Jews were taken to the Poniatowa[11] extermination camp, and they succeeded in escaping. We remained here until liberation. The two women were, Blimeh Rubinstein, and her sister-in-law, the wife of David Rubinstein (Teitelbaum). Her husband

[Page 187]

was taken from Jastkow to Poniatowa. He managed to escape from there with his father. The two women were placed in the bunker. Our landlady was unhappy about this and she began to neglect everyone. She argued that she could not serve so many people, she had little food. But we were not bothered by her neglect. We hoped that we could maybe save another two Jewish souls.

A little while later, David Rubinstein arrived at our bunker. He stayed until the partisans could find a weapon for him.

We were four women now in the bunker. Everyone had someone close in the partisans. We were always worried about the fate of our fighters. Our days and nights in the hiding place were long and lonely. We understood the insecure ground on which they stood due to the spy network the Germans had set up. By chance, they succeeded in uncovering three Poles who had the job of spying on the partisans, and handing them over to the murderer's hands. These three men went around to the villages asking about Jewish fighters. One of the farmers, a friend of the partisans, immediately informed them of this. In one village they succeeded in uncovering the Poles. They were given a hearing, and having no other choice, they admitted that they were on a German assignment. They understandably received a well-deserved punishment.

In winter, 1943, several Jewish partisans were passing through the village of Lugow, a nest of the antisemitic A.K. (Armia Krajowa–Home Army). The Poles attacked the partisans, and Itzchak Morel of Garbow fell in the battle. He was shot by his one-time Polish schoolmates.

Partisan stories

The Jewish fighters would come quite often and tell us of their successes, of their connections with various Polish fighting organizations, and about the suspicions and worries that were upsetting them. After they left, we would be seized by sorrowful thoughts, and moods. "Will we ever see each other again?" Danger lurked at every step, and at all times. And we ourselves,

[Page 188]

buried alive in the bunker, felt the flutter of death at the slightest rustle or movement coming from outside. We were convinced they were coming after us, that someone from the village must certainly have noticed that we were brought food, and had betrayed us to the Germans. Or maybe we spoke too loudly?! If we heard the German language, we felt certain that they were coming after us. In those moments, we would stiffen with fear. We didn't start breathing again until they had left the village. At such times, a ray of hope entered our living grave: Maybe we would survive after all?

We tried to drive away the difficult mood and days by talking about our relatives, friends, acquaintances. They were actually the whole shtetl, our Jewish Markuszow–the living as well as the dead. By that time, already mostly dead. In those moments we forgot that many of them were already dead, and told many stories about them, anecdotes and funny happenings. And as much tragedy as there was at the time, it was not free of comic moments. We would often, for no special reason, break out in hysterical laughter, or spasms of weeping. Yes, our nerves would give out and we were too weak to overcome them.

There was nothing to read. But we had agreed that the farmer's wife would buy a paper every Sunday. She did in fact do this, and according to German information and statements that they are moving the front lines, we understood that the war was going against them. We imagined the picture of Germany's defeat and our liberation. About the latter, we used to frequently talk a lot, although more than once we doubted we would live to see that moment. It was hard to believe that we could once again be free to move about, go to the movies, or theater. It became painfully clear to us when we heard free conversations and carefree laughter from outside that this free world outside was closed and forbidden. The longing for that lost world was particularly hard at those times–and everything appeared hopeless and tragic.

As much as possible given the conditions, we tried to observe the rules of elementary hygiene. We got toothbrushes and toothpaste. Once a week, our landlady had to get us a bowl of hot water. For this treasure,

[Page 189]

we had to conduct a long debate and negotiation with the farmer. He argued that he didn't understand at all why it was so essential to wash, since we weren't doing any dirty work. "My wife does all kinds of dirty work, yet she only needs to wash once every few months." Even with such a powerful argument, he was unable to change our minds, we would not give up the water, and so everyone got a bowl of warm water once a week. After washing, we changed our clothes that we used to wash in the farmer's house. Two of us would leave the bunker, and do the work in his house.

We only yearned for fresh air. Even though we knew how dangerous it was, we would steal out and fill our lungs with fresh air in the quiet and cold of the night. The stillness around us was sometimes broken by the baying of a dog. Once at the surface, we always held our heads high, looked at the star-filled sky, and began again to dream about God's little world, and asked ourselves for the countless times, "Why is it forbidden for us to live and breathe. Are we worse than other people or nations?"

In the month of November, my brother-in-law fell tragically. Not far from the Wole forest, a group of partisans went off to lodge at a farmer's. While someone was cleaning and manipulating a pistol that he had taken from a Pole in Markuszow, the weapon discharged. The bullet went through the hand of the partisan who was cleaning it, and through the heart of my brother-in-law, Issar Rosenberg, who only cried out, "Oi," and fell down dead. We were only told about this occurrence much later, after our persistent questions about his absence. He was one of the frequent visitors to our bunker. The partisans would give us various excuses: that he was off on a meeting with the representatives of the party, or that he had an important task to do. Until our landlord, who had gladly received my brother-in-law, complained to the partisans why they were keeping his fate a secret. Since he was known in the region as a bold and courageous fighter, the partisans spread a rumor that he fell during a skirmish with the Germans, His heroic deeds were talked about in the whole area. On more than one occasion, he would enter a village with several partisans, and no one dared to oppose them. For a while, the Germans put a high price on his head.

[Page 190]

When we got the terrible news, we knew that it represented a great loss for us. Of all the partisans, he was the most concerned about our welfare, and provided everything needed. When people came and told us he fell in battle with the Germans, I also went along with that version, even though my brother had previously told me about the true events and the reason for his death.

That same evening, they took us away from the bunker, because there was a suspicion that they knew about our bunker. One farmer, although well known by my brother, told him that he knew Jews were being hidden in the area. We moved to another location in the village of Wole. The bunker belonged to a woman farmer, a friend of the party, and it served also as a hospital for sick and wounded partisans. There was room there for eight people. As we later learned, there was also a sick partisan in the woman's attic recovering from a bad case of Typhus. He was very weak and had to stay in the hiding place until he regained his health.

As I already mentioned, the commandant of the partisan group was the Jewish young man, Yeager. He had escaped from the prisoner-of-war camp in Lublin, on Lipowa 7. At the beginning of 1944, the Polish workers' movements united. A common front was created from the RPPS (Robotnicza Polska Partia Socjalistyczna–Polish Socialist Workers' Party), PPR (Polska Partia Robotnicza–Polish Workers' Party, Communist), and other progressive elements who with their armed groups mounted a unified people's army (Armia Lodowa) that was known as AL. Because of the approach of the front line to Lublin with the victorious advance of the Red Army, larger partisan divisions began to operate in the area. Especially active were the groups on the other side of the river Wieprz, who had a tight connection to Moscow. With the help of airplanes, they received weapons, food, medicine, and military instructors. Soviet military airplanes dropped paratroopers very often to help the partisans.

Because of the new developments on the front, our Markuszow

[Page 191]

unit allied itself with the united partisan forces and began to operate far from our hiding places. We were saddened by the knowledge that their frequent visits would become rarer, and who knows if any of them would be able to come. But luck was on our side, because near to us a Soviet military landing was supposed to happen and our men had the job of being there. The commandant, Yeager, my brother, Shmuel Rubinstein, my cousin, Hershl, and several Polish partisans, among them a woman, appeared unexpectedly in our bunker. Women played an important role in the partisan movement as military liaisons. They also distributed illegal literature calling for the fight against the Germans.

Clearly, the unexpected visitors did not come with empty hands. Aside form food, they also brought encouraging news about the situation at the front. Only Yeager was not happy, and he openly said that he had a bad feeling. According to him, it seemed that terrible days were coming. Precisely because the Red Army was getting closer, the Germans would at all cost clear the way for their retreat and would clean out the partisans. The situation was becoming more complicated all the time, and there would be a lot of victims. Speaking thus, he drew a picture of how he would fall on a hill that would become his grave, and on a stone would be inscribed, "Here lies Moishe Yeager."

The partisans went to the Opole region to wait for the landing. They bade us good-bye. The next morning we heard shooting. In the evening we again had a visit. My brother and cousin brought along with them Shmuel Rubinstein, wounded in both legs. They also informed us that Yeager was dead. He died in the following way:

Upon leaving us, the fighters went off in the direction of the Wole forest, and during the day, established themselves in a house in the little village of Meszno. That same day, the Germans had searched the village before the partisans arrival. Feeling certain that the Germans would not return soon, the partisans left the house and spread out in the forest. Suddenly a woman called out, "Germans!" It seems that somebody had revealed that there were partisans here. Yeager immediately ordered them to take a position behind the hill, and opened fire from there on the attackers. When he ran out of ammunition for his rifle, he reloaded with a new magazine, and poked his head up a little above the hill. A German bullet struck him in the head.

[Page 192]

The fighters told us more. Shmuel "Bochan"[12] had bad headaches and had lain down in the house where they had been earlier. As soon as he heard shooting in the forest, he wanted to run there knowing that among the tall dense trees you were more secure than in a farmer's house The Germans saw him, shot at him, and wounded him in both legs. He fought back with all his strength, and dragged himself deeper into the forest because luckily the bones in his legs had not been hit. Not until after the slaughter, when my brother and cousin went through the forest looking for wounded comrades, did they find Shmuel in a bad way, and brought him to our bunker. They left him with us, and went back to the forest again to look for other partisans. Shmuel Rubinstein, lying in the forest got very sick, had a high fever, and according to all indications, he was now suffering from Typhus. We were not able to get him the medication required. The only relief from his pain we had was a piece of cotton and disinfectant. We cleaned and washed his wounds without having the slightest idea of how to do it. For fourteen days he lay in high fever. He became so weak, also because of the dwindling food supplies, that we were afraid for his life.

Meanwhile, we got more bad news: While crossing the river Wieprz, our partisans were attacked by Germans, and we paid with two victims. The dear boys who fell were David Ettinger and Veve Laks. It seems to me that in that encounter, my cousin, Hershl Fishbein was wounded for the second time. He was also shot in the leg, and stayed in our bunker until liberation. That same winter, there was also a badly wounded partisan, who came from Belzec, in our bunker. His nom de guerre was Stephan. He overcame the wound and other illnesses, got well quickly, and went straight back to his unit.

We remained in our bunker without money or medicine for our sick and wounded. Fortunately, our current landlady was not one of the greedy farmer women, for whom just the thought of becoming rich forced them to risk their lives and hide Jews. She did this out of purely human sentiments and good will to help the suffering and oppressed. She risked her life in the belief

[Page 193]

that she was doing the right thing. As a long-time member of the Polish Communist party she was free from racism, and behaved with tolerance toward Jews and anyone regardless of religion or nationality. She selflessly bore the heavy burden and gave aid in such terrible times, and didn't complain about her fate. After the liberation, she was murdered by her political opponents, the antisemitic and reactionary AK. I can still see before me the visage of this gentle and noble woman.

In spring 1944, when the Red Army was already on Polish territory, and their victorious advance was certain, a heavily wounded partisan came to our bunker-quarantine station. His name was Berl Bereza and during the battle at Vromblov[13] he was wounded in the head. We were now five people in the bunker– three wounded men and two girls. (Blime Rubinsein and I). My sister-in-law, and David Rubinstein's wife had left for the partisans at the beginning of spring.

The echoing sounds of Soviet artillery now reached our ears. The red Army was in the Lublin neighborhood at that time. We were drawn to go outside, to the approaching liberation, but we knew that without news from the partisans, we didn't dare to take such a step. The recovered partisans were uneasy in the bunker. Disregarding our warnings, they often went to visit farmer acquaintances, party comrades, and they would bring us news about the German retreat. Once, leaving the bunker, they saw several Germans. At first they were afraid, but it was not long before the Germans began to take off their uniforms, their backpacks, and asked for the way to Lubartow. The partisans immediately returned to the bunker, and described to us what they had just seen in the village. The next day, we learned that the Russians were in Lublin already. Several days later, some comrades came to us and together we first went to Lubartow where we met with most of the Markuszow partisans, and with the Parczew partisan group under the leadership of Yechiel Grinspan. After spending several days in Lubartow, we all went to Lublin.

[Page 194]

The underground and persecuted A.L. was now in power.

The people's militia in Lublin was mostly comprised of ex-partisans. The then bustling Lublin took in the remaining barefoot, starved, tortured Jews from the forests, bunkers, and the Aryan side. Their eyes were full of fear even though they walked around freely in the lively streets of the city. The emptied-out Jewish homes, the frequent news about the murders of survivors, and the horrors lived through brought the She'erit Hapletah[14] to Lublin where they were concentrated mostly on Lubartowska Street. The ability of Jews to recover from tragic experiences was also now wonderfully demonstrated. With extraordinary energy, the survivors began to rebuild their lives. Jewish committees and children's institutions were established. The renewal of a devastated Jewish life had begun.

Translator's Footnotes:

1. Martyred for being a Jew
2. Term for the Holocaust
3. Polish community division
4. Targowisko, Polish, market
5. Polish parliament
6. Leader of the right-wing Revisionist party
7. Literally, "May we be protected from what we can become used to."
8. Ritual slaughterer
9. Polish district
10. Lipowa 7 was a notorious forced labor camp in Lublin from 1939-1944. In November 1943 all the Jewish inmates were executed.
11. Located 36 km from Lublin
12. Nickname, Stork.
13. Phonetic transliteration. Unable to find actual location
14. Remnants of the survivors

[Page 195]

In Battle with the Nazi Enemy

Moishe Pelz, Kfar Ono

Translated by Moses Milstein

1.

On September 1 1939, when Hitler's Germany began its war with Poland, I was on active military duty in the 10th Ulaner regiment stationed in Bialystok. Our regiment receive an order to move to Lomza to set fire to the city in case it fell into German hands. After, we moved back to the river Niemen where we encountered a Jewish partisan group. They persuaded us, Jewish soldiers, to lay down our arms because the Red Army was due to march into western White Russia.

M. Pelz, writer of these memoirs, after liberation

When the rumors of such agitation came to the major, he openly ordered two Jewish soldiers to be shot, in order to remove any desire to follow the partisans,

[Page 196]

mostly Jewish soldiers from the Polish army, who because of antisemitism and persecution were forced to leave their units.

My unit, where I was the only Jews, arrived at Grodno. There we saw Soviet tanks. The officers issued an order that we should go into battle against the tanks with swords alone. Understandably, such an unequal contest did not last long. We all ran away in great panic. Not until the border with Lithuania did the regiment reform, taking in the beaten- up and fleeing military groups. In the new regiment, they spread antisemitic leaflets, and every Jewish soldier was cynically given to know his origin. "Zido Komuno!"[1] –was heard at every occasion.

It appears that the officers finally realized that from such an army they would not benefit. So they lined us up, and asked who was sick or wounded. These were immediately sent to hospital. The rest were paid, held for three days, and then ordered to go wherever they wanted. Me and 16 other soldiers rode away on the cavalry horses. Near Ostrow, we came on Soviet tanks. The Russians confiscated our horses, and told us to go home. They also told us to carry a white kerchief–the symbol of capitulation.

2.

After wandering about, I came to Bialystok, and went to see my townspeople–the brothers Beinish and Israel Migdal, sons of the lumber merchant, Isaac Migdal. They had been living for the last few years in Bialystok. Unfortunately, they weren't able to tell me anything about our shtetl. The lack of knowledge and uncertainty about the fate of my family drew me to Markuszow. I set off for the river Bug on foot. Since the bridge had been blown up, I returned to Baranowicka. Jewish militia in the city connected me, as a freed Polish soldier, with the local Soviet authorities, and I arrived in Brest-Litovsk via Bereza in one of their automobiles. The city was flooded with refugees from western Poland. I looked for my townspeople but found no one. Many refugees however knew that Markuszow had been bombed, and was completely burned down. This news strengthened even more my desire to go home.

[Page 197]

I went to Wlodawa. The Lublin Jews who were there tried to dissuade me from going to Markuszow. They described the German atrocities in Lublin and in other places warning me of the danger. I allowed myself to be persuaded and returned to Brisk. There, the Soviets arrested me, because I was still wearing the uniform of the Polish army. When the detainees were being transported to the railway station in order to be sent to another place, I was able to slip away from the transport. I got work in a mill and temporarily settled in.

I did not, however, stop thinking about my birth shtetl. The fact that I had no news of Markuszow threw me into despair. I was strongly drawn to go home to my parents, and siblings from whom I had been separated for many months because of my military service. Once, by chance, I met a fellow townswoman in the street, Rivkah Zilberman. She told me she had come from Markuszow, and that since my parents had been sure that I had been killed at the front, and I was no longer among the living, they sat shiva for me. That made it clear to me that I must, at all costs, get to Markuszow.

Along with my friend who had served in the same regiment as I, a resident of Kuzmir, Shmuel Rosenblit, we left for Domaczewo. With the help of border smugglers, we crossed the Bug and found ourselves on German-occupied Polish territory. We set off through the forest, and to our great surprise, we were stopped by a Soviet patrol. We were taken to a guard station where there were many Jews. Many of them had been accused of smuggling watches. The following morning, they asked us where we intended to go. As I had earlier learned that they sent you in the direction opposite to the one you wanted, I said I wanted to go to Russia. They therefore, put me with the group that was selected to go to Germany.

On December 20 1939 we crossed the river Bug in boats. As soon as we touched the shore, the same farmers who had been paid well for crossing the river, attacked us, beating us mercilessly, and stole everything. We barely got away with our lives. Not until night did we reach a small house in the forest, ate something, and for the rest of the night wandered on until Parczew. There we hired a female Jewish

[Page 198]

carriage driver to take us to Lubartow. After driving on for a few minutes, we were stopped by three Germans.

"Are you Jews?"
"*Co pan gada?*"[2] We answered back in Polish.

The Germans let us go, and we arrived at Lubartow. We did not want to go into the shtetl knowing that there was not one Jew left there. We went off to Markuszow on foot. In the village of Wola Przybyslawska we encountered the wife of Kafe Zisel. I asked her to prepare my parents beforehand for the news that I would be coming home shortly.

3.

At the end of December 1939 I arrived at my hometown having left one and a half years ago. The ruins of the burned-down and bombed houses made it difficult to find the way home. Only in the center, by a miracle, a few houses stood, and among them–our house. I directed my steps there. On the way, I met several shtetl Jews who greeted me warmly, like a "guest from another world." And who can describe the joy, emotions, and deep experiences of my parents and the whole family who saw me hale and alive, after having sat shiva for me. They led me into the house with love and tenderness, and many Jews in town came by to wish my parents mazel tov, and a sholem aleichem to me. And just as they wanted to know what was going on in the wider world I had just come from, so I burned with curiosity to learn everything that had happened in the shtetl since the outbreak of the war. I learned about the great wave of refugees that had rolled through Markuszow in the early days of September, the march-through of the retreating Polish army, and the frequent bombings with incendiary bombs that destroyed the shtetl. After the first flight over Markuszow, the majority of the Jews fled to the surrounding villages. My parents had hidden in Staroscin. When it had quieted down a bit, they came back to only ruins. Even the German authorities could not establish themselves in Markuszow because of a lack of suitable houses. They headquartered in Garbow, 5 km from us. Thanks to the German absence, the Jews could move around freely and occupy themselves with

[Page 199]

food supply. Markuszow and its surroundings were always known as a wheat center. Transports to starving Warsaw took place in those days. A number of Jews did good business from it. I related my experiences and then asked, "Why are you still here?" I told them that I came from a land where people walk around with their heads held high, and there isn't the fear like with local Jews, that the only goal I had for coming back was to take my family over the river Bug, and get them settled on Soviet soil.

A number of Markuszow Jews wanted to tear themselves out of the German control, but the fear of a closed border held them back. I succeeded in persuading my brother, Eliyahu, my brother-in-law, Velvl LOTERSTEIN, and several other Jews to go to the Bug. The river, already frozen was strongly guarded on both sides. They returned disappointed and despondent. I did not, however, give up on getting away from the Germans, and I strongly pleaded with my parents they should let my younger brother and I leave. My parents, like most Jewish parents in those turbulent times, did not want to be separated from their children. It was hard to oppose the parents' desire–and we stayed put.

4.

Winter 1940. Huge blizzards blocked the roads. The Germans settled themselves in the new shul building in Markuszow. They began to detain Jews for certain kinds of labor. At first–peeling potatoes for their kitchen. After–clearing the snow from the road. They also took women, youngsters, and old people for this work. They apportioned a section of road for each person, and established a standard for how much needed to be cleared in a day. While grabbing Jews they would beat them and constantly shout "verfluchte Juden."[3]

With time, they stopped grabbing Jews on the street for labor, and turned the job over to the Judenrat. From the Gestapo and gendarmerie in Pulawy an order arrived to create a Judenrat in Markuszow. To our astonishment, the Jews in the shtetl received complete freedom

[Page 200]

to determine its composition. It was constructed along the following lines:

Shlamke Goldwasser–president (he was a grandson of of the Markuszower rav), Itzchak Fishbein–secretary (ex-representative of Betar commander, a young man), and as member–Mechl Wiener, ex-chairman of the Markuszow community, Chaim-Yosl the shoichet, and Sender Fishbein (Vevi's). Now the Judenrat required the Germans to go through them if they wanted Jewish workers, and they would supply them. A list of work-capable people was made, and during the great frosts, they were forced to clean the Markuszow-Pociecha road. After, they brought large rocks to this place and Jews had to break them up to provide material to widen the Warsaw-Lublin road. We received work cards that allowed us to buy bread from the Polish baker. The overseers for the work were Poles from Silesia who behaved very badly toward the Jews, but with bribery and alcohol (they liked drinking) it was possible to somewhat soften the stony hearts.

After finishing the roadwork, we were taken to the train station to Pulawy where we unloaded heavy rocks from the freight cars.

Lives were at risk in the shtetl under the German occupation. Many Jews had returned and had begun to rebuild the ruined homes. Most of the time the building material consisted of wood, tin and even lime. This was of course illegal building activity. The bribed Polish police was aware of this but kept silent. There were two informants, Poles, who used to tell the Germans everything. A significant bribe forced them too to ignore certain events.

The Germans frequently demanded geese, butter, eggs, and whiskey from the Judenrat. These demands used to be made every Monday, when the market took place. The cost of such "gifts" was high, and Jewish Markuszow had to cover all the expenses. For the price of these food packages, it was often possible to avert subsequent anti-Jewish decrees.

5.

The decree of requiring the wearing of arm-bands did not pass us by either. Every Jew over the age of 12 had to wear the yellow armband with the Star of David.

[Page 201]

Children of 12 were considered of work age, but the Judenrat succeeded in making it lighter: only 14-year-olds and up were to be sent to work. German demands, however, always increased. The more they got the more they wanted. The Judenrat's coffers emptied out. It was hard to keep up with the murderers' desires. The Judenrat had to tax the better-off Jews who brought the money with little enthusiasm to the treasurer of the Judenrat–Shlamke Goldwasser. He bought the packages for the Germans.

Then an order came out from the Pulawy labor office to send out 35 Jews to work in the Janiszow camp near Kuzmir.[4] The Judenrat was able to negotiate the number. Twenty-three Jewish youths from Markuszow, and I among them, went off to Janiszow.

The camp was on the banks of the Vistula, surrounded by barbed wire. We worked under the supervision of Ukrainians, and one SS officer. Our work consisted of digging canals and ditches to regulate the flow of the Vistula in order to prevent flooding. We were half-naked while digging the sandy earth, and thinking about the end nearing when we would be exchanged for another group. We also worried about those left behind in the shtetl from whom we had been torn away. The system instituted in the camp did not permit for too much introspection. Five AM–the call to wake up. They counted to verify the number of slave-laborers. After, we made coffee with the river water, and got a half of a kilo of bread for the entire 24 hours. Arriving at the work site, everyone was given a section of canal and ditches to dig, or to fill the bulwarks of the Vistula. After a 9-hour workday, when the work assigned was completed, we marched back to the barracks where we received a bowl of soup. Thanks to the food we brought from home, we did not suffer from hunger. We also bought food for money in Janiszow. Our beds consisted of planks, 3 tiers. We covered ourselves with the blankets that we had brought with us. The barracks were unheated, and a biting cold ate at everyone's bones. While bathing in the river, we washed our lice-filled shirts.

They did not beat us in the Janiszow camp, although from time to time they made us line up and perform exercises, or run, or

[Page 202]

forced us to clean the place within 5 minutes.. There were also Jews in the camp from Wawolnica, Kurow, and Konskowola.

6.

When the first 23 workers had left the shtetl, the Judenrat promised to exchange them for another in a month's time. Our parents did not want their children to work away from home, torn away from their homes. After we had been working in the camp for two weeks, the Judenrat member, Chaim-Yosl the shoichet, traveled to Janiszow on a broad wagon pulled by two horses, and brought food and clothing for us, as well as "presents" for the overseers. Chaim-Yosl assured us that the agreement would be kept, and we would be freed when the time came and another group would be sent. When the four weeks passed, and there was no news from Markuszow, four of us, after bribing the guards, went to Januszow in order to telephone home. Jews lived freely in Januszow, didn't wear armbands, carried on business unmolested, and didn't even know about the forced labor by Jews in occupied Poland. The Jews of Janiszow at the time still wore their beards and did not feel at all the harsh anti-Jewish ordinances.

I went to the post office and asked them to call my father to the phone at the Markuszow post office. In a few words, I told him about our conditions in the camp, and asked when they would exchange us. My father replied that he does not rest and was always demanding of the Judenrat that they keep their word.

The Judenrat kept their word, and were only 7 days late. After 5 weeks of working in the Januszow camp, 15 other youths from Markuszow replaced us. For providing such a small number, it was necessary to intervene with the labor office in Pulawy and a larger bribe. I made my way home.

Pesach 1941. German soldiers appeared in Markuszow. In groups, they went into Jewish houses. In one house they found the son of Chaim shoichet hiding in a closet, and shot him then and there. A big panic ensued in the shtetl, because there was nowhere to run to anymore. We were surrounded on all sides. When the Germans finally left,

[Page 203]

we consoled ourselves with the fact that it had only cost one Jewish life. Almost the whole shtetl took part in the funeral of the murdered Jew, and the sorrow over the young life cut down mixed with fear of the future.

7.

On the eve of the outbreak of the German-Russian war (July 22 1941)[5], military echelons, autos, tanks, artillery and encampments stretched constantly through Markuszow. During such passes through, the Jews would lock themselves in their houses or in hiding places. Day and night, we heard the loud noises of the war machines, the singing and cries of the soldiers traveling to the front.

Once, such a military echelon stopped in town. Everyone locked themselves in their houses and prayed that the uninvited guests leave as quickly as possible. In the late hours of the night, we heard banging on Jewish doors, and we were all scared to death. German soldiers were dragging young girls from their beds, and were doing whatever they wanted to them. Markuszow Poles helped them in this contemptible work, showing the Germans where to find pretty Jewish girls. The next day we were still locked up all day in the houses afraid to go out in the street as long as the Wehrmacht was still there. They finally left the shtetl and we could breathe easier.

The moment Germany began the war with the Soviet Union, antisemitism became much stronger both from the occupying power, and from the local Polish population. The bigger the success on the battlefield, the more extreme anti-Jewish decrees became. During the first winter of the Russo-German war an order was issued that all Jews had to give up their furs to the German army. He who did not carry out the order would be shot.

All the ways to get to the German authorities with whom we used to be able to deal with and to negotiate were cut off. The Markuszow Poles also openly and impudently expressed their impatience with the Jews, wanting to get rid of them faster. There was another reason for this: many Jews had hidden their possession with the Christians. So they were keen to inherit Jewish wealth as soon as possible.

[Page 204]

8.

In spring 1942, 5 trucks with gendarmes arrived in the shtetl and ordered all Jews to go into their houses. The elder called out the Judenrat, and ordered them to immediately make a list of all Jews, without exception, who were in the shtetl. The chairman of the Judenrat, Shloime Goldwasser, managed to get the Germans to postpone the list for another day. Of course, moving the date, even one day, cost the Markuszow Jews a lot of money.

The next day we already knew that that same night the Germans and Ukrainians had surrounded the neighboring town of Korew, and the Jews there were taken away to an unknown destination. Several thousand Jews were thus torn from their homes, and sent to their death.

The following day, the Judenrat was called to Pulawy and calmed down by telling them that there was no danger threatening Markuszow Jews. Their only desire was that every Jew in Markuszow, young and old, should be ready to work wherever he was sent.

We were not allowed to rest for long. As soon as the murderers left Korew, they came to Markuszow and ordered all the Jews to appear at the square opposite city hall. The order stipulated that any Jew found in his house would be shot. From early on, we saw parents and their young children going to the city square. By 7 AM the whole shtetl was assembled there. Three cars carrying gendarmes and Ukrainians quickly arrived. Their order was curt: to arrange ourselves in rows–men, women and children separate. A lament arose. Unhappy mothers, despairing fathers and confused children were separated, but quickly began to search for each other with wailing and cries. The murderers stood with their weapons pointed and rubber truncheons and sternly made sure their orders were carried out. Everyone was filled with fear, because no one knew the goal of the bandits. This time the hellish spectacle did not last long. They surrounded the group of older people and led them to the shul building. There they remained under strong guard. The rest were told to go home. They quickly left this tragic place and many then left the shtetl.

[Page 205]

The captives were then led to the train station in Naleczow on foot.[6] Those who had no strength to walk were shot along the way. In that way the Markuszow water-carrier, the wife of Pinchas Israel Itche's, Yehoshua-Tuvye Friedman, and others whose names I can't remember now were killed. When the driven Jews arrived at the station, they were immediately forced into freight cars that were already waiting, and took them to an unknown destination.

9.

After the first transport was sent out, it was forbidden for the remaining Jews to live in the center of town. They stuffed us into the back streets. The crowding in the small rooms was extraordinary. Over 10 people were forced to live in one room. There was not even enough room for a bed. Everyone slept on the ground. Those able to work were taken to work every day: paving the road to Klody, or unloading freight cars in Pulawy, mostly–large rocks.

Locked in the ghetto, we often saw trucks traveling in the direction of Lublin. Cries from the trucks were heard, and from time to time, shooting. Jews in other shtetls were locked up in ghettoes.

In order to exist, we began to sell off things, because Markuszow farmers did not want to sell a kilo of potatoes for money. They only demanded merchandise, things, especially valuables. We now had to access the things hidden with the Poles they were loath to return. They knew that Jewish wealth would belong to them. Hunger and need reigned in the houses of the ghetto. Added to that, the baker, Shifra, was arrested because several loaves of bread were found in the cellar. She was taken to Pulawy, to the Gestapo, and each one of us was afraid that they would shoot her there. They also called the Judenrat to Pulawy, and we felt that a difficult fate hung over our heads. Shlomke Goldwasser returned from Pulawy and reported that Shifra the baker would be freed. We imagined to ourselves how much money and gifts such a freeing had cost. It didn't bother the Germans to let their victim go

[Page 206]

for a few more days. They knew that sooner or later we would be killed. That's how they played their cat-and-mouse game.

Since the case with the baker, everyone was afraid to have any spare bread. They therefore bought small coffee grinders to grind corn or wheat kernels, and secretly bake rolls on the glowing stove. While doing this, someone from the household would stand watch to make sure no uninvited guests showed up.

10.

On may 7 1942, the Judenrat secretly informed us that, whoever was able, should save himself, because according to the sad news, on the 8th of May, the shtetl was to be emptied of Jews. Most of us knew what that meant. As a result, we quickly packed our bags and ran to wherever our eyes could carry us. For various reasons, the Markuszow Poles did not display much enthusiasm for helping us hide, and everyone was on his own. My parents and brothers went to the Babawisker forest. Through the night, almost all the Jews left the ghetto. My brother and I stayed not far from the shtetl in the hope that we might be able to save something from our home. But we were not successful this time. When day was dawning, we left for the village of Dabrowica, in the Jastkow gemina where our sister, Feige-Malke Letterstein was living. As soon as she saw us, she broke into tears, and asked about our parents. Unfortunately, we didn't how to answer her. After calming down, we explained that the Jews from the shtetl had run off in all directions, and that our parents had gone to the Babawisker forest. From there they would go somewhere further. I told my sister that our dear mother asked us to separate, because she and father, being older people, could not do what we younger people could. We always had a lot of respect for our parents, and in this case too, we obeyed our mother. After spending a day with my sister, I went back to Markuszow via back roads to find our parents. We now had the opportunity to see how the Markuszow Poles, especially the youth, spied along the roads and in the forests in order to discover Jews

[Page 207]

and hand them over to the Gestapo. They were rewarded for that. So proceeding with the greatest care, we came to a place where two Markuszow *shkootzim*[7] sprang out. They related how Gestapo were looking for Jews everywhere, and that we had better get away from there as quickly as possible, it was awful here. For this information they requested a reward: to give them the money we had on us. They were Bogdan Opolski and Heniak Zgodzinski. To the question posed by my younger brother, whether they wanted all that we possessed, one of them answered, "Tak Zydzie!" (Yes, Jew!)

In a flash, we threw ourselves on them both, and beat them so well that they lost their enthusiasm for our money. We continued on our way, and we came to a forest where there were many Jewish families. They reported that our parents were on the other side of the forest. My father just asked for a little water to drink, and declared that all were exhausted, and could not go on further. We would stay in the forest and what God decides will be.

We did not, however, want to leave our parents. We succeeded in changing their minds, and at night we all went out on our way. That same night we got to Dabrowica, and settled the old one in at our sister's. In the villages of the Jastkow gemina, they had not yet started to deport the Jews. My two brothers worked as carpenters in the village and received food for us all.

11.

At the end of June 1942 an order was issued that all Jewish residents of the Jastkow gemina had to present themselves to Belzec where they would be settled. As the farmers learned about this new decree, they no longer wanted to keep Jews, because to do so meant the death penalty. There was no other choice than to transfer to Belzec. About 100 families in the area had no other recourse. My sister and brother along with my parents decided to go away to Belzec, and whatever would happen to them would also happen to the children. I decided that I would go to another village in order to find a bunker for my family.

[Page 208]

At that time there was a nobleman's estate where there were young Jewish people working. Since there was a Gestapo detachment on that estate, 100 people were needed for field work. I decided to stay there.

That same evening, my younger brother, Motl, came and told me about the tragic fate of the Jews who were taken to Belzec. They were transferred to Lublin to the Majdanek death camp. At Belzec, armed

Germans and Ukrainians were waiting and shot children and old people on the spot and drove the others into trucks. It's impossible to imagine such a bloodbath if you did not see it with your own eyes. My brother managed to sneak in amongst a group of young Poles, invited them for a coffee, and there over a glass of alcohol, waited out the storm.

We also quickly established that I would stay on the estate, and he would go to the forest where the first partisan groups were beginning to be established.

12.

About one hundred boys and girls were found on the Jastkow estate. We worked hard in the fields from 6 AM until 12 without any breaks. For lunch we would come to the courtyard. Our overseers were Poles, armed with rubber truncheons. We slept in a separate house surrounded by barbed wire. The food was not of the best, but we hoped it would not get any worse. At night, we were guarded by the Polish workers, and it was hard to get out of the place. Nevertheless, one night I risked it, wanting to see my brother, and also to find out about the partisans. Aside from this, I knew many farmers in the area, and I wanted to get some provisions for me and the guys. I was present along with everybody at the morning roll call, but it seems someone betrayed me, because I was called out of the ranks, and given fifty blows of the rubber truncheon. They immediately lay me down on a bench, pulled down my shirt, and they rained fiery blows on my back. I had to bite my lips and not cry out, because that meant a greater punishment. Blood spurted from the open wounds, but I had to go to work the following day.

News came to the estate that

[Page 209]

partisans were operating nearby. The Germans behaved more strictly with us, we were surrounded by guards while working, and particularly at night. Six armed Ukrainians did not take their eyes off us. In spite of the strengthened watch, it was made known to me at lunch that my brother was in the dining room. He had come with three other partisans to our barrack where we slept, because there was no one there at the time, and they told our girls who worked in the kitchen about the reason for their coming. At lunchtime, the girls let them into the dining room because no outside people came there. The six[8] partisans had small arms. If my memory does not deceive me the six partisans were: Motl Pelz, Itzchak Plashowitzer, the brothers, Yosef and Lazar Kozak, Shaul Wichter, and Yerocham Gothelf. They were ready to take with them several men from the estate. We held, however, that it would be worthwhile waiting in order to organize ourselves better and go to the forest in a larger group. Afterward, we learned that the same night the partisans left us they had a run-in with Polish police and drove them off. At the same time, they warned the police if they didn't interfere with the partisans, they would be left alone.

13.

The regime on the estate became harsher. We sensed a difference in the behavior of the Germans, Ukrainians and Poles to the Jews. The overseers began to display callousness and hooliganism. Once when we were returning to the barracks from the fields, one of us sat down next to the fence to rest. Without warning, a Ukrainian shot him and killed him on the spot. The actual bosses of the estate, the SS, on hearing the echo of the shot came running, and after they were told that a Jew was shot, they enthusiastically lauded the Ukrainian murderer. Still not appearing to have settled down from the event, they took a sick comrade from the barracks with the promise that they would take him to the hospital. They, however, took him 2 km away from the camp, and shot him in the field. Now we understood the intentions of the murderers, and we began to consider various plans to get away to the forest and join up with the partisans. Before that could happen,

[Page 210]

we began to smuggle weapons into the camp itself. Our goal was to come to the partisans with weapons n hand. In such cases, every new fighter was welcomed with open arms.

As soon as we received our first pistol, there was some thought of attacking the Ukrainians, taking their weapons, and escaping to the forest. After going over all the details of the plan, it became clear that we were putting the lives of a hundred Jews in danger, because not everyone was capable of participating in an open battle and escaping the camp. There were also some men and women there. Therefore it was decided to leave the camp one at a time. I was the first to say goodbye to friends and comrades. In the month of November 1942, while the Ukrainians were asleep, I stole out of the barrack and disappeared in the darkness of night. It was even dangerous to be out on the roads, because snow had fallen and all my footprints were visible. But going back was not an option. I went off to the Jastkow forest, and from there to the Wole forest where our partisans were supposed to be found. According to the sign and address my brother, Motl, passed on to me during his visit to the camp, I went to the farmer, Smolak, and gave him the password, "Kozaks" (that was what the partisan group called itself, after the name of a resident of the village Wole-Przybyslawska). This farmer was connected to the partisans. Smolak told me to wait until night when the partisans would come and link up with me. He led me to the forest where I met many Markuszow families that were hiding in bunkers.

The people told me that they have been set up in the bunkers for over a month. The Germans had not shown themselves in the forest the entire time, and relations with the farmers were not bad. The farmers provided food, and through the partisans they received news from the outside world. The partisans arrived in the forest around 8 o'clock in the evening. I was overjoyed to see my bother, Motl, and our friend, Yakov Gothelf. They brought greetings from other Markuszow Jews who were hiding in various places. They took me to the Kozlowka forest, not far from Kamionka.

14.

A new world was revealed to me here. Right at first arriving, I saw the partisan group which consisted mostly of Markuszow

[Page 211]

Jewish youth. There were two Russian officers with them who had escaped from German imprisonment. It was really cold then, and all of them were sitting around the fire frying pig fat. There were also two girls in the group–Manye LOTERSTEIN and Sima Bronska. I was right away given a French rifle, and put on guard duty next to a tree. The rest went to sleep. After four hours I was relieved, and I went to rest for the first time in my partisan lair: a shallow ditch in the snow, my jacket on the ground, and my coat as a cover. The cold did not permit sleep, but there was no choice.

In the morning, the camp woke up. Every partisan got his ration at breakfast: a piece of bread with pig fat, and a little hot water from melted snow. After eating, we began to work out plans for the day. I described my life on the Jastkow estate, and proposed that we should get all the Jews out of there because danger threatened them. I explained that the guards were Ukrainians, and they practiced target shooting on the Jews. It would be right to rescue our brothers from there, transfer them to the nearby Wole forest where other Markuszow Jews were to be found.

15.

End of September 1942. On a cold, frosty day, several of us left the forest, off to the neighboring villages with the goal of acquiring weapons and distributing them to the forest dwellers who were living in bunkers and striving to join the armed camp.

We came to the village of Saslawic late in the evening. According to previous information, we had the address of a farmer who had weapons. Because of the bad weather and the late hour, we spent the whole day at the farmer's. However, we held the farmer and his wife under house arrest, because we had a suspicion they would inform the Germans of our visit. On the second evening, we freed the farmer and left his hut in spite of the big snowstorm. Ten at night we went to another farmer who was supposed to have a rifle. The snow whipped our faces, and the wind whistled fearfully. We got to the place, surrounded the house, and David Ettinger and I went inside. We left

[Page 212]

Itzchak Fishbein and Yerachmiel Rubinstein on the road to guard, and Shmuel Laks stood at the window. As soon as the farmer opened the door, Yechiel Gothelf and Hershl Fishbein came in after us. We demanded the farmer give up his rifle that he had hidden from the first days of the war. The farmer denied having any kind of weapon, but we gave him to understand in a partisan way that it would be healthier for him to give up the instrument–until he took us to the stable to dig up the rifle. In the meantime we heard a shot, and a few minutes later we confirmed that Shmuel Laks had fallen down dead at the window. We opened fire, but without a target because the night hid everything. It was clear that we had to leave this place as quickly as possible. We placed the dead body of the partisan on a sled and took him to the nearest woods. We dug a grave with our rifles

Markuszow partisans in Lublin after liberation

From left to right: Chane Kestelman, Mordechai Kerschenblatt, Moishe Pelz, and Shmuel Rubinstein

And laid the fallen fighter in the freshly dug grave. We had to get away from there as fast as possible, because there was a German post nearby. Later we did confirm that the Germans removed the body of Shmuel Laks–the first victim of our group. He left behind a wife and child.

As soon as we got back to the forest, Laks's wife, Leah Bronska from Markuszow, asked us about Shmuel. We wanted to convince her that he had left with another group of partisans. But she had a premonition that the worst had happened, and she said that she could not imagine her husband would not first want to see

[Page 213]

his wife and child. She broke into spasms of weeping and it moved us all so much so that we decided to tell her the truth as bad as it was. Great was the tragedy for Leah Bronska and we felt how ineffective our words were of consolation and assurances that we would always remember our fallen comrade, take revenge for his young life, and take care of the orphaned wife and child.

16.

Right after this, a resident of Staroscin, Yosef, came and in tears related how farmers from his village had found some of the hidden Jews, and with clubs in their hands, had driven them to the German station in Markuszow. We immediately grabbed our weapons and headed out to the road leading to the shtetl being certain that we would succeed in freeing the captives. Unfortunately, the road was empty and our brothers were already sitting behind bars in the Markuszow jail ("kozeh")

It was a Sunday afternoon. From our stakeout we could see the farmers returning from church to their warm homes. We could not let go of the pain and trembling over the fate of the imprisoned Jews. We made a reckoning of what it meant for them. We returned to the forest and ordered all those who had no weapons to go to another forest. We had a mind to teach the farmers who had helped the Germans in their murder business against the Jews.

Before anything else, we planned an attack on Markuszow jail, and freeing the captives. We knew, however, that there were German gendarmes in the shtetl, and that such an action could fail. So we had to give up the plan, and began the search for those farmers who exchanged the life of a living Jew for a half-kilo of sugar–the German payment to their helpers. When the farmers learned that Jewish partisans were looking for them, many hid, and in most of the cases we did not succeed in uncovering them. So we set fire to the houses of those traitorous farmers, made attacks on the village, and let the residents understand that Jewish life was not worthless. The nearby villages now understood that handing a Jew over to the Germans was associated with mortal danger, because in the forest there was a well-armed Jewish partisan unit that would take revenge.

[Page 214]

Later we learned that the following day, Monday, in the middle of market day, gendarmes arrived from Pulawy. Under machine gun guard, the captured Jewish families were taken to the cemetery, made to remove their clothes and stand naked next to an open ditch, and were shot. The Germans invited the farmers who had come to the market to this "spectacle."

Simcha Ettinger before being shot managed to shout, "My son is in the partisans, and he will take revenge for shedding innocent Jewish blood!"

The oldest son of Simcha Ettinger, David, was in the partisans with me, and always wanted to be the first at the most dangerous missions. He fell along with seven comrades in March 1944 just before liberation.

17.

In 1943 we joined the well-organized partisan army of the Polish workers' parties (AL). Their headquarters were in Warsaw, and from there they carried out partisan actions across the country. We also heard that not far from us, in any case, in the Lublin region, there was another Jewish partisan group. One day, a colonel Miatek, representative of the AL came to see us, spent a few days with us, and proposed carrying out important acts of sabotage against the Germans. In order to demonstrate our readiness to join with the AL, we took his suggestion to tear up the rail lines at Motycz, because military transports to Russia went through there. The line was guarded by Ukrainians, but since they knew that there were partisans in the region, they hid at night and didn't carry out the usual patrols.

We left the forest and went off in the direction of Motycz. On the way we passed by the village of Garbow where there was a mechanical factory. We got in there, took various implements and French keys. Then we went to the train embankment. Four of us began with extraordinary swiftness to unscrew the screws that held the rails together. After completing the work, we quickly withdrew, hid not far away, and waited. After half an hour, with noise

[Page 215]

and commotion, the train arrived. When it came to the sabotaged spot, it went off the rails. The German echelon was now lying destroyed. There were dead and wounded soldiers under the smashed cars. Who can describe the joy that reigned on looking at the destruction to which we had contributed for the first time?

18.

Our group (battle name "Holodi") began to carry out new sabotage acts against the Germans. We lurked on the highways, shot at German columns, killed and wounded their soldiers, destroyed many autos. For the Germans it was now hard to move wherever we were. From time to time we would organize attacks on forces, communities, and recruit posts, destroying the mobilization papers to dig trenches, for forced labor in Germany, or for contingents of products for the German army. We destroyed a bunch of dairies, and for a while, freed the farmers from providing milk and butter for the Germans. At the first indication that a village was getting ready to hand over a consignment of pigs to the occupier, we went into the village, confiscated the pigs, and divided them up among the partisans and the impoverished villagers. In such a case, of course, we left the farmers a message that we, Jewish partisans, had seized the pigs, and distributed them to those who fight against the hated enemy. Our reputation and authority grew greatly among the farmer population. Now we were shown sympathy and help from all sides.

The German occupation power thought differently. They did not want to make peace with the idea that a frank and free partisan group should rule in their hinterland, especially a Jewish one. They began to prepare major attacks against us. First they sent Polish police with scent dogs, afterward, Ukrainians to search the villages and alert the Germans to any movements. There were, however, farmers friendly to us, especially among the prior members of the communist party. Those farmers let us know in advance of any appearance of German soldiers, or their Polish or Ukrainian helpers. In that way we knew who, when, and how many, asked about us, and sometimes, also about certain plans of the enemy against us. Such information, received in time, always made us able to

[Page 216]

stay away from the given place, and avoid crossing the path of the Germans which would not always end with our victory. But more than once we forced to mount a defense, and not let them into the forest. We knew that German soldiers, who demonstrate so much discipline, and criminal efficiency in cities and villages, become big cowards when they see a forest. That's why they changed to a different tactic: they would set fire to the woods when there was even a suspicion of partisans being there. They would also set fire to fields of wheat if they thought that fighters were hiding among the stalks.

19.

The growth of the partisan movement under the influence of the leftist parties, as well as the constant advance of the Red Army at the fronts, activated a series of avowedly fascist organizations of a military character in occupied Poland that were ostensibly fighting the German occupier, but whose entire energies and strategies were actually engaged in murdering individual surviving Jews in cities and forests. These groups, known under the name of AK (Armia Krajowa)[9] and NSZ (Narodowe Sily Zbrojne) (National Armed Forces), organized in many villages, fields and forests lairs and observation posts in order to spy on the Jewish partisans, and then mercilessly exterminated them. Our situation got more difficult, because now we had to deal with an enemy that knows the ground, and the environment, well, and also benefits from the support of the local population. In order to make it harder for them to find us, we agree to split into two groups. One group went to the forest, and settled into a well-masked bunker with two entrances. For someone uninformed about the existence of the hiding place, it would be impossible to discover. Twenty-eight boys and girls from our shtetl settled in there, and found a refuge for several weeks.

Three friends and I later left the bunker and went to the village of Ozarow to a farmer acquaintance of Yechiel Gothelf. He lived in the colony, and in a free empty field there stood a lone little house. We dug a bunker there, and lived in it for over three weeks. In that time the Germans carried out several raids in the village and

[Page 217]

the colony. Once, we could hear them talking, and could sense them sticking bayonets into the ground around the hut. They were very close to us, but since the entrance was in the outhouse, the Germans had little enthusiasm to search in such a place too much. And maybe it never occurred to them that people would want to hide there. Aside from that, snow covered the whole neighborhood, and wiped every sign of the underground bunker. We were lucky this time–and the Germans left with nothing.

Christmas 1943, we decided to get out of the bunker and find food for ourselves and for the ones hiding in the forest. All four of us went to the estate of the nobleman, Gutanow, whose owner was now a German. We stole two pigs, in order to give one to our host, the Ozarow farmer, and the other to take to the forest. At one AM we got on a sleigh and took off. The snow was deep, and a cold wind blew. But for us it was not a bother, because everyone was adept at handling the cold and the blizzards.

While riding along in the freezing night, we saw two figures in the distance. We quickly descended from the sleigh, lay down on the ground, and when the two approached closer, we yelled out in Polish, "Don't move, hands up!"

With hands in the air, the people began to get closer, and we immediately recognized our Markuszowers: Shmuel Melhendler, and Israel Meir Rosenzweig. With great joy they began to kiss us, and didn't know how to express their joy at this unexpected reunion. They related that now, exactly like every other night, they were looking for a place to spend the night at a different farmer. They had heard from the farmers about a Jewish partisan group, and their only goal was to meet these armed Jews. Our question, if they were ready to go with us, was met with a denial, because each one had a family hidden in various places, and they had to care for them. Shmai Melhendler's mother, and her younger brother, Motl, were hidden in one place, and Israel-Meir's sister and father were at another place. Their only desire was– weapons. We granted them a pistol with 7 bullets and asked them

[Page 218]

to be careful. We said good-bye and went on further to the bunker in the forest. This time it so happened that we drove through the fields of Garbow. Suddenly we saw a larger group of armed people. We jumped off the sleigh, took a position on the ground, and saw that the others were doing the same. They were yelling at us to come closer, and we yelled at them to come to us, hands up of course. It occurred to one if us to ask for a sign that they were Jewish partisans.

"Amcho?"[10]
"Amcho!" a joyful voice replied.

They were 8 partisans from the forest bunker we were now traveling to with this fortune: a slaughtered pig. We all embraced, and this night was one of wonder: in such terrible times, two encounters in a field, and with our own…But the news we received disrupted our joy, and our fists clenched. According to a denunciation by the soltis,[11] Germans, armed to the teeth, accompanied by Polish police, Ukrainians and dogs, entered the forest, found the hiding places, pumped in smoke, and asphyxiated everyone.

This is how yet more Jewish heroes from Markuszow were killed.

20.

We went to stay with a farmer, and began to hatch various plans. One thing was clear to us: we had to leave the Garbow area, because they knew too much about us in the whole area. Every one of us was known, and further operations in the region were filled with danger. We quickly decided to transfer to the Lubartow neighborhood, because there were big forests there. But even there we were not destined to spend much time. After spending several days there, the Germans discovered our new place, and began their persecutions. On a dark night, we left Lubartow with the greatest precautions, crossed the river Wieprz, and got to the village of Przypisowka which was under the control of the Polish Workers' Party. There was also found a strong fighter contingent of the AL, led by the famous partisans, Yanek and Matchek. Now we were attached to the AL, and left for Ostrow-Lubelski with the unit. The shtetl was ruled by the partisans.

[Page 219]

There were also Russian fighters there, either having come over the border, or parachuted in from airplanes. They possessed first class weapons. There was a larger unit in Ostrow under the leadership of the legendary hero from the Soviet Union, Kolpak. We approached the Russians to allow us to join a Soviet unit, because our manpower and weaponry were too puny to carry out the new tasks. Their answer was: You will get weapons, but everyone must fight on his own turf.

Several days later, we got an order to meet a Soviet airdrop delivering weapons at night. We were supposed to set fire to straw at the location to show the airplane where to drop their valuable baggage. Halfway through the night we heard a roar, and from the sky there began to fall heavy packs. As soon as the planes left, we opened the packs, and we found to our great delight all kinds of weapons suitable for partisans.

Later we found out that the following day, German airplanes were seen over the same area, and noticed a pack that had landed in a tree. They opened fire on it, and a fearful explosion occurred. That exploded the material that was meant to destroy German echelons, and damage their train communications.

Enriched by the new weapons, we headed back to the villages in the Markuszow neighborhood, because there were some Markuszow girls still hiding in several bunkers: Dina Gothelf, Bluma Rubinstein, Bella Teitelbaum, the woman, Itke, from the village of Staroscin and her seven-year-old child (They all survived, some in Israel, some in America). The danger from the Poles was now lessened in our neighborhood, because the AK had temporarily halted its murderous work against the Jews. But first we had a duty to care for our shtetl people, and to repay the farmer who had hidden them. By the end of 1943, we had found all those who had hidden in the bunkers in Wole. We provided them with food, with an encouraging word, told them about the developments on the front and–again continued the partisan march. The AL laid the most important and responsible duties on us knowing that the Jewish partisans would carry them out properly.

When we left the bunker to go over to a neighboring village, I began to experience a bad headache. I turned to my friends

[Page 220]

and asked if I could be excused for a little while, because in an encounter with the enemy, I would not be able to fight. The partisan, Isser Rosenberg z"l, (pseudonym, Ignace) went quickly to a village to find a secure place for me. It didn't take long and he returned happy to have found good quarters, I should not worry, because the partisans would not forget about me. The most important thing was for me to rest for 2-3 days and regain my strength. Isser Rosenberg arranged it with a number of farmers that each one should keep me for a given time, if the partisans failed to return quickly.

21.

I was now all alone with the farmer. The condition of my health got worse, and the headaches became greater every day. My joy was great, therefore, when a group of partisans came to visit. They related how they had managed to detain a Pole who had been sent by the fascist Polish organization, NSZ, to spy on hidden Jews and partisans. Our boys took him into the house where I was staying, and identified him as Stashek, the brother of the Markuszow barber. We took his gun away and let him go. So Isser was sitting on my bed and telling me the whole story, and showed me the confiscated weapon. In the meantime, a partisan came in, began to examine the gun, and manipulate it. Suddenly a shot rang out, and an unintended bullet shot out of the gun and into Isser's heart. He fell on my bed and breathed his last.

We quickly harnessed a horse and wagon, put the body on it, and I–half dead from the illness, the high fever, and the tragic event, was set up next to him. We left for the forest to the bunker-grave of the 28 Markuszow partisans who had been asphyxiated from the smoke the Germans had pumped into the bunker of the Markuszow Jews, and buried Isser Rosenberg as the Jewish fighter of Markuszow.

When we had given the dead man his rites, they took me to a farmer, laid me in a stable, and told the owner that I was sick with Typhus. In reality, I did have Typhus. I lay there

[Page 221]

in the stall for 15 days, without Markuszower help, almost without water, and no one believed that I would survive such a severe illness. I did however overcome the Typhus–and became healthy again. One cold night they took me away from the stable and transferred to the village of Wole, 25 km away from the place I had been until now. In that village there was a bunker where a Jewish family, Shmuel Aaron Rosenstein, his brother-in-law, Moishe, and David from Lublin (they all live now in Rishon L'Zion) were installed. Along with me, they brought the partisan, Itzchak Plashower who had founded the first partisan group with my brother, Motl (fell in battle with the Germans in 1942). The Rosenstein family behaved to me with a lot of loyalty and care in this difficult time. Thanks to their devotion I became completely healthy in 6 weeks.

Ten partisans came to take me from the Rosensteins and move over to the partisan country in Ostrow-Lubelski. In order to make such a long journey we had to create a caravan–horses and wagons and provisions. So we headed to the Kozlowka estate which was in the hands of graf Zamoyski, ordered them to harness four horses and wagons, took a pig, and left in the direction of the river Wieprz. The deep snow increased the difficulty of the trip. After driving for a couple of hours, we stopped at the village of Dombrowka, in the Lubartow powiat. We set up in several houses near the forest, unharnessed the horses, and led them into the stable. We set up a guard that changed every hour. We spent the night there, and in the morning ate the prepared breakfast. Aside from the food we had with us, we had to drink a little alcohol, the only and the best cure for partisans on the road, especially on such a cold day.

When one of us went outside, he noticed a few figures in the forest, dressed in white smocks in order not to be seen on the snowy terrain. Before he could warn us of the impending danger, we heard shooting, and we saw the stable encircled by fire. We felt we were surrounded on all sides. But it was clear to each of us that no one could fall into

[Page 222]

the murderers' hands, and so we returned fire, and tried with all our might to escape from the siege. Bullets were flying everywhere, and we saw our first victim–Veve Laks who fell covered in blood on the snow. After him, a German bullet struck David Ettinger, who finished himself off not wanting to fall into the hands of the Germnas. Then the two brothers, Abraham, and Gershon from Plaszowic fell. Seven young Poles who had voluntarily joined our group also died in the battle. Only a few of us were able to avoid death, and get away from that terrible place. We lay hidden in various places until evening, because our fear that the Germans were hunting us was justified. It was only at night, when we came to the village of Grobina and saw that everything was surrounded by flames. This was the modus operandi of the Germans: wherever they saw partisans, they destroyed everything with fire. They ordered that the dead partisans be buried in a mass grave.

Two days later, we got to our group, and related the tragedy. Shmuel Laks did not want to believe that his brother, Veve, was dead. We calmed him down and consoled him, but everyone knew that the same death awaited us all.

22.

In the shtetl of Ostrow, there was concentration of Polish, Russian, and a small number of Jewish partisans from the surrounding area. Since everyone knew the Germans were preparing to clean out the district of partisans, it was agreed to leave the shtetl, and head off toward Carpathian Russia. We were now a large army, and during the nightly marches our caravan stretched for kilometers. It is quite likely that the Germans knew about our march, because German airplanes flew over our heads and shot at us.

We came to the Parczew forests. There the Germans surrounded us, and pinned us down under strong fire for two days. Then they set fire to the forest, in order to chase us out. But nothing came of all the German plans. We suffered no losses, and at night we continued on our way to our designated target. We arrived safely in

[Page 223]

Markuszow, marched through the shtetl, and approached the Naleczow train station. There in the middle of the day, we set up camp. It's interesting that the Germans did not mount an attack. At night we continued on our way until the village of Rablow where we decided to rest because everyone was exhausted after the unending march. Around eight AM, we noticed German scout planes over the village followed quickly by bombers who dropped a lot of bombs on the village. Then a large division of Wehrmacht surrounded the village, and started an artillery barrage. Fortunately, there were many valleys there, and we could lie there hidden. As soon as the Germans began to storm the village, we were ordered to mount an active resistance. The Russian partisans, the "Tchapyevtses," had taken a very important strategic position, and kept the Germans at bay. The other groups as well took up positions, and we, the Jewish partisans defended a heavily treed terrain.

It seems the Germans had decided to definitively annihilate our partisan army that day. They brought reinforcements. We thought our situation was hopeless. Many partisans fell in battle, even more were wounded. In the middle of the chaos of battle, a group of Germans appeared not far from us. It seems they had lost contact with their unit. We opened a strong fire on them, and killed almost all of them. Then we took off their uniforms–the most important trophy for a partisan.

When night fell, the Germans lit up the whole area with rockets, and strengthened their grip on all sides of the village so that not one of us should get out alive. The situation became terrible until an order came that it was every man for himself. So we, a group of twelve Jewish partisans decided to break through the German lines of fire. We went towards the valleys, but we quickly came under fierce fire. We decided to attack then–and to our good fortune, we broke through the German attack and–out of danger. On the road, we met another group of Jewish partisans who had two wounded: Micholai and Andzay (both now in Israel). All together we came to the village of Wojciechow at midday, acquired some horses there, and went to our old place–Wole forest. In the bunker

[Page 224]

we settled the wounded and told our girls about the events of the Rablow battle–one of the largest the German army had fought with the partisans. I, as a soldier in the Polish army, who had in 1939 taken part in the battles at Mlawa, could comprehend the meaning and significance of our resistance at Rablow. We sat under a large tree in the Wole forest and talked about the previous battle. As partisans, we discussed the entire matter from the standpoint of military tactics and strategy. But we couldn't talk about this too much. We had to think about what comes next, how to search for surviving partisans, if they had succeeded in breaking out of the siege. We received news that some of our guys had made it to the other side of the Wieprz. We went off to look for them, found a few, and from them learned about another group in the Janow forests. So we went after them, with skirmishes with Germans along the way. We were very worn out and exhausted. We knew that the German army was retreating in panic, but precisely because of this, wanting to have a clean path for their retreat, they persecuted the partisans with great implacability. So it continued until liberation.

23.

July 1944. We are in the Parchew forests. Once we heard a loud noise. From among the trees, we saw heavy German artillery, machine-guns, and autos rolling along the road. We were certain they were going to surround us again. Who knows if we would be in a position to withstand the assault of such a large military force? But the Germans continued on their way. A little later, a Polish cart appeared. We stopped the farmers and asked what they knew about the increasing movements of the German army. The farmers joyfully said, "You are free! The Germans are retreating. They are running away!"

We did not believe it. The farmers assured us that they themselves had seen Russian tanks 8 km from here. As proof they pulled out a jam container which now held axle grease. There was Russian writing on the can. This time we had no doubt that the hour of liberation had come.

[Page 225]

We remained in the forest, because although the Soviet army was found near us, we could still see from our current place retreating German military without the discipline and order with which they used to distinguish themselves during their advance, when all Europe lay trampled under their bloody boots.

Markuszow partisans

(From left to right) Eisenberg, M. Pelz, M. Kerschenblatt, Sh. Rubinstein

When night fell, we no longer had any patience and left the forest in order to greet the long awaited freedom. We arrived at Lubartow where the majority of our surviving partisans were already meeting up, and acquiring various positions of responsibility in the security service of the new Poland. The sent me to Lublin. Before visiting the once capital city of a liberated Poland, I visited Markuszow in order to see who of the shtetl Jews had survived and whether they needed any help. Unfortunately, there was no one left of Jewish Markuszow. I went to Lublin where the first signs of Jewish life were beginning to be instituted. The Jews returning from the camps and forests were temporarily accommodated at Peretz House on Czwartek Street. The Jewish committee began work on 8 Rybna Street.

After the liberation of Poland, I filled various positions in the police in Lublin, Bylice and Cracow.

In 1947 I immigrated to Israel.

Translator's Footnotes:

1. Jewish communist
2. "What are you talking about?"
3. "Cursed Jews"
4. Kazimierz-Dolny
5. The actual date was June 22 1941.
6. About 13 km distance
7. term for gentile boys
8. According to the previous sentences, there were only four partisans.
9. Home Army
10. Are you Jewish?
11. Village elder

[Page 226]

With Markuszow Partisans

Nathan Westelschneider (Tel Aviv)

Translated by Moses Milstein

During the first days of the German-Polish war, Nazi airplanes bombed Markuszow, and almost half the shtetl was burned down. Our house too went up in smoke. If not for the efforts and hard work of the Markuszow firefighters with the help of the civilian population, not a trace of the shtetl would have been left.

The homeless Jews, and even those who still had houses, left the shtetl en masse and went to the neighboring villages. After things calmed down, we returned to Markuszow and lived under the occupiers.

Several months passed like this, until a decree was issued that all the Jews remaining in the Jastkow gemine were to go to a labor camp. Only young people had the right to work there. I, along with my brothers, Hershl, Itsl, Getzl, and my sisters, Feige and Perl, went to the camp. Our father and mother remained at home. We worked in the fields from sunrise to sunset. German and Polish overseers were not stingy with their blows and insults. There were also cases where they shot a Jew for the slightest transgression of the posted work rules. Terror and fear dominated the camp, and created despair and bitterness in us.

I was fifteen years old at the time. It's possible that my youth was responsible for the thought of escaping from the camp to be born in me. All my senses told me that it would be very hard for me to overcome all the violence and persecutions, or to look on as the exhausted Jews were persecuted. I entrusted my brothers and sisters with my plan to escape. They urged me not to try this, because the Germans would shoot me.

The urge to run away was, however, great. Taking advantage of an opportunity, I ran away

[Page 227]

from the Jastkow estate. By day, I hid in the fields and forest, at night–stole into a stable and slept there. But before that, I went to a farmer I knew, and begged for a piece of bread. Most of the time, I was not refused. I lived for several months like that. I used to sneak into Jastkow a few times, and meet with my brothers and sisters.

Nathan Westelschneider–in the time of the occupation

One day a decree was issued that all the older Jews who were not working in the Jastkow camp had to report to Belzec[1] within 24 hours. It further stated that any older Jew found in the Jastkow gemine would be shot. When the decree came out, I was 12 km away from my parents. As soon as I heard about the new decree from a farmer, I went straight to my parents and found them sad and desperate. They had completely changed. If I had seen them somewhere else, it would have taken me a long time to recognize them. My father asked me if I had heard the latest news. He added that the soltis[2] had told him to leave the village within 24 hours and present

[Page 228]

himself for transport to Belzec. They both begged me to go with them. "What will be our fate, will be yours." After wavering for a few minutes, I decided not to go with them to Belzec. I parted from them with an uneasy feeling. Who knows if it would be for the last time?...

Then I went off to the Jastkow estate to my brothers and sisters. I managed to get into the yard unnoticed. There I learned that my two older brothers, Hershl and Itsl, had been transferred to another estate called "Wigoda." We were sitting there telling each other about our mutual problems, when we heard the sound of machine gun fire. A riot had broken out in the camp, and it soon became clear that the whole yard was surrounded by Germans and Ukrainians, so that no one could escape. I was stunned. Nevertheless, I began to look for an exit, but everything was surrounded. It was clear to me that if they caught me, an escapee, my life would be over. I had no choice but to rely on fate, maybe it would also this time, as in other times, avail me.

I was staying with my youngest brother, Getzl, and my two sisters. The previous night was spent in fear waiting for what the morrow would bring. In the morning an order was issued that everyone had to immediately leave the estate and board the waiting trucks. Where to–no on knew. Accompanied by blows from Germans and Ukrainians we climbed aboard the trucks, and after several hours, we came to a camp called Dorohucza, not far from Trawniki. When we arrived at the camp, we were driven out of the trucks with blows, and led to the prepared barracks, fifty men in each. Since it was night, they ordered us to go to sleep.

In the morning, they conducted a roll call. We were arrayed in columns, counted, and sent off to work. What did the work consist of? It turns out that, six km from the camp, there were peat bogs. Beginning at dawn, we dug out the peat, cut it into cubes, and set them out to dry. Everyone had to meet their quota, or they were murderously beaten, and later–shot. Going to and from work was transformed into hell. We often had to run the six kilometers during which the Ukrainians used to goad the dogs that accompanied our march. More than a few were bitten by the enraged beasts. We used to march three in a row, and for the whole

[Page 229]

time, we had to maintain our ranks. Food consisted of 100 g of bread and a half-liter of watery soup with a little bran. After a day of hard work, we returned to the barracks and lay our weary bones on the wooden planks. We became apathetic and indifferent. Everyone thought we would not get out of there.

The thought of escaping did not leave me even from this well-guarded camp. This time, however, I thought about how to bring along my brother and two sisters. For several evenings we looked for a way to flee, but nothing came of it. Disappointed, we returned to the barracks. My sisters began to try to convince me to try my luck alone, and get out of there.

One dark night around one o'clock, I snuck over to the last barrack near the barbed wire, and crawled on my stomach over to the gate. I lifted the wires with the greatest care, and was ready to crawl to the other side when suddenly all the lights in the camp came on and bathed the area in light. At the same time, I heard a shot, and a bullet passed through the bottom of my jacket. I began to crawl back, but I felt the jacket burning. I quickly took off the garment, and half dead, went back to the camp where my brothers and sisters had already mentally bade me farewell knowing that the shooting and the reflectors were meant for me. I quickly got undressed and lay down in my spot as if nothing had happened. The

Germans quickly carried out searches in the barracks, found nothing suspicious, and after a few shots meant to scare everyone, the camp quieted down.

Two days later, I again tried my luck, but this time–from work. We used to take the harvested peat in carts to a place where they were cut up and dried, and at the end of the day we would turn them upside down and leave them overnight. Then we lined up in columns in order to march to the camp. When the carts did their last round, I crawled under the upside-down cart, and lay there for about a half hour. When it became quiet, a sign that everyone had returned to the camp, I crawled out of the hiding place, and began crawling on my stomach in the direction away from the camp. It became dark. I began to walk through the fields. After about ten kilometers, very tired and hungry,

[Page 230]

I came to a farmer, and asked him where I was, and which way led to the Lublin region. The farmer was a good man. He answered everything, and also gave me something to eat–bread and pork. I openly told him where I was coming from. He took me outside and by the stars, told me which direction to go. I walked all night. At dawn, a farmer I met told me I was not far from Lublin. Nevertheless, I was afraid to wander around during the day, and I hid in a field. At night, I was transformed again into the eternal wandering Jew, and about two am I came to the village of Plaszowic, went into a stable, and spent the last hours there. But in the morning there was no place to go, so I stayed in the stable. The insecure, and afflicted life that I experienced before I went into the Dorohucza camp, began again. I spent my nights in a different place than my days, and received food from more than one farmer's hands and was able to sustain life.

I lived like that for several weeks, until the Germans issued a strict order that any Pole who hides a Jew would be immediately shot and his household goods burned. Those Poles who would bring Jews to the authorities or reveal their hiding places would be rewarded by the German forces. Those Poles who still harbored a certain sympathy for the persecuted Jews were frightened by the German threats, knowing that no good would await them for helping a Jew. The more evil Poles, and there was no lack of them, were tempted by the promised kilo of sugar and the reward for a Jewish head. The danger for Jews in my situation was now greater and more serious. I therefore decided to go to my brothers who were working on the Wigoda estate in order to discuss what to do next. At night I went to the estate, came to a farm hand I knew, and asked about my brothers. He replied that my brothers had been taken away. According to reports, they were shot along the way. Shattered by the news, I left the estate and wandered with no goal or direction. One thing was clear to me: better to die in a field than return to a slave-labor camp.

Wandering like this at night I came to the village of Moszenki, went into first best stable and was looking for a suitable spot to lie down. Suddenly I heard a voice in the darkness:

[Page 231]

"Nathan, is that you?"

I approached the figure and recognized Dan Fishbein, my good friend from Markuszow. We hugged and began to dance with joy at the meeting. He described his experiences. I relayed to him everything that had happened to me lately. Then a whole host of questions about what was happening in Markuszow to the Jews there. Dan knew that the shtetl was now without Jews. They had been taken to an unknown destination. But in the forest there were some young Jews from the shtetl belonging to a partisan division. They had acquired weapons, and were now leading the life of forest heroes. This news greatly cheered, and surprised, me. I told Dan that we must at all costs get to the partisans. Dan agreed with me, arguing that if we made it to the partisans we would be saved, because the farmers would not want to help us, and even if they did, they would betray us to the Germans at the first opportunity, or kill us outright. We began to search for the Markuszow group.

This was in autumn 1943.

Dan Fishbein and I wandered over fields and meadows looking for a sign of the partisans on those dark nights. We wanted to join up with them and fight together. We slunk through the nights like shadows afraid to speak a word to each other. Suddenly we heard a noise, and marching people appeared not far from us. One behind the other. We thought they were Germans, and we stopped in fear. Nevertheless we were curious to hear what language they were speaking, because we were not completely certain they were German. Tense and stressed, we heard a few words.

It seemed to us they were speaking Yiddish. We still couldn't believe that Jews had marched by. We strained to hear, holding our breath–and again Yiddish words came to our ears. Not being completely certain they were Jews, we followed them–but at a distance of 500 meters. We were warmed by the simple thought: maybe these were the Jewish partisans the farmers used to talk about with great respect? A while back

[Page 232]

some farmers promised us that if they encountered the partisans, they would tell them there were two youths from Markuszow looking for them. It was a lucky chance that we ourselves should meet them in the field–perhaps our wandering would end?

Nevertheless, we did not dare approach the armed group. We still were not one hundred percent convinced that they were those we had been seeking for so long. Following their footsteps we went on for about a half hour, until they came to the village of Moszenki. Then we saw lights come on in various farmers' huts–a sign that the partisans had entered. I stole into a stable, stood there for a while, and began to get closer to the window. Through the windowpane, I clearly heard the guys speaking a hearty Yiddish, and I had no doubt anymore that they were ours. I wanted to go back to Dan who was waiting not far from me, and give him the news, but one of the partisans noticed me. Suddenly I heard a shout. "*Stoi! Padnie!*" (Stay! Down!) Before lying down on the ground, I saw a rifle aimed at me. On the ground, I said, "*Swoje!*" (One of us).

The partisan ordered me to get up and come closer to him. My heart began to beat rapidly, because the joy at meeting the partisans was spoiled by the uncertainty: are they really Jews? I was still speculating that they could be disguised Germans who often used to fool hidden Jews and later murder them mercilessly. But spending a lot of time thinking about it was not permitted. It was now too late. Had I made the slightest movement away, the partisan would have shot me immediately. With fear and hope I began to get closer to the armed man, who probably recognized me as a Jew, because he immediately asked, "*Amcho?*" I answered with a question, "Are you the Markuszow group?" He replied that in his group there were a lot of Markuszow youth. And still with his rifle, he

[Page 233]

led me into the Polish hut where I found some youths I knew well from my hometown: Moishe Pelz, Velvel and Shmuel Laks, Shmuel Rubinstein ("Botchan")[3], Mordechai Kerschenblatt ("Martchinek") the Morel brothers from Garbow. Among them, there was also a greater number of prisoners-of-war who, during the Polish-German war in 1939, fell into German captivity, and after having been in several camps, ended up as slave laborers in Lipowa 7 in Lublin.[4] They were trained soldiers who organized the escape from Lipowa 7. Some of them arrived in the Lubliner forests and joined up with our Markuszow partisans. Now I found the whole company seated at the table. We embraced and wept for joy for a long time, and talked a lot about our experiences. We ate our fill for supper, something we had not been able to do for years. The night passed in happiness, and the time came to set out on the road. I asked about the most senior in the group, and they pointed out an escaped prisoner-of-war called Yeager. We both approached him about joining the partisan group. To our great astonishment, we were denied. Yeager's reasons were that we had no weapons, and the partisans had no spare ammunition. We had to wait, the commandant said. If the partisans succeeded in getting more weapons, another partisan group would be established, because smaller units were more secure. In any case, Yeager promised, we would be the first to get the weapons, as soon as they could lay their hands on some rifles. The situation was, in general, tense. The Germans were persecuting us, and if we showed up in a larger group, the news would soon get to the Germans that 300 armed Jews were marching through the village. Meanwhile, seeing our crestfallen faces, Yeager consoled us, that they would set us up with a local farmer, and nothing bad would happen to us until they returned from the forest, and that they would probably take us with them to the forest.

And so it really happened. The partisans left us with a farmer who had to take care of us, provide food, and anything required. They made the farmer responsible for our fate. On one hand, we were happy that our wandering was coming to an end, and we were more or less established in a stable place. On the other hand,

[Page 234]

we could not so easily digest the fact that after so much searching for the partisans, we had to separate again–and who knew for how long. Our insistent demands to be taken to the forest were met with no answer. There was no choice but to remain forsaken again. The partisans left, and we stuck ourselves in the hiding place waiting impatiently for their return.

We didn't have to wait long. A few weeks later, my townspeople returned, knocked at the farmer's door, and the first question asked of him was if we were there, and how was our health. At that time, we didn't get to see each other. They were probably on their way to a mission. But after they left, a young farmer came to inform us that we had to report to headquarters in the village of Wole. We ran there as quickly as possible. They didn't detain us long there, and gave us weapons. They immediately began to teach me how to handle the rifle. I became a partisan!

It's hard to describe the details of forest living in a camp of armed fighters who lead a partisan life, and an underground war with the hated enemy. We used to derail German trains, and shoot at the fleeing soldiers. At night we also attacked German patrols–and always with success.

Our membership in the partisans also meant membership in the PPR–Polska Partia Robotnicza (Polish Workers' Party) the only political movement in Poland at the time that helped the Jewish youth in the forests, arming them, and fighting the Germans. Our entire Markuszow group, plus the prisoners-of-war, belonged to the PPR whose headquarters were in the village of Wole. We would meet other partisan groups in the forest practically weekly among whom there were many Jewish youth. Our group from Kamionka distinguished itself particularly. There was also a Polish partisan group from the village of Przypisowka. Thus there were partisan groups that ruled in the whole region. The Germans were afraid to show themselves in those areas.

Several months later, we received an order to go to the Parczew forests where a large partisan group from the People's Army (Armia Ludowa) was being concentrated. Our group went off to the agreed-upon spot, but before we got there we had to engage in a battle with the Germans. In truth, we didn't spare any bullets for the

[Page 235]

Nazi murderers. But several heroes from our ranks fell, among them the Markuszow Jews: Velvl Laks, and David'tche Ettinger, as well as the young Yosl from Staroscin who particularly distinguished himself as a fighter. David'tche Ettinger had been wounded in the legs, but seeing as he was in danger of falling into German hands, he shot himself. When night fell, we got away from the battle with the Germans, and went off toward our assembly point. We arrived in the Parczew forest the following day. There, a massive military camp was revealed to us with the necessary equipment, and most importantly–thousands of partisans preparing for the decisive battle. A big celebration was taking place there with the participation of general Rola-Zymierski,[5] colonel Moczer (Myetek)[6]–ex-officer of the Republican army in Spain, and the Jewish partisan leader, colonel Bolek Alef[7], and a Soviet captain with the name of Zemsto (Revenge). We also met a group of Jewish partisans from the Parczew neighborhood and from the shtetl, Wlodawa. Our Markuszow group was attached to the Fourth battalion led by captain Zemsto. The battalion, exactly like the others, was divided into platoons. Our guys remained in one platoon. We bonded with each other, demonstrated loyalty and aid, lived as brothers. We spent several weeks in the Parczew forests.

In the meantime, our army was growing. More and more Poles joined the partisan ranks. There were no more Jews in the forests. Not because they were afraid to live a partisan life, but simply because there weren't any Jews left. At that time–end of 1943, the Germans had completed their bloody work of annihilating the entire Jewish population and very few were able to escape their criminal reach. The only consolation was that the partisan army kept on growing. We were a serious force. We captured many villages and settlements. The partisan kingdom was spread over the entire region.

The front approached closer by March 1944. At the same time, Soviet partisans came over from the other side of the river Bug, well-armed and equipped with all the necessary instruments of war. Thanks to this influx, we were transformed into a large army. Previously,

[Page 236]

we had had to acquire our own provisions, and our entire arsenal consisted of a few rifles. We considered ourselves extremely lucky to get a machine gun. Now we became real soldiers from partisans. We were just missing uniforms. Everything else was like a regular army. They taught us how to use the most modern weaponry.

One day we got an order to get ready that night. We thought we would be going on a routine partisan mission: laying mines under the rail lines, or carrying out an attack on a German post. We formed into columns and began to march. We stopped after several kilometers and a high-ranking officer informed us that we would be getting weapons from Russia that evening. We were stunned by the news believing that now we would be coming into contact with the advancing Red Army. Some senior officers began to give light signals with green and red electric flashlights. About twenty minutes later, we heard the sound of several airplanes that were approaching our place. Soon white packs began to fall from the planes, and paratroopers began to jump from the flying machines. The wish occurred to me that it should have happened two years earlier so that many Jews could have been saved. For over an hour, weapons, clothing, and supplies fell from the sky. Then came the order to load everything into the waiting cars, and we drove back to our base. By daylight, there was no sign of the night-action that had given us such real aid.

It was late in the day when we got back to base. We grabbed something to eat and then fell into a deep sleep. After waking, we were ordered to form into smaller groups (*druzhines*) every one of which was provided with machine guns and automatic weapons. After getting the new weapons, the paratroopers came over to us, shook our hands and introduced themselves. They began to learn how to handle the weapons.

A while later, we occupied the town of Ostrow. We took the place without firing a shot, and set up partisan rule. We were no longer stuck in hiding places, but could walk around in the middle of the day. After dominating in that neighborhood

[Page 237]

for several weeks, we got word that Germans were coming. We immediately covered all the roads and waited for the enemy. When the Germans got close, we opened up on them with strong fire. A bitter battle raged which stretched on all day. The Germans suffered big losses, but our partisans also lost people. In my group, led by the partisan, Janowski, we lost several fighters. It wasn't until the evening that we got the order to withdraw. We moved out. Those nights we travelled about 60 km, before coming to the woods near Markuszow. The village was called Syry, near Amelin where the estate of the nobleman called Samokleski was found.

There were Germans quartered on this property with whom we began a battle, but with no result. There were no casualties on either side. In the evening, we withdrew in the direction of the Janow forests. We came to the village of Wromblow[8] between Kuzmir and Opole. No sooner had we begun to unharness the horses, than the alarm was spread that Germans were coming. We soon heard the drone of airplanes. One German airplane dropped a bomb which landed on a wagon from headquarters. The driver, the Jew Botchan from Parczew, was killed on the spot. Before we could calm down from this attack, our scouts with binoculars saw a column of Germans approaching the forest.

That was at the end of May 1944. During their retreat, the Germans wanted to destroy as many partisans as they could, and they pursued the fighters with particular relentlessness. We received an order from headquarters to take up positions in the woods. We lay down in a quadrilateral, dug ourselves in, and waited for the Germans to get closer. Many bullets from rifles, machine guns and mines were hurled at us. We did not respond with any firing. We set fire to the surrounding houses in order to light up the battlefield, and see every movement the Germans made. A Russian partisan group from the "Tchapayevski Otriad" was with us. Aside from some machine guns, they also possessed an iron patience not to respond with one shot at the attacking enemy. Not until the Germans moved closer, believing that they had killed most of the partisans, did the Tchapayevskis open a powerful concentrated fire. We already had several dead. During that attack, my best friend from Markuszow,

[Page 238]

Dan, fell heroically in the battle. He will always remain in my memory…

The battle with the Germans lasted over an hour, and often changed to a fight with bayonets. The situation was becoming unfavorable for us, and the head-commander issued an order: we must break through the German lines at any cost. Their forces were significantly stronger than ours, and we were encircled, and had to break through. A violent battle ensued, and we succeeded in breaking out of the encirclement.

The next day, the farmers told us that they saw a lot of carts carrying dead Germans, a sign that the partisans had killed many Nazis. As night fell, our fear of the Germans diminished. In the end, we were the "heroes of the night." And when they tried to bother us that evening, they received a real defeat. After this battle we left the wounded with the farmers, and held them responsible for the lives of the partisans.

Now our group had to split up. Some went off with colonel Bolek Alef. A second Jewish group to which I belonged left with captain Zemsto who, a few days later, was killed in battle while we were engaged with a division of the German army. Under the leadership of colonel Moczar, and captain Franek from the village of Przypisowka we arrived at the Parczew forests, and there we began to gather together the separate groups and reform them anew. Here we met a Jewish partisan group that had stayed in the forest a few days ago. Our battalion reformed and received an order to cross over to the other side of the Bug. That area was however flooded with Germans who were fleeing in great panic from the Russian front. It was impossible for us to force our way over the river, because the Germans were fleeing back, and filled all the roads and pathways. So we were stuck in the wheat fields and waited for the German counter current, until a farmer came and reported that the Russians were already in the nearby village of Zahajki. A few hours later, we had the honor of shaking hands with the Red Army, embracing and dancing for joy.

Together with the Russian army, we marched into Lubartow, and when Lublin was liberated, we, a group of partisans,

[Page 239]

were the first to arrive in town. The people showered us with flowers, and welcomed us as liberators. As partisans, we received the most important powers and functions of the liberated city. I began to work for the city military commander as a sergeant.

Several days later, I travelled to Markuszow with the hope of finding one of my own, or anyone I knew. Unfortunately, there was no one left of my large family. It became clear to me that I had to make aliyah to Eretz-Israel. After some wandering, I arrived in the land in 1946. But the English intercepted our ship, and all the refugees were interned in the detainee camp, Atlit. We were there for several months before being freed.

In Israel I learned a trade, and settled in with my family.

Translator's Footnotes:

1. Belzec (June 1942-March 1943) was one of the first extermination camps. It was near the Soviet border in the Lublin district. 500,000 Jews were exterminated there.
2. Village elder
3. Stork
4. Lipowa 7 was a notorious forced labor camp in Lublin from 1939-1944. In November 1943 all the Jewish inmates were executed
5. Communist party leader. Later Marshal of Poland
6. Mieczyslaw Moczar. Polish Communist resistance leader, Lodz region. Later minister of the interior, Poland
7. Gustaw (Bolek) Alef. Communist leader in Warsaw Ghetto. Later colonel in Polish army

8. Phonetic transliteration. Possibly Rablow.

My Experiences During the German Occupation
Eye-witness testimony recorded by M. Nachshon (Capa)

Eidl Fishbein (Tel Aviv)

Translated by Moses Milstein

From village to village

Panic and trembling overtook everyone at the outbreak of the German-Polish war on September 1, 1939. Everyone felt the darkness descending on Polish Jewry. Markuszow Jews were also seized by the distress. Sorrow and despair were written on their faces. People looked for a word of consolation from each other in these hard times.

On that day, I said to my husband that a hard life was coming, and in order to be able to maintain ourselves, we have to be concerned with practicalities–travel to Lublin and buy merchandise there (we had a haberdashery store). The plan did not please my husband. He argued that, in a time like this, we shouldn't go out on the road for the sake of money. First of all, you had to stay alive. If we survived, then we could get money again. I, however, maintained my position, and went off to the big city.

The panic in Lublin was greater than in Markuszow.

[Page 240]

The newspaper sellers were shouting, "The Nazi army is advancing!" "The German Luftwaffe is bombing cities and shtetls, and above all, the civilian population!" The war atmosphere in Lublin was felt at every step. Nevertheless, I was able to spend all my money on various kinds of merchandise. With the help of a porter, I brought the purchased goods to the bus station, but to my great disappointment, there was not one bus. You can understand how I felt–alone in a strange big city, in wartime yet, separated from my husband and two small children (Moisheleh and Goldeleh–six and three years old). What do you do? How do you get home? All these questions greatly worried my mind. Nevertheless, luck was on my side. After several hours of wandering around the bus station, I hired an auto for a greater sum of money, and it took me to Markuszow.

I arrived home at around three o'clock. It seems that in the early days of the tragedy, a Jewish life was still considered precious and important. Half the town had been looking out for my return. Waiting tensely they constantly asked, "Is she still alive?" My husband really took my delay on the road hard. He ran around the shtetl looking for a carriage driver to take him to Lublin, but without success. When he first saw me alive, he thought–it's *tchies ha'maysim*[1]…The children too were beside themselves with joy at their mother's return.

In that first week of the war, we were occupied with hiding the goods from the store and the Lublin purchases. We were very wary of strangers' eyes. Because we were so careful in carrying out the job, the goods lasted for so long.

On Friday September 8 1939 the neighboring shtetl of Korew was heavily bombed. It was feared that Markuszow would also be covered with bombs, because the shtetl was on a main road, and right during the first days of the war, a mighty wave of refugees from western Poland rolled through Markuszow. For that reason, the following day, Saturday, we left the shtetl and went to the village of Gutanow from where we saw the murderous onslaught of German airplanes on our homes. In that village, we spent 4 days living outdoors. On the fifth day,

[Page 241]

my husband's relatives, who lived in the village of Moszenki, came to us, and took us back with them. We stayed there until Yom Kippur.

Afterward, we left Moszenki and moved over to Bogucin where we rented a room from a farmer, and "settled in" for a whole two years. We didn't want to live in the half-destroyed Markuszow, and as long as there was a possibility for us to change our home and settle in a village, we took advantage of it…

Until the deportations of May 1942, along with all the Markuszow Jews, my husband worked for the Germans repairing the roads or building new ones. Since the deportations did not yet apply to the Jews who lived in the territory of the Jastkow gemine, we left for the village of Tomaszowice, and gave the landowner ten thousand zlotys he should take us for slave labor on his properties. Dozens of Jews from near and far were able to delay death for a while–although with hard physical labor and ransom money, and not just for the nobleman, but for all his assistants, the trainee, the steward (*zhondtse*) and other aid. We worked there from May to October 1942 when an order was issued that the nobleman had to send all his slaves to Belzec.[2]

The tragedy in Belzec

On a Saturday evening, the nobleman and his farmhands transported 50 Jews who had worked in the village of Tomaszowice to Belzec. My brother, Yechezkel Nierenberg, lived then in Belzec. In his one room, there were 50 men. They lay on the ground pressed together like herrings. Around 11 at night my husband's brother, Itschak Fishbein, knocked on the door, and related how he was coming from the Judenrat where he secretly learned that at two AM the deportation of the Belzec Jews would take place. He, therefore, advised both my husband and I to flee without fail. My husband argued that I should go, and I argued that he should run away. There was no place to hide, so we thought we would have more luck getting away separately. At the end, I allowed myself to be persuaded and I left Belzec.

I ran where? Only God knows. It was raining, the road was mud-covered, but I ran like a lunatic, until I came to a spot that even in the dark of night looked familiar to me. Yes, I recognized it–it was the train station

[Page 242]

Sadurki. From the Belzec side, the echoes of frightful shooting could be heard. I became terrified: where are my two dear children, my beloved husband? Only I, the unlucky lonesome mother, blunder around in the dark of night, hunted by everyone. Sha, I think someone is walking by. From a hidden spot, I looked at the approaching figure and I recognized Basheh Goldwasser, a granddaughter of the Markuszow rav, who managed to escape Belzec at the last minute. She told me that around midnight, my brother-in-law, Itzchak Fishbein, came to the window and pleaded with my husband to run and find me. My husband went off to Bogucin, thinking I was hiding there. My niece, Esther Fishbein, took my two children and went to the same village of Tomaszowice that we had just come from. A local farmer hid them in a haystack.

I am beside myself. I continue to blunder around the station. I am persecuted by thoughts about the fate of my nearest ones. I run into another Markuszow resident, Aharon Bauman, who escaped from the hell of Belzec. He told me of what had transpired last night in the shtetl. At around 1:30, they drove all the Jews to the market, and shot them all. Germans and Ukrainians went wild, and in the most savage way killed thousands of Jews that had been herded to Belzec. He, Bauman, with another few dozen Jews, were designated to gather the dead bodies, pile them on cars, drive them outside the town, and dig a mass grave there. Many of the bodies were still moving in their death throes while they were being thrown onto the cars, and even while being thrown into the mass grave. He managed to escape by a miracle.

Dawn is breaking. I am still blundering around the Sadurki train station. Bashe Goldwasser shows up again. Shattered, I fall into her arms with a convulsive cry, "I don't have a husband or children anymore." Like in a dream her words ring in my ears, "Eidel, we will survive the brutal Nazis, just as I saw your husband in Bogucin alive. He is looking for you."

In the stable

With the last of my strength I ran to Bogucin. Exhausted and weakened I came to the farmer with whom we had lived

[Page 243]

for two years. He led me to the loft in the stable. Half-dead I fell on the straw. It turned out that my hearing was well tuned. Although the stable was far enough from the farmer's house, I heard knocking on his window in the middle of the night. I was more than certain that my husband, Israel, was there. Without thinking, I quickly jumped down from the height and out to the yard. Who can describe my joy and luck when I saw my husband alive? My first question was, "Where are our children? Are they alive?" The answer came, "Yes, yes! Our little children are alive." And right after that my husband asked tremulously, "Have you found a place for us?" I answered yes, although it wasn't true, but I had but one desire: to see my children.

My husband took me to Tomaszowice where several stalks of straw were standing in a field–and in one of them, my two little children were lying stuffed in there. I fell on them, embraced each one individually, kissed and hugged them and tears poured from my eyes. After the first tender moments, and after stilling the yearning for the dear ones, I grabbed them by the hands and ran off. Where to? After all, I had told my husband I had a place, nu, so I ran to Bogucin. There I ordered my husband and the children to go to the same farmer whose stable I was in at night, and alone I went to the poor family, Kozak, begging the farmer's wife to take me in. She agreed on the condition that we dig a well for them. I ask her how much it would cost. She replied–3,500 zlotys. I immediately gave her 2,000 zlotys, and a piece of linen. She took it all, and said it was for two months…

So we moved into another "apartment" in the loft of a stable. Every day the owners demanded the remaining 1,500 zlotys. I assured them that as soon as we began to dig the well, we would pay the money. A few days later, the farmers went to church, and saw for themselves how, in the village of Garbow, not far from the church, Chaim Morel and his youngest son, were shot. Coming back home, the wife described the incident, and begged us to leave the hiding place. But we didn't feel much determination in her request, and it gave us hope that we might be able to stay.

[Page 244]

On the ninth day of our settling in with the Kozaks, the wife came to our hiding place and told us about a new order from the Germans that any Pole hiding a Jew would be shot along with his household, and his goods burned. On the other hand, any Pole who hands over a Jew to the Nazis would be rewarded with one kilo of sugar, and ten zlotys. Frightened by the injunction, she asked us to leave the stable. This time her tone was categorical, an ultimatum–leave immediately. In tears, we begged for a few more days until we could find a new refuge. She allowed us to stay one more day.

That evening, my husband and I left our children, and went to the village of Wysokie, to the poor farmer, Jan Saba. He was an old acquaintance of ours, and over the span of many years, had received many favors from us. I told him that my children and I were hiding in the forest, and that he should have pity on us, and let us stay in his stable. I also promised to pay him for this, because I was owed money by the farmers in the area, and he would be able to receive certain amounts from time to time. After a long deliberation the farmer told us to come the following day.

On October 3 1942 we left the Kozaks, and moved over to the new "residence" in the loft of the farmer, Jan Saba in Wysokie. The new landlord demanded rental money on the very first day. Incidentally, those were his very first words on coming up to our loft. I replied that I would soon bring him the money. The farmer wanted to accompany me, but I gave him to understand that it was not worth his while, he must not risk too much. I went on my way, walked for about one and a half kilometers, got 200 zlotys ready, came back, and gave the farmer his money. He asked me if I had any more money. I denied it, because I didn't want Jan Saba to know we had money on us. For money, the farmer was ready to do the worst things. Every few days the same story was repeated: he came demanding his money, and I ostensibly ran to the farmers to claim my debts. We have to admit that Jan Saba treated us well as far as food was concerned, and in general, behaved honorably. At Christmas, he came up to us with the best meals and a bottle of vodka, ate with us, drank, toasted,

[Page 245]

and spoke from the heart, "I really regret taking you in, but too late"…

New Years eve, 1942. That evening, loud voices from the hut were carried to our ears. We were sure that they were carrying on wildly there. But later, we learned that it was the founding of a gang of bandits. No more and no less. That's all we needed! Every night we heard the shouts of the drunken farmers, their comings and goings.

One night, when we were sunk in a deep sleep, we suddenly heard the door of the stable opening, and several voices were carried to our hiding place. Our eyes opened in fear. We thought, here is our end–but the landlord calmed us down.

The same story was repeated practically every night. In the late hours, various types of merchandise were brought in to be hidden: dry goods, slaughtered pigs, even stolen church donations. We had to sort the money, count it, put it together, and roll the coins up. Once we were brought a new item. I did not believe my own eyes: boxes of rifles and bullets. I said to my husband, "Do you hear, Israel, I think the goy will not die because of us, but the opposite–we will die because of him. This place is becoming dangerous."

We decided that I should go out to several farmers to "check the pulse." First I went to the Kozaks, and after talking to the wife, I understood that they needed money badly. The enthusiasm for taking us in was not so great. In the final analysis, it was risky. But the money tempted them, and we left the Kozaks with the conviction that we should wait for an opportunity to leave the Sabas, and move to someone else.

An encounter with Jewish partisans

At the end of May 1943, Jan Saba came again demanding to be paid for living there. We no longer had any capital. Our only possessions were several gold rings. So my husband and I went to the farmers to sell the rings and get a little money. Of course, those condemned to death do not travel the straight and narrow, but in constant fear looking for hidden paths in order to reach our goal. Suddenly, we saw ten men approaching, all armed. We stopped dead, wanting to

[Page 246]

go back, but we heard a command, "Stay where you are!" We obeyed, and when the armed group got nearer, another command, "Hands up!" We obeyed this as well. They told us to come closer. Trembling with fear, feeling it was our last moment, we began to go toward the group when my husband cried out, "Isser Rosenberg!" I studied the group, and something surprising–the rifles aimed at us were lifted onto their shoulders and the whole gang shouted with joy, "Israel! Eidl!" We fall into each other's arms, we kiss, the joy is great. It's no small thing! To encounter our dear Markuszow boys, the heroic partisans who knew how to fight the Nazi murderers. They gave us 1,000 zlotys, established a connection. We no longer felt alone and abandoned. We also sold several rings for 2,000 zlotys, and we returned "home" with a fortune of 3,000 zlotys. Of course, Jan Saba got a few hundred zlotys for our rental account, and we could continue to live in the stable.

Now it became clear that our landlord was the leader of the band of robbers. Every night, he and his company would go out on "actions" and come back at dawn with loot and booty.

Germans arrive

On a July night in 1943, the gang felt like raiding a farmer from their own village who they knew did not spend the night at home. Wearing no masks, they went to the farmer's wife, tied her up with rope, beat her badly in the process, and stole a slaughtered pig which was worth a fortune in those days. When the farmer who was robbed came back the next day, and learned about the attack, he decided to go to the Germans and give the Sabas over to them. He went to the Jastkow gemine and explained the matter. The news that the farmer, Rodak, had fingered the Sabas spread quickly through the village of Wysokie. The Sabas did not hesitate, and that same night went to the Rodaks, dragged him to a field, and killed him.

The next day, around nine AM, Jan Saba came to us in a fright, explained in panic that the Germans were coming, and begged us to get away from there as quickly as possible. We four, that is my husband, my two

[Page 247]

children and I, quickly got busy, descended from the loft, went outside, and straight away saw the Germans coming. We went to the nearest field where there was some uncut wheat, hid among the stalks, and lay there breathlessly. Suddenly, we heard the sounds of farmers cutting the field where we were hiding. The clang of the scythes and the voices of the cutters were coming closer and closer. Any second they would come to where we were lying. Through the stalks we could clearly see the faces of the farmers cutting around our hiding place that would any minute be uncovered, and four souls would end their lives.

We sat clinging to each other in deathly angst; we wanted to disappear into the earth. The reapers were getting closer----

Suddenly, a shot was heard. Then another, and a third. Then a hail of bullets. Through the thin stalks we saw the reapers running away in panic, some falling to the ground. Although we were hidden by the wheat in the field, we lay there entwined without breathing. The German bullets could also reach our hiding place. We were certain that at any moment we would experience the worst… The day dragged on without end. Every hour felt like an eternity. The sun, which was our enemy number one at the time, did not seem to want to set under any circumstances, and warmed us with its rays, and lit the place where we were lying. We did not leave the field, because where would we run to?

The long-awaited night came. The precious night, friend of those condemned to death, settled on the earth. As soon as it became dark, we heard footsteps. Both children were quivering with fear, clinging to me. I pressed them to my heart. But I heard a familiar voice, "Eidla, Eidla!" Yes, the voice of Mrs. Saba bringing us food. She sat down next to us, and in tears told us that the Germans took away her husband and her son. She was certain they would not be returning from there. She was now left with five small children.

On that stressful day, we ate nothing. The food stood untouched. We heard the complaints of the farmer's wife. Her misfortune got mixed in with what we had experienced that day. But sitting like this for long was not possible. We had to look for a new hiding place. Homeless again. Who would now let in a Jewish family?

We thanked her for everything and went away to look for a shelter. Halfway through the night we came to the Lugow colony. I told

[Page 248]

my husband and children to sit behind the stable and I went off to the farmer, Wartacz, and knocked on his window. He didn't open the door, but asked through the window if I was coming to get some merchandise (I had a few things stored with him that I used to pick up at various opportunities). I asked him to let me in; I had something very important to discuss with him. The farmer stubbornly refused to even hear about it. I broke through his stubbornness with tears and pleading, and he let me over the threshold of his house. I told him various lies. Then I gave him 2000 zlotys, two cushions, and a gold ring to let me stay until tomorrow evening. He did not, however, agree to my proposal, and his refusal was sharp and categorical. On leaving, I delivered a few harsh words, reminding him about our partisans, and this had an effect. It seems the farmer was afraid of having his household burned down. So he led me to the stable, but here I revealed the secret that I was not alone, that my husband and children were waiting not far from here. Having no choice, he led us all up to the loft of the stable. We fell asleep on the straw like free people.

Again–our partisans

The following morning, the farmer's wife brought us food, and a spark of hope stole into our hearts: Maybe they will after all let us stay in the loft? We needed so very little, our desires were so pathetic…Meanwhile, we stayed another two nights. But midway through the night, we heard a fearful howling from the dogs, and according to the angry barking, we understood that strangers had come to the farmer. Later, it quieted down, and we heard the farmer coming into the stable with unknown people. No one came over to us, and we lay the whole night awake knowing that strangers were under the same roof. The others, the night guests, were also still. At dawn, the farmer came up to us and told us that Jewish partisans had spent the night here, and that two of them were armed and standing guard in the yard. We could not get over our joy over the extraordinary news–our guys are together with us. We immediately climbed down from the loft, and heartily kissed the two Jewish heroes, and tears

[Page 249]

of joy ran down everyone's cheeks. The partisans were not only happy to see us, they quickly made sure that a chicken would be cooked for us. They gave us a large, golden signet ring, and several gold coins to find a shelter. From Wartacz, they took back without discussion, the 2,000 zlotys and the ring, and left him with just the two cushions.

At night, the partisans and us left the farmer. They went off in a different direction, and I went to Bogucin, to the farmer, Kozak, in order to beg again for a hiding place. My husband and the children stayed with Wartacz in the meantime. To Mrs. Kozak, I proposed paying 2,000 zlotys a month, took the golden ring off, and put it on her finger, promised various "goodies" if she let us stay. She did not want to answer immediately declaring that her husband was not at home, and she must consult with him. In the meantime, she led me into the stable to spend the night. When her husband returned home the next day, he agreed to take us in. I gave him 2,000 zlotys, spent the day there, and at night went to the Wartaczs for my husband and children. I came to a field about one and a half kilometers from the Wartaczs. Suddenly I heard someone calling my name, and I recognized my husband's voice right away.

"What happened, Israel?"

"When Wartacz saw you were not returning right away, he threw me and the children out"–and despondently added, "Do we have anywhere to go?"

"Yes, my dears, we're going to Bogucin, to the Kozaks."

I went to the Wartaczs to say goodbye, and on the way picked up my husband and children. In the month of August 1943, the Kozaks took us up to the stable and immediately informed us that they would not be providing any food. Hearing such a verdict hit us hard. What does it mean not providing food in the conditions under which we find ourselves? All our pleading and crying was of no avail. The Kozaks would not be moved.

"It's enough we took you in!"

There was no choice but to make peace with our bitter fate. In the dark nights, my husband and I, like birds of prey, went into the fields. With our hands

[Page 250]

we dug out potatoes, beets, carrots, and anything that presented itself. This fieldwork we engaged in until winter. After, the ground was frozen and empty of any produce. Incidentally, feeding ourselves with vegetables was not news, because we had lived without bread for the last two years.

At the beginning of November 1943, we received some dear guests: our partisans came to visit and brought several loaves of bread. The joy of our children was indescribable (as was also ours) when they saw the loaves of bread. I took advantage of the opportunity of the partisans' presence to go with them to the village of Wysokie, to the farmer Wladislaw Banaszek where a part of my merchandise was hidden.

This particular farmer wanted to inherit my things while I was still alive, threatening to kill me if I came one more time to claim my merchandise or money. Nevertheless, I now went to demand what was mine– now not alone, but in the company of ten armed partisans. My husband also came along. Coming to the farmer's property, the partisans divided into patrols of two men, and by the farmer's door four partisans. They opened the door for me. When the farmer saw me, his first question was, "You're still alive? I wouldn't have believed it…"

Yes, he was full of anger when he saw I was still among the living, and I had the feeling that any minute he would attack me. I was really scared and I cried out, "Come in!"

The door opened and four armed partisans, weapons pointed, came into the room. The farmer shouted, "Ola Boga! What have you done to me, Eidla? What have I done to you?"

"I just want my merchandise back."

The partisans asked him, "Do you have her things?"

"No!" Banaszek replied. Three times the question was repeated with the same answer. Only when a partisan brandished his weapon at the farmer did he admit that maybe there was something, but it was hard to get to, because it was buried. So the partisans grabbed the farmer by the arms and he showed us all the places where my things were.

[Page 251]

I filled two sacs with various things, and returned to our "inn" at the Kozaks and asked her to sell everything because we had no more money. Later she brought us a larger sum of money, and we could pay her for keeping us.

This living in hiding continued until February 20 1944. Then something happened which disturbed the whole region. In the village of Krasienin, 22 Jews, among them two Markuszow families, were staying with a widowed farmer. Mordechai Bleiweiss and his wife and children, and David Iberkleid (Dzedzits) and his family. On that day, the widow went to the Garbow gemine and told them that there were 22 armed Jews hiding at her place. The bunker was immediately surrounded by Germans who opened intense fire on them. Three of them were, by exceptional means, able to break out and run away. The remaining 19 Jews were buried in the bunker. All this was told to us by our landlady. Right after ending the story, she firmly stated that we had to leave the loft, she didn't want to keep us any more at any price. She also added, "If you don't leave, I will."

We knew only too well what these words meant. We quickly gathered our things and went to Wysokie, to the old place at Saba's, and without asking the owners, went up to the stable loft. In the morning, when the wife entered the stall, I came down and immediately handed her a sum of money. In truth, she was overjoyed, even burst into tears, that they were poor and had nothing to eat. I promised her all good things…The next day, she left with the money and bought all sorts of good things. To us, however, she gave very poor food, and furthermore, less and less. Every week, like leeches, they sucked money, but fed us very poorly until we figured out that a farmer with the name of Zeznik was a big advisor of hers, and that this "buddy" was urging her to keep us on a hunger diet so we should slowly perish. Stopping the food completely they could not and didn't want to, because I was ostensibly going out and getting them money every week. It was a shame to lose a steady source of remuneration. For us there was no solution, only sitting in

[Page 252]

hiding and hungering. We had one consolation–the favorable news from the front. We got it in this way:

Once a week, my husband would go to the farmer in Bogucin where we had first stayed, and from him, he got reports about the situation in Poland, especially about the conditions at the front. In this way, my husband learned that the Red Army was on Polish soil already, and that the Germans were getting hammered. At that time we were physically and psychologically exhausted. But this news gave us a breath of life. Our hearts filled with hope and consolation: Maybe we will survive after all?

The joy did not last long. Our eight-year-old, Moisheleh, suddenly fell sick. He acquired a blood-dysentery[3], began to vomit, and was burning with fever. For a long six weeks, without medication, or a doctor, in the worst conditions, we had to look on as our son became skin and bone, all color drained from his face, and see our own child expiring from sickness and sorrow. That was the most painful time of the hellish existence we went through. Unfortunately, in the last months, we had absolutely no news from our partisans. We knew only that they had gone to the Parczew forests. Thus, there was no one to expect any help from…

I remember well the day in May 1944 when we saw through a crack in our loft how the fields were covered by a green carpet, how the birds were beginning their spring song, and all nature was awaking to a new life. But only we, the unfortunate and rejected, lie on rotten straw, emaciated from hunger, and broken by our child's long illness. Yes, I mourned my unlucky Moisheleh, who was rotting alive like the straw. My only plea was that I could bury my boy in a Jewish cemetery…And in the middle of this prayer, my Moisheleh opened his eyes and with a weak voice said, "I will live! I will get better!"

Tears came to my eyes from my son's determination to struggle for life. It turns out that a sick person's plea is no small thing…My son sat up and asked to be given a drink. More than a little water to give him, we did not have. He drank it up quickly–and from

[Page 253]

day to day, you could see an improvement. Our Moisheleh got well! And a bit of health came to us parents as well…Hope was renewed!

A grave is dug for us–and liberation comes

One day we heard the terrible echo of an explosion. We ran to the crack in the stable and saw a bizarre thing: On the Lublin-Warsaw train line which was about three km from our hiding place there were overturned train cars, and a cloud of flames and smoke could be seen on the horizon. We knew it was our partisans who had done this. Several days later, we clearly heard artillery fire. I asked the farmer's wife if the front was really that close. From her angry response, I got a weird suspicion. A little while later, an open tank passed by not far from us, and the soldiers in it were talking amongst themselves. My husband said he heard them speaking Russian. I laughed at him. So he defended himself saying he must have been mistaken.

In the middle of our discussion, we saw the Saba woman and the farmer Zeznik come into the stable. In both their hands–shovels. They began to dig in the ground. Although it seemed suspicious to us, we said nothing. The next day, she came back alone and continued to dig. I asked her, "Is the hole for us?"

The answer came instantly, "Since when are you such a devilish guesser?"

The discussion was interrupted. We awaited further developments with unease.

The wife began to give us very good food. Once, seven in the morning, we were even given potatoes with sour cream–a meal we hadn't seen before our eyes for several years. We decided, however, not to go near the good food being full of suspicions, doubts and worries. Every few minutes she came over to us, and pressed us to eat, but expecting something bad, we didn't

[Page 254]

go near the potatoes. This occurred on July 28 1944. At nine AM, we heard unfamiliar voices in the yard, and the reply from our landlady, "*Nie Wiem*!" (I don't know!). Suddenly a resounding slap rang out. The wife opened the stable with heart-rending cries. I hear clearly in Polish, "Eidla, Eida!"

We clung together certain that our end was coming. Suddenly we heard again, but this time in Yiddish, "Eidl! Israel! Your cousin, Abraham Fishbein has come to free you! The Red Army has been in charge of this area for six days!"

These words rang out like a voice from heaven for us unfortunates. Is it maybe a dream? Is freedom really here? We sat frozen between dream and reality. But our cousin did not delay. He climbed up high and getting closer to us, he shouted, "Partisans have come to free you! On Saturday, July 22, the Red Army liberated Lublin, and you still lie buried here? Are you alive? Say something!"

We crawled out from our rot and dirt, threw away our death-fear, and fell into the arms of our liberator.

* * *

Our partisans, with Avramtche Fishbein, helped us crawl down from our living grave, and led us by the arms to the main Lublin-Warsaw road, stopped the first peasant wagon they met going to Lublin, and ordered him to take us to the city. They bade us farewell and we went off to the city.

Six days since Lublin was liberated, and it was impossible to walk through the streets. Masses of people flooded the city. On the sidewalks, a pressing mass, but the signs of war were very evident. Chunks of glass littered the streets. We saw ruined houses, and gaping window frames. Half naked and barefoot we got to Lubartowska Street, and our joy was boundless when we saw the first Jew. He let us know that several Jews were living in the house on 8 Lubartowska. We left to go there, found a room, hammered together a bed of planks, and all four of us lay down. Actually in freedom!…We found out that the Red Cross was distributing food. My husband went there and brought back a container of barley soup, something we hadn't tasted for a whole two years. We fell on the tasty meal, but it seems our emaciated guts could not digest the food. We lay sick for three days after.

A Christian teacher from Bogucin village found out that we were alive, and she brought me a pair of slippers as a present. The farmer, Stachura, from the same village brought us a large loaf of bread and we started to get used to eating. After a week in Lublin, we began to slowly put our lives together.

There was not, however, a day that we did not receive news about individual Jews whom the AK (Armia Krajowa–armed organization of the Polish expatriate government in London that did not accept the new Polish regime) cold-bloodedly murdered. They wanted to continue the bloody work of the Nazi murderers. We began to give serious thought to aliyah to Israel. But it doesn't happen so quickly, because my husband was meanwhile doing business, and wanted us to get on our feet a little. He used to travel to liberated Warsaw and Lodz. On November 5 1945 my husband travelled to Warsaw, and two days later– the 7th of November, some Jews came to my house with the terrible news that my husband had been murdered on the Lublin train station by the AK. Everything in me gave way. After such horrible six years, we had tasted a little freedom–and now such a fatal blow. Now I was left with my two children, alone, unlucky, forlorn…

In the new Lublin cemetery, another tombstone was placed.

My husband was 36 years old when he was killed by the hands of savages. Honor to his bright memory!

We leave Poland

After sitting shiva for my husband and our father, my husband's brother, Yosef, came from Germany. After long preparations, we came to the camp, Lampertheim,[4] in Germany via Szczecin and Berlin. After many difficult experiences, and illnesses, we left the cursed earth of Germany on December 20 1948, and traveled to the French port

[Page 256]

of Marseilles. There we boarded a ship which took us to the long dreamed-for, and yearned-for land– Eretz Israel. We arrived in the Jewish state at the beginning of 1949.

Translator's Footnotes:

1. The rising of the dead at the coming of the Messiah
2. Extermination camp near border of Ukraine
3. Bloody flux. Hemorrhagic diarrhea
4. Displaced Person's camp situated between Mannheim and Darmstadt. It held up to 1,200 people, and was closed in 1949.

Memories of Nazi Hell

Esther Fishbein-Friedman (Petach Tikva)

Translated by Moses Milstein

1.

The second Friday of the Second World War. Markuszow is overcome with panic. People are beginning to pack their meager possessions. They run away to the villages. Everyone feels that the firestorm of war is coming nearer to our small, quiet, shtetl. The main road that divided Markuszow is full of retreating Polish soldiers, and thousands of refugees marching to the east. On Saturday, the first bombs fall near the Jewish cemetery. On Sunday and Monday, the German bomber airplanes do not let the city rest. Constant flights–and incendiary bombs set fire to Markuszow, and transform this community into a heap of smoking cinders. The flight to the villages increases. I too am caught up in the fleeing current to Staroscin in order to wait out the bombs and fires.

After two days, Devorah Pelz and I returned to Markuszow in order to find out what was happening in the shtetl. A frightful picture of destruction and desolation greeted our eyes. Aside from the row of houses by the Polish school, all the other buildings were turned to ashes. The telephone poles lay on the road like ineptly felled trees. There were many bodies of soldiers and refugees lying around on the shul square. In one place, I encountered Freideleh, the unlucky mother mourning her dead son, Dovid-Leib. He was killed by a German bomb not far from the cemetery while they were fleeing to Zablecz. Markuszow suffered its first victims.

2.

Later, the Germans came to Markuszow. Since the antisemitic soldiers of the retreating Polish army had spread rumors in the villages that any farmer caught hiding a Jew

[Page 257]

would be killed along with his household, most of the farmers began to kick out the Jews who came to them for protection. As a result, a large number of them went back to Markuszow. Our family too went back to the ruined shtetl. Not far from Garbow, we encountered a group of German soldiers on a truck. Their first words were, "*Verfluchte Juden.*"[1] The whole family, most of whom had no place to live because of their burned-down houses, moved into our house which had survived. Jews began to put up huts and barracks on the site of the ruined homes, just to have something over their heads. Some began to immediately rebuild houses–a sign they wanted to reestablish themselves in the shtetl. The Germans did not let the exhausted Jews rest. They cut off their beards, insulted, cursed and beat them. Persecutions were a daily occurrence.

A while later, the Germans set up a committee over the Jewish community in Markuszow they called the Judenrat They appointed Shloime Goldwasser as president, as director members–Mechl Weiner, Yerachmiel Rubinstein, Itzchak Fishbein (secretary) Chai-Yosef the shoichet, and Sender Vevi's (Fishbein). The first German order to the Judenrat was to provide a contingent of 100 Jews for various kinds of work. In the winter months, we had to clean the section of road from Markuszow to Garbow where the Germans were. In the summer months, they used to take us to work in Kloda where we broke up rocks for road building. Every day they forced us to work, and treated us like slaves. Our humiliation was so great that we were afraid to raise our heads in front of gentiles we knew. Nevertheless, the thought that the war would end with Hitler's defeat, and that the sun would shine again on the Jewish people, never left our minds. This Jewish faith strengthened us and gave us courage in the hardest times.

3.

One evening is etched in my memory. It took place in the house of my grandfather, Shloime-Gershon, in honor of completing the end of the Talmud. This was in October 1940. My whole family, the members of the Judenrat, and some other Jews from the shtetl–altogether about 30 residents of Markuszow–came together in the greatest of secrecy at my grandfather's. Doors and windows were

[Page 258]

covered so no light would shine through. Disregarding the fact that bringing together such a large crowd in those times was life-threatening, there was no fear, because who among the participants would tell the Germans about the Talmud celebration. (To the credit of the Markuszow Judenrat, it must be said that there were no betrayers or sycophants among them who would create problems for their brothers). In a very solemn and quiet mood, my grandfather lifted up a glass of wine, blessed everyone, and wept. The entire houseful of people wept along with the old one, wishing him that next year he would survive to finish it in Jerusalem. At that, my grandfather wept even more strongly, and expressed his doubts with respect to being saved from the murderers' hands. His wish was that his children and grandchildren should avenge themselves on the hated enemy…

4.

One day, two Gestapo people from Pulawy brought an order to the Judenrat that every Markuszow Jew had to wear a white armband with a blue Star of David–a sign of their belonging to the Jewish people. Even the members of the Judenrat would have to wear the armbands, with an additional sign that they belonged to the Judenrat. At the same time, a new decree was issued: Every Jew had to relinquish all furs, even fur collars. As an example, the head of the Judenrat was the first to hand over his furs, but not all Markuszow Jews wanted to give up their warm clothing for German soldiers who were freezing on the Russian front. Those who had the slightest opportunity gave their furs to Polish neighbors for safekeeping. But our troubles didn't end there. That was only the beginning of the end–unfortunately, a rather tragic end.

Chol Hamo'ed, Pesach, 1941[2], news came that the Jews of neighboring Korew were being expelled. We waited with the greatest suspense and unease to see what would happen to us. We learned from trusted sources that the same was going to happen to us in two days time. And that actually happened: Several Gestapo arrived at city hall in an auto, called out the Judenrat, and demanded the immediate provision of 500 men.

With the help of the Polish police, the Jews were driven to the square in front of city hall, and formed into columns–

[Page 259]

separating the old, the young, and the children. They picked out a few hundred older Jews from the three columns, and sent them to the Polish schoolhouse.

During the deportation, my family and I were hiding in the Gutanow forest. We sent a Polish acquaintance to find out what was going on. After returning, he reported that the Jews who were taken to the shul were later taken to the train station from whence they were taken to an unknown destination. The remaining Jews were again ordered to work for the Germans. After this ostensible calm in Markuszow, we decided to go back home. On the way from the Gutanow forest, we met some farmers we knew who told us that the Germans had terribly beaten and even shot the Jews gathered at the train station, and had driven them into the prepared freight cars. Some of the Jews, particularly the older ones, mounted a resistance. Moishe Beinishe's (Weinriber), and Mendl Moishe's (Kandel) did not want to go on the march and begged to be shot then and there. The German beasts did the martyrs the favor–and killed them. Other Jews, as well, preferred death rather than making the tortuous journey in the whitewashed cars.

Coming to the shtetl, we encountered orphaned families. Children had lost their parents, and parents–their children. That was not enough for the Germans. Now the Jews were concentrated in one place, the entire left side of Lubliner Street.

A ghetto for us.

5.

Two months later–Shavuot 1941–the Judenrat was again required to assemble all the Jews in the gemine square. We understood that the Germans intended to make Markuszow *Judenrein*.[3] Many immediately took off to the neighboring villages and forests. Our family decided to go to Belzec that very evening. According to various reports, it was still possible to get by in that shtetl. As soon as we got out of Markuszow, we heard the rasping voice of 70-year old Velvl Rothstein, "*Yidn*! Save me or shoot me!"

[Page 260]

We approached the spot where the voice was coming from, and saw the old man lying on the ground, shot by a bunch of Poles. We applied first aid to the old man, and returned to Markuszow afraid to set off on a distant, unfamiliar road where armed Poles were lurking and completing the Germans' work for them.

Late at night, our cousin, Chaim-Leib Fishbein came and told us that it made no sense to sit in the house. We had to get out of the shtetl as soon as possible, as long as the slightest opportunity existed. About 30 Markuszow Jews left for Belzec that night. At dawn, we arrived in the shtetl of Moszenki, and found many Markuszowers there. The village of Moszenki belonged to the Jastkow gemine, and ten local Jewish families lived there. There in the village we rested from our travels. All the anti-Jewish decrees had not yet reached the local Jewish residents. Just their land was taken from them and given to the farmers. The Moszenki Jews themselves were harnessed to slave labor. The Polish police found out about the "invasion" of Markuszow Jews in the small village, and ordered all the refugees to present themselves to the city hall in Jastkow. The Moszenki Jews hid a great many of us in attics, stables, and cellars, and thanks to this, many succeeded in rescuing themselves.

I, dressed as a village girl, left at 12 noon for Belzec on foot in order to find out what was going on.

6.

Thousands of Jews driven from Germany itself were driven to Belzec, and here, in the worst sanitary conditions, found a temporary home. As identification, the Germans ordered the German Jews to wear yellow arm patches, whereas the Belzec Jews wore armbands like we did in Markuszow. If not for the arrivals and those driven there, Belzec would not have been aware that there was a war going on between nations, and that one of the biggest wars was against the Jews. The houses here were whole, unaffected, and the Belzec Jews lived in their own dwellings. They carried on business, worked, traded and believed that the current war did not concern them. Not until we, the remnants from Markuszow arrived in Belzec, and brought our misery there, did the shtetl become more upset, tenser, and waiting for further problems.

[Page 261]

Two days after our arrival in Belzec, a small number of armed Germans, and many Ukrainians, surrounded the shtetl and ordered all men from 16 to 40 to assemble at the marketplace. In that action, about 50 Markuszow Jews were taken from Belzec to Lublin to the Majdanek death camp. Among the first Jewish Markuszow victims to be killed in Belzec was my fourteen-year old brother, David, who died in the following circumstances:

When the shtetl was surrounded, my father and his brother were lying hidden in a cellar. My brother and I were standing outside. Members of the Belzec Judenrat were going around and shouting, "From 16 to 40, must assemble! Whoever doesn't show up will be shot!"

I asked the passing Judenratnik with despair, if my brother, who was not yet 16 years old, had to go. To this came the answer, "Yes, certainly, he must show up, if not, they will shoot him." Here we were just talking to my brother, and in a few minutes, he was already standing in the row of those being taken to Majdanek…

"David, we will never forget you! You left an open wound in our hearts…"

Even in Markuszow, during the first deportation, Polish acquaintances offered to hide him, but his answer was always, "Wherever my parents go, I will go."

Later, the Belzec Judenrat member who accompanied the transport to Majdanek, told me that my brother stayed the whole time with my grandfather. When he was asked how he ended up in this transport when he was not even 16 years old, he answered, "Better me than, God forbid, my father!"

7.

After this aktion, life in the shtetl became "normal" again. Every Tuesday, the weekly market took place. Belzec Jews did business, sold, bought like in the good old days. It was only bad for

[Page 262]

the German Jews whose only occupation now was selling everything they owned in order to stay alive. In their naivete, they waited for the baggage that the Germans had promised they would send after them. The situation of our Markuszow Jews, and those arriving from other cities and shtetls of Poland, was similar. We all had to survive with what we had, or by selling our last shirt. There was nowhere to go. We remained in Belzec.

In late autumn, 1941, an order was issued that all the Jews from the shtetl itself, and from the surrounding area must assemble at the shul. Since most of the Jews already knew what that signified–they weren't so quick to obey. Ukrainian and Polish police surrounded Belzec and began to search through the houses, cellars and attics. Most of the Jews found hiding were shot on the spot. Those who did show up at the assembly point, were led on foot to the Mendrewic train station 11 km from Belzec. Since we were hidden in a cellar whose windows looked out on the shul yard, we saw with our own eyes the hell endured by our unlucky brothers and sisters whose last voyage was accompanied with blows, insults, curses, and shootings on the spot.

That day, only the Belzec Judenrat was not a partner in the great tragedy. They were locked in a separate residence under a strong guard from where they were freed after the bloodbath ended. Only a few isolated shots now echoed. This was the Ukrainians killing Jews they found, among them women too, who, even with a cross on their necks, were not saved from death.

8.

Late at night, we left the hiding place, and returned home. My father's two brothers, Itzchak and Israel Fishbein, went to a village where Israel's wife was hiding. We stayed with the two children: the 11 year old Moisheleh, and six-year-old, Goldeleh.

The next day, loudspeakers announced that those Jews, who for various reasons had failed to show up at the shul square, could do it now. The new assembly point, however, was now Piusk,

[Page 263]

and that is where the remaining Jews had to go. Of course, the new decree ended with the warning that failure to do so would be punishable by death. My parents, two brothers and sister with the two children, and I decided to obey this time. Along with 300 other Jews, we were driven by the Germans to Piusk. On the way, little Goldeleh, who I was carrying in my arms, broke into loud tears.

"I want to go to mommy, the Germans are going to kill us!"

We calmed the child down. My mother said, "Goldeleh is right. This march means death. We have to run away from here."

So we took advantage of the moment when the Germans accompanying us were far from us, to move off to the side, and run across the field. We went to the village, Tomaszowice, because our uncle, Israel, was supposed to be there, and hand over his two children. But on the way, we met farmers who threatened to take us to Majdanek. We knew this was not an idle threat, but a real danger, because the Germans paid for every Jew brought to them. We begged the farmers to let us go. Crying the hardest was little Goldeleh who could speak Polish and pleaded, "Let me go to my mother…"

For the price of 500 zlotys and the ring off my finger, we ransomed ourselves from the murderers' hands, and continued on our way.

It was decided to stay sitting in the field, because it was too dangerous to go about by day. I, on the other hand, would try to get to Tomaszowice to look for my uncle. We decided that this same evening we would meet at the stable of a Tomaszowice farmer we knew. I went on my way. Coming near to Bogucin, I met a farmer I knew who warned me not to go into the village now, because there were a lot of gendarmes there looking for Jews. So I stayed lying in the field, and although night had already fallen, I still didn't dare to go to the village. It began to rain. I continued to lie in the field with my dark thoughts. Suddenly, I see two figures approaching and Yiddish being spoken. I recognized the two uncles I was going to see, by their voices. We were very happy at the unexpected meeting. The joy was spoiled, however, when my uncle reported

[Page 264]

that not one farmer was willing now to hide a Jew. He added in a resigned way, "There is no other option, but to report to Piusk."

I did not agree, and the decision about this horrible question we left for later. For now, it was important that everybody should meet up at the agreed-upon spot. When we showed up at the stable, the farmer did not even want to hear about letting us in. There was no choice but to return to the field and hide in a haystack that had been set up by 30 Markuszow Jews when they had been working for the Tomaszowice nobleman. We all crawled into the straw and settled in. The next day, my uncle, Israel, with his wife and two children went to a farmer they knew with the hope of finding a shelter.

9.

Another family came to the Markuszow colony in the hay stack: Esther-Breindl Huberman and her family. We spent two months like this in the haystack. At night, I would go to farmers I knew, and buy food. I told them we were hiding not far from Belzec. The snow was awful, because footprints would persist in the snow and could have betrayed our hiding place.

And that's what actually happened. Once a farmer told me that they already knew in the village that there were Jews hiding in the stack, and they would have to kill them. So we quickly had to come up with another hiding place, because our lives were in danger. So I went to Belzec to get some news, and look for a bunker.

In Belzec, I found a new ghetto of 600 Jews who were locked up in the synagogue and in some nearby houses. The previous Judenrat and the Jewish police were the only rulers. There was no way to get into the ghetto, because it seemed to the locked-up Jews there that every newcomer was liable to present a danger for them. But with a lot of connections and still more, money–from 10 to 15 thousand zlotys–the Belzec ghetto doors would open. My mother and sister were there, and I went to them for advice and help. My mother sighed–and could only

[Page 265]

do one thing: take my eight-year-old sister. So I brought the child there during the day. So now almost every day, I made the 16 km trip there on foot from the haystack to Belzec and at night, the same distance back. My job was to provide food for those in the ghetto and in the haystack. Dressed like a farmer, and with their expressions and appearance, it was easier for me to travel in the hate-filled environment where death for Jews lurked around every corner.

The haystack was close to the road. One Sunday, some village boys approached, and one of them opened the entrance and shouted, "Oy, look everyone, Jews! We have to tell the Germans who are here on the road."

In truth, we had seen Germans on the road. We began to negotiate with the boys. We managed to buy them off for several hundred zlotys they should keep mum. It now became clear that we had to get away from there.

10.

At night, we went to the village of Tomaszowice. A fellow resident of the haystack (who stayed there, by the way) told us that there was an abandoned, lonesome little house in Tomaszowice where his family had hidden, and it could now serve us as a hiding place. So we settled in there, and at night I went to some farmers I knew. They told me that Germans and Ukrainians were looking for hidden Jews in all the villages. We were surprised by other news, however: that in the nearby Wole forests there was a Jewish partisan group, and among them--many youngsters from Markuszow.

So we went to the Wole forest, and a new world was revealed to us: Our hometown youth, armed and full of the courage to live. They led a free life in the forest, and when the Germans attacked, they fought back with weapons in their hands.

On Chanukah 1943, the Germans carried out a big raid. The Wole forest was surrounded. The murderers opened with heavy fire, and then succeeded in getting to the bunkers where many

[Page 266]

Markuszow families were hiding. They came to our bunker as well, and threw in grenades. Since they fell on sandy soil, they did not explode. A polish policeman from Markuszow opened the bunker, and we heard him say, "Stifling air, but no people" and he shot several rounds into it. Since my mother, Rivkeh, was standing near the ladder that served as an entrance to the bunker, several bullets went through her legs. She died in terrible agony, in the evening. I will never forget my blessed mother who was so savagely murdered by the Germans and their Polish accomplices!

Curse the murderers! Eternal remembrance of my mother, a"h!

When the shooting ended, the Germans called to the Jews to get out of the bunkers, that nothing would happen to them, they would only be taken to work in Konskowola. Some allowed themselves to be persuaded, and left the bunkers. Then the unfortunates were lined up in a row and shot in the forest. At night, we, the survivors, got out of our hiding place, and buried the bodies in a mass grave.

That night, we paid the last respects to the sixty victims of Nazi murder in the Wole forest.

After this tragedy, we stayed in the forest for another three days. Later we went to Belzec and stopped in Markuszow along the way. When we got to the haystack, we found the dead body of Israel who had not wanted to leave the place. He had been stabbed in several places. We decided to bury him. Lying on the haystack, we saw several farmers approaching with shovels in their hands. We heard one of them say, " We didn't mean him, Israel. We were supposed to kill those who were hiding here, especially the black girl (meaning me). Now, we have to keep together. Wherever we see a Jew, we will immediately take him to the police station."

The farmers dug a grave in the field and put Israel in.

We decided to go to Belzec once more.

[Page 267]

11.

There were several hundred Jews in Belzec ghetto. We managed to get in there, and along with everyone else, we cleaned the snow off the streets, and did other kinds of physical labor. For this, all we got was soup. We bought our own bread.

On May 8th 1943 the ghetto was surrounded, and they forced out two hundred men and one hundred women, and took them to the camp at Budzyn. The rest were shot in the ghetto, among them–my youngest brother, Nechemia, z"l.

As soon as we arrived in Budzyn, they immediately ordered us to line up for roll call, and pulled out the elderly and the children in order to kill them. When they took the woman, Baltche Hopfeld's, two little girls away, the hysterical mother resisted, and at the end begged them to take her with the children. The murderers obliged her...

The camp was not far from Krasnik (near Lublin). There were airplane factories there in which Jews worked. Other than that, there were also rest houses for soldiers and officers of the Wehrmacht, and some camp people had to serve them. There were also German families evacuated from the bombarded areas of Germany. Jewish women filled the job of house servants in their homes.

The camp itself was surrounded by barbed wire, but not electrified. The guard was composed of Ukrainians. The commandant was Oberscharfuhrer Feix[4], a German or a Pole from Silesia whose sadism threw fear into everyone. At the time of my arrival in Budzyn, there were about 2,000 men and women, mostly from Warsaw and other areas of Poland. There were also two Jewish commandants: over the men– a certain Stockmann, a prisoner-of-war, from the ghetto of Konskowola, but he was originally from Grodno or from those areas. For the women–Regina Zemel from Zakrzowek.

Both behaved not badly to the internees. That helped somewhat lessen the hard regime of the camp we had to strictly observe.

[Page 268]

We had to get up at 4:30 am. At around 5:00 am, we got black coffee in the kitchen, At 6:00, roll call. We all had to stand at attention, and Feix himself counted the imprisoned. He beat people at every roll call, and if any of the camp Jews did not appeal to him, he shot them on the spot. After roll call we were marched under strong Ukrainian guard to work. The men–to the factories. The women–to housework. In general, we women benefited from greater movement, and didn't suffer from hunger. At around 5:00, we returned to the camp, and received a liter of soup, and 200 grams of bread. But before this, there was another roll call to make sure nobody had disappeared during work.

We could not bring any outside food into the camp. Once during an inspection, they found a piece of butter on a young boy. The boy–Hershman from Belzec–was immediately shot. Another time, they found a piece of bread on a Warsaw Jew. Feix ordered him to strip naked (this was on a freezing December day), and go around the camp carrying a heavy girder. Feix would also punish Jews for their ostensible unsanitariness. On the coldest days in winter, he would lead people to the water pump near the kitchen, and pour cold water on their naked bodies. At 9:00 pm, the signal for sleep was given. We stretched out on planks, three rows high in the barracks.

Once a Belzec Jew, Abraham Zang, escaped from the camp. A roll call was immediately ordered. Feix pulled ten young kids from the ranks and shot them. A few weeks later, my uncle, Abraham Leichter, and his son, Nechemia, ran away. At the evening roll call, Feix again chose 8 men and 2 women, locked them in a cellar, beat and tortured them, starved them, and on the third day was planning to shoot them. In the meantime, an order had come that Feix was to leave Budzyn. In the middle of the night, he ordered a roll call, hung a huge banner "To each his own," and good-naturedly declared that in honor of his leaving, he was granting the life of the ten Jews.

Feix's replacement was Oberscharfuhrer Axmann. There were cases of escape under him too. This time, a Belzec Jew, Kerschenbaum. Axman had a different punishment than his predecessor. He ordered the shooting of all the family members of the escapee.

[Page 269]

The Ukrainians took Kerschenbaum's two brothers out of the line and shot them in front of everyone's eyes.

12.

In spring 1944, a large shipment of plank beds from the liquidated camps in Poniatowa, Trawniki, as well as clothing from Majdanek, arrived in Budzyn camp. The boards, which had come from the liquidated camps, were covered with hundreds of inscriptions in Yiddish, Polish, and Hebrew. "Take revenge on the Germans!" "Do not allow yourselves to be slaughtered!" "Rise up and defend yourselves!" Don't let yourself be fooled into the barracks like we were. Now they are shooting us!"–and other inscriptions with names, dates, words of farewell from men to women, women to men, from parents to children, and from children to their mothers and fathers. We were shattered by the shipment of wood that day which unequivocally gave us to understand that the same end awaited us too.

The next day, fully loaded cars with camp clothing arrived in Budzyn. Since they did not take us to work that day, and we had been left in the camp, everyone understood that the end was coming closer. They would certainly do the same here as in Poniatowa and Trawniki. Everyone was uneasy. At night, 30 men cut the wires and escaped. The Ukrainian guards saw the escapees, and alerted the German command, which ordered them to immediately open fire on everyone–on those who ran away as well as those of us who were inside.

The next day we saw a wagon fully loaded with dead bodies being led out of camp–victims of the night's shootings. Then they ordered us to put on the striped clothing and transferred us to another camp three km away from the current one. We did the same work, but under a stricter guard. The wire fence was now electrified.

In summer 1944, when the Red Army was already on Polish territory, a large transport of men, women, and children was transferred to Majdanek. The rest–about 1500 people–were transported in freight cars to Wieliczka, to the salt mines, close to the infamous death camp, Plaszow. I worked there until liberation.

Translator's Footnotes:

1. Cursed Jews
2. Period between Passover and Sukkot
3. German term for 'cleansed of Jews'
4. SS Oberscharfuhrer Reinhold Feix. Commandant at Budzyn, December 1942 to August 1943

[Page 270]

The Hero of Majdanek

Testimony of the Markuszow Jew, Gedalieh Glozsheiner (now in New York) – taken and recorded by Rivkeh Nachshon (Capa)

Translated by Moses Milstein

As someone born and raised in Markuszow, I feel it is my holy duty to record in our yizkor book the truthful events in the Lublin death camp, Majdanek, where just before liberation, a young Jewish man, my

Tzadok Garfinkle

tradesman colleague, and personal friend, displayed such heroism, refusing to allow himself to be taken like a sheep to the slaughter. I heard this story from several surviving Jews from Majdanek whom I met in liberated Lublin when I arrived there as a soldier in the Soviet army. But I want to tell it in a certain order:

As a boot maker, it was hard for me to find stable work in our shtetl, so I settled in Lublin and stayed there until the outbreak of World War Two. When the Nazis occupied Lublin

[Page 271]

in the latter half of September 1939, I escaped to Russia. It would take days, and it would still not be enough, for me to relate all the experiences I endured during the war years. As soon as the Russo-German war started[1], I volunteered to join the Red Army, and in various fronts, participated in relentless battles. I was badly wounded in the arm at Smolensk, and stayed in hospital for many long months. When I regained my strength, and recovered from the difficult experience, I read in the press that the Red Army was already hitting the Nazis on Polish territory. I reenlisted in the army, and I managed to get into a tank division. Through battles, clashes, scouting, and often unhindered, my tank regiment took Chelm, and prepared for a quick attack on Lublin.

Our tanks advanced forward, and I recognized the entrance to Lublin via Lubartowska Street. My heart beat faster wanting to advance ever more quickly over the streets where we had spent so many years. And maybe someone I knew had survived, although I already knew about the Nazi murders. Suddenly my tank stopped. About fifteen men appeared on the road, emaciated, pale, in rags. We jumped out of our tank. I saw that the men were Jews, and astonished, I asked them what they were doing there. One of them hastily explained that they had been hiding in the bushes for three days waiting for the Red Army. They had escaped from Majdanek, and this, thanks to the heroism of a young Lubliner man.

"Who?" I asked with curiosity.

"Tzadok Garfinkle," was the answer.

This name brought to mind a tremendous amount of memories of Jewish Lublin where, together with Tzadok, I had lived through days of joy and pain in the workshop, in the street, and in society. I asked the men to describe the incident to me in detail. One of the survivors related:

"Tzadok Garfinkle," as an experienced tradesman, was the head-master in the leather workshop at Lipowa 7 where Jewish prisoners-of-war worked for the Germans. Every morning, two SS people led him from Majdanek where he was living with his wife and child, to the work site. In the evening, he was led "home" by the same guards. Three days ago, armed SS men came to our barracks, and took away about 30 Jews, among whom was Tzadok Garfinkle. We well knew that this meant we were being taken to the ovens, because according to the Germans' behavior,

[Page 272]

it was clear that the Russians were near. Sensing their end, the murderers wanted to also end the lives of the remaining Jews. Now we were sure we were at the end of the road. We were getting closer to the gate. Suddenly something surprising happened. Tzadok Garfinkle, with his strong arms, lifted up one of the SS accompanying us, and threw him to the ground with tremendous force. Tzadok tried to avoid getting bayoneted and threw himself on the Nazi with the same speed with which he had lifted up, and slammed the Nazi down, and literally tore him to pieces. The rest of the Nazis finally realized what was happening and started to shoot. Riddled with bullets and covered in blood, Tzadok fell on the Nazi and breathed his last.

Those of us who found ourselves in the transport to the crematorium took advantage of the commotion and began to run. The murderers shot after us, killed several Jews, but those of us, who you see now, managed to get here, and we hid under the bushes for three days, outdoors, without food or water, until the noise of your tanks announced the liberation, and we ran to meet you. This was possible thanks to the bravery of Tzadok Garfinkle, a rare example of resistance under the conditions of Majdanek."

Translator's Footnote:

1. The Germans invaded the Soviet Union on June 22, 1941 in Operation Barbarossa

[Page 272]

Two-Week Period of Partisan Life

Shmuel Rubinstein (New York)

Translated by Moses Milstein

1.

The conditions of life in America do not allow me to give an exact and comprehensive report on the struggle of the Markuszow partisans carried out over a period of two and a half years against the German enemy. I will therefore just describe a period of two weeks that generally reflect our struggle and the painful road on the way to the day of liberation.

Actually now, March 30, 1954, as I write these lines, ten years have passed since the death of my two friends and fellow fighters from Markuszow, the unforgettable David Ettinger (Dudek), and Veve Laks (Vladek), the son of Leibish Beck. At the same time, Moishe Yeager, the commander of our otriad named Emilia Platter, also fell.

[Page 273]

We were the only Jewish partisan group operating in the Lublin area, and everyone in the whole region knew we were Markuszowers. Of course, the Germans had only one designation for us–bandits, and promised big rewards for capturing us alive.

2.

Om March 12 1944, we were withdrawing from a very successful operation of the night before against a German post in the village of Jamy not far from Lubartow.

The Germans, fifty men strong, armed with heavy and light weapons were stationed at every entrance to the village. We were informed of this by a woman farmer who spied for us. At around 9:00 pm, we carried out an attack on the Germans. After a two-hour battle we entered the village, and counted 36 dead Germans. We took off their uniforms, took their weapons, and withdrew from the village with one of ours dead. This time we had to withdraw further, because we expected hard sanctions from the Germans. We also warned the farmers to leave

Shmuel Rubinstein as a Polish officer after liberation

[Page 274]

the village for a few days, because the Germans would not let such a defeat go, and they would take out their anger on the village.

The next day, we were 40 km from Jamy village, and we received news from the wireless radio that on March 13th, we would receive for our use, people, weapons, and money via an airdrop. We just had to prepare a suitable place for the drop. The people were coming directly from Moscow, and had an important mission to carry out in this area. It was not hard to find such a place, because we were not new to airdrops. We straightaway agreed on a spot. On schedule, and under our cover, the Soviet airplanes dropped people and packs of weaponry, and things necessary for the partisans.

On March 14th, we had a meeting with the newly arrived instructors. They advised us that our first task was to transport two of their people to the Kielce region to prepare an espionage and diversion action against the retreating Germans. We knew that the way from the Lubartow region to the Kielce region involved crossing the Vistula, and would not be easy. We understood the importance of getting the two instructors to the other side of the river, in order to be of use there to the Russian army.

We set off at night. The darkness was lessened by the snow falling, which also made our movements more difficult. We had one goal: to get to the Vistula as quickly as possible. I decided that, on the way, I would visit the bunker in Wole where there were Markuszow families hidden with a farmer. Among them were my sister, Blima, my sister-in-law, Beileh, and Dina and Ita Gothelf. After I had given them a little food and the most important news, I returned to the agreed-upon place where the rest of my company was waiting for me.

Together we continued along, and on March 15th in the morning, we came to the village of Meszno. There was no better place to wait out the day, because Meszno was a small village surrounded by forest on all sides. There were 60 of us, among whom the Markuszowers were: Mechl LOTERSTEIN (Michal),

Shmuel Laks ("Dzad"), Mordechai Kerschenblatt (Martchin), Yechiel Gothelf (Heniek), my brother, David Rubinstein (Stach), David Ettinger (Dudek), Veve Laks (Wladek), Hershl Fishbein (Woitek), the writer of these lines (pseudonym, Sevek), the commandant of the group, Moishe Yeager, and others. We were well armed, and on coming into the village,

[Page 275]

we immediately took over two huts that were standing at the edge of the forest. The farmers told me the truth that, because of the sunny day, we could not march further and had to wait there until evening. Whether they wanted to or not, the farmers had to receive us and give us aid. In the final analysis, we were also fighting for Poland's freedom, and denying us help meant courting danger. They just asked that we not post guards outside, because it might draw the attention of a passerby who would then alert the Germans. The farmer himself was ready to keep watch outside, while we stayed indoors and watched through the windows to see who was coming around. We agreed to that. We brought straw into the house to lie down on and rest. The farmer went outside right away, to keep an eye out. We ate, lay down with our weapons as pillows, stretched out on the straw, and left Hershl Fishbein (Yechiel Sender's son) on guard. It was four in the afternoon, and we hoped that, barring interruptions, we could get a couple of hours of rest.

3.

I was suffering from bad headaches then and fever, but I did not ask for any medical help knowing in advance that there wasn't any available. Our only remedy for all the illnesses in the forest was alcohol that the Russians used to supply us. I was therefor happy to have the opportunity to sleep a little.

No sooner had our eyes closed, than Woitek wakes us with a cry that a light was seen in the window of a hut. Our commandant, Yeager, Woitek, and I, raced outside to find out the reason for the sudden illumination. As it turned out, several farmers had returned from a party in a neighboring village, and turned the lights on in their houses. We calmed down and went back to our location.

How long I slept then, I don't know. Woitek woke me again, but this time more hastily than before. I clearly heard him say in Polish, "Guys, get up quickly, get your weapons because the Germans are here in the forest." We quickly made an analysis of the situation

[Page 276]

we found ourselves in now. A false step, or hasty actions, threatened death. We didn't have time to get completely dressed; we gathered our weapons, ready for any eventuality. Since we didn't hear any shooting, we relaxed and finished getting dressed. A farmer reported to us that 16 harnessed carriages of Germans had come up to the forest and then continued on deeper on foot. Every second wagon had a machine gun. Clearly, the Germans were coming after us. Nevertheless, we supported each other by telling jokes, in order to drive away the unease and sad thoughts. Suddenly, we saw a column of Germans coming out of the woods about 300 meters from us, guns ready to shoot. We quickly went out the window to the yard so the Germans would not see us, and took up positions behind the barn.

"No shooting," Yeager ordered, "Until the Germans are 20 meters away."

This was the right command in the situation, because the only effective thing we could do was to fire suddenly on the Germans, and then quickly withdraw. With bated breath, not feeling the cold, we lay in the snow. The column of Germans leaving the forest was still not ended. We saw them marching one behind the other. We, of course, could not allow the farmer and his family to leave, or our shelter would have been exposed immediately.

In the meantime, we checked our rifles, which in a few moments, were to play such a crucial role in our destiny. The column of Germans, sixty of them, got closer.

Our astonishment grew as the column did not wend its way over to our direction, but marched through the whole village and went off to nearby Staroscin. Soon we saw plumes of smoke and flames of fire from some huts. As the farmers later explained, the village was punished for failing to provide food for the Germans.

Seeing that the threat was not directed at us, we decided to move to the forest, so that we did not put the hospitable farmers in danger. We camouflaged our positions, and sent off a guard on horseback for observation. Here in the forest, my headache returned more intensely, and I waited for the return of the scouts with the news that the Germans had left the village, so that I could

[Page 277]

return to the hut and rest. A short time later, our two partisans returned and reported that the Germans had finished their arson activities in Staroscin, and were off to another village to deal with those farmers for failing to provide their quota. Since my headache was not going away, I drank another glass of whiskey, and asked my friends to allow me to lie down in a hut. Maybe I would get better. I yearned for the warmth of a home that would maybe drive away the illness. My friends did not reply, but when I got up to go, they assured me that in case of danger they would alert me immediately. I struggled again through the deep snow with my best friend–my machine gun–on my shoulder. It had shown me already so much help and loyalty at difficult moments. I came back to the same farmer we had left two hours before. I told him I didn't feel well, and I had to lie down, but not in a soft bed where I would fall into a deep sleep. I lay down on the hard bench, the rifle hanging from my neck, and asked the farmer that, in case of something suspicious, he should quickly wake me, so that I could join the company in the forest. I fell asleep.

4.

How long I slept, I cannot remember at all. I remember exactly how I quickly awakened, and felt an emptiness in the house. No farmer, wife or his children. Although my head was aching mercilessly, I oriented myself quickly, and determined that things were not normal, because where was it heard of that children should leave the house on such a cold winter day. I forgot about everything, and the solitude brought me to my feet. With my gun at the ready, I approached the window, and saw how the village looked deserted. Not a living person. None of our guards, and the farmer who was supposed to stay at the edge of the forest had disappeared. I went outside with the greatest of caution to orient myself to the situation. I stood still for a while deciding on which direction to go. Suddenly the stillness was interrupted by the loud noise of machine guns shooting. I reckoned it was coming from the depths of the forest. It was clear now that I didn't have a moment to lose, but that I had to find a way to save myself, because any rash step could be the end. It was clear that my friends were now engaged in battle with the

[Page 278]

Germans. Nevertheless, I decided to go to the forest knowing from experience that the trees are the best protection for partisans. There was a 200-meter field between the yard and the forest. I had to crawl or run through that distance unnoticed by the Germans. I ran a few meters and then threw myself down on the snow in order to make my way–crawling on my belly, the rifle somewhat above my head. The forward progress was slow, my strength beginning to give out. I got up again and ran some more. But the deeper snow made it almost impossible. At that moment, I heard shooting, and bullets flew over my head from different sides. I was caught in a boiler, surrounded on all sides.

I fell to the ground, aimed my rifle and returned fire on the enemy. It was quite possible that the Germans wanted to take me alive, because they began to edge over in my direction. Seeing that my bullets hit their target, they also lay down on the ground, and continued to shoot at me with more intensity. I took advantage of the moment when they were changing their position to continue creeping to the forest. My rifle was doing its job, but I was planning to save the last bullet for myself, because falling into their hands was the end, but with terrible tortures and pain. I stood up and again ran the few steps that separated me from the forest. I could find shelter there, because the Germans knew that death lurked behind every tree. I was almost at the edge of the forest, just one more effort, a few more steps–and I am saved.

My calculations were premature. Not far away, a band of Germans with fixed bayonets ran towards me. I heard a shout, "Drop your weapons, hands up!" No, I did not obey the savages. My answer was a burst of bullets. The Germans hit the ground again; I used the moment to run. But where to? I could not go back to the field. Another group of Germans were lurking there. Deeper into the forest was impossible, there were bayonets and bullets waiting there, leaving only running along the edge of the forest. I ran with extraordinary speed. I heard the familiar melody of machine guns. At that time, March 15th 1944, I could readily distinguish the difference in sound among the various types of weapons. My legs carried me forward. But not for long. I felt a warmth, and then a wetness, in my boots. Both leg were pierced by bullets. Done for. I couldn't take another step. I fell to the ground and prepared for the final battle. I loaded my rifle and got my hand-grenades ready. My revolver as well lay ready in my pouch.

[Page 279]

It would have to finish me off. I lay there and waited for the enemy. But wonder of wonders! No one appeared. The stress of waiting and the moments that had just passed took away the pain in my wounded legs. I didn't feel the blood running. I lay on the now, the sun blinding me, thinking it was a shame to die on such a nice day. But if I had to say goodbye now to life–I would send some more bullets into the Nazis. But it was quiet as if nothing had happened. I looked at my watch with the conviction that it was certainly three in the afternoon, and that night would soon fall and shelter me under its dark wings. My watch, however, said it was only 9:30 am. Now I began to feel the open wounds in my legs, the dripping blood, and general weakness. I still had to make an effort to get closer to the forest. I was already inside, among tall pine trees, when I saw a pile of twigs on the ground. I would rest there. There was no talk of going further. I tore strips off my shirt and bandaged the wounds. After applying first aid, I lay down under the branches. I lay there for three hours in great pain. The stillness around during that time meant the Germans had withdrawn. I now had to come up with a plan on how to get out of there, deal with my wounds, and continue my partisan life. One thing was clear: crawling back to the village was out, because the situation I found myself in would not be better with the farmers than with the Germans. When night fell, I crawled toward the road, and with weapon in hand, I waited for a farmer to pass by, and force him to take me to another village. Crawling on my belly, I suddenly heard the quiet sound of boots squeaking on the snow. I readied my rifle and lay there waiting. A few steps away from me, three of our partisans passed by: Shmuel Laks ("Dziad",) Yechiel Gothelf ("Heniek,") and Hershl Fishbein ("Woitek.") I could not utter a word from great joy and surprise. My friends were getting further away. I lay there in despair in case they hadn't noticed me. A thought flashed through my mind: maybe I should shoot, and attract their attention. I quickly understood that a shot could betray me and my friends. The Germans could hear it as well. However, I didn't see another way out. I took out my revolver, lifted it in the air, and put my finger on the trigger. It seems that Hershl Fishbein must have turned around, because I heard his voice calling the others. They gave me first aid, re-bandaged my wounds, and began to tell me about the events of the day.

They rightly evaluated that the group of Germans that had attacked us in the field,

[Page 280]

had been sent there to keep us focused solely in their direction, while another group attacked us from the rear. Both German groups, however, met with stiff resistance. After our situation became more complicated and dangerous, Moishe Yeager ordered us to withdraw. Just he and Hershl Fishbein would try to hold back the attacking Nazis. Clearly, both knew that such an action meant certain death for them. Yeager and Fishbein continued to shoot at the Germans while the rest of the partisans looked for better positions in order to open a concentrated fire on the enemy, and allow the two to retreat. As soon as Yeager took the first steps back, a German bullet pierced his heart, and he fell down mortally wounded, able only to shout at Hershl, "Woitek, save yourself, I am done for."

Woitek just managed to drag him away, and right after, our commander breathed his last.

5.

The three partisans took me to the village of Wola Przybyslawska not far from Markuszow, and settled me in with the woman farmer, Nalewejek, where in addition, my sister, sister-in-law, Dina and Ita Gothelf were hidden. I lay there at the farmer's for several weeks almost unconscious, with high fever, and poor expectations of surviving. In any case, the farmer woman told me later that she was certain that I was going to die. Nevertheless, I got back on my feet, and returned to our partisans in order to continue the battle up until liberation.

I will never forget the day of March 15 1944 when we forever lost our dear friend and commandant Moishe Yeager; when we experienced such a severe attack by the Germans; when I was wounded in both legs, and left a lifelong memory. And another thing–that day, the Germans had to retreat with six dead while we lost one–Moishe Yeager.

Notwithstanding the terrible blow the Markuszow partisan group had received by the loss of our commandant, and by my inability to continue to take part in missions, the group did not give up its stated goal: to extract revenge for Jewish blood. Just a few days after the battle at Meszno, they got together at a village near Lubartow in order to further consider ways to

[Page 281]

get the two parachutists from Moscow over to the other side of the Vistula. About 15 men, among them the Markuszowers Mordechai Kerschenblatt ("Martchinek"), Shmuel Laks ("Dziad"), Mechl LOTERSTEIN ("Michal"), David Ettinger, z"l ("Dudek"), and Hershl Fishbein ("Woitek") got the two parachutists safely to the location, and returned to their base in a village not far from Ostrowce in an area known as a partisan kingdom.

On the night of March 29th to 30th 1944, they marched single file, one behind the other, in order not to leave many footprints on the freshly fallen snow. After marching all night, they came to Grabina Kolonia near Lubartow. This settlement consisted of five huts surrounded by forest on all sides. In the morning the partisans knocked on the first door, and although they didn't get a clear answer from the farmer about a welcome reception, the partisans entered his house. Actually, the farmers at that time found themselves between a rock and a hard place. The fear of the partisans was no less than the fear of the Germans, but not more, because they were filled with hatred and contempt for the Germans, whereas for our guys there was a certain sentiment if not sympathy on the part of the village population. After sating our hunger, we lay down on the prepared straw with the weapons at our side. Around 11:00 am, the watch woke up the partisans to eat what the farmer's wife had prepared from their produce. In general, the partisans behaved like the well-known expression, "Where the Gypsy sleeps, he does not steal." The guys ate up the home-cooked meals, and waited for the coming night to again go out on our way. In the end, we had made it through half a day already, and what concerned the second half, we worried less about, because it gets dark early in winter, and every passing day is just a victory for partisans.

Around one am, when the partisans were cleaning their weapons, and chatting amicably about various things, a loud cannon blast was heard. One of the five huts instantly caught fire. It seems a *snariad*[1] had hit it. We immediately grabbed our weapons and looked for a good position. The cannonade did not, however, stop, and in the space of a few minutes, all the huts were standing in flames. In such a situation it was hard to find a secure place from which to defend, especially as the shooting wasn't stopping. The Germans were probably well prepared for the attack. As soon as the artillery barrage began, the machine guns began to spit

[Page 282]

in the direction of the partisans. They tried to advance on all fours in the forest, and had actually gained several dozen meters. David Ettinger and Veve Laks were badly wounded in the legs. It was impossible for the whole group to move out. Wladek and Dudek knew that they were preventing the rest of the company from seeking shelter in the woods. They therefore begged the group to get away without them, and they would attract the attention of the Germans with their fire.

The partisans insisted they could take the two wounded to the forest. They, however, refused. Their knees were shattered, and knowing the hopelessness of their situation, they had one goal now: saving their friends. So they lay on the snow reddening with their blood, and thanks to their firing and the shots of the retreating, the rest succeeded in penetrating further into the forest. They breathed more freely. But the sounds of machine gun fire meant that the German attack was not over. But they also heard the shots fired in reply by the two wounded friends–a sign they were alive and not allowing the Germans to take a step forward, making them pay with their lives.

After having gone several kilometers from the site where the two fighters remained, they decided to wait until things quieted down. After a while with no further sounds of shooting, they went back to the previous place, but not directly. That would have been too risky. So they took a circuitous route, and came to a village to find out from the farmers about the situation.

The farmer they stopped at told them with emotion and reverence about the last minutes of Dodek and Wladek, how they had killed dozens of Germans before they died. The Germans took the adult men from the village to dig trenches. They then used the farmers as a shield against Jewish bullets. The farmer reported that as soon as the Germans opened fire on the partisans, they forced the farmers to stand in the foreground and screen the Nazis. When the shooting from the partisans died down, and the attackers thought that many of them had been killed, they told us to stand aside, and they went to finish off the remaining Jews. We just heard a few shots. Suddenly it became very quiet. Nothing from the two was heard either. Now the Germans were completely certain that no partisan was left alive.

[Page 283]

When they got to the place where two red flecks of blood stood out, and saw the partisans lying there motionless, they let out a triumphant cry. Suddenly, the two corpses came to life. Their hands, as if on command, hurled grenades, and a large number of Germans said goodbye to their murderous lives. It's true that Dudek and Wladek also died from the grenade explosions that they themselves flung at the Nazis. But their death was paid for manifold times with the death of many Nazis.

Tears appeared in the farmer's eyes. Words failed him to describe in detail the Jewish bravery that he and other Polish farmers witnessed. When we let the farmers go back home, they talked only of the actions of the two well-known partisans, and spoke their names with great respect.

This is how on March 30 1944, two of our Markuszow fighters ended their lives. Their heroic death served as inspiration for continuing the fight against the murderers.

* * *

I only selected a two-week period of our partisan life, because in that time we lost good comrades, and dear sons of the Jewish people.

Honor to their glorious memory!

Translator's Footnote:

1. I have not been able to find a translation for snariad

Jewish Partisans in the Armia Ludowa

Michal LOTERSTEIN (Paris)

Reprinted from "Dos Buch fun Lublin."

Translated by Moses Milstein

1.

The shtetl of Markuszow had about 3,000 people, about 2,000 of them Jews.

In September 1939, the Germans bombed the shtetl and almost the entire shtetl was burned down. The residents fled to nearby villages. When the Germans occupied the shtetl, the residents

[Page 284]

returned, but had no place to live. They lived in cellars, and holes. The better off began to rebuild their homes with several families occupying each one.

The house that we lived in was also burned down, and my mother, sister, and I moved into my aunt, Dvoireh Laks's, house along with their family.

I worked on road building for a German company, "Baumer and Lesh," that the Judenrat had assigned me to. And from this we supported ourselves.

I did not, however, want to work for the Germans, so I later went to a village to work for a farmer.

In April 1942, the Germans issued an order for all the Jews to assemble at the gemine[1] square. We already knew from other shtetls what showing up meant, so many young people fled from the shtetl. Only a few older men and women and a few youth showed up.

The young people were, however, immediately let go, and the rest were brought to the government school building (powszechnie) where they were held overnight. My friend from the shtetl, Itche Grushchanski, lived at his grandmother's with his mother and two sisters. His father was in America. They supported themselves on what the grandmother and grandfather earned. Itche loved his grandmother very much, so he went to the Germans and asked to change places with her, to go in her place. The Germans did actually take him, but they did not set the grandmother free. And so about 400 people were taken to Opole. Many were shot along the way.

The next day, a group of people went out to collect the dead, and bury them in a Jewish cemetery.

From then on it was quiet in the shtetl; no Germans were seen. It was the quietest time. This lasted for three weeks.

At the beginning of May, another order came out that all Jews, without exception, had to assemble. The order was given to the Judenrat, who made known to us a day before, that the following day they would have to assemble, and they added on their own, that whoever was able should save themselves. And this actually happened. During the night, many Jews left the shtetl for good, and hid in the villages and forests.

[Page 285]

My sister and I fled to the farmer I had been working for. My mother left with my aunt and her family. After four days of hiding, we went to find our family, and we found them in Kamionka near Lubartow. There were more Jews there.

Three days later, the Germans conducted a raid in Kamionka and took me, and a lot of other Jews, to a camp at Leczna. We travelled on foot for 40 km. The Germans rode in wagons, one in front, and one in back, and us in the middle. The wagons went very fast, and we had to run. If someone, however, was unable to keep up, he was shot by those in the rear wagon. Someone asked along the way if he could move a little to the side and do his business. He got permission, but as soon as he stepped out, he was shot.

Along the way, we once stopped at a well to drink water. Everyone was suffering from thirst. It was mid-day in the month of June, and going along in such a hurry it was understandable that everyone rushed to the well. The Germans used that as a pretext to beat everyone over the head with rubber truncheons.

In Leczna, we worked on a farm, straightened out ditches, built a firing range, etc. One day, the Germans noticed bees in a tree. So they ordered one of us, a man in his fifties, to climb up the tree and deal with the bees. It was a very tall tree. They brought a ladder, and ordered him to climb to the top. When he reached the top of the tree, the Germans took away the ladder and he fell to the ground breaking his arms and legs. The murderers still ordered him to stand up, and when he was unable to, they put him in a small wheelbarrow, took him to the river Wieprz that flows by there, and threw him in…

After three weeks working there, I ran away.

I went to Kamionka to see my mother, and again went to the villages to hide from the Germans who were looking for me. But in a little while, the shtetl, Kamionka, was made judenrein, and wherever you tried to run, the same thing was repeated. There was no place to turn to. At that point, my mother bade farewell to my sister and I, and asked us to hide somewhere. She herself, not wishing to be a burden, went off to the designated place in Belzec[2] near Lublin.

I hid in various villages until I came to the Wole forest near Markuszow. There I found Jews from the shtetl. However, I suddenly became sick. I felt terrible pain in my chest, and could hardly move. I knew of a place where my uncle, Mendl Ettinger, and his family, were hiding, and barely made it up to the attic of a farmer. But that same night, two young Poles with rifles came to the attic, dragged us down outside, put us up against the wall of the houses, and threatened to shoot us. They didn't say a word being afraid we would recognize them. They communicated with gestures. So they showed us with their hands that they wanted money, pointed the guns at us as if to shoot us if we didn't give them money. My uncle and I easily recognized the guys. One was the brother of the farmer who my uncle gave all his money away to, even building him a house. That very farmer had refused to let my uncle spend the night there a few nights before. The young guys, it seems, followed my uncle to find my uncle's hiding place, and now they were coming to extract money from him. We didn't give them any money, however, and they went away. They were Bronislaw Kozak, and Boleslav Banaszek, both from Przybyslawica.

This confrontation with both of them was useful to me later. Thanks to that, I was taken into the partisans. It happened like this: After I left my uncle after that night, I ran into a few of my friends: Shmuel Laks (in Israel today), his brother Veve Laks (fell in battle with the partisans), and Shmuel Rubinstein. We had already heard of partisans in the forests, and we were looking for a way to get to them. A couple of days later, we met several partisans at a farmer's–three Russians, and a Pole. We asked them to take us with them. They turned us down because they had no weapons for us. So I went off to see the two guys who had attacked us. We took their rifles, and took off for the partisans. I also took along with me my sister and her friend, Sima Bronski, 22 years old. They were both killed later along with 40 more Jews, as I will later relate.

2.

My partisan life began in November 1942. My sister and her friend, my three friends:

[Page 287]

the Laks brothers, Shmuel Rubinstein, and I left for the Zalbe-Zeks forest. Forest life began full of hardships, danger, lurking in lairs, small *zemliankes* (bunkers dug in the earth). Often, very often, we had to sleep under the open sky. In winter, we would sometimes wake up covered in snow. We often had to lie in mud, or crawl through swamps. We were often hunted and persecuted by an enemy immeasurably stronger and better equipped. It was a hard and terrible life yet full of inspiring and exalting battle.

When I think back on those days, after so many years, I don't remember the struggles, the stresses, the dangers. I remember, though, and will never forget, the high-minded feeling that we all shared when we took a rifle in our hands, and became free people because of that. We defended our lives, our human dignity, and our honor. We not only defended our lives and our honor, but we took revenge for all our dead, for all our murdered families, for our entire people. We helped to defeat and destroy this very war machine, the bloody Nazi powers.

Maybe at that time, when we were in the forest, those thoughts were still vague, but we felt it to be true. Above all, we were driven by the thought, "Never surrender! Resist!"

The beginning was a difficult one. We were 7 men in all, and we had 4 rifles and 20 bullets in total. We lived in the Kozlowka forest (Lublin territory, 7 km from Lubartow) from where big actions could not be entertained. We treated each bullet like a gem. It was our only guarantee. Our main activity was to procure food. That was not so easy in those days. We often had to threaten with our weapons to get a piece of bread or a piece of pork. We only left the forest at night.

The partisan movement in those months was not widespread. We had no connection to other groups. Slowly, the situation began to change. A big change came in December 1942 when about 100 Jewish prisoners-of-war escaped from Lublin, from the Lipowa 7 camp. They were trained soldiers and came with some weapons. Their leader was Koganovitch who later fell after a short

[Page 288]

time, about 6 weeks later. The prisoners divided themselves into smaller groups, and established ties. Most of them fell heroically in the countless battles that took place in the span of two years.

Our group also received about 10 men from the ex-prisoners-of-war. Now we were a force. The leadership of our group was undertaken by a trained warrior, a Soviet first-lieutenant (starshi lieutenant) from Kharkov who escaped from German imprisonment. We called him Toliek. His memory is cherished by all the partisans of that neighborhood.

At the same time, there was another group in the area led by a Markuszow young man, Kerschenblatt. That group consisted of 12 men, operated not far from us, but did not stay together long. In December 1942, or January 1943 they were betrayed by the farmer they were staying with. Of the twelve men, ten fell in battle with the Germans. Kerschenblatt and one more joined our group.

We knew the neighborhood extremely well, and under Toliek's command, our group developed an active agenda. I soon experienced my first battle. It happened like this: Our commander, Toliek, ordered us to take away a machine gun 12 km from us. We were 5 men. When we got to the spot, day was already beginning. Someone noticed us, and informed the Polish police that were based 5 km away. The police soon arrived and the shooting began. We easily drove away the 7-8 policemen who ran away accompanied by the jeers of the farmers. That same day, we marched 25 km, and in broad daylight, crossed the Lublin-Warsaw road being cleared of snow by the farmers. Around them were stationed German guards. The Germans were so surprised that they didn't dare stop us. When we stopped to eat something a while later, the Germans attacked us.

This time it was a more serious fight than with the police. For the first time, I heard bullets whistling around me. I shot in the direction the bullets were coming from, as if half-asleep, but at the same time all my senses were weirdly alert and tense. After about three quarters of an hour the shooting stopped. The Germans withdrew. The road was clear. But one of us, an escaped

[Page 289]

prisoner-of-war from Lipowa, was wounded in the leg. He died soon after from his wounds. At that time, we had no way to help the wounded, no drugs, no medical help.

The next day we were back at our base. Toliek praised us a lot. We were very proud of our first trial under fire. That same day, however, we were forced to leave our base, and go deeper into the forest. A German division which was coming from the front for rest, was combing through the neighborhood seeking partisans and Jews who were hidden in the forest.

From October-November 1942, the Wole forest, 5 km from Markuszow, was home to about 500-600 hidden Jews, most from the small shtetls in the Lublin territory. When the decree to go to Belzec came out, they fled to the forest and to the very small villages. They had no weapons. The partisans helped them with food and money as they were able, but more than that they couldn't do. There were not enough weapons. Just a few of these hidden Jews survived the war.

I personally know 60-70 Jews, men and women, who survived the war in the Parczew forests. The partisans helped them with food, and even left a rifle and ammunition with them to defend themselves. A rifle was worth more than anything then.

The significance of a weapon became especially clear that day. That same day, actually, when the Germans captured 50-60 unarmed Jews in the forest, they also attacked a bunker where there were also 6 Lipowa prisoner-of-war. The 6 boys defended themselves heroically. They caught the hand grenades the Germans threw in and threw them back. With their machine guns, they were able to block the entrance to the bunker, and hold them off for 8 hours. When it got dark, the Germans had to withdraw. Only one of the heroic boys–with the name of Stengl–died of his wounds. The other five survived.

In the winter of 1942-1943, we carried out a bunch of actions along with another group of 10 armed Jews led by Ephraim Bleichman. The group had earlier operated in the Lubartow-Kamionka area. We used to meet regularly several times a month. One time, a few of us were at a farmer's. We ate, and drank

[Page 290]

some whiskey. Around 8:00 am, a car suddenly arrived in the farmer's yard, and two Germans came into the yard demanding eggs, and butter. Without waiting for an answer they proceeded to go into the house. We didn't even have time to look around. Quick as lightening, two of us got behind the door. As soon as the first German opened the door, Ephraim Bleichman stabbed him with a bayonet. The second German had a machine-pistol (automatic). He ran out and began to defend himself. We chased after him. One of us, a small young kid, grabbed the long, tall German and began to wrestle the automatic from him. Meanwhile we came up. We killed the German immediately. That's how we stole our first automatic weapon.

In February 1942, we created a new bunker with all the "comforts." That means, a store of water, plank beds, etc. There were about 10 of us partisans. About 30 young Jewish kids, mostly Lubliners, lived on the base with us. They had no weapons. There were also several girls among them including my sister.

At the time, we got connected via a farmer with the leader of the underground PPR[3] (Polish worker's party) in the area. We knew him by the name of Genek. Through him, Toliek got connected with the Armia Ludowa organization (the left-oriented Polish partisan movement which was led by communists), and through it was selected as the director of all the partisan groups in the Lublin-Markuszow-Lubartow triangle. The Jews hiding in the forest also came under his command. Toleik was planning to begin large diversion activities against the enemy, but fate decided otherwise.

After having been there for a few weeks, a group of four guys went off to get a machine gun. They took 4 of our 10 rifles, and promised to return in three days. When they had not returned, Toliek sent me, two Jews and a Pole out to look for them. We left at 3:00 am. After a two-day search we located them, and told them that Toliek wanted them back immediately. They finally agreed, and after two days we all went back to our base. When we got there, we were greeted by a strange, sinister quiet. With beating hearts, we approached the bunker. But nothing remained, everything flattened to the earth.

[Page 291]

A terrible feeling enveloped us. We began to run hither and thither, not wanting to believe that all our friends were dead. But we quickly learned the horrible news. Six hours after we had left, strong German forces surrounded the bunker. There were machine guns on all sides. There was no possibility of getting out of the bunker. The armed ones defended the bunker until the very last. The Germans then distributed straw around the entrance, and set it on fire. The smoke filled the bunker and suffocated the people. Those who had not suffocated were finished off by the Germans. Everyone was killed, the six partisans and the thirty unarmed kids. Among the dead were my sister, and our commander, Toliek. This occurred on February 19 1943.

3.

Eight of us were left. We chose an escapee from Lipowa, Yeager, as commander. First of all, we had to get through the winter. But we were not satisfied with the concerns of merely existing. The desire for vengeance seethed in us. We began to look for new alliances. Two Poles, escapees from Germany, came to us. Through the winter months, we had a series of smaller skirmishes with individual policemen or Germans. We had one clash with a group from the AK[4] (the Polish military organization led by the government-in-exile in London) which had killed two Poles in Litwinow (Pulawy powiat).

In spring 1943, we finally found Genek and renewed contact with the Armia Ludowa. Genek sent us to a certain place where, he told us, Mietek, (underground name of colonel Moczar) the leader of the whole partisan movement in Lublin territory, was supposed to be coming. We went to the designated place, and met Mietek. He brought underground newspapers, proclamations, and also relayed greetings from a big Jewish partisan division under the leadership of Chil. (Captain Chil, alias Yechiel Grinspan).

Our group was given the name, "partisan group under the name Emilia Platter," the name of the renowned female Polish fighter. Mietek advised us to stay on our base in the meantime, and lead the actions from there. From that point on, we knew we were no longer alone. One month later,

[Page 292]

the well-known Jewish partisan leader, Bolek (Colonel Aleph), came to visit us. Our base was in the Parczew forests on the other side of the river Wieprz. On the other side, there were Polish groups, and Captain Chil's group. We developed active sabotage tactics.

We frequently carried out attacks on the Polish police, on German cars on the roads, and derailed German troop trains. At first we unscrewed the rails by hand. Later we got explosives.

Our group now consisted of 10 men. There were among us people with various political convictions. As far as I can recall, it never led to political discord. We lived in brotherhood, closely connected by the daily struggle.

Soon, Ephraim Bleichman's group united completely with ours. We were now 17 men. Right on the first day of Bleichman's group arriving, we had occasion to repel an attack in the village of Lugow by the NSZ (Narodowe Sily Zbrojne–a fascist Polish organization that collaborated with the Armia Krajowa and the Germans).

We continually strengthened our war actions. We blew up German trains with the aid of 16 kg unexploded airplane bombs that were lying around here and there from 1939. Through all of summer 1943, we conducted big and small operations. We operated in an area with a diameter of around 60 km. Sometimes we got as close as a couple of kilometers from the city Lublin.

I would like to describe several of these battles.

In summer 1943, we attacked my hometown, Markuszow. The Germans had established a barter facility where the farmers would bring eggs and receive sugar. We had an order to attack the station, and to divide the sugar with the farmers. While leaving, we were attacked by a German division. It was already getting dark, and in the darkness, we were able to break through their lines. One of us, a Kamionka lad who had the automatic, was killed. Two men were wounded, one lightly, the other seriously. The latter is in Israel today (1952). It is a mystery to me how he could have overcome his serious wounds. (When I last saw him, he still had a bullet in his body).

[Page 293]

I also remember an attack we conducted in the summer of 1943 on a small German garrison in Gut Leszic (on the border between Pulawy and Lublin powiats). This particular garrison had always interfered greatly with our sabotage activities. We decided to get rid of it. Our connection in the village was the blacksmith who gave us information on the garrison: Every morning farmers would come to the fields to dig potatoes. The guards were used to them. We had to take advantage of the opportunity to get rid of the guards, and kill the rest. We left with sixteen men. Shmuel Rubinstein, and a young Polish partisan volunteered to disarm the guards. We hid in the wheat field. While disarming the watch, the Pole fired a shot. The Germans heard this, and began shooting. The shooting lasted for two hours, and we had to withdraw. We killed one German. We had no losses ourselves.

Relations with the farmers improved considerably at that time. In February 1944, we received the order to go to the base in the Parczew forests where Captain Chil's group was located. The Polish groups also left with us. When we got there, we encountered a lot of Russian and Polish partisans.

Soon after arriving, we received a mission to lead two paratroopers across the Vistula at Opole. Eight of us partisans went: 5 Jews, 2 Poles, and 1 Polish woman. After traveling 5 km, we stopped at a house near Wole forest. In the morning, I was on guard, and I saw a line of Germans coming out of one side of the forest. I woke up the gang. The Germans, however, passed quietly by, went further into the village, and set fire to a house. We took advantage of the opportunity, and went into the forest. We lay there for 3 hours. Then we sent out a scout. But as soon as he left, the Germans appeared as if from under the earth. Shooting began. We got up on a hill, and defended strongly. Bullets flew around us. Our commander, Yeager, lifted his head up for a second in order to take ammunition out of his bag. He gave a shudder and fell down dead. It wasn't until it became dark that we got out of there.

I have to relate the following episode: My friend, Shmuel Rubinstein, felt very bad that day. It was the start of Typhus. He fell asleep and didn't hear the whole commotion. When he

[Page 294]

awoke, there was no one in the house anymore. He picked up his rifle and went out. What did he see? Germans everywhere. But Shmuel didn't panic. Instead of running away, which would have meant certain death, he grabbed his rifle and began shooting. The Germans, who were no less surprised than he, were confused for a moment. He used that moment to get into the forest. He was, however, wounded in both legs, and had to lie down. He had hand grenades and a pistol. The Germans were afraid to go into the forest. At night, as we were passing by, we heard him call, "Stop, or I'll shoot." We recognized his voice, and were greatly relieved. The Germans were no longer here. We hid Shmuel with a farmer while his wounds healed, and at the same time, he got over his Typhus.

When we got back to the base, our group of 4 Jews and 2 non-Jews received an assignment to accompany the Polish activists, Drobner (a leader of the PPS), Hanneman (PPS), Osubka Morawski, and Spichalski, across the front. They took them across the Bug to a Russian partisan group and came back safely. Of the 4 Jewish comrades, I remember Wladek Wohlstein (today, 1952, in Israel), and Morel (in Poland). I don't remember the other two.

In March 1944, while returning to the previous base, we had a hard, loss-filled, battle with the Germans. There were 16 of us. The Germans arrived around 3 in the afternoon. When we ran out of our quarters, bullets came flying at us from three sides at once. The Germans also fired at us with light field-artillery. That was the first time we experienced what artillery fire was like. For the first time, confusion arose among us. One hundred meters from me, my comrade, Veve Laks was lying down his knee shot through. He was unable to move anymore. He pleaded that we take his rifle and leave his pistol at his side. He defended himself to the last bullet, which he saved for himself, so that he would not fall into the enemy's hands alive.

In the same heroic manner my comrade and cousin, David Ettinger, of Markuszow fell. He shot himself with his last bullet.

A bullet slammed into the cartridge belt I was wearing. It is a miracle that the bullets I was wearing did not explode and blow me to pieces. None of the bullets were any good after.

[Page 295]

Of the 16 men, 7 were killed, and 6 wounded. Only three emerged unscathed.

4.

On May 15 1944, Rola-Zymierski[5] visited our base. He gathered all the groups on the base together and gave a speech. There were about 600 of us then, 400 Russians, and 200 Jews and Poles. There were about 40 men from captain Chil's group. Rola-Zymierski promoted me to corporal. Soon after, we received the order to leave the Parczew forests and transfer to the Janow forests. 20-30 men were left from captain Chil's (Yechiel Grinspan) group.

Several hundred men left. We were not badly armed, and we had a radio. The first leg was from Parczew to the Kozlowka forest. From there we went over to the Wole forests. There, for the first time, the Germans shot at us from airplanes. At the same time, strong German divisions surrounded the forest.

At 6:00 am, a big battle began which ended with a big victory for us. Thirty to forty Germans were killed. From the forest we saw how the German airplanes were landing to pick up the wounded officers. We would have killed them all, but they were protected by a river on one side. After a 14-hour battle, the Germans retreated. We had only one casualty.

From the Wole forests we travelled all night to the Vistula. Four in the morning, we came close to Naleczow in the village of Rablow. We had barely got ourselves set up there when 6 German planes flew in and began shooting at the village. We all ran out to the field. The airplanes were flying very low. Their bullets caused a fire in the house where the general staff was quartered, destroyed the radio, and killed the operator. Fortunately, there was a small forest nearby. We went in there. The airplanes continued to circle over the forest shooting it up with bullets. Soon the trees were no more than sticks, but this was only an introduction. Cars with German soldiers began arriving from the SS Viking division. They also had light field artillery. They assaulted the forest for a couple of hours, shrapnel exploding around us. Six airplanes constantly circled

[Page 296]

over our heads, sending volley after volley at us from their machine guns. Our order was not to respond, but to conserve ammunition. A few hours later, our commander, Captain Zemsto, ordered us, with incendiary bullets, to set fire to the village behind which the German artillery was positioned. Maybe the Germans had not properly set up their artillery, because the shells always flew over our heads. We waited like this until night. Seeing as we did not respond, thinking perhaps we had all been killed, the Germans ordered an attack in the evening. They entered the forest. We were waiting for that. Our nerves were stretched to the limit from lying for hours under bombardment. Now they could be released. We began a fusillade that it was a pleasure to see. Like savages, we threw ourselves on the Germans, clubbed them with our rifle butts, with sticks, stabbed them with knives. Frightened, they began to raise their hands in surrender. But it did not help them. We killed around 150 Germans. We lost 40 men killed or wounded.

Our situation was still terrible. Leaving the forest was impossible. We were surrounded by a numerically stronger and better-equipped enemy. Captain Zemsto therefore ordered us to split into groups of 10 men. Every group had to take one wounded and break through the encirclement. The plan actually succeeded. A lot of the groups managed to break out in the Janow forests, and some, including our group and our commander, returned to the Parczew forests. Captain Zemsto, however, did not get there. While withdrawing, he was killed by an errant bullet.

After returning to the base, we had to reorganize our groups again. They joined us (together with captain Chil's group) temporarily to the large partisan group, commanded by the Soviet general, Baranowski. Now the partisans were no longer isolated clusters, but a well organized, well-armed, disciplined army led mostly by Soviet officers parachuted in. We were now in the thousands. The following episode was characteristic of the new situation: One day, the Germans attacked our headquarters, and threw a couple of grenades into the building. Someone said they should abandon the position, but Boronowski said,

[Page 297]

"Those days are over. Russians do not retreat anymore."

5.

During the few weeks we were in Baranowski's otriad, we found ourselves in a hard fight with the German forces. Our group was stationed as the vanguard on a road, when quite unexpectedly, we were attacked by Germans. After a battle during which we lost 6 men, we were forced to withdraw back to the main force in the forest. Soon German airplanes arrived and began to bomb the forest. The bombs, however, failed to create any great damage as they exploded over our heads upon touching the leaves of the trees. Near us, there was a strong, Russian combat otriad, commanded by colonel Charney, (distinguished by the title, "Hero of the Soviet Union"). We dug trenches. The Germans tried to break through a few times, but our machine guns kept them away. About 100 dead Germans lay around our trenches. Many Jewish lads distinguished themselves in the fighting.

As day broke, Charney and his otriad left the forest for the village. The partisans went up on the roofs and fired at the German rear. We could now leave the forest and return to our base in the Parczew forests, accompanied and protected by Soviet airplanes.

In May 1944, a group of 80 paratroopers landed from the new Polish army created by the Soviet Union. Their leader was, as far as I can recall, major Klim. They didn't stay long, and soon went to another neighborhood. After the above-mentioned battle that we carried out in Baranowski's otriad, the paratroopers returned after they had fulfilled their mission. We were now in captain Chil's group along with 50 men, and they took us out of Baranowski's otriad again and joined us back to the battalion in the Armia Ludowa commanded by Mietek.

6.

The front got closer every day. A paradoxical situation was created. The closer the front came, the harder conditions became for the partisans. Between the German and Soviet

[Page 298]

armies, the field was getting smaller and smaller, and the partisans had less and less space to maneuver. Aside from that, the Germans now had their big forces here, their armies from the front with artillery, tanks, and aviation. Nevertheless, we now developed battle activities larger than if they had not been there. We had already participated in open battles against entire divisions, destroyed trains, blown up bridges behind German lines, and captured and destroyed German ammunition and supply storehouses.

The last few weeks before liberation, a Polish colonel, Grzegorz, took over the command of the section we were part of. Our headquarters and base were now in the shtetl, Ostrow.

At that time, several German divisions that were coming from the front carried out a huge raid against the partisans, surrounding the entire forest. There was no exit from any side. Our group was behind a cemetery. Suddenly, we were confronted with very strong German force. After a firefight of about a half hour, we withdrew to the Parczew forest which was full of partisans then. The Germans had surrounded the whole forest. Bitter struggles erupted everywhere. The Germans tried to break into the forest and "clean it out." The partisans on their side wanted to break out of the encirclement. Baranowski and his Russian otriad succeeded in breaking out. The units of the Armia Ludowa received the order to carry out the often well-proven tactic of breaking into smaller groups, and get out like that. Our unit of about 100 to 150 men came up against such strong opposition that we had to retreat into the forest. Night had fallen, and in the darkness we lost touch with each other. We ended up 8 people (among them captain Chil's brother and wife). We spent the night in the forest and vowed to break out no matter the cost. When we got to the edge of the forest the next morning, the Germans had gone. We soon found the others.

Now the situation became very strange. We had been hearing the cannonades day and night of the Russian artillery getting closer. Our hearts were jumping for joy in anticipation of the impending liberation. But at the same time, we were getting squeezed between the two fronts. We could not move. There was shooting from every direction. It was good to remember that we had fought up to

[Page 299]

the day of liberation, and it was hard to be lying somewhere immobile while bullets from the Germans and Russians shooting at each other were flying over our heads. All this time we had had no fear of death. In truth, we never even thought of the fact that we could die. But now the desire to live, and to finally see liberation, was great. Once we lay a whole day in a meadow while the Soviets and Germans carried on a duel. Luckily, the bullets flew over us. At night, we went on further. In the morning, we saw a column of German tanks. We quickly went back into the forest. The tanks went by, but one stayed behind. When we approached with drawn weapons we saw that the crew was already dead.

Around us, shooting was still going on. On the next day, it became quiet. A bizarre, unusual silence we had not heard for weeks. We met a farmer who said, "You can come out now." The Soviet army was there. We were liberated a day before Lublin. We were near Wlodawa at the time.

The Soviet army received us very well. The soldiers and officers embraced us and kissed us. By the 26th of July, my friends and I were already in Lublin.

It felt strange for us to see a big city, walk through the streets, live in a house with furniture, with electric lights, and see women wearing city clothes. But the war was still going on. Before anything else, we had to continue fighting the enemy. There was little time to think of anything else.

Our partisan life was ending. We felt that we had carried out an important mission. We not only saved our own lives, but we took revenge for our dead, and saved the honor and dignity of our people.

I am certain that many Jews would have taken part in the partisan movement if they could have overcome the difficulty that was the most important at the beginning: where to get weapons. A rifle, a revolver, in 1942 those were the most valuable things. A lot of young people would have become partisans in the little shtetls I was personally familiar with had they had weapons. Later, at the end of 1943 and in 1944 there were already enough weapons. But by then, the Germans had already concluded their bloody work. In the Lubliner territory, there were virtually no Jews left…

Translator's Footnotes:

1. Municipal administrative division
2. Belzec was the third largest extermination camp
3. Polska Partia Robotnicza
4. Armia Krajowa. Home Army. Perpetrators of many Jewish murders.
5. General Rola-Zymierski,1890-1989, communist agent and leader of Polish Army created by Soviet Union.

[Page 300]

A Group of Partisans at Plouszowice[1]

Alter Rasset (Paris)

Translated by Moses Milstein

At the first deportation to Belzec[2], I found myself with my mother among the unlucky who were sent to their death in this camp. My father alone was hiding in the "*kryjowka*"[3] he made himself in the house.

As we approached Belzec, and saw the camp from a distance, my mother and I ran away, and in spite of the fire the Germans opened on us, we managed to get to the village of Plouszowice near Lublin.

In that village, a farmer hid us in a hole in the ground where he usually stored his potatoes in the winter. We stayed in that hole for about 6 weeks, until one night father met a farmer he knew well when he went out looking for food. The farmer hugged and kissed my father and reminded him of the time when he, Reuben Rasset, had helped him out during a hard time, lending him 80 zlotys to buy wood to finish his house. He repaid it a while later.

He displayed a readiness to hide us from the Germans. Incidentally, the farmer was a big crook and a swindler, and interestingly, such farmers displayed the readiness to sacrifice themselves to help a Jew.

At first, the wife was against her husband's plan, but later, when my father gave them money for everyone, she became a little softer.

It's possible that the farmer knew my father had money and helped us for that reason, but the fact is there were Poles who betrayed Jews when the money ran out. Fortunately, it was different in our case.

We dug a large hole in the stable. It had one entrance. There was always a special scaffold of lime that fit into the entrance hole, and was covered with straw above.

We lived through the war, with certain interruptions, in that hole, until the Soviet army entered Lublin.

[Page 301]

About those interruptions, I will relate several episodes that I remember.

There were other Jewish families in the village of Plouszowice aside from our family of six, which, just like us, survived the war in hiding. The farmers in the area around us knew about that, but none of them could point out, not to the Germans and not to the collaborators, our hiding place.

In the area of the village, Plouszowice, several Jews founded a partisan band under the leadership of a certain Mordechai from Markuszow who they called Martchinek (Mordechai Kerschenblatt). This Martchinek and his partisan band, in which there were many Markuszowers and Lubliners (Unfortunately, I don't remember their names), constantly carried out attacks on the farmers, and forced them to give them food and weapons. The farmers had to comply, but at the same time they were looking for a way to get out of it.

One day, when the whole band of partisans was in a farmer's house, he sent his daughter out to the Germans to inform them of the opportunity to destroy the partisans.

The SS quickly surrounded the house and began to shoot with machine guns at the partisans. Martchinek, the leader, was the only one to get away from the shooting and hide in a neighboring stable.

The Germans saw this, and wanted to set the stable on fire. They did not, however, carry out the plan, not wanting to bring harm to the farmers. They left the farmers on guard with the task of killing Martchinek as soon as he left the barn.

Martchinek left the stable several hours after he saw the Germans leaving. The farmers came at him with axes and scythes, but Martchinek had a few grenades with him and killed about 15 of them, and forced the rest to flee. Then, for revenge, he set fire to several farmers' houses.

While running away from there, he came on another of his band, Itzchak, who had managed to escape from the German raid.

Both found out about our hiding place, and came to us. We, of course, hid them. The farmers, however,

[Page 302]

found out about this, and wanted to force our landlord to turn us all in.

Our farmer did not want to give us up, but after he and his family started to receive beatings, he ordered us to leave the hiding place.

We had no choice but to obey.

Martchinek suggested we go to the forest nearby where there were Jews hiding in bunkers. We did not go along with his suggestion, but hung around the village for six weeks before the previous farmer took us back in.

A while later, Martchinek came to see us again, and told us that the Germans had found out about the hiding places in the forest where he suggested we go, and had set fire to all the bunkers, and killed all the Jews.

With the arrival of the Red Army, we left our hiding places, and with our own eyes we saw the Germans that the Russians had captured in the death camp, hung in Majdanek. We lived to see the day of vengeance.

Translator's Footnotes:

1. From the Book of Lublin.
2. Belzec was the first killing center in Operation Reinhard. About 500,000 Jews were killed there between November 1941 and December 1942.
3. Polish word meaning "hiding place."

My Child Wanted to Live
(Memories of the Occupation Years)

Esther Zilbering

Translated by Moses Milstein

Before the German killers occupied our shtetl, they first sent their messengers and harbingers–bomber airplanes, against a defenseless population. The same was repeated in Markuszow: Murderous air attacks from German airplanes on a small, defenseless shtetl that, from the military standpoint, had no significance. The bombings were always so intense and deadly that we wanted the Germans to march in already rather than suffer the hell of constant flights. It was not until the killers had occupied the whole region, that the bombings stopped. Now the enemy was more real, closer, and its murderous trade was carried out using other methods.

[Page 303]

Sholem Maidener had a daughter who was beautiful, but mentally ill. The parents guarded the unfortunate girl like a precious jewel, especially during the occupation. The family lived in the Christian neighborhood. When the Poles brought the news to the Germans about the mentally ill girl, the murderers went straight to her house, dragged her out to the street, stripped her naked in the snow and cold, and began to pour cold water on her. The desperate mother begged the Germans to leave the poor sick girl alone. She received a brutal answer, "Don't be so upset. You'll get your daughter back. When she's dead. We will kill all the Jews, like dogs!"

When I saw the savagery of the Germans toward the sick girl, and heard such words, it became immediately clear to me that we could expect nothing good from these degenerates. They would certainly carry out the threats about "killing the Jews like dogs," and I began to think immediately about various plans on how to flee from the shtetl.

In 1940, I went to the village of Bogucin, and I managed to get in with a farmer. I lived for a whole year in the village, and hardly felt there was a war going on. We got on so well with the farmers, that they even promised us that in case of danger, they would do everything to save us. They kept their word. As soon as an order came to the *soltis*[1] that the remaining Jews must assemble at a certain place, he informed us of that immediately so we could go and hide. That was at the beginning of April. We went to the village of Szebrowice. After being there for 6 days, another order came that all Jews in the Lublin region had to assemble in Belzec. A ghetto would be established for us there. I did not want, under any circumstances, to be separated from my old mother, sister, brother, in-laws and children. That was why we decided that all of us would report to Belzec, because there was no place to hide anymore.

Since some Bogucin farmers owed us money, my husband and I were going to go there to collect our debts. We were getting ready to go when we suddenly heard our 5-year-old say, "I'm not staying alone. I want to go with you."

We, the parents, did not think it was a good idea, because the road was full of dangers. Better to leave such a baby at home. But the child cried hard, and my sister spoke up,

[Page 304]

"If a child is so determined at a time like this, it has to be taken to wherever the parents are going. Maybe it is fated that you will survive on account of the child."

Friday at midnight, we set out on the road. We knocked on farmers' huts, they opened their doors, but not one debtor would give us any money. They all argued that come Monday, after the market, they hoped to make enough money to repay the debt. There was no choice but to wait until Monday.

Monday, very early, Goldeleh Aaron Leib's, knocked on our door, and straight away told us the shocking news: the Jews who had showed up at Belzec were no longer among the living. Among them– our entire family who could not wait for us after we went away to Bogucin, and went to Belzec. We were shattered by the news, and did not know what to do next.

Later–a new order: If a hidden Jew were found in the village, the farmers would be killed, and their houses burned down. This news was brought to us by the farmers. My child said, "Mameh, are they going to shoot us? Why?"

"No my child, they're not going to shoot us. The Germans won't do anything bad to the Jews."
"Not true, mameh. The kids I was playing with in the village told me they're going to kill all the Jews."
I didn't know how to respond. I asked, "You won't cry when we are lying hidden, and there won't be enough food?"
"I don't want any food. As long as we will be hidden from the Germans. I want to live!"
The child hugged me with her little arms, and began to kiss my cheeks passionately. Tears flowed from both our eyes.

But there was no place to go, or to hide. We crept into a stable without telling the farmer. That meant– staying without food. We sat there for a few days ensconced in the straw. Hunger gnawed and thirst burned. The child cried softly so I would not see or hear. But it could not go on long like this. The child called out one day, "Mameh, it would have been better to go to Belzec. I wouldn't be feeling any hunger now."

I also came to the conclusion that it would certainly have been better to die rather than to hear such words from a child. However, I had to decide: to live or die. At around 2:00 am, we left the stable. It was winter. The snow had

[Page 305]

covered everything. The cold bores into our bones, and we feel its bite. The farmers are asleep, everyone in their own bed, feeling secure, unlike us, condemned to death. We marshal our courage, and I knock at the door of a farmer I know. He opens the door, and on seeing us, he says, "If you're still alive, you will survive."

We break out in tears, and beg him to have pity on us, to allow us to get into a hole in the ground where we could wait out the hard times. He agrees, just asking if we have enough money. I reply that money we didn't have, but if it becomes necessary, we will work something out. The farmer agreed to make a bunker for us on the condition that whatever we have to sell, we should give to him, because he doesn't want us personally to do it, and end up betraying us and him. He proposed selling everything himself and giving us the money. It was clear to us that he wasn't concerned so much about our survival as the money. There were many cases in those days, especially in 1942, when the farmers first took the money from Jews, and after killed them themselves, or betrayed them to the Germans. I knew of the case of Ber-Mordechai Mattes's who gave a large sum of money to a farmer to hide him. Then the farmer led him to the forest and murdered him. As we reminded ourselves now of this fact, we felt that the Bogucin farmer who we were asking for help, who was displaying friendship, was actually after our money. So we got away from him, and again began to blunder around in the cold and darkness of night, without a goal, without a purpose. The child had no energy left to walk. We carried her in our arms, and we were falling on our feet ourselves.

Another hut. A familiar farmer. We know he is very poor, but for that reason we knock at his door. He greets us quite warmly, but he explains that by hiding Jews he not only places himself in danger, but also the lives of his children. We begin to plead. Knowing how pious he is, I promise him that if we survive the war we will convert, and he will be our godfather. The idea appeals strongly to the farmer. He says we are really not like other Jews, and we should change our religion. But as concerns letting us in, he doesn't want to jeopardize his entire family.

My daughter, who spoke Polish very well, started to cry, and began to beg the farmer to protect us.

"I'm not leaving here. I'm afraid they're going to shoot me. I want to live!"

[Page 306]

I added "Better to die quietly with you here, than die at the hands of the Nazis."

These last words could even move a stone. The 18-year-old son of the farmer, who had been listening to our discussion, began to beg his father to take us in. Finally the farmer let himself be persuaded. He just warned us that he couldn't give us any food, because he himself was a pauper. His son called to my husband, and the two of them dug a hole in the stall. Alive, we let ourselves down into the grave.

We lived in that grave for one and a half years. From time to time, my husband would get out at night, and go to farmers he knew, and acquire food. But we didn't enjoy the meager food, because we were always getting reports about the death of our very nearest ones. That's how they brought me the terrible news that my brother, Avigdor, had been killed–then that my cousin was also no longer among the living. They found him shot to death in the middle of a field. One sad tiding after another. We also were not sure we would survive, because death lurked around every corner.

On July 24 1944 we left our grave. You can imagine our appearance, the wildness, dirt and pallor of our faces. In such a situation, after such horrible experiences, the first minutes of freedom could not be received with the proper reaction. After sitting in a grave for such a long time, our emotions had become blunted, our spirits broken, and constant sorrow gnawed at our hearts. I am unable to relate everything that we went through. But the fragments described above mirror generally those hard days when our child, together with us, struggled for life, and in that struggle, we emerged the victors.

Translator's Footnote:

1. In Poland, a village magistrate

[Page 307]

Two Sisters Speak
Fradl Zilberman-Oshenked and Rivkeh Zilberman-Kesselbrenner

Testimony recorded by M. Nachshon (Capa)

Translated by Moses Milstein

Experiences of Fradl Zilberman

After the first bombardment, my family, like most of the Jewish residents of Markuszow, fled to the villages. We lived in Wole for over six weeks, until one day in October 1939, Germans came to our place in the village, confiscated our few poor possessions, and one of them pointed his rifle at my mother demanding to know here my father was. If he does not receive the right answer, he will shoot. My frightened mother picked up a child in her arms and began to scream. This time, the Germans did not carry out their threat. After stealing our most valuable things, they left.

That visit from the Germans, moreover in a small quiet village where it seemed we could wait out the first stormy days of the war, made me think of running further, of abandoning this place where the German boot rules and brutally crushes human dignity. I was 19 years old then, and leaving home seemed to me to be a frenzied fantasy. I told this to my parents when I was sharing my thoughts with them. Nevertheless, my parents, who I was strongly attached to, were unable to dissuade me. The only question was: where to run to? Could I, a young girl, embark on such a dangerous road alone?

Since I had a married sister, Rivkeh, in Miechow, I decided to go to her for advice. I went off to Miechow on foot, and there my sister told me that the Germans had taken her husband to work in Kamionka, in a camp for Jews, after beating and torturing him. He had to do forced labor–

[Page 308]

and without food. Later, they took the Jews to the river, made them take off their clothes, and go into the water. It was the end of October, when the weather was very cold. They forced them to stand in the water for several hours.

As soon as my brother-in-law returned safely home, as a result of the torture he had experienced, and from observing what the Germans were capable of doing to the Jewish people, he got together with several friends, and they went to the river, Bug, the border then between Russia and Germany.[1] When we got the news that they were on the Russian side, we two sisters went to join them. At the Bug, the Ukrainians refused under any circumstances to take my sister's baggage, and having no choice, I stayed with it on this side, while my Rivkeh went by boat to the Russian side.

I returned to my parents in the village with my packs. I went to Markuszow practically every day, and whichever of my friends I met, I urged them to run away from the Nazi hell. I myself didn't want to risk such a difficult journey alone. I wanted to try it again, and I wanted someone to come along with me. The consensus among most Jews then was that the first wave of terror would pass, and Jewish life would accommodate itself to the occupation. I did not believe this, and tried to argue another view, but without success.

After a month in the village and Markuszow, a Jewish man came to us from the "other side" bringing a letter from my sister and brother-in-law. They begged me to take the baggage, and immediately leave with this man. He would take care of everything involved in getting to Russia. My parents agreed to my trip this time, because as anxious parents, they wanted their older daughter to have a few things. She was then pregnant, and since she had just begun a life of wandering, every household thing was needed.

On November 10 1939, I parted from my parents and brothers. Many tears were shed at the separation. Everyone was filled with the fear we would never see each other again…My father accompanied me until Miechow, and since we couldn't find a vehicle to the Bug, I stayed in the shtetl over Shabbes. There I was visited by a young man from Markuszow, Yechezkel Iberkleid, who told me about the sudden German visit to Markuszow. The SS had ostensibly been looking for weapons in Jewish houses, and used the opportunity to beat and torture many Jews, loot their houses

[Page 309]

and threaten the worst. This story strengthened my decision to get away from German rule. On November 14th, I finally left Miechow, and headed for the Bug. For the second time, I found myself in the border town of Slawatycze hoping to get across. When we were already at the riverbank, just about to get into the boats, Germans arrived and took me and my sister's baggage to a border post. After two weeks of stressful attempts, I was able to save myself from the murderers' hands, and I finally got over the Bug, and arrived at Damacava. From there, it wasn't difficult to reach Brisk (Brest-Litowsk) where my sister and her husband were located.

Brisk was a giant refugee camp then where you could see refugees from the occupied territories of Poland everywhere, in the streets, schools, private homes, and other public buildings. Homelessness was widespread. It was hard to find a place to lay your head even for a lot of money. My relatives and I spent four weeks in a synagogue. This made us one of the lucky ones with our own little corner.

Finally, my brother-in-law was able to find somewhere for us to live. We found work, and it seemed like our lives were stabilizing a bit. Meanwhile an epidemic broke out among the refugees. Not, God forbid a sickness, but an obsession with going back home affected everyone. The difficult living conditions, the frequent unemployment, and the nomadic life made people forget about the German problem, and they began to think about and prepare for going back to the German occupation. There was another motive involved. There was a constant gnawing longing for the relatives left behind on the other side of the border. The lines were long at the registration office for returning to Poland. We too were infected by the "home epidemic," and were waiting for the call to return to where we had come from.

Yes, such a call did come…But instead of going home, one night, they took me out of bed, and drove me to the Brisker prison. After two months behind jail walls, they took me and a lot of others in a troop train to deep Russia. After a month of travelling, we arrived at a camp in Novosibirsk. There were already 500 Russian women in the camp, mostly criminal lawbreakers. We were considered political prisoners, and most of our women worked in the sewing workshops. This lasted until September 1941 when the Polish citizens

[Page 310]

benefited from the amnesty. I had the address of my sister who had been sent to Komi-A.S.S.R.[2] After a year's separation, we reunited emotionally, and joyfully. After various periods of wandering around, we arrived in middle-Asia, and worked in a kolkhoz[3] harvesting cotton in the fields, and later, in a tailor cooperative. There I met my current husband. We began to build a family.

In 1945, I came to Poland with the repatriation wave. There a son was born to us who we called Moisheleh. The joy of the new birth was spoiled by the hospital days. There were also several Polish women in my room in the Krakow hospital where I was confined. They, not knowing I was Jewish, spoke frankly, and although I had known about the role of a large part of the Polish population in helping the Germans carry out the annihilation of Jewish life, their current antisemitic language seemed crazily wild to me now in the liberated Poland. These women frequently and frankly expressed their regret that there were still so many Jews left alive, and shared memories from the horrible time when they killed our brothers and sisters. On the eighth day, when the doctor arrived and asked me if I wanted to circumcise my son, I replied with a categorical, "Yes," and added that I wanted to call the child Moishe! My neighbors looked around. I can imagine their horror hearing those words from me…

We quickly left Poland, and arrived in Eretz-Israel in March 1949. Our wandering came to an end.

Rivkeh Zilberman adds:

I was living in Markuszow at the beginning of 1939. Later, my husband and I went to Miechow-Lubelski. The first days of war in September did not affect us that much. But when Markuszow was bombed and burned down, my parents. Israel and Sima Zilberman, moved over to us for a short time. The whole family was together. Everyone wanted to believe that we could maybe sit out the difficult days of war in a little shtetl like Miechow.

It didn't take long for the killers to reach our shtetl. They grabbed a few Jews, among them my husband, and forced them to clean the filthy streets with their hands, to crawl on all fours while they were beaten with clubs, kicked, insulted and cursed at. Later they

[Page 311]

drove the unfortunates away in trucks, saying they were going to drown them in the Vistula. They did not carry out their threat. The Jews were taken to a camp in Kamionka where they were starved for 5 days. Not until they were falling on their feet exhausted from hunger and abuse, did the Germans give them some bones without any meat on them. The victims threw themselves on the bones, and bit into them with their last bit of strength in order to get something out of them to still their gnawing hunger. Then, the Germans appeared with cameras and captured the horrifying picture. To the Germans, this picture was supposed to show the savagery and uncultured nature of the Jews, their greediness for food, and how they behaved when they were around food.

When the unlucky men returned home, most of them decided: Away from here!

Even if it involves smuggling yourself over borders, a foreign country, Russia, living a nomadic life, anything but being subjected to such humiliations and calamities, or being an object of sadistic enjoyment. My husband too categorically declared he would not remain under Nazi rule. So he went away by himself to the other side of the Bug in order to send for my sister and I in a short time.

The experiences and events of crossing the border, and the harsh conditions of refugee life in Brisk have already been described by my sister. After traveling on the troop train to the east, over a span of four weeks, and a three week trip on water, we arrived at Komi-A.S.S.R., at "poshilyek"[4] number 92, where there were a lot of arrested Kulaks who had opposed collectivization. We became forest workers. In the barracks, constructed by the refugees themselves, everyone got their corner. We made it through 14 months of exile. At the agreement between the Soviet government and the Polish refugee government of General Sikorski, we were amnestied. Most of the refugees decided to go to the warmer countries in middle-Asia, but they couldn't establish themselves in the big cities, and with no other choice, we went to work in the Kolkhoz cotton fields.

The hard work conditions in the forest, and the exhaustion of the trip in the changed climate had a fatal influence on

[Page 312]

everyone's health. I spent 7 months in hospital, and then paid a terrible price–our five-year-old daughter, Sureleh, died. The death of our child overwhelmed us.

In 1944, my husband's brother found out about us, and managed to get us over to him. He lived in Dzhambul (Kyrgizia)[5]. We settled in not badly there, and a child was born to us. The repatriation migration after the war brought us to Lublin from Russia. Although we knew about the great tragedy, it was hard to believe that there was no one left of our seven brothers and sisters. I mustered my courage, and travelled to Markuszow. Yes, the shtetl was living a normal life, only without our Jews. Not a trace of Jewish Markuszow remained.

We travelled to Szczecin, settled in there in summer 1950, and we were successful in making aliyah to our country of Israel.

Translator's Footnotes:

1. The border between Ukraine and Poland.
2. Komi Autonomous Soviet Socialist Republic located west of the Ural Mountains. Site of many gulags
3. Communal farm
4. Russian–village, settlement
5. Today, Jambyl, Kazakhstan

[Page 312]

My Experiences During the Occupation

Testimony recorded by M. Nachshon (Capa)

Esther Kitenkaren-Grossman (Ramat Gan)

Translated by Moses Milstein

Friday September 8 1939, Hitler's airplanes flew over Markuszow bringing bombs, fire, destruction, and human victims. The panic then was great. People fled in all directions. The goal–to get away as far as possible from the hell spreading death and destruction. The Polish population looked for shelter in the small woods (Burek) nearby, while the majority of the Jews fled to the neighboring villages. For the first time, there were no Shabbes candles burning in Jewish windows on Friday night.

My parents and the whole family did not have the opportunity to leave the house. That evening, my fiancé, Levi, had come from Korew. He told us about the air attacks on his shtetl, and that it had entirely been burned down. Jews from Korew also fled to the villages. His parents went to Bogucin. My mother asked him to arrange horse and wagon for us so we could get away. He went immediately away to fulfill her request.

[Page 313]

Early Saturday morning, a farmer from Bogucin arrived with two strong horses in harness, and asked us to get in the wagon as quickly as possible. A ray of hope appeared to everyone. It was, after all, safer in the village than in the shtetl. Maybe we could sit out the stormy times there? We started to gather the most important things, when our parents declared, "We're not going. We will not desecrate the Sabbath!"

The children began to plead and cry. But our pious parents were set against travelling on the Sabbath. My father issued a stern, but for us, a holy, order, "*Kinderlach*, you get up on the wagon. We are staying here, and nothing bad is going to happen to us."

Father commanded…We the children, the small ones as well as the adults, had too much reverence and respect for our father to contradict him with even a hint or a word, even in such a fateful moment. Father was everything for us–teacher, and educator, respected father, and the very highest authority. Children did not want to engage in debate with him, primarily out of respect for his piety and faith.

The first one on the wagon was my sister, Temeh, with her son and two little children–Itche Mayer'le, and Hershele. She asked of me, "Esther, take the children and get up."

I called them in their order: "Shaindele, Tsvi'ele, Yehudit'l, Tsadok'l, Itche-Mayer'l–everyone get on the wagon. Father said to do so!"

I sat on the wagon and reminded myself that there was one name of our household I hadn't called out, our dear brother's, Alter-Leib. He was then in the Bialystok yeshiva–and God will protect him from evil.

Upon arriving in Bogucin, we went straight to the residence that my fiancé had prepared for us at a farmer. The next day, Sunday, we heard the loud reverberations of bombs. The farmer we were staying with, went up on the roof and yelled, "Markuszow is burning!"

The news left us shaken. The worry about our parents left behind was transformed to fear that something had happened to them. I left the younger children under the supervision of my older sister, and Levi and I set off for Markuszow. We broke through smoke and flames to get to our house.

[Page 314]

It was whole, undamaged, but we didn't find anyone inside. After running around the shtetl and asking those who had stayed, we found our parents in an orchard not far from Markuszow. We returned to the house, and sat on the threshold all night watching the fire consume Jewish property, destroying years of toil and effort. That night, we were not the only spectators of the Jewish destruction. Many Markuszow residents had come back from the villages to the shtetl, and experienced horror and fright, especially after the news that Yakov Glasman's two children, ten-year-old Aharon, and 8-year-old Moishe, were torn apart by bomb shrapnel.

Early Monday, our parents and us returned to Bogucin. Now the whole family was together.

A week later was Rosh Hashanah. In neighboring Lugow, a minyan was created at Leib's the village's Jew. My father went over there to daven. There he met the Markuszow cantor, Moishe Weinriber, who davened this time with a special feeling. There was a reason for it–torn from home, rootless, in war with a savage enemy.

Before Yom Kippur, my father gathered the whole family, and we returned to Markuszow. My fiancé's family also came along, and everyone settled into our house. At that time, many Jewish families were resettling in the shtetl, although the Nazis were already ruling over Markuszow. The fear of the Germans was so great that during Yom Kippur, when they were praying in the house of Chaim Shoichet (the besmedresh had burned down) the devils came by and asked what kind of meeting was going on. After we told them it was a house of worship, they went away. But the Jews ran away after they left, in the certainty that the Germans would bring tragedy.

The Jewish population of the shtetl felt the brutal hand of the Nazis on a daily basis. Cleaning the streets, the city hall, the toilets were now the jobs of the Jews. The work was always accompanied by beatings, cursing, and humiliation. A little later, the Germans ordered the creation of a Judenrat composed of seven people: Michal Weiner, Pinchas Liebhober, Shlomke Goldwasser, Chaim-Yosef Kuropatwa (shoichet), Mendl Ettinger, Simche Ettinger, and Yitzchak Fishbein. To help the Judenrat, several policemen were chosen from the Markuszow Jewish youth. The duty of the Judenrat was to provide a contingent of workers every day on the demand of the Germans;

[Page 315]

to receive and carry out all the orders and decrees affecting the Jewish population; and to levy fines or contributions for the local German rulers.

Winter 1940. When the roads were covered with snow, the Judenrat had to supply a greater number of Jews to clean the covered roads, plazas, and streets. The intent of the murderers was not to carry out important work, but rather to torture and debase the Jews of the shtetl.

Business was practically dead. From sheer fear of the occupiers, the Jews did not want to engage too much, or to show themselves with merchandise at the market. Although my parents' factory and shoe store survived, they did not carry on any business. But we still had to live. As result, many shtetl Jews carried on a secret business bringing different kinds of merchandise to the villages in return for produce. This was all done at night, because no one would dare to be seen on the roads in the daytime.

It was also hard with bread. The only Jewish bakery in the shtetl consisted of part of an oven from Moishe Baker's (Kaveh) bakery. The bread was actually baked under the open skies, because the wooden bakery building had burned down in the first bombardment.

* * *

Spring 1940. New decrees against the Jews. The first–shaving off the beards. This was a severe blow for religious Jews. In addition, everyone had to wear a white armband with a Star of David.

My father decided not to shave off his beard. He therefor went to Baranow, to Beile, the oldest daughter. After six weeks there, he was forced to return, because the decree had reached even that remote village. The murderers were still not satisfied with the harsh limitations, and now forbade Jews to leave the shtetl. They warned they would immediately shoot any Markuszow Jew they found outside the shtetl. We could rely on their carrying out the warning. But who can exist in the locked-down shtetl? So Jews used the darkness of night, and risking their lives, they slunk like shadows to the villages just to ensure a pitiful existence for themselves and their families.

In the summer of 1940, my father got together with my future father-in-law, and they agreed that my wedding to Levi should take place in the month of Kislev. I was not

[Page 316]

especially delighted by the agreement, because getting married during Hitler's regime meant taking on a big and difficult responsibility for family life in the harsh conditions of the occupation.

But my father wanted it so…Our wedding took place on the agreed-upon schedule. We rented a house on the edge of the village, on the Lublin side. My husband worked for the Germans all winter. His job was to clean the snow off the roads.

Pesach is coming, the holiday of freedom. But instead of freedom, we were enslaved by a much worse and gruesome Pharaoh who was already set to disturb our lovely holiday. On the second day of Pesach, Chaim Shoichet's son, Shloime Goldstein, was shot in his home. He had been hiding when the Germans came in and asked for women. He replied that there were no women there. The Nazis shot him on the spot. The murder of an innocent Jew created great panic in town. We looked on the future again with unease and worry, picturing the worst.

In summer 1941, we learned about the German attack on Russia.[1] In the first days of the war, we were witness to big military transports rolling through the shtetl. When German war vehicles or armies came through Markuszow, the Jews would hide in their homes, afraid to show themselves in the street.

Once on an autumn evening, the door of the Judenrat opened and a German officer appeared. He ordered us to immediately prepare a truck loaded with cheese and butter for the soldiers marching to the east. Of course, the Jews had to bear the expense of the contribution, which was not the first (and also not the last). At every opportunity, the Germans demanded various gifts, mostly foodstuffs.

I want to take this opportunity to remember that it was actually during the years of occupation that my oldest sister, Beileh, gave birth to two children: Itche-Mayer, and Rucheleh. I point this out because, in the first ten years of her marriage, my sister did not have any children. My father was overjoyed that after such a long interval, his oldest daughter had brought him grandchildren. They brought him great joy, and he believed in better times. But suddenly he became sick, and developed angina. At that time,

[Page 317]

it was impossible for a Jew to get medical help, much less any medication. He lay in bed for only a few days, and then on the 28th of Shvat he gave up his gentle and holy soul. All the children felt a horrible loneliness. He was a protector we strongly depended on in these stormy times. His death strongly affected the children, but more so our mother, Malke-Leah. It was hard for her to even find consolation in the children and grandchildren. Life had no appeal to her anymore. When on the last day of Pesach the order came for 500 people to be deported from Markuszow, she was the first to go to the town square. With her also went my sister Temeh, her husband, Yakov Warrenheiser, and their child. The words of my mother, who was very worried about me, still ring in my ears today. I was pregnant then. My mother knew that in the first deportation in Korew, the murderers killed the pregnant women first. She now begged my husband to take me to a village, to a friendly farmer. He immediately carried out her wish. We went on foot through the "*laches*"[2] of the shtetl. On coming to Zelig's fishpond, we heard cries of distress and shots being fired. We understood that the murderers were already in the shtetl carrying out their bloody business.

Around two in the morning, we came to Garbow, and went off to the farmer, Jan Wartacz. We told him what was happening in the shtetl, and asked him if we could stay with him. After much hesitation he agreed. We stayed in his house, but our minds were troubled: what is happening to our near ones in the shtetl. Are they still alive? Why did we forsake them? We are nervous and jumpy, constantly looking at the clock. It is six pm. The worry and anxiety grow larger. We beg the farmer he should drive over to Markuszow and find out what's going on. Two hours later he returned. His report shattered us. "There are no Jews in the shtetl." We don't believe him, and ask him over again, to get more details. The farmer reported that at the beginning the Germans had ordered all the Jews to assemble at the town square. There they carried out a selection, picked out 500 older men and women, and interned them in the school building, letting the young go free. It seems that those who were not shut up in the school have left the shtetl, because no Jew can be seen there.

We could not sleep all night, and begged the farmer

[Page 318]

to travel to Markuszow again. When he returned from his second visit, he told us that he had learned that the 500 Jews had been driven on foot to the Naleczow train station. They were accompanied by Germans and young Poles who beat the unfortunates with clubs. Their blood seeped into the dusty road that stretched for eight kilometers. In this manner the following were killed: Moishe Beineshe's (Weinriber), Benyomin-Yosef Eisenberg and his wife, Itche-Mayer Roguski and his wife and child, Chantche Fiertog, the widow, Malke Glasman, Itche Chane-Roise's, and others.

Later we learned that the Judenrat had paid a Pole handsomely to follow them and find out what they did to the 500 Jews. He returned after several days and reported that the unfortunates were stuffed into freight cars, tightly packed-in, without a drop of water, taken to Belzec, and killed in the forests there. About other details, he had no knowledge.

We spent six days with Jan Wartacz. The news came to us that the Markuszow Judenrat gave the Germans sixty thousand zlotys to leave the rest of the Jews alone. "Leaving alone" in those days meant– hard work on the roads under the strict supervision of the Germans, and their Polish or Ukrainian accomplices. We decided to return to the shtetl, and do the slave work on the roads like everyone else. This lasted four weeks, from after Pesach to Erev Shavuot, 1942.

* * *

On May 8th, an order came for all Markuszow Jews to assemble at the town square again. Everyone already knew the significance of such a decree. There was an outbreak of panic and at the same time thoughts of saving oneself from the murderers' hands. The surviving Jews, with the exception of about 20 to 30 men, decided to flee wherever they could. Those that showed up were sent off to Konskowola. My husband and I decided to go to the village. On the way to Gutanow, we encountered Isser Schneidleder, Ber LOTERSTEIN, Mordechai Mast, and other Markuszow Jews. Together we decided to first hide in the Gutanow forest. We had barely

time to catch our breath, and to sit down to rest under some trees, when a group of young Poles from the

[Page 319]

neighborhood, armed with large clubs, appeared. They demanded money from us. We could not give them any money because that would have had fatal results. The *shkootzim*[3] swung their clubs and hit my Levi in the head creating a deep wound. Then they ordered us to walk, and they led us around all day. Once they were convinced they weren't going to get anything, they handed us over to the Gutanow soltis in the evening. He was well acquainted with Ber LOTERSTEIN, and Isser Shneidleder. He gave them a wink they should go to his stable. Since I was pregnant, I moved over to Ber and his family, and together we went into a small stable. A Pole appeared right away and demanded money. Ber gave him a few hundred zlotys. I had no money on me, so I took off my wedding ring, and gave it to him.

Then the soltis explained that it was dangerous for him to let us hide there. We had to leave the stable. At 12 midnight we left Gutanow for Lugow, to the farmer, Michal Pietrak. We spent the night there in the loft of his stable. He brought us food in the morning. After stilling my hunger, I decided to go look for my husband who had fled wounded into the Gutanow forest. I decided to go to Bogucin. Arriving there, I began to ask the farmers about Levi Grossman, because practically everybody knew him. A farmer told me that Levi had paid someone 500 zlotys top take him to his sister who lived in Belzec. The German authorities still allowed Jews to exist there.

When I got back to the loft in Lugow, I discussed going to Belzec with Ber. We could not decide. But because I was pregnant, the farmer was afraid of complications, and he himself decided to take me to Belzec. On Sunday they dressed me in farmer clothes, harnessed the horses to the wagon, and travelled to Belzec.

* * *

After staying for eight days with my sister-in-law, Chaneh-Tobe, my first daughter, Chaneleh, was born on June 1 1942. The joy of the birth was mixed with sorrow about her future.

A week later the Germans issued an order

[Page 320]

demanding a contingent of 500 Jews. The Belzec Judenrat, of course, did not want to hand over its own local Jews, so they sent out their police to capture the newcomers who had come from elsewhere. The Judenrat emissaries carried out their work efficiently. But luck was with us for now. We found a place to hide. On July 1 1942, my husband met with several Markuszow Jews in Belzec: Simcha Ettinger, Ber LOTERSTEIN, Yitzchak Fishbein, and a few more. They discussed the situation knowing in advance that in further aktions, which would definitely follow, they would be the first victims. There was word that the Tomaszowice nobleman, who was a good acquaintance of Ber LOTERSTEIN, had the right to employ Jewish workers. So it was decided to send him to the landowner. The latter agreed to take 20 families on his estate for the price of 500 zlotys per work card. He immediately ordered the village Jew, Avremeleh Tomaszowicer, to prepare space for 20 families. We were already on the site by July 15th. We were the following families: Simcha and Sarah Ettinger and their children; Ber and Feige LOTERSTEIN and child; Israel and Eidl Fishbein and children; Yosef and Rivke Fishbein and children; Yitzchak Fishbein, the Glasman brothers; and the children of my uncle Binyomin Capa; Mindl, Ruchel, Freide Rubinstein-Iberkleid with her husband, Avrum and children; and the two sisters, Leah and Nechama Weiner, the daughters of Leibish Pesach; and others whose names I can't remember.

We worked alongside the owner's farm hands, but accomplished more than them, although they received the full salary, while we didn't get enough to eat. There's no need to even mention clothing. Thanks to our stay with the landowner, a few more Markuszow Jews managed to hide with us and avoid certain death for the moment. Our life went on this way almost all summer, until October 5 1942. On Saturday, we went to work like every other day, not knowing that the nobleman had received an order from the Germans to send everyone to Belzec the following day. When we got back to the compound that night, the soltis, with a stern tone, read out the order, and declared that the work at the estate was at an end.

So a few of the shtetl Jews got together to consult on what to do next. One thing was clear: not to take a bullet, but to dodge it. That same Saturday evening, we split up. Me, my husband, his sister, and our child; Simcha Ettinger and his family; Ber LOTERSTEIN and his family; Freide Rubinstein and her family. Our first journey

[Page 321]

was to Bogucin village. Terribly tired, we arrived at the house of the friendly farmer, Stanislaw Gnieczak. Our hearts were as bleak and dark as the night outside. It was midnight, and we wondered if he would let us in. Would he open the gate to the stable or stall? My husband knocked on the window. The farmer opened the window and was inclined not to let us in, but he was ashamed in front of my husband. It seems the many years of acquaintance, even friendship, did not allow him to refuse. He told us to go up to the attic over the room. There, with our four-month-old baby, we spent the night.

* * *

In the morning, the farmer showed up and openly stated that he was afraid to keep us there. Since my husband had found out that, in Korew, his hometown, there was a work place where, along with the chairman of the Judenrat, Avrumtche Goldberg, there were 40 Jews employed. Levi sent his sister there to find out if we could come work there. A. Goldberg was a good friend of my father-in-law, a"h. So he ordered us to come, but without being able to work. After a day with the farmer, we went to Korew via the back roads. We spent a hard month there as illegals. We "hung around" the 40 workers. One day, the Volksdeutsche informed us that the 40 needed to assemble at a given place. We already knew what that meant, and we quickly got out of town knowing that such a step was associated with great danger. That's why we decided to separate for a while. Separately, it might be easier to find a way to get by. I went off to Plinek,[4] a village near Markuszow, with my child in my arms. Incidentally, I came there for the first time, didn't know anyone, and no one knew me. Despairing, and resigned, I sat down at the river's edge. My unlucky child cried with fearful yowls, and her cries more forcefully described the tragic situation we found ourselves in. My parents, whom I was very strongly attached to, were no longer among the living. I had had to separate from my husband. Now I sat by the water, lonely, friendless, unlucky, with no goal or way out. I wondered, where will help come from? My tearful face was reflected in the river. I turned my head around, and saw an older Christian woman. I stopped her, and asked her if she wasn't, by any chance, coming from Korew. She answered yes, and to my further question about what was happening there, she said she had heard talk that, today, the last Jews had been shot. After this bitter news, I asked her if I could go

[Page 322]

to her house to warm the baby, because night was falling. She was not enthusiastic about it, and said she was afraid of her husband. After pleading and crying for a while, she said to go with her.

Coming into the hut of the old couple, Shikora, I felt immediately better. I felt a warmth in the household, and alongside it, a ray of hope. Maybe my Chanaleh would survive. I unwrapped the child, and her shining, beautiful little face, it seemed, had an effect on the farmers. The old lady began to fuss over the baby; heated up some milk. I saw how the baby greedily drank the milk and ate some bread. My heart was overflowing with joy, and it seemed to me that only here, with the childless couple, could my Chanaleh survive the dreadful times. I screwed up my courage and asked the farmer's wife if she didn't want to keep the child. It was the only way to avert danger. They did not respond immediately. But their reaction momentarily made me feel better, because I was now feeling the happiness of my child.

That same evening, I had another happy surprise. My husband appeared in the Shikora's cottage. They allowed him to spend the night. So we went off to the stable, and made our bed next to the cow.

The next day–another surprise. My husband's sister showed up. But the news she brought filled our hearts with lead. The forty Jews had been shot.

We got on very well with the old couple. They agreed to keep us for a little while for money. This agreement was dictated more by profit than by pity. The loft over the cow shed now became our stable living place, and we hoped to stay there as long as possible, because the old couple behaved very well to us, and did not stint on food. The cold, however, ate into our bones. We could have borne this affliction as well, but for a five-month-old baby, it was hard to endure. She cried terribly when her diapers were changed. We saw her pain and suffering, and lived and felt them with her. Chaneleh was oblivious to the danger of death that threatened us every minute with her crying that could be heard in the village.

After three weeks in the loft, old Shikora came and invited us to eat in the house. We immediately understood that such a sudden invitation meant eviction. In those circumstances, it meant the same as

[Page 323]

death. Like those condemned to death, my husband, his sister, me and little Chaneleh came to the farmer where a set table was waiting for us. The asked us to sit and eat. We took our places at the table, but didn't touch the prepared food.

"Why are you not eating?" asked old Shikora. "You have to eat well now, because you will soon have to leave."

The words struck us in the very depths of our souls. The specter of homeless wandering looms. We know the taste of it. We try to avert the fearful decree, but the old man keeps talking in a sincere tone, "My house stands near the road. Yesterday, a neighbor came by and asked, 'Why are we hearing a child crying? Everyone knows you don't have any children.' I tried to divert him with various excuses, but the neighbor interrupted me, 'Michale, you are bringing tragedy to your house and to the whole village.' He went away angry. Don't you understand what this means? It means certain death for me and my old wife, a burned down property, and in the process the neighbors will be burned too. To avoid this tragedy, you must leave this place right away."

Now we saw that our fate was sealed. My husband still had something to say. "Well, we are already lost…But seeing as you don't have any children, take the little creature. The child will bring you joy in your old age."

We thought that the couple really wanted the child. They quietly discussed it, exchanged meaningful looks, and at the end, both of them, crying and sobbing, declined to take the child. Their only reason was fear. We understood that further talk would be of no use.

How then to save the child? The thought tortures and won't desist. Without talking about it, we each understood that the baby could only be saved if she was separated from us. If we left the child in a house, she would have a better chance to survive than in our aimless wandering, full of danger. Since my husband and his sister decided to go look for a new shelter, I begged the farmer to let me and the baby stay another few hours, until my husband comes to bring me to a new place. Michal Shikora hesitated, then agreed. I said good-bye to Levi, and we discussed what place to meet at should he fail to come and get me. We parted.

[Page 324]

I stayed in the house with the child. My brain was completely engaged with the baby: how to save her? How to prevent the death of a child that has just come into the world? Leaving her with good people was certainly a way out, but the pain of separating will be great, and who knows how long we could endure it. Nevertheless, leaving Chaneleh with a farmer was better. If luck was with the parents, and they survived, we would collect her back, and raise her in the Jewish way. But where do you find this good farmer who would want to keep a child in these savage times. Can we find someone in whom pity will triumph over fear and evil? If such a person can't be found, I think further with dire consequences–will we have to maybe abandon her? A shudder passed through me at the very thought of such a possibility. But what then to do? Maybe abandon her at the Shikora's house? They would take her. Then Chaneleh would be saved. And if not?

My thoughts were interrupted by the farmer's words, "Your husband said he would be back in a few hours. Night is coming. It hurts me very much, but you will have to leave. At night, unwelcome guests are always coming, and your presence could bring us trouble."

"You are right"–I sighed–"Good night and thanks for everything."

* * *

I left the old people's house.

It was the evening of November 11 1942. I went down the hill to the road. There were farmer's cottages on both side of the road. Smoke was coming from the chimneys, and with sorrow and disappointment, I thought of the warm secure houses, about children who have a home and a bed there, plentiful food, and the tender care of their parents. Only my child and I are condemned. Where to go, whom to depend on? I glance at Shikora's hut that only a few weeks ago had seemed to me like a lifejacket in a stormy sea. But what do I see? Yes, the old couple was standing at the door and watching me go…

I went further on my way, opened the gate of a fence. The owner, a young farmer lady, saw me and asked what I wanted. "A drink of water," I replied. "Go, get out of here," she began to scream. "Get away. I don't want to see you around here!"

[Page 325]

    I left the yard chased away like a dog. It began to snow. What to do? How do I protect the child from the cold? The thought of leaving the child in some house was renewed with greater power. I thought: my father is standing on the other side of the fence and is saying, "Esther, come in." He removes a plank from the fence and displays a little room in the yard. I run over there. It looks to me like the altar where Abraham laid Isaac. Should I leave my little daughter there? I want to lay her down, but my arms don't obey. I press Chanaleh to me. "No, I will not be separated from my only child. I will take her with me." I want to go on my way, but my father appears again, and I see his index finger pointing at the shed. His lips whisper, "Lay the child down here…you will be saved. All of you will be saved…"

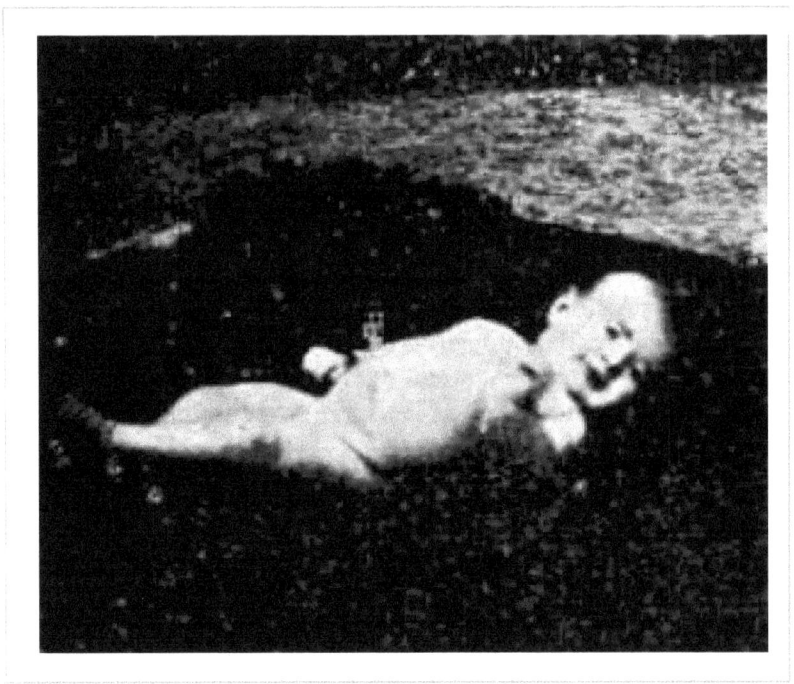

Chaneleh Grossman, 5 months old,
photographed 8 days before she was placed
in the village of Plinek

    After a while–my only treasure is already lying outstretched near the shed. I parted from my child. With disheveled hair, and disordered thoughts, I left the yard with the same narrow exit that my father broke open for me. I went way from the place where I had abandoned my child…

    Physically drained, and spiritually broken, I ran without a goal, with no direction. I lost all sense of time or place. I had no awareness of whether I was going east

[Page 326]

or west, north or south. Maybe I'm delivering myself into the hands of the enemy? But now there is no enemy either. If any thoughts at all occur, they are of my abandoned child. My disordered thoughts focus on my only little daughter. The anxiety over her fate obliterates any fear for my own life. Will she be lying there in the snow? Maybe a compassionate hand picked her up?

Suddenly, I tore myself out of my frozen state. With open eyes, I look around at my surroundings. There seems to be a familiar building. Yes, it's the Kaliner[5] water mill. I now became aware of the great danger threatening. The Kaliner farmers were always known for their antisemitism. The Jew who fell into their hands during the occupation was not to be envied. Fortunately it was already dark. The night gave me a little security, and I quickly got out of that awful spot. I went quickly to Markuszow, and arrived at the shtetl which seemed dead at night. I slunk by the houses so as not to be seen. I was mostly scared of the dogs. Their barking could quickly betray a stranger. I was now a stranger in the town of my birth where I had lived for years. I managed through side streets to come to the house where I had lived after the wedding. My landlady, Janka Trombicka, recognized me at once, and allowed me to come into the house. Here, in the light, she noticed my appearance, and said frankly that I gave the impression of not being normal. I told her about the abandoned child. I didn't want to live anymore after that deed. Janka said, "Estherke, you did right. Your child will live and you will be able to hide."

She took me up to the attic, made me a bed, and brought me food. As tired and hungry as I was, I did not touch the food. I was also unable to close my eyes and sleep. My unhappy child's face was always before my eyes. Who am I? I asked myself for the thousandth time. Can I still carry the name of mother after having abandoned my flesh and blood? I lay there all night with those thoughts, unable to fall asleep for a second.

Janka Trombicka came up in the morning, and brought food, but when she saw that I had not touched anything yesterday, she began to shout, "What's going on with you, Esther? Why don't you eat? You look terrible. You put the fear in people with your appearance."

I answered her resignedly,

[Page 327]

"Listen to me, pani Trembicki! I am going straightaway to Plinek. I must reclaim my child. I don't want to live without Chanaleh."

The Christian woman explained to me that it made no sense to go now to save the child. My showing up in the village and demanding my daughter would only betray her origin, and both of us would perish. "Better, Estherke, to go find your husband at the agreed-upon place, but not now in the daytime, but when night falls."

With a broken heart, I had to recognize that this woman was right. I remained in the attic for the day, and as soon as it got dark, I went to Garbow. There they told me they knew nothing about my husband, so I went to Bogucin. But I didn't recognize the village. I ask an older farmer passing by where I was, and he said it was the village of Lugow. It was then I realized that my memory and my mind had suddenly left me. I asked the farmer to explain to me how to get to the Bogucin colony. He explained the route to me, and through roads and back roads, I set off running again. In normal times, the way there would have taken not more than a half hour. Now I wandered for four hours. After such a long and tiring day, I gave no thought to danger. As soon as I saw the first cottage, I knocked on the door and asked about Levi. The whole village of farmers knew him, and had he been with any of them, I could have been certain that I would get the right information here. Yes, he had been there, but he left. Several farmers confirmed this. Nevertheless, I found him at the farmer, Karol Drozd. Levi told me that the situation was not good, because several farmers refused to hide him. Karol Drozd too would not hear of it. I begged the farmer to let me wait there. He did not reply. I sat there all day. The farmer never asked me if I wanted anything to eat. My husband explained that the farmer wanted me to leave right away. He had told his sister openly to get out. We began to cry and beg the farmer not to condemn us to the angel of death. Our tears were useless. Levi called him to another room, handed him a larger sum of money, and that had an effect. He agreed to allow just my husband and I. He did not want to hear about the sister, for any price. As soon as he got the money, he drove her out of the house, not letting her stay for one more minute. He showed us both to the potato pit in the yard. That would be our

[Page 328]

hiding place. We let ourselves down into our new "house" covered with a straw roof. There was no question of being able to stand up there. The farmer handed us a little food two times a day, but it did not agree with us. The thought of abandoning the child, and the homeless wandering of the sister did not leave us for a second.

* * *

Our life in the pit, the living grave, meant days of despair and sleepless nights. Farmers kept bringing news of Jews, who had been hiding in the surrounding villages, betrayed. We were certain that, any day now, the same would happen to us.

On December 23 1942, a day before Christmas Eve, our landlords demanded we leave the pit. Like most of the superstitious farmers, he did not want to be together with Jews on this holiest Christian holiday. They were convinced it was a transgression to be found with Jews on such a holiday. We saw that no amount of pleading would help; the farmer was determined to drive us out. We left for the Wole Forest to one of the bunkers where my sisters, and other Jewish families from Markuszow and surrounding areas were hiding.

I met my two sisters, Tzviah, and Yehudit, my brother, Itche Mayer'l and my cousin, Tobe. I got tragic news there. My sister, Shaindl, was shot a few days before by the Germans when she went to the village to acquire food for the children. My 18-year-old brother, Hershl, was found frozen to death in a hole.

After hiding in the bunker for about two weeks, we began to feel the cold and frost that seeped in from outside. That would not be so bad, but what about the snow? It began to fall, covering the roads, and each step out of the bunker left footprints and betrayed our hiding place. Getting food turned out to be one of the most terrifying things. My husband and I decided to go to Bogucin, and create a shelter for us and the children.

Sunday night, January 7 1943, we again visited several farmer acquaintances, and asked them to hide us in exchange for money, but we were refused everywhere. We spent the night in several places, and Monday morning we went out again to try our luck. This time at our farmer, Karol Drozd. We were ready to pay, and brought up

[Page 329]

our old friendship. The wife shook her head, we thought that she had changed her mind.

"You don't need a hiding place for the children anymore. We were at the market in Markuszow today. The farmers talked about the Germans discovering bunkers in the Wole forest. They, and Polish policemen, surrounded the hideouts, emptied their bullets into them, and when they ran out of ammunition, they placed straw around the entrances, lit it, and the suffocating smoke completed the murders.

We heard the bad news with heavy hearts. Now the Wole forest too had stopped existing. The few Jews who had sought protection under the dense trees were no more. We could not spend much time thinking about this, and as for mourning–of course not. We repeated our request, but the Drozds were unyielding in their refusal. Where to go? To whom to go? I remembered Janka Trembicka, the Markuszow resident who said a while back, that in case of need, I should call on her. We snuck into the shtetl like thieves in the night, and barely made it to her residence. Knock on the door? We were afraid. We showed ourselves at the window. Janka saw us. She approached the window and yelled, "*O la Boga*,[6] Estherke!" And she quickly added, "Get away from here. You cannot be here for one second. *Ja chce zyc!*" (I want to live).

We stepped back a few feet. We asked ourselves, "Is there no corner of the world where we can lay our heads, rest our weary bodies?" My husband reminded himself of the farmer, Stanislaw Burek. We went to his house via the back roads to where an old chicken coop stood. In the summer it held chickens, but now, in winter, the chickens were transferred to the warmer stable. We crept into the coop. It seems that they had heard a suspicious sound in the house. The old mother-in-law came out, and recognized me and shouted, "Estherke, where did you come form? You know nothing about what happened today. There were a bunch of Jews hiding in a bunker. They had decided to temporarily set themselves up in a nearby unfinished building in order to mislead the Germans in case they came to search the hideout. It seems that someone saw them moving to the unfinished building. As soon as the Jews began to settle in there, farmers showed up,

[Page 330]

tied up the terrified Jews' hands and feet, and threw them into wagons like calves, and took them to the gemine authorities in Markuszow.

She knew the Jews well and listed their names: Simcha Ettinger, and his little girl, Blumeh; Mendl Ettinger; Tobe Schwartz; Yitzchak Schwartz, his wife, Leah, daughter, Tobe; Sheva Rubinstein and her little girl Sarah, Yoineh Teitelbaum; Dvoireh Rosenberg. The 18-year-old son of Simcha Ettinger tried to run away, but the farmers ran after him and cut his head off with an axe…

In the middle of the old lady's story, her son-in-law, Stanislaw Burek, appeared and without any introduction, he asked where we were coming from and what we wanted. My husband said we had a little gold for sale. We wanted him to find a customer, and take care of the thing. Since day was beginning to break, we asked him not to drive us away. He gave us a price for staying in the chicken coop for 8 days. We agreed. He immediately brought some straw, put it in the coop, and also provided a good meal.

Burek reported that Ber LOTERSTEIN had stayed with him several times and had asked about us.

Sunday evening, our landlord said that tomorrow, Monday, was market day… A lot of German gendarmes come then to the shtetl, and with the help of Polish collaborators, they search the houses. We had to go away that night. If it became hard for us, we could return.

That meant–homelessness again. No amount of pleading would help. If we are ordered to leave, we leave. No one cared that my husband had a high fever, that there was no place to go. So we crawled out of the chicken coop and went on our way without a destination. Our feet carried us on their own to the Garbow colony. There were farmers we knew there. Perhaps one of them would show some compassion for unlucky hunted Jews? But better not to be seen by anybody. No farmer must know if there are Jews hidden. We crawled into the stable of Stanislaw Filipek. Bundles of wheat and straw filled the giant granary. We climbed up to the top, our goal was to stuff ourselves as deeply as possible into the straw so no one could see us. Higher, higher, snuggling into the straw, finding a little rest. Suddenly we heard a question in Yiddish. "Who is there?"

We recognized the voices of Shloime and Itzchak Morel, sons of Chaim Morel. They helped us get up in the straw. We asked about

[Page 331]

their parents. One of the sons told us that several Polish policemen, actually very good friends of theirs, grabbed the old couple, and openly shot them by the church. This happened in fact, on a Sunday, when farmers from 18 villages of the parish had got together, and in front of everyone's eyes they put to death two more Jews. In fact, that will be our fate. Germans themselves don't have to be our killers; they have others to rely on…

The next morning, quite early, we heard movement in the stable. From the words we overheard it was clear that the farmer was getting ready to thresh. The doors of the stable creaked open. We heard them harness the horse to the carriage, and the machine began to swallow sheaves of wheat. The stable began to empty out. The Morels had expected this. They moved over to the unthreshed straw, and made a new hideout. Forewarned is forearmed. Suddenly the noise of the machine stopped. The farmers sat down to rest. They rolled some cigarettes, lit them, and began to talk. As was the custom in those days, their favorite theme was Jews. They talked about the case of the Morels. The farmers expressed their happiness over the shooting of the old couple. We lay there stunned. Have people become so transformed into beasts? These very farmers had been the very closest friends of the Morels. They did business with them, borrowed money, came into the house and shared many things. Now they openly expressed their joy at the death of two Jews.

One farmer reported that Leibush Grossman (he meant my husband–Levi Grossman) was wandering around the neighborhood. In addition, he expressed the hope that, in a couple of days, we would catch him too and get rid of him…And they talked about this cold-bloodedly, calmly, as if it involved the life of a rat…

* * *

We had the good fortune of staying in the stable for a week. Our food consisted of a loaf of bread that we shared.

To continue to live like this was impossible. The Morel brothers decided to go to the Wole Forest, to the partisans, mostly Markuszow youth. They said farewell to us. We remained alone and didn't know what to do. Since we suspected that the farmer would continue threshing the wheat, we moved over to the loft over the cow shed. There was a ladder outside against the loft. I used to creep down at night and take some beets from the pit where the farmer stored them.

[Page 332]

The beets were the only nutrition we had to sustain life. In the meantime it began to snow. The leaky roof let in the snow and the cold. Out of fear that the ladder would rot in the snow, the farmer took it away, and away went the chance of getting a few beets. It was clear; we had to go again. But where to? We had spent two weeks in the barn, and one week in the stable. But where do we go now? We remembered that our Markuszow acquaintance, Stanislaw Burka had once told us to go to him in an emergency. We ran to Markuszow. The snow was falling continuously, the night was fearfully dark. We went on for several hours then realized we were lost. We were actually in the Gutanow forest. We plodded through deep snow all night, and reached the shtetl at dawn. Stanislaw Burek greeted us with a sour countenance, and quickly informed us that it was dangerous to stay with him. Seeing as it was day already, he allowed us to stay until evening in the chicken coop. After, we had to leave. The farmer told us that my husband's sister comes often to him. He gave her a loan of 500 zlotys on our account, and she was now at a farmer's in Plinek village.

We crawled into the coop. At ten in the morning, Burek came running demanding we leave the place right away. The danger was great, because showing ourselves during the day meant certain death. But what should we do? We ran to the Markuszow cemetery through the "*laches*." We lay hidden by my father's tombstone. We envied those who had died a natural death. Their shtetl accompanied them to their eternal rest. Who will accompany us? By what violent means will we be killed?

With such dark thoughts, we waited for our very best friend–the night. Hungry, frozen stiff with the cold, we left the cemetery and began walking in the snow, without a destination. We have to decide: clearly, we have to return to the cowshed. But where do we get a ladder to climb up to the loft? As we were engrossed in thinking about the loft and the ladder, we didn't see what was happening on the ground. Until my husband realizes that we are in the middle of the village. In fear, we began to creep by the walls of the huts, until we got to the hut of Jan Wartacz. Here we had to settle two things: getting a ladder that would allow us to climb up to the loft, and the two comforters we had left at the farmer's that we had to get back. They would always be useful in such cold and snow. We hid in the stable waiting until whichever of the

[Page 333]

landlords comes first. Knocking on the door is dangerous. At dawn, the farmer came to get straw for the animals. He thrust the pitchfork hard into the spot we were actually lying. He nearly pierced my husband's head. The shining tips of the hayfork passed a millimeter by Levi's head. We held our breath, did not make a sound. When the farmer left we could breathe easier. We decided to wait there until night. When it had just begun to get darker, we heard the farmer's wife let herself into the stable to milk the cow. My husband threw the ladder out of the stable, and went off to the wife to get our comforters back. Greatly surprised, she returned our goods.

My husband with the two comforters, and me with a big heavy ladder set off.

Only 3 kilometers separated Garbow and the colony. We were sure we would be there in a half hour. This was around 6 pm. No sooner had we taken the first steps than a thick snow began to fall, and evolved into a blizzard. Forward progress became difficult, hands were frozen, bodies stiff with cold. Adding to that the blizzard whipped in our faces, and we couldn't see where to tread. With superhuman effort, laden with the comforters and ladder we continued onward not wanting to stop to rest for a second. Suddenly, I saw my husband drop his pack, and stretch out on the snow. I ran over yelling and coaxing him, "Levi! Levi! What's wrong with you? I heard a quiet reply, "I can't go on anymore…I have to sleep now." No sooner said, than he was asleep. I knew, however, that this could not happen, because sleep in such a terrible night, on the snow no less, is certain death. With the last of my strength, I began to tear at his clothing, shaking him and trying to wake him up. I barely got him to awaken. We looked around, and saw the sky beginning to redden in the east. Was that possible? We had left Garbow at 6 in the evening. Did we blunder around all night? Did the 3-kilometer trip take 11 hours? My husband looked at his watch. Yes it was 5:00 am. What to do. Not far from us, we saw a few trees. It seemed to us that they belonged to Filipek's property. With the last bit of strength, we dragged ourselves to the stable, put up the ladder, and– up to the loft. We wanted to pull up the ladder so it wouldn't betray our presence. Our bodies did not comply. We made another effort, another pull on the ladder–but without success. Half dead we fell on the straw and fell into a deep sleep. We slept for twenty-four hours.

[Page 334]

We opened our eyes hungry and frozen. It was day. We must not be seen anywhere. As soon as night fell, my husband went down from the loft, and went straight to the Filipek's house. He asked for food.

"Who are you, where did you come from?"

He told them a few lies and…and asked again for food. They invited him to the table. He swallowed the fatty potatoes, thanked them for the meal, and asked them to cook up two kilos of millet kasha. "We're going a long way," he explained, and gave her 100 zlotys for her to cook a chicken. She returned 20 zlotys change, and promised to have the chicken tomorrow. My husband said goodbye to the hospitable couple and left with the warm kasha the wife had put in a bag. He left the house, and after going through the yard, he kept walking a ways so as not to attract suspicion. Then later he doubled back, climbed up to the loft, and handed me the food. I fall on the warm millet, and ate with great appetite. We stilled our hunger, and refreshed our souls.

The next evening, my husband went down to the farmer's wife again, but here–a new surprise. She spoke in anger about the great sin we are committing against her, why do we want to kill her. She told us that yesterday morning she had noticed a strange ladder in the stall, and immediately went to tell her father. She reckoned that unknown guests, certainly Jewish partisans, had spent the night in the loft. Now when my husband showed up in the evening, her suspicion fell on him. "When you left here," she said, "I cleared the frost from the window with my breath, and saw you go a little ways, and then return to my shtetl. I went and told my father again that Leibush and his wife were hiding at our place. My father is very fond of you, although the day before he wanted to tell the local police commandant that lives with him about the uninvited guest. But now he regrets it. Especially since the commandant and the few policemen are not in the village having gone to Pulawy for several days. But the danger for me is great; you know that the Germans killed my husband. You will bring catastrophe on me now. You have to go away from here right away."

Levi began to plead and weep for the woman, told her about our hopeless state, that we have nowhere to go. He tells her that I'm in the loft, sick, with frozen infected hands.

[Page 335]

A feeling of pity was awakened in the farmer, and she tells him to get me down from the loft, and she would do something for us. As soon as I got in the house, she smeared oil on my hands, bandaged them, and said, " There is an empty stable in the field that belongs to my father-in-law. The best thing would be for you to move over there. My father will take care of getting food for you. Even if it doesn't work out, none of us will be endangered, because the stable is in an empty field."

We took the two comforters and went to the new spot. There was a chicken coop in the stable. We put two bunches of straw in it, and covered ourselves with the comforters because we were shivering from the cold.

The next day, Saturday, around ten in the morning, we saw through a crack two young farmers coming towards us with axes glistening on their shoulders. We stiffened with fear. There is a disaster coming. The gate of the stable opened with a bang, and we recognized the voice of the young Tkatch, "Leibush, come out!"

My husband began to howl, and began to beg the *shkootzim*[7] to have mercy on us. They don't want to hear about it. Their murderous intentions are clear. I feel that I have to do something. I go out of the coop, take the golden signet ring off my finger, put it in the shaygets's hand, and ask him to leave us alone. It seems that my pleas and tears moved the murderers. They put their axes down, and told us they were giving us just one week to stay in the barn, after which we had to get out. Seeing such a change, I mustered my courage to ask for food. They promised to bring food tomorrow, Sunday, when all the farmers were in church. So it came to pass. Sunday, before noon, they threw in a sac containing several loaves of bread, and two bottles of milk. Monday, the older Tkacz himself came playing the good landlord, covered the open areas, did repairs of the barn, and without uttering one word, left.

We lay stiff with cold and with dulled thoughts. The nightmare of the days past disappeared in view of the present danger. Here it comes now. We hear footsteps, the gate opens, and in the still of the night we hear the voice of the young Tkacz, "Leibush, you have to get out of the stable at once. They're going to be coming here tomorrow to work, and you know what that means."

Yes, we had a good understanding of what that meant.

Fatigued from hunger,

[Page 336]

bodies dehydrated from living for days without water or cooked food, we took the comforters–and again forced to wonder. Where?

We went off to the Bogucin colony, and not asking the landlord, we went into the stable belonging to Karol Drozd, a lame farmer. We crept up to the loft and stayed there for three days without eating or drinking. We felt that hunger and cold were now capable of putting an end to us.

There was a woodshed not far from us. When Drozd's daughter went in there for wood, my husband decided to show himself to her, and beg her to bring her father to the stable. The girl got really scared when Levi appeared, she even began to scream, but my husband calmed her down. She promised to send her father. A little later we heard the thumping of his crutch in the stable. Karol Drozd called Levi for a talk, and asked about certain issues. We knew Drozd was a poor farmer. He was unable to work the few acres he farmed because of his crippled legs, so he relies on workers. We proposed to him that he should keep us with him, and provide food. And for this, he would be rewarded. The farmer quickly agreed. He stipulated it was only for a month, because the wheat would have to be threshed then. It was agreed that we would say with him for 100 zlotys a month. To the farmer's credit, it must be said that he treated us very well, and thanks to the food and his good behavior, we revived somewhat. The month went by quickly, and although we had a promise from the farmer to take us back after the end of the threshing, we had to now leave into the unknown.

* * *

At the end of February 1943, the cold frosty nights had one good attribute: no moon. The darker it was, the better for us alienated people. We trudged in the snow. The road led to our Markuszow. Suddenly a small figure comes toward us. We wanted to avoid her, but it was too late already. The person goes by and says, "Levi!"

We stopped in our tracks. Who recognized us in such a dark night? Yes, it is Rivkeh, my husband's sister. Before we could even embrace her she said all in one breath,

[Page 337]

"Your Chaneleh is alive. She is staying with the old Shikora couple…

Sweet music fills my bones. My head is spinning, but my spirit feels so good, so light. Chanaleh lives. I don't know what is going on. I only hear someone begging me, "Esther, Esther! Get up, have pity on yourself. You must be strong. It is terribly dangerous on this spot. You have to muster your strength, so we can go look at our child. Come to Markuszow."

My husband was right. We had to go see our little swallow. I made an effort, they helped me get up off the snow, and after some time walking, we came to the shtetl. Markuszow is a cemetery for us. So we actually walked among the tombstones, lay down there, and decided to wait for Rivkeh. Here no one will be able to overhear our sister's telling of how Chanaleh was saved:

On November 11th, when Esther lay the child down in Wladslaw Zachniaz's yard, I happened to be there in hiding. There was a party in the farmer's house, because he and several of his friends were celebrating Poland's independence day. Being a little drunk, he went out to the yard, and heard a baby crying. He picked up the swaddled baby, and took it in the house. The farmers present there, quickly sent someone on horseback to maybe find the woman who had abandoned the child. The rider got to Kalen, and asked about a wandering woman, but no one could tell him anything. So they reported it to the soltis in the village of Plinek, and he ordered them to take the child to the gemine in Korew, or else, the entire village could end up in trouble. The Zachniaz farmers, old Shikora, and the soltis immediately went to Korew. The commandant of the Polish police happened to be away, so the gemine clerk decided to put the child into the jail cell, and told the farmers to return the next day. The child was yelling fiercely, and the secretary's wife was so moved that she took the child to herself, fed her a little warm milk, cleaned her up, and changed her. The secretary meanwhile phoned the gendarmerie in Pulawy. Early Monday, two Gestapo showed up to find out what was going on. Their first question was if this was a Jew. The others replied that there are also plenty of Christian women now wandering over the roads, and abandoning their children. One of the Gestapo had a brilliant idea. He took out a coin and showed it to the child. She stretched out her hands to the money. "You see," the German triumphantly shouted, "A Jew is cunning, the child

[Page 338]

is already attracted to money." The other Gestapo proposed trying another method. He showed her a cigarette lighter. Chanaleh wanted to grab it as well. The second German came to the conclusion that you can't know for sure. And the proof–every child is attracted to shiny objects. Furthermore, the lighter was lit; they even held it close to her little face, but she wasn't afraid and wanted to touch the fire. The Germans then decided to send the child back to the village. So that it wouldn't be a burden for one family, they said everybody should look after her for one day. Here the soltis spoke up, "You can't take a child to a different place every day. Therefor…"

The impatient German interrupted him, "Do what you want."

The soltis and several prominent farmers decided to give the child to the childless, old Shikora couple. "I know," Rivkeh ended her story, "that the Shikoras are looking after her like their own child. Chaneleh lacks for nothing…"

Levi and I are overjoyed. For three months we saw death before our eyes so often, said good-bye to life more than once. The child lives, she is healthy, and if the war ends and one of us is alive, we will reclaim the child and raise her Jewish.

Nice dreams, bright hopes. But where do we go now? Waiting for victory here, among the tombstones, was an impossible thing. We were again in despair. Our sister does not lose her wits. She believed she could arrange a hiding place for us with the neighboring farmer. She warned us not to go to Markuszow, to the Bureks. She thought it was better for us to go back to Garbow, to Karol Drozd. She would find us there, and bring us to our new quarters.

We separated from Rivkeh. After a night of wandering, we arrived at Drozd's. we explained to the farmer that we have a shelter, but it will take several days for it to be ready. We agreed that for 250 zlotys, we could spend the few days in our old habitat–in the loft of the cowshed.

We lay covered in the comforters, wondering whether our sister would be able to convince the farmer to take us in. The short winter days are frightfully long. On the fifth day, Rivkeh shows up with the good news that Stanislaw Wiejek agreed to take us in.

[Page 339]

Now the joy was boundless. We will be close to our child. Maybe we would see Chanaleh from a distance? My hear beat faster at just the thought that I will see our child. We waited impatiently for night, our savior and redeemer.

Around 10 in the morning Mrs. Drozd appears on the ladder. She told us breathlessly that the Germans were in the colony, and we must get out right away. But right away; she won't listen to another word. All three of us climb down from the loft. Where to direct our feet? About a kilometer away, we see several piles of manure out in the field. But how do we get there? The blizzard had darkened the brightness of day. We crawled on all fours to our goal. With our last strength we crawled on our bellies on the snow. Our hands became stiffened with cold, our feet–blocks of ice. Only our bodies are hot from the great strain. The manure pile got closer, just a little bit more–and with our stiffened hands we tore at the frozen pile in order to get in. Finally we sat there in the manure, shielded from stranger's eyes, teeth chattering, exhaustion and cold overtaking us completely. We dug deeper into the manure, waiting for night. When it arrived, my husband ran back to say good-bye to Karol Drozd.

* * *

We began to walk to the Bogucin colony. To get to Plinek, a 15-kilometer road awaited us. In normal times, it would not take more than two hours. But we heard the echoes of shots and saw people marching in some places. Perhaps they are Germans? Or maybe fighters of the A.K., or bandits who behave toward Jews exactly like the Germans? In any case, every suspicious noise interrupted our march. We arrived in Plinek at dawn. Rivkeh took us to the farmer, and introduced us. Wiejek made an unsympathetic impression on us. He looked like shabby and lazy. At the first meeting, his wife, who gave the impression of being half-mad, called him a "*lajdak.*"[8]

We agreed on a price. For 1000 zlotys a month we were to get food and a hiding place in the stable. It seemed to us that we would have a relatively peaceful time. But it was not destined to be. Our half-crazy landlady used to become very talkative on certain days. At those times, her mouth would not shut. She talked up a storm.

[Page 340]

We were very afraid she might start to blab about Jews. Fortunately, in her monologues, she talked about everything, except we didn't exist. That's the way the first month went–our pockets were empty. There is no money. We asked the farmer if he would keep us for my fur coat. He agreed, but without food. We gave him 25 zlotys for 50 kilo potatoes. Every day, he took 10 potatoes and cooked them for us. From this, my husband and I subsisted.

But even the potatoes end. We are left with no resources. Rivkeh visits us once a week, but she has nothing to be able to help us. True, we are owed some money from farmers in Bogucin and Garbow. But how do we get to it? Leaving a hiding place is always dangerous. Farmers in the village could notice a stranger leaving Wiejek's *gospodarka*[9] --and we're done for. But we, nevertheless, have to collect the debts, because sitting idly means perishing. The best is the evening, because there is a little movement in the village, and two more people passing through will not be so noticeable. Now, we are outside the village, and along the narrow rail lines that lead to the Garbow sugar mill, we set out.

That was at the end of March 1943.

Not far from the village of Zablocie, we suddenly saw coming toward us, a tall man smoking a cigarette. We wanted to turn back, run to the side, but it was impossible, because there was water on both sides of the rails. Turning back was risky, because the man could shoot after us. Without talking about it, we walked toward the man wanting to avoid him. We were already a few steps past him, when we heard a shout, "Levi! Levi!" We were very startled, but the man turned around to us and asked, " Levi, you don't recognize me? How come I recognized you right away?" we still didn't know who he was, although the voice was very familiar. Finally, we heard his name, Aharon Rubinstein, a Markuszow Jew. To his query as to where we were going, we replied, to Garbow-Bogucin. He warned us not to go there, because lately there had been a skirmish in those places between Jewish partisans and farmers. They were shooting for hours. The neighborhood was agitated, and we sensed strengthened patrols in the area. Aharon Rubinstein relayed how he had been hiding in a haystack for the last 6 days without food or water. Now he was on his way to Bronice to the magnate Laniewski to get some money owed him. My husband warned him not to go there, because they had recently killed several Markuszow Jews: Nachum Fiertog,

[Page 341]

and Mechl Weiner and their families. To his question about where we were staying, we told him with a friendly farmer in the village, Plinek. Our landsman proposes going with us, money would be no problem. We explained to him that it was not so simple. In the end, the farmer has to agree to take in another Jew–and obviously, he would not want to. Rubinstein was however determined to go with us, and having no choice, we went back to Plinek.

In the middle of the night, we knocked on the farmer's window, and he came out frightened, knowing that we were supposed to return in two or three night's time. When he saw Rubinstein, his panicked question, "What happened," comes out in a shouting why did you bring me a third. He didn't want to hear about taking in one more. He was ready to drive us away, because he was afraid to be hiding Jews. "The Germans," he reasoned, " don't give you a pat on the cheek for this." The farmer thought that the Jew we brought was a partisan, those the Germans called "bandits." In anger he said, "What, a *bandzior*[10] I needed?"

We begged the framer to go into the house, and there with tears and weeping we tried to convince him to have pity on unfortunate people, and not drive them into the arms of death. Let the newcomer stay until tomorrow night, and he would be well rewarded. Finally, we were able to break through the stubbornness of the farmer. He agreed to keep the third for just one day.

The next day Aharon Rubinstein had a talk with the farmer, and promised to pay him 1000 zlotys a month for himself alone. That means the same sum we had to pay for the two of us. Because of that, the farmer changed his behavior to us, exhibiting more care and interest in the new "client."

This situation obtained for three months. The time came to leave the place. Like in all similar cases– quickly, unexpected, and in great haste.

One day, a Jewish girl came to Wiejek from Korew. She was dressed as a village girl. The goal of her visit–to collect a debt from our landlord. The result was that, in that moment, a danger appeared in his yard, and it was soon spread around the village, that there were Jews on Wiejek's property. The farmer only found out about it the next day when he went for guard duty at the city hall in Korew. (By German orders, the farmers had to guard the city hall every night) Wiejek overheard the other farmers in the guard talking about hidden Jews in Plinek, and that it would be

[Page 342]

the right thing to do to immediately inform the gendarmes. The farmer secretly left the guards, and ran to us with the unconditional demand that we leave. We asked him, where to, but the farmer knew that danger threatened him, and that his entire farm would go up in smoke, and he and all his household would be shot.

Having no choice, we left the stable

After several obstacles, we arrived at the Bogucin colony, travelling the 15 km road. We found a ladder, and at 1:00 am, we went up to the loft of our old acquaintance, Karol Drozd. Without his knowledge, of course. It so happened that early the next morning, it occurred to the farmer lady to look for something in the loft, and she discovered us right away. She began to shout, "*Zlaszto stad!*" (Get out of here). We begged her to call her husband, but she wouldn't hear of it. She fell into a bigger rage, and threatened to tell the neighbors that Jews stole into her loft. With these words, she left.

Depressed, we stayed where we were. Moving out from here by day would result in our certain death. Then, her daughter came to get some wood from the shed. Levi went down to beg her to call her father. The young farmer also reacted with hysterical screams, and threatened us with the worst. Nevertheless, she sent her father. We heard his crutches banging on the cement floor of the stable. I went down to him, and with tears, I begged the good farmer to allow us to stay just two more weeks, until we could return to the previous hideout we temporarily had to leave. He agreed to let in just me and my husband. As for the third, Aharon Rubinstein, he did not want him to stay for even one minute. We explained to the farmer that the third is very capable of paying. He is owed money by the farmers, and even by the magnate, Broniewski. We promise Drozd 500 zlotys for us, and the same from Rubinstein, and this for only two weeks. The farmer did not want to give in. We argued for a long time with him using various arguments– until he let himself be convinced, and he underlined, not more than two weeks.

All three go back to the loft.

After fourteen days, the farmer informed us that they were going to repair the roof of the stable. We had to get out–and the sooner the healthier. In the meantime, my husband's sister, Rivkeh, visited us, and told us

[Page 343]

that in Plinek no searches had taken place at all, the village was quiet, and it was quite likely that we could return to the previous place. So we went off to Plinek. Wiejek was happy knowing that every month a little sum awaited him.

The first night, my sister-in-law stayed with us, and at dawn, she went to her hideout. She returned a few days later, and told us that quite by chance, she saw our child. The old Shikora woman was carrying her in her arms, but her clothes were quite tattered. Rivkeh also promised to see us twice a week and bring bread that she received in a larger portion.

```
From left to right: Esther Grossman-Kitenkorn, her rescued
little daughter, the farmer lady, Shikora
Standing center: Levi Grossman
```

We were, however, concerned at that moment for the fate of the child, and we decided to send the Shikora couple a few hundred zlotys, ostensibly from unknown people, in order to dress the little girl better. The plan succeeded, and as Rivkeh reported to us later, she saw Chanaleh dressed nicely. That was a big consolation in those difficult times we experienced then through lack of food.

One evening, we overheard a conversation between our

[Page 344]

landlord and his brother-in-law. He was bragging that he lacked nothing now that he was hiding Jews. Revealing such a secret in those days meant–putting us in danger, because everyone wanted to share in extracting money from Jews. That same evening, we decided to leave this place, and move over to Karol Drozd's loft (in the Bogucin colony).

Chanaleh Grossman,
the rescued child-now in Israel

No sooner said than done. Wednesday night Levi and Aharon went there, after coordinating with us that if they failed to come back soon, Rivkeh and I should go there Saturday night.

At the agreed-upon time, my sister-in-law and I arrived at the colony. Before we could even enjoy the reunion, Levi told us the following story: "Around midnight, I knocked on the lame farmer, Karol Drozd's door. He received me quite amicably, served bread and sour cream–

[Page 345]

a meal I hadn't eaten for years. We had hardly finished swallowing the last bite of the delicious meal, when we heard a commotion outside. The farmer said that several sleighs with strangers arrived, and he asked me to hide under the bed. I crawled under the spot he showed me, and at the same time, I heard knocking on the window, with an order to open it fast. I lay under the bed in fear of death, although according to the answer that the farmer gave, I understood that they were partisans knocking. Karol Drozd shouted through the window that Germans are expected momentarily to demand their allotment, and if they find anyone staying with him–he is lost. "We're not afraid of the cursed Germans," was the reply from the other side of the window. The farmer opened the door, and an armed man appeared. He examined every corner of the rom with an electric flashlight, and looked under the bed. "Why are you hiding from me?" I heard in a homey Yiddish voice. "Levi, do you not recognize me?" It was the partisan, Moishe Pelz. He helped me crawl out from under the bed, and we heartily kissed. Then more partisans came in, all Markuszow boys: Isser Rosenberg, Shmuel Rubinstein, Shmuel Laks, David Rubinstein, and others. The joy at our reunion was extraordinarily great. They asked about you, Esther, and about our baby. We sat at the farmer's house almost all night, and we took turns asking each other about various issues. They stayed for the day, and Isser Rosenberg gave me a souvenir–a leather briefcase that once belonged to a Polish landowner. To his question as to whether I need money, I thanked them. The partisans left in the late evening, and I felt so good that our Markuszow youth roamed over field and forest, weapons in hand, ready to take on a powerful, pitiless enemy.

* * *

Karol Drozd agreed to let us hide in his stable. All three of us took to the work, supported the dugout with beams and lumber, and achieved a pretty good hideout. There we lived in a group of three until the end of May 1944 surviving more than once moments of terror and death angst. Once a relative of the landlord, a 21-year-old Pole came to us, and threatening us with a revolver, he took our watches, and the last of our money.

[Page 346]

Until the worst happened. Especially since the good news from the front had reached us, and the hopes of being free began to seem real. Karol Drozd came to us with his daughter, and categorically demanded that my husband and I leave the stable. By his tone, we felt that this time, we could not avert the bitter decree. We also tried to get A. Rubinstein to lobby for us–but without success. We left the stable dejected and embittered. A. Rubinstein remained in the place.

Majdanek was already in flames… Times were so terrible that even the boldest farmers were afraid to stick their heads out.

The two of us wandered on the Lugow-Garbow road. Suddenly we saw a man with a rifle. We began to run. My husband threw himself on the ground disappearing among the stalks. I heard a cry in Polish, "Stay still!" I see a rifle aimed at me "Are you a *Zhidovke*?"[11] the stranger asked me. "Yes," I answered resigned. "Who is your husband?" "Leibush Grossman," I said quietly. "So you're the wife of Leibush. I almost shot you both. I think he just ran away from you. Where is he? I'm very fond of your husband. I know you don't trust me. You don't actually have to tell me where he is right now. Take this basket of cherries, and take some to him. But go carefully. The road is now full of danger."

The armed man went away. Then I found my husband, and I told him about the extraordinary meeting. We both continued on our way. But where? Sha, let's go to Plinek–specifically to the farmer holding our child. After a night of wandering through fields while bullets and even rockets are flying over our heads, we arrived at dawn in Plinek, and knocked on the door of the old Shikora couple.

"Who's there?" we heard from behind the door.

"The parent of the child," we both answered.

The old man opened the door, and very lovingly welcomed us, and honored us with a good meal. We didn't want to go near the food, and asked him about the child.

"She's sleeping now with the "*matke*."

On tiptoes we went into the other room, and saw our two and a half year old Chanaleh, her eyes shut, lying in the arms of the old Shikora. Her breathing was calm and a bright smile appeared on her little face. Maybe Chanaleh had felt the presence of her real parents?

[Page 347]

And maybe she's just dreaming about them? The child continued to sleep her quiet sleep. It was just us who felt complete joy, and sublime good fortune looking at our rediscovered child. As quietly as we entered the room, we left it. The farmer led us into the stable, wished us goodnight, and told us consolingly that we won't have to struggle much longer, the front was getting closer and the Russians were chasing the Germans nonstop.

Again in hiding, but how different from all those other hiding times. We see our child every day, but Chanaleh cries, doesn't want to come to me… "*Ja chce do matki*," (I want to go to my mother)–Chaneleh begs, and the mother in her mind is the old farmer…

After two weeks at the Shikoras, we suddenly began to hear artillery fire, and the sound of hundreds of airplanes carried to our ears. Now it rang like the most beautiful music. We knew that it meant the end of the occupation, and our troubles. That Sunday, there was a terrible rainstorm. Nevertheless, old Shikora did us a favor and drove to Korew to find out what was really going on at the fronts. He returned and told us that the shtetl had already been liberated, but that the Germans had returned a day later. That's why he advised us not to leave the shelter yet, but to wait for a week or two, because you can never predict what happens at the front. We took the good farmer's advice–and remained in the stable.

On Monday, farmers returned from Korew to Plinek, and reported that they had seen massive columns of Soviet military going through in the direction of Warsaw. Lublin was already liberated. And Markuszow as well. We decided to go to Markuszow. There we met with Jan Burek who looked at us as if we had returned from the other world. I then went to my father's grave and told him that we have been left alone, forlorn, because all our close ones have been killed by the Nazi murderers.

The next day we travelled to Garbow, to our farmer acquaintance, Wartacz. He received us cordially, gave us a good meal, and harnessed a pair of horses so we could go to Lublin. There, in the once police-commissariat on Zielona Street, which was now the headquarters of the militia, we met many Markuszow young people, the security guards of the city. Yankl Kesselbrenner helped us get settled in a room on Lubartowska Street. My husband got employment with him, and I went to

[Page 348]

Plinek three times a week to see my child, and bring toys and treats. Until the moment came when I asked old Shikora how much she wanted for returning to me my flesh and blood. She did not want to hear of it. I gave her to understand that I could take Chanaleh back with the help of the police. She understood that the matter was a losing one for her, and after long negotiations, she returned my daughter to me for the price of three pigs, two pair of boots, and two fur coats. For most of the two years–from November 11th 1942, when I laid Chaneleh down by the Shikora's fence–until now, Novemebr 17th 1944, when I got her back, a stormy and tragic period had been lived through. But we didn't want to dwell on the past, because the luck of finding our child was so great, so moving…

Overjoyed, I returned to Lublin, and the father too lived to rejoice in the rescued child. After several months in Poland, we travelled to Germany–at that time practically the only way that led to Eretz-Israel. In 1949, we arrived in the Jewish land so yearned for.

Translator's Footnotes:

1. Germany broke the Molotov-Ribbentrop non-aggression pact with Russia, and launched Operation Barbarossa in June 1941.
2. A grassy lawn area
3. Young gentile punks
4. I believe Plinek is the Yiddish version for the village of Plonki, 3 km SE of Kurow
5. Kalen, 3 km east of Plonki
6. Oh God
7. Young gentile punks
8. Polish, scoundrel
9. Farm
10. Polish, thug
11. Jewish woman

[Page 349]

Miriam LOTERSTEIN

Translated by Moses Milstein

The daughter of Ber and Faige, born in 1939 in Markuszow, saved from death thanks to the efforts of our partisans

In 1943, before they were killed by the Nazi murderers, her parents managed to give their little daughter to a farmer they knew in Gutanow. A little while later, the farmer, whether out of fear of betrayal, or out of wickedness, threw the child away in a field. It was winter. By chance, a farmer who had been gathering wood in the forest, passed through the field. He took the child back to his house, saved her from the cold and hunger, and kept her with him.

Since the Markuszow partisan bands were already active at that time, they became interested in Miriam LOTERSTEIN's fate, and found out where she was. From that point on, the child was handed from one farmer to another with the agreement of the partisans who paid for her support, and took an interest in the fate of the little orphan.

After liberation, the child was reclaimed from a farmer, and taken to the first Jewish orphanage in Lublin. Miriam had been very neglected in that time, and it took a lot of time and effort before the child got back a human face. Thanks to the rescue-aliyah of Poland, Miriam was taken to Switzerland, and after a health recovery stay of several months, she made aliyah to Israel. Now she is in the *Kvutsah Neve Eitan*,[1] in the Beit She'an Valley.

Translator's Footnote:

1. A *kvutsah* is a collective agricultural settlement, precursor of the kibbutz.

[Page 350]

In the Partisan Movement

Shmuel Laks (Tel Aviv)

Translated by Moses Milstein

On Sunday September 3 1939, as the first transports of retreating Polish soldiers and fleeing refugees were starting to be seen in Markuszow, the shtetl was bombed. In the span of two hours, incendiary and explosive bombs laid waste to half the houses. At that time, we were operating a bakery in which we continued to bake bread all day and night for the army and the civilian population. Afraid of looting and theft, we did not leave Markuszow during the bombing, although the majority of the residents fled to the neighboring villages. When we finally saw the results of the attack–the dead, and wounded, the burned down houses, all of us who had stayed in the shtetl were seized by panic, and fled in all directions. Sunday evening, we also left Markuszow. Early the next morning, I went back with my younger brother to the shtetl to see what was gong on. It just so happened that another aerial bombardment began. So we both ran to a potato field, and waited for the aerial attack to stop. When the killers of the air had left, we entered the shtetl, and the first shocking picture revealed itself to our eyes: a human body without a head. We quickly went away to the burning houses to see if we could help save someone. A little later my father, mother, younger brother and the rest of the family members arrived in the shtetl. We helped the wounded, and with putting out the fires. As we affirmed, the first Jewish victim was Fradel's four-year-old girl who had run into a field and was chased by an airplane shooting machine guns and shooting innocent people. The child was badly wounded and died later.

Our rescue efforts were too weak in the face of the flames from the incendiary bombs. People fled again from the village. Whoever managed to

[Page 351]

save a few things from a burning house, wrapped it up quickly and ran off to a village. Our family went to the village, Wola-Przybyslawska, and arranged accommodation with a farmer we knew, a blacksmith. We had no financial means to live on. Fortunately, the farmer was a good old friend, and he didn't demand any money for our support. He was a steady customer of ours, who bought bread from us all year, but didn't pay until after the harvest. That was why he was now displaying trust and credit. We understood, however, that this could not go on for long. In the midst of the greatest tragedy, we had remembered to bury a little matzah mill in the ground. We dug up this treasure, and brought it to the village. Thanks to this mill, we were able to bake bread for the farmers from the grain the farmers brought to us. We, the young ones, milled the grain, and my father ran the bakery. In this way, we provided bread for the framers and the evacuated Jews.

-2-

When the war operations ended, most of the Jews came back to Markuszow. Everyone began to rebuild according to his means. We fixed up our house. Because the oven had not been burned; we baked bread again.

While still in Wole, groups of young people carried around plans to escape to Russia. Believing that no Jew can be safe around Germans, the youngsters dreamed about smuggling themselves across the border to Romania, and from there, sailing to Eretz-Israel. There were some among them who had already joined up with the second aliyah in Sniatyn, but had had to return to the shtetl when the war broke out. To this group of "Romanians" belonged Shmuel Rubinstein, Dovid'che Ettinger, Chaim Goldschlager, Fishl Schildkraut, and me and my younger brother. Fishl Schildkraut had planned to bribe the border guards, because he had already had success in crossing the border. We wanted to leave home on bicycles without the knowledge of our parents. But not everyone had a bike, and it was necessary to raise money so the whole group would have bicycles. Money was no problem, because there were some wealthier kids in the group. We could not, however, get another two bicycles. Nevertheless, we decided to take them riding double, in order to leave no one behind. Our baggage

[Page 352]

had to be just a change of shirt. The preparations for the voyage were made in top secrecy.

One evening, the guys called me out and told me they had found a rifle. We smeared it with Vaseline, wrapped it in rags, and hid it in a tall tree that was standing near the main road, in the certainty that no one would think to look for weapons at such a spot. In the process, we thought that if our trip to Romania should not succeed, a rifle like this could come in handy…The next day, we learned that some military had stayed in the nearby forest. So we went off there with the hope of finding weapons. We searched all day, but found nothing. It's likely that farmers had been there before us.

On the eve of our departure, our parents found out about their children's plans. The matter became complicated, because in those difficult days we did not want to go against our parents' wishes, and leave them alone. Of our entire group, only Simcha Ettinger, and Aharon Rubinstein succeeded in getting a carriage, and after a while on the road, they returned reporting that it was impossible to get any food along the way, even for money. It was their opinion that we should not undertake such a danger-filled journey. Their information, and the opposition from our parents, resulted in our giving up the entire plan, even though we desperately wanted to travel to Eretz-Israel.

-3-

The first entry of the Germans to Markuszow resulted in the death of Chaim Goldschlager, a resident of Staroscin. He had begun to run as soon as he saw German military vehicles. The murderers shot after him, and killed him. If we had not yet had an exact idea of what the Germans were, the murder of Chaim Goldschlager opened the eyes of many of us to see the occupiers in their true light.

Life in the shtetl, in the meantime, went on in "normal" ways. We began to organize our lives again, worrying about employment, money. Germans marching through bought from Jews, and actually paid for everything, and we wanted to believe that we would survive the war-years like this.

The Wehrmacht began to go closer to the Soviet border. Gendarmes began to show up in Markuszow, and there was more supervision of the shtetl that lay on the main route of German military transport.

[Page 353]

The shtetl became less homey, uneasy. People wanted to run, but the optimists dissuaded them, and related, although with true facts, that German soldiers often gave chocolate to the children, and from time to time, cigarettes for the older ones. In the meantime, fleeing became difficult. Jews coming back reported that the way to the Bug was becoming impossible, people were beaten and bayoneted on the road. Crossing the border was hopeless. The returnees themselves tried to establish themselves in the shtetl. Business was actually booming thanks to trade with Warsaw and other places that Markuszow supplied wheat and other agricultural products to. Some Jews did very well. People began to improve their houses and dwelling places. The impression was that the tempest of war had passed through already.

Soon, however, they limited Jewish trade. Markuszow Jews could not budge out of Markuszow more than a radius of 5 kilometers without special permission. So some Jews took Poles as partners, and continued business on a big scale.

German rule in the shtetl began to harden. The Judenrat that had been created, first of all, had a duty to supply a contingent of laborers. Until that point, the Germans would snatch any Jew they encountered on the street for forced labor. We already knew that between 7 and 10 in the morning it was healthiest to hide. In catching Jews for work, carrying out searches, and attacking Jews, the Volksdeutsche distinguished themselves for their evil. Jews were also forbidden to be outside at night, or to walk on the main road, just in the side streets.

-4-

My brother and I couldn't tolerate these restrictions, especially to be forced to sit at home in the evenings. So we arranged for work at a German company, Schtrassen and Brikenbau, in Garbow. I was employed in the lock division, my brother, in the carpentry section. Thanks to the workplace, we acquired certificates that protected us from being dragooned for labor, and we had the right to be out at night. The majority of the youth of the shtetl were taken for hard work in Pulawy unloading rocks at the train station, or other work.

At the job, we worked for 8, 10 or sometimes 12 hours a day. The manual laborers were badly treated. They were beaten

[Page 354]

at every opportunity. Only three tradesmen were treated not badly, Finkelstein, my brother and I. Our salary was 1 zloty, 20 groshen an hour, like the Poles, with the difference that our earnings went to the master "for a drink." But for us the important thing was the work paper and not their money. Thanks to the chance to go out at night, we could arrange for flour for the bakery, and my father was free of slave labor thanks to his running the bakery.

Friday night, when we really wanted to go home to our parents who were waiting for us impatiently and nervously, the master always had an urge to get drunk, and with us of all people. So we would sit for hours drinking, and not until late at night did we get to go home on foot. The next day, Saturday, the drunken master would come to the shtetl, and start chasing Jews with his loaded revolver. He also threatened to shoot the chairman of the Judenrat, Shliamke Goldwasser. I calmed the master down, and even took away his revolver.

A while later, the master was transferred to an SS division, and another came in his place. At the same time an order was issued not to employ any Jews for paid work. Nevertheless, my brother and I got paid under the same conditions as before, i.e, that the earnings went into the master's pocket. We had to get drunk with him too. After this particular master was transferred to the "death organization," where no Jew was allowed to be employed, he was ready to take me along as a Pole. I refused, however, not wanting to be separated from my parents. We remained in the shtetl.

-5-

With the outbreak of the Soviet-German war, the situation in the shtetl became significantly worse. Gendarmes began to run riot in Markuszow, and run roughshod over the Jews. One of the gendarmes, a certain Nepert, used to beat and curse every Jew he encountered. He would barge into a Jewish house, take the best of whatever out of there, and command the person to clean the toilet with his hands. More than once, he ordered them to eat the filth.

Once, they called my father to the authorities. When he went there, he ran into Nepert. The killer called my father into a separate room, and murderously beat him with a truncheon so badly that my father had to spend six months in bed. The entire burden of running the bakery

[Page 355]

now fell on my mother and the children. Even the youngest child, 7-year-old Noah, felt that he had to help out the family, and he did it well.

That same Nepert took great care that no Jews would attend the Monday market. As soon as a Jewish merchant saw the killer coming from a distance, he quickly grabbed his bit of merchandise and took off, so that a little later, when Nepert had gone, he could return to the market. In a lot of cases, the merchandise was left on its own, because the frightened Jew preferred to save his life.

During Nepert's rule in Markuszow, the most pious Jews had to shave off their beards, and the traditional Jewish hats changed for the farmer's "*Macziewuke.*" Still today, I can see before my eyes, the completely changed appearance of the very pious Yomele Yosef's without his beard and the cap on his head.

At that time German punitive expeditions appeared in the shtetl whose actual job was to mobilize Polish youth in work battalions ("*jonakes*"). Nevertheless, they did not let any opportunity go by to harass the Jews, breaking into their homes, and hideouts, and abusing the unlucky. Even a work permit issued by the German authorities did not protect the Jews from the sadists. Even my brother and I, possessors of a card from a German firm, were once caught for labor. We managed to get out of it and hid in an attic from which we could see what they were doing to the captured Jews. They took them to Antek Czepa's orchard where there were telephone poles prepared. The Germans ordered that two Jews should pick up such a long heavy pole, and lift it up and down until they fell from exhaustion. When they finished their sadistic games with this group of Jews, they went off to capture others who were ordered to perform a different kind of "sport:" Every one of them had to jump fully clothed into the fish pond in the orchard, and take the frogs out of there. The Germans claimed that the frogs were disturbing their sleep, so they had to be destroyed.

-6-

One day, gendarmes and Jewish police from Lublin arrived in the shtetl, and demanded a contingent of young Jews for labor.

[Page 356]

The Judenrat replied that they could not obey this order, because all the Markuszow Jews, especially the younger ones, had stable jobs. At the same time, our Judenrat managed to inform the Markuszow Jewish policemen that they should warn the shtetl youth about the danger, and to hide themselves, because there would probably be a hunt for them. As in many other cases, the Judenrat wanted to buy off the Germans, but without success.

The hunt actually soon began, but the killers could only catch two Jews. Most of the youth hid in the *laches*,[1] near the railroad tracks. One Jewish policeman from Lublin noticed the runaways, and went off after them to detain them. He managed to grab one of our youth by the arm (I don't remember his name now), but this particular servant of the Germans was properly beat up, and left with empty hands, and went back to where he had come from.

The two captured Jews were taken to Majdanek where they stayed for one month. Thanks to a large bribe, the Judenrat managed to bring them back to the shtetl. We saw two living skeletons. Each one had lost about 20 kilos in body weight.

Our Judenrat gave serious thought to establishing a permanent employment place for Markuszow Jews, so they wouldn't be subject to the caprices of the local and foreign killers who got great satisfaction from grabbing Jews for labor.

After major efforts, a work place was established in Kloda, 5 km from Markuszow thanks to the bribing of the German authorities in Pulawy with a large sum of money. The work consisted of digging rocks out of the ground, and in most cases, reburying them again the following day in order to remove them once more. The elder there, a Pole, got his tip, and thanks to that, the conditions were not the worst.

A while later, we were forced to send about 40 men to the Janiszow camp. In order not to create the impression in the shtetl that only kids from poor families were being sent there, the first group sent there came from better-off families. Then they were exchanged for another group.[2]

[Page 357]

-7-

On Pesach 1942, the Judenrat received an order to provide a list of 500 Jews, together with the people. The Judenrat thought that in order to save the youth, the parents should voluntarily report themselves. There was a great commotion, because we felt that we were supplying the angel of death. And we knew one other thing: the 500 would not quench the Germans' thirst for Jewish blood.

A tragic debate began in Jewish homes: to show up on one's own, or wait to be called. The killers only cared about the quantity, the number that had to match. For us Jews, it meant tearing away from the family one of its members, our own flesh and blood, to sacrifice oneself for others.

That evening in our house is well etched in my memory: my whole family–grandmother, parents, three brothers, three uncles, and three aunts discussed the fatal decree affecting such a large number of Jews. The first to speak was my grandmother, Ruchel Laks, who because of her piety and adherence to kosher laws, lived in our house.

"Kinderlach, I have already lived my life. The few years I have left to live, are not worth anything to me, especially in these bitter times. I will be the first to register, and let's hope you will all be saved by this.

None of us wanted to agree to this. The next morning early, grandmother was the first to get up, and she went straight to the gemine place where the Jews were supposed to assemble. The rest of the family members fled out of the shtetl to wait out the storm.

In the evening we returned home. A Pole we knew told us that it was quiet in the shtetl now that the Germans had gone. The next day, the rest of the Jews who had fled returned to Markuszow frightened and ready to leave again should danger approach. The Judenrat asked several young people to go to the road to Naleczow on which our parents and brothers and sisters were driven yesterday, in order to pick up the dead bodies and bury them in a Jewish cemetery. Shmuel Rubunstein, Motl Pelz, Dovid'che Ettinger, me and my brother, provided with a special permission from the gemine authority, set out on the road of death of the Markuszow Jews.

[Page 358]

It was Friday, and it was pouring rain, and the muddy road made walking difficult. We asked about the marching Jews at practically every house. We wanted to have a clearer picture of their last journey. They told us that the Jews were transported to Przybyslawska on wagons that the farmers had to supply. In Przybyslawska, they were ordered to get off the wagons, and they were driven further on foot on the soaked Polish road, but through the mud only, preventing anyone from walking on a dry place.

At Kolonia Gory we noticed a fresh pile of dirt, like a grave. A farmer told us that, on that spot, a Jew who had been shot was buried yesterday. We made a sign, memorized the spot, and continued on, even though our permission was only to Kolonia Gory. A few hundred meters farther on, we saw another grave–and that was an order for us to continue. We believed that one of the Jews had surely left a letter or a sign of some kind. In the village of Olefin we came across various papers, and among them–names from siddurs, chumashes, and other religious books. And another grave. We really wanted to know which of our hometown Jews was covered by this foreign earth for eternity. So we went to the soltis to ask for permission to remove the buried body. He required a written permission from the gemine, and we could only dig up the body and identify it. We had to make do with asking the farmers about the appearance of the person who was buried there yesterday on that spot. According to their description and signs, we understood that this was the fresh grave of the Markuszow cantor, Moishe Beinishe's (Weinriber).

In the meantime, it had become darker, and we had to return home and bring the bodies of the Jews who had been shot. Aside from that, we knew that any delay would cause profound worry back home. We got horse and wagon from the soltis in Gory, took the bodies of Yehoshua Tuvieh's, and Shifra Leibke's from the graves. Before we had set out, the Judenrat told us we were to leave the bodies at Asher Beigelman's house. We did so, and went to the Judenrat with our report.

That Saturday after the deportation was terrible, full of unrest and sorrow. There was someone missing in every Jewish home. There were no illusions that the same fate awaited the Jews still alive.

[Page 359]

-8-

Not long after the first deportation, we again got the sinister news about having to assemble at the gemine square. We also heard about the disaster carried out by the Germans in neighboring Korew that became empty of Jews. So we left Markuszow now instead of going to the gemine place. My father and youngest brother hid at a Pole they knew in Markuszow; I, my mother, and other brother went to a cellar in the shtetl itself. We could certainly have left the shtetl, but we were motivated by curiosity to see what was happening, and that's why we stayed in Markuszow. Someone however betrayed us, and several Markuszow firemen, led by my onetime classmate, Soral, took us to the gemine place where there were another 50 Jews who had been captured like us. They took us to the previous ghetto in Konskowola. At that point, Konskowola was completely Judenrein. Right away the next day, we started to think about running away from there. We left on the road to Markuszow, and there we saw a transport of Markuszow Jews. So we decided to return to the shtetl we had just left, because in the passing transport, we noticed our father and brother. We met them in Konskowola and they told us that having learned about our being sent to Konskowola, a group of Markuszow Jews decided to go there in order to meet up with their own people, and be together with them. We were greatly upset by these events, because we weren't supposed to voluntarily hand ourselves over to the German animals.

In the meantime, an order was issued that all the Jews found in Konskowola had to, within the space of one hour, assemble at the synagogue. It was not hard to figure out what that signified. And although there was no point in hiding, because the noose was being tightened around our necks more and more, we also didn't want to hand ourselves over to the murderers. The designated hour meanwhile was coming to an end, and we did not know what to do. So my brother and I climbed up to an attic to have a look at the neighborhood. Perhaps we could find a way to flee. It turned out, however, that the entire shtetl was surrounded by Ukrainians, and there was no chance of leaving the shtetl. So we went to the synagogue. There were about 1000 Jews gathered there, driven here from the surrounding shtetls.

[Page 360]

Suddenly the sound of Yiddish singing came to our ears. We distinctly heard Chasidic melodies. Some of us ran to the windows, and saw hundreds of Jews from Miechow on the synagogue street, with sefer-Torahs in their arms, dancing and singing. Of course, they were doing this on the orders of the killers.

As soon as the Miechow Jews had gone, armed Germans and Ukrainians broke into the shul courtyard, and ordered the Jews to get out. Two SS were stationed at the door inside, and another two outside. One of the Germans outside hit every exiting Jew on the back and shouted, "To the right!" We rarely heard the word, "left."

After this selection it turned out that of the 1000, only 17 were told to go left. Among the 17 were several Markuszowers: two sons of Yehoshua Greier, Avrum Zukerman, and my brother and me. The rest of the Jews, those on the right, were taken to the Pulawy train station. We, the 17, remained in the shul building. Suddenly we heard a shot, and the scream of a child. It seems that a young Jewish child had been left in the shul, and as soon as one of the killers saw this, he quickly took the young life. We were ordered to collect the body and hand it over to the Jewish police in Konskowola. This we did.

The 17 were not prevented from moving around freely, and I wanted to take advantage of this to take my condemned parents and younger brother out of their group. Getting our parents out was out of the question, but we could have easily got our brother out. Our parents convinced him to run away with us, but the young man stubbornly refused arguing that he didn't want to leave the parents alone, and wherever they went, he would go too. I went back to Konskowola, looked up a Pole I knew, and asked him to follow (for money, of course) the transport of deported Jews, and see what happens to them. Three days later he returned, and reported that, from the Pulawy station, the Jews were taken away in sealed freight cars. He followed them until Lublin, but further, he could not go. It was forbidden to approach the freight cars, and the presence of a stranger in a small train station, even a Pole, would have aroused suspicion.

[Page 361]

-9-

We remained in Konskowola, and were employed building an airfield outside Pulawy. We had to remove the topsoil, and flatten out the whole site. This kind of work required both knowledge and physical endurance. My brother and I quickly caught on to the gist of, for us, the new profession, and the overseers had reason to be happy. For that reason, we didn't lack food, and their behavior towards us was good. The few Markuszowers now kept close together.

One time at work, I noticed my cousin, Shmuel Rosenberg, walking between two Polish policemen. I knew he had been hiding in the village of Wole, and his appearance here accompanied by police did not signify anything good. I gave him signs that he should escape and mix in with our group of workers. He was unable to do it. Later, I found out that he was discovered in his hiding place, and shot in Pulawy.

I got a new job in the camp. I drove the small locomotive that pulled carts. My job was to bring the empty carts in time to the excavator machine that quickly filled them with earth, and bring them to another place where young girls were waiting who then overturned them and emptied them out. Once, while discharging the soil, one of the carts got stuck. The two girls who were supposed to tilt the cart made superhuman efforts, but the mass of iron would not yield. The rest of the girls ran over to help, but their combined efforts were not successful due to their poor diet and the harsh conditions. I saw the crowd at the cart from my little locomotive, and felt that danger threatened because we were staying too long on one spot, and the excavator had already prepared another load. I jumped off the locomotive and quickly ran over to the immobile cart, and gave it a push so that it turned over, and the earth spilled out. The German overseer, who did not spare whacking people across their backs with his thin rod, hit me with all his strength across my back so I immediately felt blood from top to bottom. I went back on the locomotive in pain and anger, and set off with such force that the carts jumped off the rails. The hard work of putting them back on the rails was done accompanied by blows and curses.

[Page 362]

I later told the head master about the incident, and he actually consoled me and promised to make efforts on my behalf to make it easier for me in the camp. He was even prepared to take me back and forth to work in his car, because we walked the road to the airfield, one hour each way.

The physical pain of the blows, and the moral suffering caused by the gross behavior of the new overseer, made me think that I couldn't go on very long, and I would probably have to find a way to escape. Coincidentally, at that time, a large transport of Czechoslovakian Jews arrived. Since they arrived on a Friday, and with a lot of baggage, we sat down to table and celebrated a Friday evening with candle blessing, challah, wine and other good food. The Slovakian Jews were strongly convinced that their home was only temporarily changed, and they would quickly be freed to return to their old homes. We, the local Jews, saw things completely differently. The fact that they brought Jews here from so far away demonstrated to us that Hitler's paws reached everywhere, and that the death sentence on Jews did not mean only Polish Jewry. It was possible that the murderers had already finished with the Jews of Poland, and now they could be employed with the annihilation of Jews from other European countries.

I determined to escape, and told my brother and Avrum Zukerman about it. Both agreed with the plan, and it was decided that I would be the first to go. If they hadn't received any news from me in eight days, they were to come after me to Belzec.

I hit the road at dawn. The hardest was to get out of Konskowola. I barely made it to the valley near the shtetl; lay down there for a little in the grass still wet from dew. After a brief rest, I combed my hair like a *shaygetz*, and cautiously continued my march. I was supposed to get to Wawolnica, and from there to Loki, from where it was easier to get to Belzec. Along the way, I avoided several older farmers, and asked some young shepherds in which direction to go. I had a list of villages that lay along my route. Around noon, I approached Wawolnica, and began to think that it was very dangerous now, in the middle of the day, to be going through the shtetl. Waiting until night meant sleeping outside, not eating, and most importantly, adding another day or two to the journey.

[Page 363]

Without realizing it, I had come to Wawolnica, gone through the back streets and out the other side of the shtetl. I kept going and came to a crossroads. One sign read: Lubki–11 kilometers. I went in that direction through a quiet country road, and arrived there in the evening. One mustn't stop though, danger lurks from every corner. I kept going, and late that night I found myself in the village of Wojciechow. I suddenly felt a gnawing hunger, but knocking on a door now would be dangerous. There were still 6 km to the Kolonia. Although it was late, I decided to continue on my way. I took the switchblade out of my pack, opened it up, and felt somewhat safer. I came to a cottage, knocked on the door, and to the question from the farmer of where I was coming from, I told him I was a Pole from outside Lublin who had run away from the "*Junaken*," (Polish youth organization working for the Germans). The farmer believed me, gave me a good meal, and even proposed I spend the night. I thanked him, and explained that I wanted to reach Milocin tonight to deliver greetings from a Junak who had been alongside me at work. The farmer gave me a loaf of bread with lard and wished me good luck. I thanked him with a real Christian "*Niech bedzie Pochwalony Jezus Chrystus*" (Praise be Jesus Christ), and happy and full, I quickly headed off to Belzec. I knew the city, and went in via back roads, and got to grandmother's house where everyone embraced me, and asked about the family. I did not want to hide the fact of my parents' death from them. I could not sleep a wink that night. The knowledge tortured me: maybe I was responsible for my parents' death?

I got up in the morning, and went about the shtetl to find out what was going on. It became clear to me that Belzec was awaiting the same fate as all the shtetls with a Jewish population, although the local residents (and others too) wanted to convince themselves that they were different. I decided to go to a farmer I knew in the village, and take care of my brother, who was supposed to be coming in a few days, there. The farmer received me in quite a friendly manner, and proposed I stay and work. That appealed to me very much. The farmer even entrusted me with the keys, but after a few days I concluded his wife was stealing from him, and that could get me in trouble. So Sunday I asked

[Page 364]

them to take me to her father, because I wanted to settle my brother there. She asked me to harness the horses and she came along. The old man lived in Plouszowice. He welcomed me warmly, and asked about the family. I told him about everything, and he straight away showed his readiness to receive my brother. He would treat him like his own child, he said.

The next Sunday, my brother did arrive from Konskowola, taking almost the same route I had. I soon took him to the old farmer and asked him to find me another place, close to my brother. Since the old man was greatly respected by his children, he immediately ordered the oldest (and richest) daughter to take me in. So I went over to the new place in Tomaszowice, 4 km in all from my brother. It didn't take long before we acquired papers to be allowed to be employed as field workers. The bosses were exceptionally happy with our work, and the farmers strongly praised the work we carried out, emphasizing often that we were certainly not Jews.

-10-

One Friday evening, our boss came back from the city, and told us about the German decree that all Jews found in the Lublin area must report to Belzec. As in every such decree, it ended with the threat of death for anyone not obeying the occupier. At this, the farmer informed me that I could no longer stay with him. I told him that I first had to consult with my brother and the rest of the Jews, among them many Markuszowers working in the area. I actually did go off to the nearest village, came into a house where some Markuszowers were living, and I saw Jewish men, women and children sitting at the Shabbes table, with the candlesticks, and candles, and weeping. The bitter news had reached them too. They well knew what reporting to Belzec meant. That was why everyone resolved not to go to Belzec, but to save themselves however they could.

Later I met my brother, and we both decided not to accede to the demands of the Germans. We had a talk with our boss, and asked him to get us weapons. He refused. We then asked him if he would allow us to stay for three days, until things quieted down. To our surprise, he agreed, but he just wanted that his family knew nothing about it. We crawled up to the loft full of straw, and settled in there. Through the cracks, we saw

[Page 365]

a group of Jews being led to the city either because they had no place to hide, or they got tired of wandering homeless. Voluntarily or driven by armed farmers our brothers went to their death.

After three days in the loft of the hospitable farmer, we decided to leave. But where to? We set out late at night. Coming to Wole, we went to a farmer we knew, and asked him to let us stay the night. He agreed on the condition that the door of the barn stay open, so that in case something happens, he can say he knew of nothing. But only for the night. Tomorrow we had to leave. He can't risk his life, or the lives of his family, and his whole farm. Having no choice, we accepted his condition, and from then on, for weeks after, our wandering life continued. We did not spend our nights in the same places as our days. By day we lay hidden on the peat fields, at night, in a barn in a field, or close to a farm. In our wandering, we often came across other unfortunates like us, but in larger groups with more family members. From them we learned how one night young armed Poles from Przybyslawica came and looked for hidden Jews, took their money, raped the girls and women, and promised more such visits.

We understood that this sort of wandering served no purpose for us. We thought constantly about weapons. We even wanted to buy them from various farmers, but with no success. In the meantime, the wandering continued. You were lucky if you found some hay or straw in a field, because the farmers had caught on to the uninvited night guests, and they all locked the stables. And he who found a safe place to sleep, did not want to tell anyone, because too many people skulking around would only arouse suspicion and bring disaster. So we sat around idly all day in the forest, although our thoughts were always about the partisans, without even knowing exactly what that meant.

Once as we sat in the forest roasting potatoes, someone we knew from the city showed up, and invited us to a farmer's cottage. There we saw three people sleeping, and next to them–rifles. Our eyes shone with joy, our hearts beat faster. Are they perhaps the partisans we were looking to join? Will this be the end of our wandering over fields and forests? But our landsman quickly corrects us. They were just homeless Poles

[Page 366]

who were taking advantage of wartime for robbery purposes, and inasmuch as their area of activity was the region where Jews were hiding, they had not yet bothered us, and were in friendly relations with the partisans. There were, however, among them two Russians, escaped prisoners of war who had weapons and belonged to a partisan band. We were very envious of them, and dreamed of acquiring a rifle or a Nagan.[3] Nevertheless, we asked them to take us with, without a weapon, in the hope that being with the fighters we would somehow get our own rifle. The partisans would, however, not hear of it. Without weapons, nothing happens.

Mechl LOTERSTEIN said that while he and other friends were hiding in a loft, armed farmers approached, took their rings and other things. He knows the farmers, knows where they live, and it would be worthwhile to pay them a visit, and take their weapons. Said and done. At night, several guys went to the farmers'. They took my brother along too. I waited for them all night in fear and anxiety, and finally saw them return–healthy, cheerful, and the most important–with three rifles. After they acquired real rifles, they gave their old used gear to those who wanted to join the partisans. It was decided that Shmuel, Mechl, and my brother would go with the partisans. I stayed to continue my homeless wandering, but always with the hope that I would one day be worthy to get my own rifle.

Several weeks went by without any news from the partisans. I began to inquire about them from farmers, and used the opportunity to ask them if they could buy or find a revolver or a rifle for me. Unfortunately, I was refused everywhere. I went to the forest where many Jewish families from Markuszow and elsewhere were hiding. The poorest of the Jews, with no financial means, were hiding out here. They subsisted on only potatoes that they dug out from the fields during the night, and then roasted over a fire. In most cases the families were broken, storm of war separating them so no one knew where they were, even though they could have been hiding quite near. I remember that I met in the forest at that time Simcha and Yosef Kopitke and their families, Yidl Schwartz and his family, both Markuszow shoichet's and their families, and others.

Leaving the forest at Meszno, I met Aharon Shmuel Zalman's and

[Page 367]

we discussed weapons. He was ready to sell me a rusty rifle, with missing wooden stock. For 400 zlotys, I took the bargain off his hands without the slightest conviction it would lead to anything. I went back "home," put the rusty piece of iron in a can of naphtha, and then began to tinker with a knife to carve out the stock. I fell asleep in the middle of the work. I dreamed that I owned my own rifle, a new one, a real automatic, and all the partisans envied me. When I woke up, the dreaming was over, it was back to harsh reality. After 24 hours in the naphtha, I took the metal out, tried to take it apart, but the rust had so eaten into the metal that I had to return it to the naphtha. After another 24 hours I tried it again, this time with more success. I was finally able to move the bolt. After much effort, I took the rifle apart in pieces, wiped everything dry, smeared each piece with Vaseline, and began to put the weapon back together–a job I had never in my life done before. I don't know how long it took but I was suddenly the owner of a rifle…I stroked the wood, the cold metal, and my heart was full of joy and hope. I waited for news of the partisans so I could join them. And suddenly there was an opportunity: a Russian came for Manye LOTERSTEIN who was hiding with us, and I used the moment to go with them. This time no one refused me out of respect for the rifle.

-11-

It didn't take long to learn the most important tenets of the partisan Torah. The first–how to "occupy a position." You look for a farmer cottage that is separated from the other village houses, and is close to a forest. Going in there as well as out only happens at night. If there were one or more partisans, the farmer and his household would be put under house arrest, unless they had urgent work to do in the field or in the garden, but close to the house so the partisans could see them. In the case where the farmer had neighbors or relatives visit, the guest must also be placed under house arrest. The partisans and the farmer's families must eat together, and behave well, not offend them in anyway, except when they openly display unfriendliness. Second–a partisan had to know how to orient himself by the stars at night, know every tree in the forest and use them in their wandering, not to use main roads, but paths in the fields,

[Page 368]

or forest trails. Eyes and ears must always be alert. Don't be in a hurry to use your weapon, avoid shooting too often, and while walking in the woods, to be very careful stepping on the dry twigs that crack under your feet and make noise. Don't leave a sign of your presence walking through the forest, know the bird calls, don't get lost in a dark night, and in the case of someone getting separated from the group, know where the closest meeting point is.

We learned about all the partisan ways from our commandant, Tolek, a Soviet officer who had escaped from German imprisonment. He transformed our otriad, composed of people who had never held a rifle in their hands, into professional, trained fighters. We were located in the Kozlowka forests, and led our partisan life.

Once, the news came to us that in the Wole forests big raids were carried out which resulted in the deaths of the hidden Jews there. So we went off there to find out how much truth there was in the rumors, and maybe we could help our unfortunate brothers. We found out that the forest overseer, (*lesniczy*) and some local farmers carried out an action with their own hands, and captured several Jews, before the rest fled to other places. Someone raised the idea that we should rescue the captured Jews, but the majority, and commandant Tolek, spoke out against such an action. We were not yet battle capable, and it would be a huge risk with such small numbers, and poorly armed people. Aside from that, we didn't know exactly where the captured Jews were.

We returned to the Kozlowka forest. A while later, we learned about the great destruction the Germans had perpetrated in the Wole forest. They killed almost all the Jews who had been hiding in the bunkers. We left for the place where our nearest ones had been killed in the most horrible manner. We walked over what were now the graves of the Markuszow Jews. Pictures, documents, clothing of the dead were strewn about the forest. While leaving the forest, we saw along its edge, the naked little bodies of two children of around two and three years of age. The younger child was lying on the body of the older one. We went to a farmer nearby and asked him to bury the children, which he did.

It became clear that only by increasing our strength, and improving our weapons could we effectively lead the partisan war.

[Page 369]

We got news that there was an armed Jewish partisan band in the Kozlowka forests. There were other partisans quartered with a farmer, Kozak, who were called "Kozaks" after their landlord. We sent a messenger to the Kozlowka fighters to propose uniting–it was, however, rejected. The situation worsened. The farmers began to show displeasure with the fact of armed Jewish partisans in their environment. That was why we were inclined to unite with the underground communist party, because that meant political, and moral help and also a supply of weapons, and a changed relationship with the farmers who were close to the communist movement.

We therefore gladly received the invitation from a certain farmer, Smolak, from the village of Wole, who promised to connect us with the partisans, and simply legalize us. We would submit to a unified behavior and discipline, and carry out missions, and not be exposed to all the dangers of a smaller, unorganized group. We accepted the invitation, and every Thursday, we took part in meetings. Above all they taught us to carry out education of the farmers we came in contact with, to organize them to fight against the Nazis.

At that time, there was a debate in the Polish underground movement about the forms of struggle against the occupier. While the P.P.R.[4] was for immediate actions against the Germans, the B.Ch. (Batalion Chlopski–farmers' battalion) maintained it was too early, and the nationalist organizations like the N.S.Z.[5] and the A.K.[6] urged waiting "with rifles at their feet." Our appearance in the villages agitating for immediate defense actions created a reaction in these organizations who wanted to delay the response, and they threatened us Jewish partisans with the worst if we did not stop our education activities. We therefore had to move to a different area where we were not known as Jews. Our territory increased somewhat, and we received weapons as well. At one meeting with young farmers, the idea was broached of each partisan with weapons being allowed to bring along one more unarmed.

-12-

One day we were lying hidden at a farmer's in Syry. Our dream then was to occupy our own comfortable hideout ("*skritke*") in the forest and not

[Page 370]

have to always be looking for quarters with different farmers. Sitting around the table, we began to talk about how to build such a bunker, secure it well, store food, and take in our own people even those with no weapons. Suddenly we heard a noise through the window, and we saw a huge column of Germans with machine guns, mortars, and even small artillery pieces, marching close by us in the cottage toward the forest. Tolek ordered us to hide in the house, and in case of danger everyone was to defend himself individually. One of us remained at the window to watch the marching enemy. After they had left, we got an order to march following their footsteps. The distance between us and the marching Germans was a few hundred meters. We heard a lot of shooting and reckoned that it was the Germans combing through the forest. We waited for night impatiently, certain that the uninvited guests would retreat. That was what did happen. Thanks to our proximity to the Germans, we knew about their movements and were witness to their leaving the area. But here we made a small mistake. The next day they returned, but in a neighboring forest. But most of the Jews there had already left for another place, and the raid did not harm them much.

-13-

Once it had calmed down in the area, we began to build the bunker. It consisted of two large holes, four by 10 meters each, separated from each other at a distance of 10 meters, and connected by a zigzag tunnel. The holes were covered with several layers of big trees, a lot of earth was piled on top, and planted with young pine trees. From the top it was completely impossible to know that there were two bunkers there. The entrance was designed so that a sapling could be removed along with a section of soil.

We moved into the hideout in autumn 1942. We brought in a lot of food, clothing and two jugs of alcohol. Isser Rosenberg and his wife, Chana Gothelf, were also in our hiding place. They had been in a bunker along with their sister, Dina Gothelf until now. As much as I can recall, occupying the bunker were the following people. Tolek, Aliosha, Wladek (my brother), me, Shmuel Rubinstein, Isser, Michal Yakov Gothelf, Yehoshua Teitelbaum, Yerachmiel Rubinstein, Moishe-Velvl Kestelman, Itzchak Fishbein,

[Page 371]

the two escaped prisoners-of-war, Gatz, and Yeager, Manye Schwartz, Manye Laterman, Simeh Breinsky, Zlateh Kestelman, Sureh-Beileh Kestelman, Bunieh and Tovieh Teitelbaum.

A strict regime was carried on. We could only leave the bunker at night with the permission of the commandant. Our precautions went so far that when a farmer's carriage brought us products, it was not allowed to stop near the bunker, but had to throw the things out while continuing on its way so that no traces of the horse's hooves remained. And in winter, when we went out to collect provisions, we returned only during blizzards so that the snow would obliterate our footprints.

This hideout was like the Garden of Eden for us where we could relax our strained nerves. We were not, however, allowed to rest for long. The party sent a messenger of its own and we were unhappy with that, not wanting anyone to know about our *skritke*. Another time, Mordecahi Kerschenblatt and Yuzek Reich showed up at our hideout, and they told us that the partisans hiding at the Kozaks were killed during a German raid, and they were the only ones who managed to escape. Tuvieh Kandel was also among the arrivals. The three survivors stayed with us, but they were impatient. Something was driving them from the place, and they asked the commandant for three more people, because there was a possibility somewhere to buy some weapons. We accommodated them, and my brother, Martchinek and I went along. It was a nice night even though it was snowing which covered us in white completely. In Wole, we got a sled from a farmer, and went off in the Tomaszowice neighborhood. We stopped and stayed in Bogucin, and then continued on to the Tomaszowice Kolonia to farmers we knew, rested, and then went to see the place where so many of our nearest ones had been killed. We examined each place wanting to learn from their failures the reasons for the tragedy so that we could avoid them in case of emergency.

As regards buying weapons meanwhile, nothing was happening. The farmer dragged it out from one day to the next, even though we had money to pay him. Resigned, we decided to return to the forest bunker. It was a starry night, and a snowy whiteness was spread over everything. Suddenly we saw a sleigh coming toward us. We quickly lay down on the ground.

[Page 372]

The people approaching did the same. Both groups prepared to fire. We heard a cry, "*Stoi, haslo!*" When the others also cried, "*haslo,*" we recognized the voice as one of ours. By a hundredth of a second we had missed creating victims on both sides. It turned out that my rifle had been aiming at my cousin, who was with Yeager, Isser Rosenberg, Michal Gatz, and the farmer, Kopica. The commandant had sent them out to look for us, because they were worried about us in the bunker. We decided to go back with them right away. We were only going to stop in the village for a while for supper, and to change horses.

-14-

After changing the horses, we continued on our way hoping to get to the bunker, and rejoice with our own people. But the deeper we got into the forest the more worried the farmer, who was driving us with his horse and wagon, became. We promised to let him go soon, but he asked to be let go right away. We found his behavior suspicious and when we subjected him to questioning as to why he was in such a hurry, he stammered that two days ago a big raid had been carried out in the forest, and according to what he heard, all the people hiding in a bunker had been killed. We did not want to believe this bad news. We let the farmer go, and went straight to the house of the forest overseer. (*Gajowa*).[7] He confirmed the horrible news and added more details:

A strong punitive expedition had been combing through the entire forest for two weeks, until they found the well-masked bunker. They hit it with mortars, shot in with heavy weaponry, but without result. So they hit on the idea of digging an entryway into the bunker. As soon as a German appeared near the hideout, he was immediately eradicated. So the murderers enlisted dozens of farmers from the villages to dig a tunnel. It did not last long, however, because they had to stop working at night. When it became dark, the Germans retreated and returned in the morning. On the third day of digging, after the murderers realized the senselessness of the plan, they dug small holes near the bunker, placed straw within them, and set fire to it. The smoke suffocated most of the bunker inhabitants. Those who were still gasping in their death throes, the Germans shot.

[Page 373]

From the forest ranger to the bunker was only two kilometers. But our feet would not carry us after hearing the horrible news. After two hours of walking, we got to the spot that had seemed such a secure home just a few days ago. The earth around looked like it had been ploughed up by bullets, digging, and human feet. Our heads were lowered in sorrow, and grief enveloped us. We understood: the enemy is a merciless one. He has pronounced a death sentence on us that brooks no appeal. We now also have to be without compromises and sentimental feelings. The forces are really unequal, but we cannot lay down our arms. On the contrary, we needed to acquire more weapons, make more frequent attacks on the Germans, harass them more, and the most important–take revenge for the blood spilled.

Now a mass grave of dear, kind comrades and brothers-in-arms, townspeople, and acquaintances stretched before our eyes. Our hearts beat faster, anxiously, fists were clenched, but also despair stole into our consciousness. It seems our commandant, Yeager, felt the change in the handful of fighters left. He asked for silence, even though no one had even breathed yet. His order was a brief one: to honor the memory of the fallen with a rifle salute. Everyone lined up, and at the same time opened the bolts, inserted a bullet, and a powerful boom was heard in the forest.

That was our partisan Kaddish on the fresh graves of Markuszow Jews. Yes, according to ancient Jewish custom, we did not forget a tombstone. We inscribed the date and the tragic event on a fallen tree, and enveloped in a bitter silence, we left that place and went to the village of Syry.

-15-

After the death of the inhabitants of the bunker, most of whom were partisans, the behavior of the farmers changed radically. They knew that our camp was now a small one, shrunken, beaten up. They decided not to let us into the villages anymore, much less show up on the threshold of their cottages. To that end, they hung bells in every village which were rung in alarm at the sight of any partisans. We had not expected such a blockade and excommunication. Considering there was nothing to lose, we decided to teach a lesson to a village of farmers–maybe they would stop their battle against us. We knew that the most aggressive

[Page 374]

and antisemitic village was Gory, because most of the local young men had served in the Polish army, and after the defeat in 1939, they came home with weapons. We decided, therefore, to march through the village in the daytime, and respond with fire if any if the farmers tried to mess with us, or ring the bell. We also knew that they would not use their weapons in the middle of the day for fear for their women and children. The success of such a march through would mean that we had demonstrated our strength and courage not submitting to fear and terror of the farmers.

And that indeed came to pass. The residents of Gory looked on amazed and surprised as a Jewish partisan band marched through their village, and not one of them dared to open his mouth. It seems they understood our determination–and it was a clear one: their village would be burned down if they attacked us.

Not far from Gory is the village of Gutanow. We went in that direction, and as soon as we reached the first houses, we heard the bells ringing. There was no choice but to still forever the zealous farmer pulling the string of the alarm bell and tear down the bell. Approaching the Gutanow woods, we came upon a strong division of German and Polish (Granatens) police. We opened fire trying to penetrate deeper into the woods in order to later cut through the Lublin-Warsaw main road, and look for shelter in the village of Leszic. Here too the bells rang, but not as a reception for partisans, but as an alarm and warning that banished and hunted people have shown up in the village. In a quick march, we reached the woods, because we only felt secure there, even though hunger and fatigue had robbed us of the slight feeling of safety. After resting, we went off to the nearest cottage to find something to eat. There we were attacked with concentrated fire. So we had to run away again from this terrible place.

Our battle with the surrounding villages for recognition went on for months, until we decided to invite a few smaller partisan groups to march with us through several larger places and show our strength. We also let the soltises[8] know that if the villagers attacked us, they would die together with the partisans. This helped. Fantastical news began to spread about our strength. One farmer even claimed that he alone had seen over 1000 Jewish partisans…

[Page 375]

-16-

Finally a break came in the behavior of the surrounding village populations to the partisans. Now every farmer knew that if he had to prepare a consignment for the Germans–whether a pig, dairy products, or wheat, he first had to inform the soltis, who then informed the partisans. So we would go to the farmer's home, and leave a note that the partisans had confiscated the pig that the farmer had actually in the meantime buried in a secure place. Then a commission came and confirmed the partisans' raid and theft of the articles destined for the consignment. The result was, the Germans got nothing, the products remained with the farmer, and our image and authority grew immensely. The peasants come to us now for various issues. It was impossible to keep up with so many requests. So we had a talk with the soltises, and told them that the partisan bands will hand out a certain number of blank certificates confirming our confiscation of consignment articles. For this we claimed the right to take whatever food we needed for ourselves.

Now we even dared to levy contributions on some landowners and wealthier farmers, and to help the impoverished farmers with this money. Here the A.K. mixed in, and made known their opposition to the contributions, and that they, the underground fighters for Polish nationalism were ready to guard the gentry's estates, and their possessions. To that we replied that it's a waste of time for them to post guards on the estates, because on the fields of the gentry there are plenty of stacks of wheat or hay, and we will make them go up in smoke if they mount a resistance to the partisans' demands.

It appears that the A.K. group in the area had determined to liquidate us. Once there were thirty of us quartered in the Bogucin Kolonia. Among them were many Markuszow people: Chaim Gothelf, David Ettinger, Moishe Pelz, Hershl Fishbein, the writer of these lines, and others. Suddenly a strong fire was directed at us. We succeeded in getting outside with no losses, and getting into the woods nearby. When night fell we decided to find out who attacked us. It turned out that it was no other than local Poles of the A.K. who took upon themselves the German business of annihilating Jewish partisans. A while later, we got the trustworthy news that the headquarters of the A.K. were in the court of the nobleman himself. So we began negotiations with the magnate with no result. Finally we gave him an ultimatum

[Page 376]

demanding a meeting on Saturday with all the gentry in the neighborhood to put an end to the shooting at each other, and the murder of hidden Jews by A.K. members. If not–we would declare war on the estates of the gentry–and let the chips fall where they may. It was clear that a lot depended on the success of the negotiations.

Negotiators elected on the partisan side were: Yeager, Gatz, Shmuel Rubinstein, Isser Rosenberg, Hershl Fishbein, and myself. We were supposed to have sat at one table with the gentry, and reach an agreement about a ceasefire. We were accompanied by two more groups, separated from each other by a distance of half a kilometer, ready at any moment for any eventuality or surprise.

At the designated time, we went to the courtyard where the negotiations were to take place. The other two groups came behind us. Arriving at the "*spoldzielnie*,"[9] (consumer cooperative), we noticed a large number of farmers at the place. It was still light out, and we shouted loudly, "Hands in the air!" The crowd fled, looking to take up positions. We warned them against it, and threatened to open fire. They stopped still in the middle of running. Their commandant took a few steps forward, and declared his willingness to negotiate. From our side, Yeager stepped out. Both approached each other, shook hands, and agreed to invite one more from each side to the talks, in order to consult with them. Our first demand was: Only the four people leading the negotiations should remain at the spot. The rest must leave. Now the farmers were embarrassed when they saw only four men from our side leaving.

Both sides discussed how the official meeting was taking place in the tavern, and not in the courtyard as previously decided. One of us and one of them went to see the magnates to invite them to the consultation. A half hour later, in a separate room in the tavern were assembled: the count of Milocin, the noblemen from Bogucin, Tomaszowice, Palikije, and two paratroopers from England, and several prominent farmers, officers of the previous Polish army. Our side was represented by the partisans named above. The negotiations were stormy, and we sat the whole time with our hands in our bags where we had loaded pistols, our fingers on the trigger…Our partisans were waiting outside with grenades ready.

At around two am, we reached an agreement whereby the Palikije magnate had to pay the partisans 50,000 zlotys.

[Page 377]

Weapons they didn't want to contribute with the excuse that they themselves were an underground group in need of weapons. The magnates had to pay us a sum of money every month for our needs. We committed ourselves to take nothing from the farmers other than food for our use, and only with the permission of the farmer himself.

In this way we assured for ourselves freedom of movement and recognition from the A.K., implacable antisemites and opponents of armed struggle against the Germans if not conducted through them exclusively.

Now we could think about engaging the number one enemy in battle–the Hitlerist occupiers.

-17-

And we let the Germans know about the existence of the partisans. Every night we would shoot up some part of the Warsaw-Lublin road. We aimed only at the cars, not the Germans, because their warning, and unfortunately, the reality, was that for every German killed all the villages in a radius of 8 kilometers would be burned, and the farmers shot. In the meantime, complaints were coming from many farmers about the actions of a small German garrison in Leszic that was stealing produce from the farmers, demanding huge consignments, and harassing the farmers no end. We decided to liquidate this bunch. With the help from the farmers we knew every detail about the Germans–where they slept, where they kept their weapons, and when the most suitable time to attack them was. After we got the necessary information, we left at dawn for Leszic with the intention of taking the Germans alive. We just had to neutralize the one guard walking outside. Every partisan was given a role in the action.

In the meantime everything is going well. The guard is already dead. We send a farmer to the sleeping Germans to suggest to them that they should surrender without a shot, because they are surrounded by partisans. The farmer returned with a positive answer. We approached the spot where the Germans were found in order to disarm them and take them prisoner. It seems that the Germans regretted their capitulation, and as soon as three partisans got near the window, they opened fire on them. Hershl Fishbein was immediately wounded, and the trophy rifle he had just taken from the guard fell to the ground. One of the partisans carried him to a tree, laid him down there, and then started firing at the Germans. Hershl Fishbein was suffering terribly from his wounds. He thought his intestines were spilling out.

[Page 378]

He takes his pistol and puts it to his head. I see him about to press the trigger. In really the last second I managed to run over to him, and wrenched the revolver from his hands. I undid his clothing and showed him he did not have a big wound. I ordered my uncle, Shmuel Zilberman, from Belzec, to take Hershl to the woods nearby. He does so, and I continue the firefight against the Germans. True, we could set fire to the barrack they're in, but we have to reckon with the farmers against whom the Germans would direct their reprisals of revenge for burning their soldiers alive. Continuing the shooting for a long time we also couldn't, because German help might come, and we would be lost. The order therefore came to retreat, and to continue the battle with the enemy under better circumstances.

-18-

The "Gwardia Ludowa" which changed its name now to "Armia Ludowa"[10] carried out wide-ranging actions against the Germans who were getting beaten at the Soviet front. Partisan activities of different groups increased. We too were not idle. Once we were given help from the Przybyslawska group to blow up the train line outside Lublin. Another time, we carried out a similar action by ourselves.

The winter of 1943 approached. Two partisans from our group–Moishe Pelz (Martchin) and Yosef Plashowitzer (Yuzhek) came down with typhus. That was dangerous, because if it spread, it would be as dangerous as the Germans for us. The first thing we had to do was to isolate the sick. We took them to two farmers, and made them responsible for the lives of the sick. To care for the sick, we left my brother, because he had already had typhus, and he was immune to the infectious disease. We had to think about a more secure hideout for them. Once the sick had improved, having gone through the crisis, we asked a group of Markuszow Jews, who had a well organized *skritke*, to take in the two partisans. They agreed and we went back to bring them to the new place. As soon as night fell, we laid our two comrades on a well-cushioned bed of hay in a sleigh and covered them with blankets. After travelling for a few kilometers snow began to fall so heavily that we lost our way. The snow

[Page 379]

got deeper, the horses sinking in up to their bellies, and it was really hard for them to move. Our sick companions began to moan. In spite of the warm coverings they were shivering from the cold. We removed our coats and put them on the sick. By the duration of the trip, we figured it was about to become day. And in reality, we heard the roosters crowing. With our last bit of strength we turned the horses toward the village, helped push the sleigh, and knocked on the first cottage. We explained to the farmer who we were, arrested the entire family, because we intended to spend the whole day here, and not leave until evening. Having no choice, the farmer agreed. We relaxed in a warm house, ate well, helped the sick to clean themselves up and rest up. At night we went on further, and arrived in peace at the Markuszow Jews at whose bunker we left the two sick comrades.

Once, several partisans went to a village to secure provisions. When my brother heard about this, he immediately said he had a bad feeling about the outcome. The next day we actually got the news that Shmuel Trapper, and Itzchak Morel had been shot by farmers. We quickly discovered the reason for their death, and decided to teach the murderers a lesson. So we went to the village, and set fire to the stable and cottage from which they had been shooting at our friends. But the murderers had in the meantime run away, and our revenge didn't reach them.

-19-

In the meantime we received an order to report to the Parczew forests. We had, however, to postpone carrying out the order until our two friends were completely healthy again. When they had recovered, we set off to the designated location. On the way, we stopped at a village whose name I can't remember now. There a lady farmer from the partisan movement told us that there was another Jewish partisan group active in the neighborhood, and that they would be in the same village as us tomorrow. The next day we actually did meet several Jewish partisans, who did not receive us very friendly, and we couldn't even figure out who they were and where they came from.

In the forest, we were ordered to join up with Captain Yechiel's group. We tried to explain our opposition to the agreement, but without success. We preferred to operate in a neighborhood where we knew every road and path, including the population. Here we found ourselves in a foreign, to us, environment.

[Page 380]

My brother and other partisans had to bring some Jewish survivors here. I and several other fighters had to go on a sabotage mission: to blow up a glassworks, and a bridge near Wlodawa. A hundred of us set out, and several days later we returned to the base with our tasks completed, and three German prisoners. My brother and his group of fifty had still not returned. Ten days had passed since their departure–and no news of any kind. I ran to headquarters every day to ask for news, but they didn't know what to say. Suddenly, by chance, I overheard some Polish partisans saying that there had been a big battle, and that it was likely that fifteen of our fighters had died. I returned to headquarters and asked them for a horse and an escort up to the river Wieprz. I would go on further by myself, because I was anxious about the fate of my brother. They calmed me down with the promise that if there were no news in 3 or 4 days, headquarters would send me on an official mission to find out about the fifteen partisans. Waiting the few days stretched on like an eternity.

On the fourth day, quite early, while I was still sleeping, Michal and Yuzhek came to see me. Both sat down on my bed not wanting to wake me. As soon as I opened my eyes and saw the two partisans, it immediately became clear to me that they had bad news. I shouted wildly, "What happened?!" They calmed me down, told me that several fighters had returned, and that my brother was only wounded. I tore out of bed, and raced to the headquarters to demand a clear answer. They knew my brother well there, and knew that I was ready to go through fire for him. They could no longer withhold the truth, bitter though it was. They calmed me down and I heard the story:

The fifteen men went to get several hidden Jews that the farmers no longer wanted to keep, and at the same time, to get food for the girls in the bunker. This all went smoothly. On the way back, they stopped in the village of Grabina. Around 12 noon, their watchman saw a white figure sneaking out of the forest. Suddenly, more such white figures got closer to the village, and began to surround the cottage where the partisans were staying. Our watchman didn't panic, and immediately began to fire on the Germans, at the same time waking up the sleeping partisans. A heavy firefight developed. The Germans, however, had a mortar, and one round got through the window into the house where our fighters were. They got out of the house, and when the surrounding buildings began to burn,

[Page 381]

they escaped to the field, and everyone had to look after himself. Suddenly, a shot went through my brother's arm. He joked, saying to Michal, "Look, the Germans made a hole in my new coat."

A few minutes later, the clatter of heavy machine guns was heard. A series of bullets put him on the ground, several bullets entering his abdomen. He felt his last moments were coming. He begged Martchin from Konskowola to take his new rifle that he had a while back received from Tolek for excellence. He just wanted them to leave him a pistol and a grenade. Every German trying to approach was met with an accurate bullet from his pistol. When several Germans at once attacked him, he flung the grenade at them. When he was out of ammunition, and down to one bullet, he put the pistol in his mouth and put an end to his life. David Ettinger (Dudek) died in a similar way.

My despair and sorrow at the death of my brother was great. I wanted to convince myself that if we had been together maybe this tragedy would not have happened. This idea tormented me, and in order to quell it, I volunteered for all the missions that headquarters decided to carry out, and to ask them to put me in the active groups. Revenge–was the only answer to the murderers of my brother.

-20-

Now we were a combat group of fifteen, almost all Jews. Our task was: to periodically blow up the train line leading to Minsk. At every kilometer along the line, the Germans had placed observation posts and fortified points. It did them little good, however. Every night we blew up the rails at a different point. Once we succeeded in capturing a post with eleven Germans, and brought them back alive to headquarters.

At that time, we were supplied with weapons from Russia. Airplanes with ammunition would appear at predetermined locations, and drop their valuable burden. Automatic weapons and bullets were now no longer scarce. Our group was mainly entrusted with meeting

[Page 382]

the weapons drops, and we would get the transport to headquarters in the best of shape. Once we entered an area where the A.K. had a large unit stationed. We did not know their password (*haslo*) and the first guard post threatened to shoot us if we continued. We did not show any fear, and demanded that two of ours be taken to their headquarters. After long negotiations with the commandant, we achieved our goal: the password, and permission to carry out our mission, and to return safely to our base. Here they received us with great ceremony, because they thought we had been killed.

We received an order to unite with the big partisan army of the legendary hero, Kalfak, whose base was in the Carpathian mountains. We set out on our way, met partisan divisions named Wanda Wasilewska, and a group of Czapijewces (called Czapijew), crossed the river Wieprz, and reached our sector. We decided to quarter in the village of Syry. It seems the Germans had information about our march and attacked us in Syry. After the bitter struggle, during which a German general, a specialist in war against partisans, was wounded, we withdrew under the cover of darkness, because the order was to get to the Carpathians as quickly as possible. Out of caution, we divided ourselves into two groups: the otriad, W. Wasilewka, went off on its own. We, the Markuszow partisans, along with the Czapijewces (1,000 men) went in the direction of Konskowola through Markuszow where we stayed a whole day. The following night, we went further on foot while the ammunition was loaded onto wagons. We arranged our baggage train in the village, Vromblov.[11]

-21-

Friday, when the camp was still sunk in sleep, an explosion was heard. Then a second, and a third. Airplanes dropped several bombs on the camp, and then an artillery barrage began. Staying in the camp was terrible. We felt that the Germans had discovered us, and there would be a bitter battle. Headquarters issued an order to evacuate to the woods nearby where there were valleys. The woods, however, were not dense; there were no more trees than there were fighters and horses. It had, however, one important quality:

[Page 383]

tanks could not get in there because it was full of gorges. We lay there helplessly and watched as six more German airplanes approached, dropped their bombs, and before they finished their job, other planes came right after. The artillery too boomed continuously, a sign that the Germans had decided to give us the ultimate blow. After noon, our scouts informed us that big reinforcements of German infantry were approaching the woods, probably to surround and annihilate us. As a result, we got an order to divide our force into four, and each group would defend one side of the woods. We constructed a defensive quadrant with a reserve of automatics that was to be ready to help out any group finding itself in trouble. Around four in the afternoon the cannonade suddenly stopped. The Germans were preparing to attack. With bated breath we heard their orders, and saw from our observation posts, a dense mass of well-trained soldiers, officers at the head, were closing quickly on the woods. Their steady gait, the rifles aiming, and the loud orders bore witness that the Germans were sure that very few partisans were left alive after the heavy bombardment and artillery cannonade. We let them believe that, not moving around, and not betraying our presence. When the beasts were at a distance of 10 meters from us, we opened a concentrated fire on them, and dead German bodies lay stretched out on the ground. Their advance was interrupted. They began to retreat in panic, but the officers' orders forced the soldiers to renew their attacks. It was repeated several times with the same result. Night was approaching and the Germans were not big heroes, especially in a forest. They did, however, have us well encircled, held in a vise, and we could be sure that early tomorrow morning they would renew their attempts to destroy us. Our leaders ordered us that we should try to break through the blockade at night, and at any cost. A vanguard group was chosen which would battle through the German ring, and allow the rest to get away. But before this, we gathered together the 27 wounded, and we gave them help, and made arrangements for continuing on further. We quickly buried three fallen partisans, in the knowledge that the German victims in the Vromblev battle attained hundreds.

The dark and quiet of the night was interrupted by our gunfire–a desperate but determined attempt to break out at any cost. In the darkness, the besiegers did not display much

[Page 384]

efficiency. Most of us got out of the woods, but in split-up groups, with no connections, everyone on his own.

-22-

At dawn, we encountered several survivors near the village of Tomaszowice. We decided to go to the village of Wole, where we would certainly find a connection to headquarters. Unfortunately, we weren't able to find out anything in the village. We had to travel to the Parczew forests. We delegated three partisans to get the details and then inform us. The three went off to the Parczew neighborhood, and met the only headquarters member, Kolka, a known antisemite. He did not permit the three to return, but told them to stay there. When they refused, he wanted to disarm them, but our emissaries resisted. Later they discovered that not far from that spot, there were higher ranked Soviet officers responsible for the partisan movement. So they reported to the higher authorities, and told them about the antisemite. The officers took the three partisans under their protection, and permitted them to return to us. If truth be told, we had little enthusiasm for going to the Parczew forests; we knew the antisemite, Kolka, very well. Therefore, we stipulated that we would not be subordinated by this Jew-hater. A number of farmers from Przybyslawica, who also belonged to the general staff, promised us protection. Thanks to their promise, some individual Jews who had survived the Vromblov battle were added to our group, and we left to continue our partisan life as a larger unit. We reformed our units anew, and on May 3rd it was decided to carry out a partisan army parade in the village of Debi in the Parczew neighborhood. After the parade, which had demonstrated our reawakened power, they organized a dance party in the village. Along with Russian partisans, we danced and partied all night.

The next morning, our group received an order to escort General Rola-Zymierski to the partisan otriad called Wanda Wasilewska, from whence he flew back to Russia in a special airplane.

While accompanying general Zymierski, we liberated the shtetl, Ostrow-Lubelski, which remained under our rule until the German retreat. At that time,

[Page 385]

German deserters began to appear, because they felt the catastrophe at the front, and looked for safety, ironically, with the partisans. There were also spies among them sent by the Wehrmacht in order to find out about our forces, and then finally annihilating us to make the road clear for their retreat. Once, a German approached us and reported that one of their generals wanted to see us. At the appointed time and place, the general actually showed up. We handed him over to the Baranowski otriad, which delivered him to Russia. But at the same time, we felt that the Germans were preparing to hit us. We often captured German spies. At that time, about 80 paratroopers arrived with the most needed weaponry, medicine, food and ammunition. We knew that about 90% of them were Jewish, but they didn't especially acknowledge it. The shtetl, Ostrow, and the surrounding neighborhood was now full of partisans whose numbers certainly reached around six thousand. We believed that such a force was capable of going into battle with the Germans, and fight as well as a regular army. We received trustworthy information, however, that the Germans were encircling the whole area, and that the circle was getting smaller by the day. We had to prepare for a defensive battle. Various smaller and larger groups were appearing in the forest, a sign that the German encirclement was getting closer. Our group, mostly Jewish and from Markuszow, received an order to protect the shtetl. Ostrow, and we set up our firing station in a windmill. From there, we were to shoot at the enemy as it was nearing the shtetl. The order specified that after fulfilling our task, we were to return to the forest where everyone had a designated position. The Germans actually did begin to attack Ostrow during the day, but they had to withdraw with big losses. A soon as night fell we went to the forest, because we were low on ammunition. The position designated for us was among the most exposed, and accessible to tanks. We waited for the enemy all day. But he didn't show up. In the evening we saw general Baranowski and colonel Czarny come by. We asked them what explained the quiet, and their appearance here. The answer was a surprise: We had to retreat, because some of the Poles had betrayed us, and deserted their posts. We could not believe such bad news. So we went to headquarters but there was no one there. Even the Russian groups had disappeared.

Were we, the 100 partisans, left to fend for ourselves? All signs pointed to yes. We decided to break out of the encirclement at night,

[Page 386]

and move to another place. Remaining in the forest, or even mounting a defense against thousands of Germans meant certain destruction. The darkness allowed us to move forward, although we didn't know the way then. So we went on without direction, and that led to my finding myself alone. I wandered around all night, and at dawn I ran into one of our partisans, Franek. Two together was comforting, especially since Franek knew the location of the meeting place. So we set off there, but got lost along the way. Luckily, we met a farmer in the forest who was very afraid of us. He wept and begged us to let him go, he was a father of five children. We forced him to go forward. He took us to two lakes and said that there was a way through that was not marked on any military map, and so there are no Germans there. We let the farmer go, and went to the rendezvous point where we encountered the large partisan group we had lost at night. We all agreed to get out of the forest by the way of the two lakes. But before anything else, we drank a lot of water because we had not eaten or drunk for 24 hours. We began marching forward with the greatest caution, and came to a village where we went to the first farmer, and he gave us food. In the middle of stilling our hunger, news came that there were tanks in a neighboring village. No one had any enthusiasm for leaving the delicious meal after such a long fast. We ate up quickly–and out to the field so we wouldn't be discovered in a village that had received us so hospitably. Had the Germans caught us in the farmer's house, the entire village would have had to pay a harsh price: farmers shot, and houses and fields burned. We lay in a field of clover waiting for night. But the day dragged on long. Suddenly we heard the noise of tanks getting closer. There was no doubt they had discovered us, and the heavy German machines wanted to crush us. We lay there with grenades to receive the enemy. Alongside the tanks, soldiers were coming, their rifle barrels really close to us. Suddenly, however, airplanes appeared and the tanks quickly drove away. Clearly–we were at the very front, between two armies. That was the worst place of all.

Night finally fell, and we had one goal: to notify the headquarters of the Soviet army of our existence– and then we would be saved. A farmer told us that the Soviets were already here in the nearest

[Page 387]

village. In that village, we also found our general staff who told us we were to occupy Ostrow-Lubelski. We became again the rulers of the shtetl, and when the Soviet army arrived, we marched into Lubartow, and temporarily took power. With the liberation of Lublin, we were the first Jewish partisans who had the honor of marching into the liberated city. The most responsible positions in the security service, and government were entrusted to us. I worked in the *voivod*[12] police command.

Like most of the Jews in Poland then, I was determined to leave this land, and go to Eretz-Israel. After a series of wanderings over Polish cities, Germany, and Austria, I came on the famous ship, *Altalena*,[13] to the just recently reestablished state of Israel.

Translator's Footnotes:

1. According to a description on p. 15, the *laches* was a grass covered lawn area with low trees and shrubs where young people would congregate, and sheep and goats were grazed.
2. For more details about the Janiszow camp, see the memoirs of M. Pelz (ed.)
3. Automatic pistol originally Nagant M1895
4. Polska Partia Robotnicza
5. Narodowe Siły Zbrojne. Fascist antisemitic organization
6. Armia Krajowa. Fascist antisemitic organization
7. Polish. Gamekeeper.
8. Village magistrates
9. Cooperative
10. People's or Folk Army
11. Phonetic transliteration. Unable to identify modern location.
12. A voivod is similar to a province
13. The Altalena Affair was a violent confrontation between the IDF and the Irgun in June 1948.

[Page 388] Blank [Pages 389-397]

List of the Jews who Perished During the Occupation

(Markuszów, Poland)

[Page numbers refer to the original book]

Transliterated by Judy Petersen

Family name(s)	First name(s)	Gender	Marital status	Name of spouse	Remarks and additional family	Page
א Alef						
IBERKLEID	Simcha	M	Married	Devora	and family	389
IBERKLEID	Devora	F	Married	Simcha	and family	389
IBERKLEID	Aharon	M	Married	Rachel Leah		389
IBERKLEID	Rachel Leah	F	Married	Aharon	and family	389
IBERKLEID	Yechezkel	M	Married	Sarah	and family	389
IBERKLEID	Sarah	F	Married	Yechezkel		389
IBERKLEID	Shmuel	M			and family	389
IBERKLEID	Avraham	M	Married	Pesse		389
IBERKLEID	Pesse	F	Married	Avraham	and family	389
IBERKLEID	Avraham	M	Married	Frayde		389
IBERKLEID	Frayde	F	Married	Avraham	and family	389
IBERKLEID	Chaim Gershon	M	Married	Rivka		389
IBERKLEID	Rivka	F	Married	Chaim Gershon	and family	389
IBERKLEID	Leibel	M	Married	Devora		389
IBERKLEID	Devora	F	Married	Leibel	and family	389
IBERKLEID	Gitel	F			and family	389

IBERKLEID	Chaim	M			and family	389
IBERKLEID	David	M	Married	Shprintze	and family	389
IBERKLEID	Shprintze	F	Married	David	and family	389
EISENBERG	Binyamin	M	Married	Teela		389
EISENBERG	Teela	F	Married	Binyamin		389
ANGLUSTER	Herschel	M	Married	Chaya Ita		389
ANGLUSTER	Chaya Ita	F	Married	Herschel	and family	389
	Esther Henne	M				389
EIDELSTEIN	Eliezer	M	Married	Channah	and family	389
EIDELSTEIN	Channah	F	Married	Eliezer	and family	389
EIDELSTEIN	Shimon	M	Married	Dina	and family	389
EIDELSTEIN	Dina	F	Married	Shimon	and family	389
EIDELSTEIN	Henech	M	Married	Channah		389
EIDELSTEIN	Channah	F	Married	Henech		389
EIDELSTEIN	Rivka	F				389
OSHINSKA	Bineh	M	Married	Moshe		389
	Aytzikel	M	Married	Gitel	tailor. And family	389
	Gitel	F	Married	Aytzikel	and family	389

ב Bet

BERENBAUM	Yakov Shlomo	M	Married	Sheva	and family	389
BERENBAUM	Sheva	F	Married	Yakov Shlomo	and family	389
BERENBAUM	Itsche	M	Married	Channah Roizeh	and family	389
BERENBAUM	Channah Roizeh	F	Married	Itsche	and family	389
BAUMAN	Aharon	M	Married	Sarah Esther	and family	389
BAUMAN	Sarah Esther	F	Married	Aharon	and family	389

BREINSKY	Moshe	M	Married	Beile	and family	389
BREINSKY	Beile	F	Married	Moshe	and family	389
BLEIWEISS	Chaim Yossel	M	Married	Channah Roizeh	and family	389
BLEIWEISS	Channah	F	Married	Chaim Yossel	and family	389
BLEIWEISS	Mordechai	M	Married	Devora	and family	389
BLEIWEISS	Devora	F	Married	Mordechai	and family	389
BLEIWEISS	Gershon	M	Married	Breindel	and family	389
BLEIWEISS	Breindel	F	Married	Gerson	and family	389
BLEIWEISS	Mordechai	M	Married	Rivka	and family	389
BLEIWEISS	Rivka	F	Married	Mordechai	and family	389
BLEIWEISS	Itsche Leib	M	Married	Sarah Gitel	and family	389
BLEIWEISS	Sarah Gitel	F	Married	Itsche Leib	and family	389
BLEIWEISS	Yisrael	M	Married	Hinde		389
BLEIWEISS	Hinde	F	Married	Yisrael	and family	389
BRATTEN	Mendel	M	Married	Perl		389
BRATTEN	Perl	F	Married	Mendel		389
BRATTEN	Mechel	M	Married	Chaya		389
BRATTEN	Chaya	F	Married	Mechel	and family	389
BARENHOLTZ	Mordechai	M	Married	Esther		389
BARENHOLTZ	Esther	F	Married	Mordechai		389
BEIGELMAN	Asher	M	Married	Channah		389
BEIGELMAN	Channah	F	Married	Asher	and family	389
	Berl	M	Married	Neche	and family	389
	Neche	F	Married	Berl	and family	389
BLEIWEISS	Mordechai	M			Father's name David Yekel	389
	Beile	F	Married	Shaul	and family. Mother's name Kayla GOLDSCHLAGER	390
	Shaul	M	Married	Beile	and family. Wife's maiden	390

name GOLDSCHLAGER.

ג Gimmel

GLASMAN	Yeske	F			and family	390
GLASMAN	Shmuel	M	Married	Pesse		390
GLASMAN	Pesse	F	Married	Shmuel	and family	390
GLASMAN	Yankel	M	Married	Fraydel	and family	390
GLASMAN	Fraydel	F	Married	Yankel	and family	390
GLASMAN	Leibel	M	Married	Sima		390
GLASMAN	Sima	F	Married	Leibel	and family	390
GLASMAN	Yechiel	M	Married	Chaya		390
GLASMAN	Chaya	F	Married	Yechiel	and family	390
GLASMAN	Yehuda	M	Married	Esther Malka		390
GLASMAN	Esther Malka	F	Married	Yehuda	and family	390
GLASMAN	Yisrael Moshe	M	Married	Elke		390
GLASMAN	Elke	F	Married	Yisrael Moshe	and family	390
GLASMAN	Chaim	M	Married	Gitele		390
GLASMAN	Gitele	F	Married	Chaim Gershon	sister and family	390
GLASMAN	Yosef	M	Married	Chaya Sarah		390
GLASMAN	Chaya Sarah	F	Married	Yosef	and family	390
GLASMAN	Yakov	M	Married	Channah		390
GLASMAN	Channah	F	Married	Yakov		390
GLASMAN	Asher	M			and family	390
GLASMAN	Ovadia	M				390
GLASMAN	Bracha	F			and family	390
GLAZSCHNEIDER	Motel	M	Married	Esther		390

GLAZSCHNEIDER	Esther	F	Married	Motel	and family	390
GLAZSCHNEIDER	Shmuel	M	Married	Gitel		390
GLAZSCHNEIDER	Gitel	F	Married	Shmuel	and family	390
GLAZSCHNEIDER	Golde	F			and daughter	390
GLAZSCHNEIDER		F			daughter of Golde	390
GLAZSCHNEIDER	Moshe	M	Married	Beile		390
GLAZSCHNEIDER	Beile	F	Married	Moshe	and family	390
GLAZSCHNEIDER	Gershon	M	Married	Malka		390
GLAZSCHNEIDER	Malka	F	Married	Gershon	and family	390
GEIER	Yitzchak	M	Married	Channah		390
GEIER	Channah	F	Married	Yitzchak	and family	390
GOLDSCHLAGER	Nechemia	M	Married	Leah		390
GOLDSCHLAGER	Leah	F	Married	Nechemia	and family	390
GOLDSCHLAGER	Yitzchak	M	Married	Mirel		390
GOLDSCHLAGER	Mirel	F	Married	Yitzchak		390
GOLDSCHLAGER	Shimon	M	Married	Reizel		390
GOLDSCHLAGER	Reizel	F	Married	Shimon		390
GOLDSCHLAGER	Moshe Yossel	M	Married	Rivka		390
GOLDSCHLAGER	Rivka	F	Married	Moshe Yossel	and family	390
GOLDSCHLAGER	David	M	Married	Pesse		390
GOLDSCHLAGER	Pesse	F	Married	David	and family	390
GOLDSCHLAGER	Aharon	M	Married	Chava		390
GOLDSCHLAGER	Chava	F	Married	Aharon	and family	390
GOLDSCHLAGER	Gitel	F	Married	Peretz		390
GOLDSCHLAGER	Kayleh	F			and family	390
GOTHELF	Abish	M	Married	Malka		390
GOTHELF	Malka	F	Married	Abish	and family	390
GOTHELF	Kalman	M	Married	Tzotel		390
GOTHELF	Tzotel	F	Married	Kalman	and family	390

GOTHELF	Yakov Yosef	M	Married	Esther Malka		390
GOTHELF	Esther Malka	F	Married	Yakov Yosef	and family	390
GOTHELF	Berish	M	Married	Malka		390
GOTHELF	Malka	F	Married	Berish		390
GOTHELF	Golde	F			and family	390
GOTHELF	Kalman	M	Married	Tzotel	lived in Garbów (Lublin district), Poland	390
GOTHELF	Tzotel		Married	Kalman		390
GOTHELF	Mordechai	M			and family	390
GOTHELF	Rachel	F				390
GOLDMAN	Pinchas	M	Married	Grine		390
GOLDMAN	Grine	F	Married	Pinchas	and family	390
GOLDMAN	Golde	F				390
GOLDSTEIN	Binyamin	M	Married	Rachel		390
GOLDSTEIN	Rachel	F	Married	Binyamin	and family	390
GOLDSTEIN	Avraham Chaim	M			and family	390
GOLDSTEIN	Chaim	M	Married	Tzirl		390
GOLDSTEIN	Tzirl	F	Married	Chaim	and family	390
GOLDSTEIN	Berish	M	Married	Beile		390
GOLDSTEIN	Beile	F	Married	Berish	and family	390
GRIVALD	Chava	F			and family	391
GREIER	Yehoshe	M	Married	Frayde	and family	391
GREIER	Frayde	F	Married	Yehoshe	and family	391
GOLDBERG	Yosef	M	Married	Bashe		391
GOLDBERG	Bashe	F	Married	Yosef	and family	391
GOLDBERG	Shimon	M	Married	Sima		391
GOLDBERG	Sima	F	Married	Shimon	and family	391
GOLDWASSER	Fraydel	F				391

GOLDWASSER	Peretz	M	Married	Matel	Rabbi. And family	391
GOLDWASSER	Matel	F	Married	Peretz	and family	391
GOLDWASSER	Shlomo Shlomke	M	Married	Roiza		391
GOLDWASSER	Roiza	F	Married	Shlomo Shlomke	and family	391
GOLDWASSER	Neche	F			and family	391
GOLDINER	Chava	F				391

ד Dalet

DECKERMACHER	Moshe Hersch	M	Married	Pesse		391
DECKERMACHER	Pesse	F	Married	Moshe Hersch	and family	391
	David	M	Married	Hinde		391
	Hinde	F	Married	David	and family	391
	David	M	Married	Rivka	tailor	391
	Rivka	F	Married	David		391

ה Hey

HUBERMAN	Miriam Dina	F				391
HUBERMAN	Melech	M	Married	Esther Breindel	and family	391
HUBERMAN	Esther Breindel	F	Married	Melech	and family	391
HOLTZHENDLER	Tanchum Moshe	M	Married	Rivka		391
HOLTZHENDLER	Rivka	F	Married	Tanchum Moshe	and family	391
HOLTZHENDLER	Sheva	F			and family	391
HOFFELD	Baruch	M			and family	391
HOFFELD	Baltsche	F			and family	391
HOFFMAN	Moshe	M	Married	Breindel		391
HOFFMAN	Breindel	F	Married	Moshe	and family	391

HOLTZMAN	Sarah	F			and family	391
HOLTZMAN	Yankel	M	Married	Neche		391
HOLTZMAN	Neche	F	Married	Yankel	and family	391
HOLTZMAN	Yitzchak	M	Married	Channah		391
HOLTZMAN	Channah	F	Married	Yitzchak	and family	391
HERSCHENHORN	Herschel	M			and family	391
HENDLER	Chaim	M	Married	Ita		391
HENDLER	Ita	F	Married	Chaim	and family	391

ו Vav

WASSERMAN	Chaim David	M	Married	Perl Bina		391
WASSERMAN	Perl Bina	F	Married	Chaim David	and family	391
WASSERMAN	Asher	M	Married	Hinde		391
WASSERMAN	Hinde	F	Married	Asher	and family	391
WASSERMAN	Itsche	M	Married	Channah Leah		391
WASSERMAN	Channah Leah	F	Married	Itsche	and family	391
WESTELSCHNEIDER	Leah	F				391
WESTELSCHNEIDER	Betzalel	M	Married	Rivka		391
WESTELSCHNEIDER	Rivka	F	Married	Betzalel		391
WESTELSCHNEIDER	Moshe	M	Married	Gitel		391
WESTELSCHNEIDER	Gitel	F	Married	Moshe	and family	391
WESTELSCHNEIDER	Natan	M	Married	Henne		391
WESTELSCHNEIDER	Henne	F	Married	Natan	and family	391
WESTELSCHNEIDER	Noach	M	Married	Fraydel		391
WESTELSCHNEIDER	Fraydel	F	Married	Noach	and family	391
WESTELSCHNEIDER	Elke	F			and family	391
WESTELSCHNEIDER	Channah	F				391
WICHTER	Yakov	M	Married	Reizel		391

		Shlomo					
WICHTER	Reizel	F	Married	Yakov Shlomo	and family		391
WICHTER	Natan	M	Married	Maleh			391
WICHTER	Maleh	F	Married	Natan	and family		391
WICHTER	Avigdor	M	Married	Tzipora			391
WICHTER	Tzipora	F	Married	Avigdor			391
WICHTER	Herschel	M	Married	Frayde			391
WICHTER	Frayde	F	Married	Herschel	and family		391
WICHTER	Moshe Shalom	M	Married	Perl			391
WICHTER	Perl	F	Married	Moshe Shalom	and family		391
WICHTER	Efraim Yehuda	M			and family		391
WICHTER	Mordechai	M			and family		391
WICHTER	Shmuel Yankel	M	Married	Leah			391
WICHTER	Leah	F	Married	Shmuel Yankel	and family		391
WASSERSTROM	Eliezer	M	Married	Breindel	and family		391
WASSERSTROM	Breindel	F	Married	Eliezer	and family		391
WASSERSTROM	Gershon	M	Married	Gitel			392
WASSERSTROM	Gitel	F	Married	Gershon	and family		392
WASSERSTROM	Gershon	M	Married	Chava			392
WASSERSTROM	Chava	F	Married	Gershon	and family		392
WASSERSTROM	Nechemia	M	Married	Tova			392
WASSERSTROM	Tova	F	Married	Nechemia	and family		392
WASSERSTROM	Sarah	F					392
WEINSTOCK	Yechezkel	M	Married	Beile			392
WEINSTOCK	Beile	F	Married	Yechezkel	and family		392
WEINRIBER	Moshe	M	Married	Mintsche Devora	Cantor		392

WEINRIBER	Mintsche Devora	F	Married	Moshe	and family	392
WEINER	Michael	M	Married	Rachel		392
WEINER	Rachel	F	Married	Michael	and family	392
WEINER	Laybish Pesach	M	Married	Frayde		392
WEINER	Freyde	F	Married	Laybish Pesach	and family	392
WEINER	Ite	F	Married	Laybish		392
	Laybish	M	Married	Ite	and family	392
WACHENHEISER	Yakov	M	Married	Temma		392
WACHENHEISER	Temma	F	Married	Yakov	and family	392
WETZER	Reuven	M	Married	Shprintze		392
WETZER	Shprintze	F	Married	Reuven	and family	392
WEINTZICHER	Yisrael	M	Married	Tova		392
WEINTZICHER	Tova	F	Married	Yisrael	and family	392
WEINTZICHER	Yehoshe	M	Married	Ite		392
WEINTZICHER	Ite	F	Married	Yehoshe	and family	392
WEINTZICHER	Gitele Male	F			and family	392
WEINTZICHER	Yosef	M	Married	Bashe		392
WEINTZICHER	Bashe	F	Married	Yosef	and family	392
WAGSHAL	Hillel	M	Married	Scheindel		392
WAGSHAL	Scheindel	F	Married	Hillel	and family	392
WEBERMAN	Herschel	M	Married	Henne		392
WEBERMAN	Henne	F	Married	Herschel		392
WEIZMAN		M			Rabbi. and family	392
WOLF	Ber	M	Married	Malka		392
WOLF	Malka	F	Married	Wolf Ber		392
WEISENBLUM	Pinchas Piniale	M	Married	Leah		392
WEISENBLUM	Leah	F	Married	Pinchas Piniale		392

WEISENBLUM	Chaim	M			and family	392
	Velvel	M			son in law of Tanchum	392
WALLACH	Laybel	M	Married	Rivka		392
WALLACH	Rivka	F	Married	Laybel		392

ז Zayin

ZILBERMAN	Yisraelke	M	Married	Sime		392
ZILBERMAN	Sime	F	Married	Yisraelke	and family	392
ZILBERMAN	Mordechai Yosef	M	Married	Tzviya		392
ZILBERMAN	Tzviya	F	Married	Mordechai Yosef	and family	392
ZILBERMAN	Bentzion	M	Married	Scheindel		392
ZILBERMAN	Scheindel	F	Married	Bentzion	and family	392
ZILBERMAN	Aharon	M	Married	Tova		392
ZILBERMAN	Tova	F	Married	Aharon	and family	392
ZILBERMAN	Yechiel Hirsch	M	Married	Mirel		392
ZILBERMAN	Mirel	F	Married	Yechiel Hirsch		392
ZILBERMAN	Perl	F				392
ZEIDENBAUM	Moshe	M	Married	Esther		392
ZEIDENBAUM	Esther	F	Married	Moshe	and family	392
ZILBERING	David	M	Married	Gitel		392
ZILBERING	Gitel	F	Married	David		392
ZILBERING	Noach	M	Married	Perl		392
ZILBERING	Perl	F	Married	Noach		392
ELIEZERS	Zlata	F	Married	Yosef Moshe	and family	392

ח Chet

CHAIM	Yisrael	M	Married	Rachel	father in law of Ayzik	392

				MIGDAL		
CHAIM	Rachel	F	Married	Chaim Yisrael	and family	392
	Channah	F	Married	David	maiden name FALIKS. Father's name Bine	392
	David	M	Married	Channah	and family	392

ט Tet

TEITELBAUM	Shlomo	M	Married	Pesse		392
TEITELBAUM	Pesse	F	Married	Shlomo	and family	392
TEITELBAUM	Yitzchak	M	Married	Leah		392
TEITELBAUM	Leah	F	Married	Yitzchak	and family	392
TEITELBAUM	Menashe	M			and family	392
	Yosef	M	Married	Leah		392
	Leah	F	Married	Yosef	& family. Maiden name FRARBERSTEIN. Father's name Aharon Leib	392
	Yankel	M	Married	Yocheved		393
	Yocheved	F	Married	Yankel		393
	Yankel	M			and family. Occupation listed as kasha maker.	393
	Yakov Mordechai	M	Married	Rivka		393
	Rivka	F	Married	Yakov Mordechai		393
	Yechiel	M	Married	Breindel	son in law of Yehoshua GREIER.	393
	Breindel	F	Married	Yechiel		393
	Yankel	M	Married	Perl	Son in law of Itsche WASSERMAN	393
	Perl	F	Married	Yankel		393

כ Kaf

KATZ	Reuven	M	Married	Yocheved		393
KATZ	Yocheved	F	Married	Reuven	and family	393

ל Lamed

LOTERSTEIN	Shmuel	M	Married		and wife	393
LOTERSTEIN	Channah	F				393
LOTERSTEIN	Noach	M	Married	Frayde		393
LOTERSTEIN	Frayde	F	Married	Noach	and family	393
LOTERSTEIN	Melech	M	Married	Bashe		393
LOTERSTEIN	Bashe	F	Married	Melech	and family	393
LOTERSTEIN	Wolf	M	Married	Feige Malka		393
LOTERSTEIN	Feige Malka	F	Married	Wolf		393
LOTERSTEIN	Yocheved	F			and daughter	393
LOTERSTEIN	Yakov	M			and family	393
LOTERSTEIN	Temma	F			and family	393
LOTERSTEIN	Mordechai	M	Married	Feige		393
LOTERSTEIN	Feige	F	Married	Mordechai	and family	393
LOTERSTEIN	Yishayahu	M	Married	Rachel		393
LOTERSTEIN	Rachel	F	Married	Yishayahu	and family	393
LOTERSTEIN	Hinde Nechama	F				393
LAMBERG	Frayde	F			and family	393
LAMBERG	Moshe	M	Married	Blima		393
LAMBERG	Blima	F	Married	Moshe	and family	393
LAMBERG	Yitzchak	M	Married	Sarah		393
LAMBERG	Sarah	F	Married	Yitzchak		393
LIEBHOBER	Simcha	M	Married	Scheindel		393
LIEBHOBER	Scheindel	F	Married	Simcha		393
LIEBHOBER	Pinchas	M	Married	Scheindel		393
LIEBHOBER	Scheindel	F	Married	Pinchas		393
LIEBHOBER	Hinde	F	Married		husband and family. Father's name Pinchas	393

LAKS	Meir	M	Married	Rachel		393
LAKS	Rachel	F	Married	Meir		393
LAKS	Yechiel Moshe	M	Married	Devora		393
LAKS	Devora	F	Married	Yechiel Moshe	and family	393
LAKS	Leybish	M	Married	Hinde		393
LAKS	Hinde	F	Married	Leybish	and family	393
LAKS	Pinchas	M	Married	Sarah		393
LAKS	Sarah	F	Married	Pinchas		393
LEDERMAN	Aharon	M			and family	393
LUSTMAN	Berl David	M	Married	Yocheved		393
LUSTMAN	Yocheved	F	Married	Berl David	and family	393
LUSTMAN	Yosef	M	Married	Rivka		393
LUSTMAN	Rivka	F	Married	Yosef	and family	393

מ Mem

MELHENDLER	Yisrael	M	Married	Rivka		393
MELHENDLER	Rivka	F	Married	Yisrael		393
MELHENDLER	Shimon	M	Married	Bracha		393
MELHENDLER	Bracha	F	Married	Shimon	and family	393
MELHENDLER	Chaim	M	Married	Ite		393
MELHENDLER	Ite	F	Married	Chaim	and family	393
MAST	Moshe	M	Married	Rodeh		393
MAST	Rodeh	F	Married	Moshe	and family	393
MAST	Mordechai	M	Married	Rivka Perl		393
MAST	Rivka Perl	F	Married	Mordechai	and family	393
MAST	Herschel	M	Married	Chaya		393
MAST	Chaya	F	Married	Herschel	and family	393
MAST	Yakov	M				393
MINDEL	Ayzik	M	Married	Chaya		393

MINDEL	Chaya	F	Married	Ayzik	and family	393
MANDELZWEIG	Lazar	M			and family	393
MANDELZWEIG	Leybish	M	Married	Channah		393
MANDELZWEIG	Channah	F	Married	Leybish	and family	393
MALTZ	Chaim	M	Married	Miriam		393
MALTZ	Miriam	F	Married	Chaim		393
MILLER	Leybish	M			and family	393
MOREL	Channah	F				394
MOREL	Chaim	M	Married	Channah	lived in Garbów (Lublin district), Poland	394
MOREL	Channah	F	Married	Chaim	and family. Lived in Garbów (Lublin district), Poland	394
MARCHEWKA	Shmuel Avraham	M	Married	Malka		394
MARCHEWKA	Malka	F	Married	Shmuel Avraham	and family	394
MOSHKOABLIT	Shimon	M	Married			394
MOSHKOABLIT		F	Married	Shimon	and family	394
	Mendel	M	Married	Dina	and family. Father's name Ayzik	394
	Dina	F	Married	Mendel Itzikels		394

נ Nun

NUDELSTEIN	Tuvia	M	Married	Sarah Esther	and son	394
NUDELSTEIN	Sarah Esther	F	Married	Tuvia	and son	394
NUDELSTEIN	Yisrael	M	Married	Devora	and family	394
NUDELSTEIN	Devora	F	Married	Yisrael		394
NIERENBERG	Yossel	M	Married	Sarah		394
NIERENBERG	Sarah	F	Married	Yossel	and family	394
NISSENBAUM	Leah	F				394

ע Ayin

ETTINGER	Mendel	M	Married	Ite		394
ETTINGER	Ite	F	Married	Mendel	and family	394
ETTINGER	Efraim Yehuda	M	Married	Elke		394
ETTINGER	Elke	F	Married	Efraim	and family	394
ETTINGER	Yoel	M	Married	Mindel		394
ETTINGER	Mindel	F	Married	Yoel	and family	394
ETTINGER	Gershon	M	Married	Ite		394
ETTINGER	Ite	F	Married	Gershon	and family	394
ETTINGER	Moshe	M			and family. Father's name Yosef	394
ETTINGER	Leybish	M	Married	Esther Malka		394
ETTINGER	Esther Malka	F	Married	Leybish	and family	394
ETTINGER	Yossel	M	Married	Scheindel	yoel	394
ETTINGER	Scheindel	F	Married	Yossel	and family	394
ETTINGER	Shifra	F				394
ETTINGER	David	M			Father's name Tuvia	394
ETTINGER		F			Father's name David Yekel	394
ETTINGER	Moshe	M	Married	Feige		394
ETTINGER	Feige	F	Married	Moshe	and family	394
ETTINGER	Leybel	M	Married	Matel		394
ETTINGER	Matel	F	Married	Leybel	and family	394
ETTINGER	Simcha	M	Married	Sarah		394
ETTINGER	Sarah	F	Married	Simcha	and family	394
ETTINGER	Sarah	F			and family	394
ETTINGER	Yosef	M	Married	Naomi		394
ETTINGER	Naomi	F	Married	Yosef	and family	394

פ Peh

FIERTOG	Pinchas Piniele	M	Married	Channah		394
FIERTOG	Channah	F	Married	Pinchas	and family	394
FIERTOG	Aharon	M	Married	Beile		394
FIERTOG	Beile	F	Married	Aharon		394
FIERTOG	Herschel	M	Married	Ite		394
FIERTOG	Ite	F	Married	Herschel	and family	394
FIERTOG	Nachum	M	Married	Ite		394
FIERTOG	Ite	F	Married	Nachum	and family	394
FIERTOG	Yisrael Itsche	M			and family	394
FREIDHEIM	Bayrech	M			and family	394
FREIDHEIM	Tzadok	M	Married	Feige		394
FREIDHEIM	Feige	F	Married	Tzadok	and family	394
FISHBEIN	Yitzchak	M	Married	Feige Leah		394
FISHBEIN	Feige Leah	F	Married	Yitzchak	and family	394
FISHBEIN	Moshe Velvel	M	Married	Tova		394
FISHBEIN	Tova	F	Married	Moshe Velvel	and family	394
FISHBEIN	Yisrael	M				394
FISHBEIN	Zishe	F	Married	Beile		394
FISHBEIN	Beile	F	Married	Zishe	and family	394
FISHBEIN	Yechiel	M	Married	Feige		394
FISHBEIN	Feige	F	Married	Yechiel	and family	394
FISHBEIN	Yechiel Motel	M	Married	Henne Leah		394
FISHBEIN	Henne Leah	F	Married	Yechiel Motel	and family	394
FISHBEIN	Sender	M	Married	Bashe		394
FISHBEIN	Bashe	F	Married	Sender		394

The Destruction and Heroism of the Town of Markuszow

FISHBEIN	Moshe	M	Married	Leah Ite		394
FISHBEIN	Leah Ite	F	Married	Moshe	and family	394
FISHBEIN	Sender	M	Married	Chaya Esther		394
FISHBEIN	Chaya Esther	F	Married	Sender	and family	394
FISHBEIN	Mordechai Gershon	M			and family	394
FISHBEIN	Shlomo Gershon	M	Married	Shifra Leah		394
FISHBEIN	Shifra Leah	F	Married	Shlomo Gershon	and family	394
FISHBEIN	Tzadok	M	Married	Feige		395
FISHBEIN	Feige	F	Married	Tzadok	and family	395
FISHBEIN	Betzalel	M	Married	Feige		395
FISHBEIN	Feige	F	Married	Betzalel	and family	395
FISHBEIN	Rivka	F			and family	395
FISHBEIN	Leah	F			In the Yizkor book the name "Dan" is written, it is unclear whether this is the name of the husband or the father.	395
FRABERSTEIN	Aharon Leib	M	Married	Male		395
FRABERSTEIN	Male	F	Married	Aharon Leib	and family	395
PELWEBER	Yisrael	M	Married	Esther		395
PELWEBER	Esther	F	Married	Yisrael	and family	395
FINGERHUT	Yankel	M	Married	Channah		395
FINGERHUT	Channah	F	Married	Yankel	and family	395
FINGERHUT	Yitzchak	M			and family. Father's name Herschel	395
FINGERHUT	Moshe	M			and family	395
FINGERHUT	Yakov	M	Married	Chaya		395
FINGERHUT	Chaya	F	Married	Yakov	and family	395

FINGERHUT	Moshe Gershon	M			and family	395
FINGERHUT	Eliezer	M			and family	395
FINGERHUT	Menashe	M		Henne		395
FINGERHUT	Henne	F	Married	Menashe	and family	395
FINGERHUT	David	M	Married	Bella		395
FINGERHUT	Bella	F	Married	David	and family	395
FINGERHUT	Yisrael	M	Married	Chaya		395
FINGERHUT	Chaya	F	Married	Yisrael	and family	395
FINGERHUT	Yitzchak	M	Married	Rivka	Tailor	395
FINGERHUT	Rivka	F	Married	Yitzchak	and family	395
FINGERHUT	Berl	M			and family	395
FIERSTEIN	Shaul	M	Married	Malka		395
FIERSTEIN	Malka	F	Married	Shaul	and family	395
PFEFFERKORN	Velvel	M	Married	Channah		395
PFEFFERKORN	Channah	F	Married	Velvel		395
FELDBERG	Avraham	M	Married	Beile Esther		395
FELDBERG	Beile Esther	F	Married	Avraham	and family	395
FLAMENBAUM	Moshe	M	Married	Shifra		395
FLAMENBAUM	Shifra	F	Married	Moshe	and family	395
FRIEDMAN	Tzadok	M	Married	Fride		395
FRIEDMAN	Fride	F	Married	Tzadok	and family	395
FRIEDMAN	Yehoshe Tuvia	M	Married	Perl Leah		395
FRIEDMAN	Perl Leah	F	Married	Yehoshe Tuvia	and family	395
FRIEDMAN	Aryeh	M	Married	Leah		395
FRIEDMAN	Leah	F	Married	Aryeh	and family	395
PELZ	Shlomo	M	Married	Sarah		395
PELZ	Sarah	F	Married	Shlomo	and family	395

PELZ	Itsche	M	Married	Pesse		395
PELZ	Pesse	F	Married	Itsche	and family	395
PELZ	Eliyahu	M	Married	Pelle		395
PELZ	Pelle	F	Married	Eliyahu	and family	395
FISCHMAN	Meir	M			and family	395
FAJGA	Binem	M				395

צ Tzadik

ZUKERMAN	Yakov Hersch	M	Married			395
ZUKERMAN	Scheindel	F	Married	Yakov Hersch	and family	395
ZUKERMAN	Yerachmiel	M	Married	Channah		395
ZUKERMAN	Channah	F	Married	Yerachmiel	and family	395
ZUKERMAN	Butsche	M	Married	Feige Male		395
ZUKERMAN	Feige Male	F	Married	Butsche	and daughter	395
ZUKERMAN	the daughter	F				395
TZIROLNIK	Moshe	M	Married	Rivka		395
TZIROLNIK	Rivka	F	Married	Moshe	and family	395
TZIROLNIK	Perl	F	Married			395
		M	Married	Perl	and family	395
TZAIG	Yankel	M				395
TZERESHNIK	Eliyahu	M	Married	Scheindel		395
TZERESHNIK	Scheindel	F	Married	Eliyahu	and family	395

ק Kof

KERSCHENBAUM	Laybel	M			and family. Known as "the Kaiser [emperor]".	395
KERSCHENBAUM	Moshe Velvel	M	Married	Leah		395
KERSCHENBAUM	Leah	F	Married	Moshe Velvel		395

Surname	Given	Sex	Status	Spouse	Notes	Page
KERSCHENBAUM	Moshe	M	Married	Channah		395
KERSCHENBAUM	Channah	F	Married	Moshe	and family	395
KERSCHENBAUM	Yakov	M			and family	395
KERSCHENBAUM	Binyamin	M	Married	Chaya		395
KERSCHENBAUM	Chaya	F	Married	Binyamin	and family	395
KERSCHENBAUM	Reuven	M	Married	Ruchama		395
KERSCHENBAUM	Ruchama	F	Married	Reuven	and family	395
KANDEL	Pinchas	M	Married	Sima		395
KANDEL	Sima	F	Married	Pinchas		395
KANDEL	Avraham	M	Married	Sheva		396
KANDEL	Sheva	F	Married	Avraham		396
KANDEL	Henech	M	Married	Chaya		396
KANDEL	Chaya	F	Married	Henech	and family	396
KANDEL	Avraham Chaim	M	Married	Leah		396
KANDEL	Leah	F	Married	Avraham Chaim	and family	396
KANDEL	Yakov	M	Married	Mindel		396
KANDEL	Mindel	F	Married	Yakov	and family	396
KANDEL	Mendel	M	Married	Chaya		396
KANDEL	Chaya	F	Married	Mendel	and family	396
KANDEL	Yisrael Ber	M	Married	Gitel		396
KANDEL	Gitel	F	Married	Yisrael Ber	and family	396
KANDEL	Pinchas	M	Married	Ghelle		396
KANDEL	Ghelle	F	Married	Pinchas	and family	396
KANDEL	Yankel	M	Married	Rivka		396
KANDEL	Rivka	F	Married	Yankel	and family	396
KANDEL	Shaul	M	Married	Tzipora		396
KANDEL	Tzipora	F	Married	Shaul	and family	396
KANDEL	Serke	F			and family	396
KESTELMAN	Feivel	M	Married	Sarah		396

KESTELMAN	Sarah	F	Married	Feivel	and family	396
KESTELMAN	Tanchum	M	Married	Chentsche		396
KESTELMAN	Chentsche	F	Married	Tanchum	and family	396
KESTELMAN	Heschel	M	Married	Channah		396
KESTELMAN	Channah	F	Married	Heschel	and family	396
KESTELMAN	Avraham	M	Married	Golde		396
KESTELMAN	Golde	F	Married	Avraham	and family	396
KESTELMAN	Motel	M	Married	Breindel		396
KESTELMAN	Breindel	F	Married	Motel	and family	396
KESTELMAN	Sarah	F	Married	Motel	and family	396
KESTELMAN	Aharon	M	Married	Scheindel Nechama		396
KESTELMAN	Scheindel Nechama	F	Married	Aharon	and family	396
KAPITKO	Yosef	M			and family	396
KAPITKO	Aharon	M			and family	396
KITENKORN	Chaim Yona	M	Married	Malka Leah		396
KITENKORN	Malka Leah	F	Married	Chaim Yona	and family	396
KOPELMAN	Yosef	M	Married	Shifra		396
KOPELMAN	Shifra	F	Married	Yosef	and family	396
KOPELMAN	Tova	F				396
KUROPATWA	Chaim Yosef	M			and family. Ritual slaughterer and examiner.	396
CAPA	Binyamin	M	Married	Zissel		396
CAPA	Zissel	F	Married	Binyamin	and family	396
CAPA	Perl Bina	F	Married	Itsche Meir		396
KRAZEH	Melech	M	Married	Rachel Leah		396
KRAZEH	Rachel Leah	F	Married	Melech	and family	396
KLEINMAN	Wolf Ber	M	Married	Malka		396

KLEINMAN	Malka	F	Married	Wolf Ber	and family	396
KLEINMAN	Yisrael	M	Married	Pesse		396
KLEINMAN	Pesse	F	Married	Yisrael	and family	396
KERSCHENBLATT	Tzipora	F	Married	Chaim	and family	396

ר Reish

RUBINSTEIN	Chaim Yehoshe	M	Married	Scheindel		396
RUBINSTEIN	Scheindel	F	Married	Chaim Yehoshe	and family	396
RUBINSTEIN	Michael	M	Married	Malka		396
RUBINSTEIN	Malka	F	Married	Michael	and family	396
RUBINSTEIN	Herschel	M	Married	Sheva		396
RUBINSTEIN	Sheva	F	Married	Herschel	and family	396
RUBINSTEIN	Shalom	M				396
RUBINSTEIN	Rivka	F			and family	396
RUBINSTEIN	Shalom Wolf	M	Married	Ite		396
RUBINSTEIN	Ite	F	Married	Shalom Wolf	and family	396
RUBINSTEIN	Natan David	M	Married	Shprintze		396
RUBINSTEIN	Shprintze	F	Married	Natan David	and family	396
RUBINSTEIN	Chaya	F			and family	396
RUBINSTEIN	Mirel	F	Married	Aharon	and children	396
ROGUSKI	Shlomo Mordechai	M	Married	Teela		396
ROGUSKI	Teela	F	Married	Shlomo Modechai		396
ROGUSKI	Yisrael Itsche	M	Married	Ite		396
ROGUSKI	Ite	F	Married	Yisrael Itsche	and family	396

ROTTENBERG	Eliyahu	M	Married	Frayde		396
ROTTENBERG	Frayde	F	Married	Eliyahu	and family	396
ROTTENBERG	Simcha	M			and family	396
ROTTENBERG	Moshe	M	Married	Reizel		396
ROTTENBERG	Reizel	F	Married	Moshe	and family	396
ROTTENBERG	Avraham	M			and family	396
ROTTENBERG	Binyamin	M			and family	396
ROTTENBERG	Avraham Chaim	M			and family	397
ROTTENBERG	Moshe	M			and family. Father's name Aharon Chaim	397
ROTTENBERG	Yitzchak	M			and family	397
ROTTENBERG	Moshe	M			and family. Father's name Eliyahu	397
ROTTENBERG	Mordechai Aytzik	M	Married	Shprintze		397
ROTTENBERG	Shprintze	F	Married	Modechai Aytzik	and family	397
ROTTENBERG	Mordechai Yosef	M			and family	397
RIK	Eliyahu	M	Married	Machle		397
ROTHSTEIN	Machle	F	Married	Eliyahu	and family	397
ROTHSTEIN	Velvel	M	Married	Channah		397
ROTHSTEIN	Channah	F	Married	Velvel		397
ROTHSTEIN	Yehoshe Mendel	M	Married	Yocheved		397
ROTHSTEIN	Yocheved	F	Married	Yehoshe Mendel		397
ROTHSTEIN	Bentzion	M	Married	Channah		397
ROTHSTEIN	Channah	F	Married	Bentzion		397
ROTHSTEIN	Devora Rivka	F				397
ROTHSTEIN	Moshe	M			and family	397

ROTHSTEIN	Reuven	M			and family	397
ROTHSTEIN	Chaim Aytzik	M			and family	397
ROTHSTEIN	Yankel	M			and family	397
ROTHSTEIN	Mordechai Meir	M	Married	Malka		397
ROTHSTEIN	Malka	F	Married	Mordechai Meir	and family	397
ROTHSTEIN	Moshe Gershon	M	Married	Hodel		397
ROTHSTEIN	Hodel	F	Married	Moshe Gershon		397
ROSENZWEIG	Yakov Hersch	M	Married	Neche		397
ROSENZWEIG	Neche	F	Married	Yakov Hersch	and family	397
ROSENBERG	Shmuel	M	Married	Devora		397
ROSENBERG	Devora	F	Married	Shmuel	and family	397
ROSENBERG	Ber	M	Married	Sarah		397
ROSENBERG	Sarah	F	Married	Ber	and family	397
ROSENBERG	Yitzchak	M	Married	Mirel		397
ROSENBERG	Mirel	F	Married	Yitzchak	and family	397
ROSENSTEIN	Sheva	F			and family	397
REIS	Sarah Rivka	F			and family	397
RIVKA	Yisrael	M			Father's name Shalom	397

ש Shin

SCHILDKRAUT	David	M	Married	Bracha		397
SCHILDKRAUT	Bracha	F	Married	David	and family	397
SCHILDKRAUT	Ite	F	Married		husband and family. Father's name David	397
SCHILDKRAUT	Simcha	M			and family	397
SCHECHTMAN	Itsche	M			and family	397

	Chasid					
SPIVAK	Noach	M	Married	Hinde		397
SPIVAK	Hinde	F	Married	Noach	and family	397
SPIVAK	Laybish	M	Married	Golde		397
SPIVAK	Golde	F	Married	Laybish	and family	397
SPIVAK	Abish	M	Married	Esther		397
SPIVAK	Esther	F	Married	Abish	and family	397
SPIVAK	Laybish	M	Married	Ite		397
SPIVAK	Ite	F	Married	Laybish	and family	397
SCHNEIDLEDER	Avraham	M	Married	Rivka Neche		397
SCHNEIDLEDER	Rivka Neche	F	Married	Avraham	and family	397
SCHNEIDLEDER	Isser	M	Married	Bashe		397
SCHNEIDLEDER	Bashe	F	Married	Isser	and family	397
SCHWARTZ	Gedalyahu	M	Married	Leah		397
SCHWARTZ	Leah	F	Married	Gedalyahu	and family	397
SCHWARTZ	Yidel	M	Married	Rivka		397
SCHWARTZ	Rivka	F	Married	Yidel	and family	397
SCHATZ	Shmuel Leib	M			and family	397
SCHEINER	Avraham	M	Married	Gitel		397
SCHEINER	Gitel	F	Married	Avraham	and family	397
SMOCHHENDLER	Naftali	M	Married	Hodel Hadassah		397
SMOCHHENDLER	Hodel Hadassah	F	Married	Naftali	and family	397
SHMUEL	Shemesh	M			and family	397
	Shemesh'te	F			the old	397
	Shifra Perl	F	Married	Fishele	her husband was a teacher	397
	Simcha	M			lived in Wola Czołnowska, Poland	397

[Page 398] Blank [Page 399]

Obituaries

Translations by Moses Milstein

[Page 400] Blank [Page 401]

Esther Borenholz

Mordecahi Borenholz

Yehuda-Ber Rosenberg

Freidl Brenner

Sureh Rosenberg

We will always mourn the martyred death of our parents Yakov Shimon and Ettl Brenner, brothers Kalman, and Israel, sister Freidl, uncle and aunt Mordechai and Esther Borenholz, father-in-law and mother-in-law Yehudah-Ber Rosenberg and wife, my brother-in-law Aharon, Chaim and Simcha and their families.

Ruchel and Dovid Brenner (Tevl)

[Page 402]

In perpetual sorrow for our parents Menachem-Mendl and Perl Bratten, sister Itta and her husband Nachum Fiertog and children, brother Mechl and his wife, Chayeh and the children, brother, Moishe, (died in Belgium during WWII), parents Yakov-Yosef and Esther-Malkeh Gothelf, grandparents Yakov and Chaneh Glasman, brothers Chaim and Yerachmiel, sisters Perl, Chaveh, Feige-Leah and Sureh Gothelf.

Ze'ev and Devorah Bratten (Gothelf)

Mendl and Perl Bratten with their two sons Mechl and Moishe and a grandchild

Nachum and Itteh Fiertog and their children

[Page 403]

Moishe Bratten, fell in Belgium as soldier in the American army.

Yakov-Yosef and Esther-Malkeh Gothelf her mother, Chaneh, their sons Chaim and Yerachmiel, the daughters Perl, Chaveh, Feige-Leah and Sureh

[Page 404]

Kalman and Malkeh Gothelf

I will never forget the memory of my parents Kalman and Malkeh Gothelf, my brothers Yakov, Yehoshua, Avrum, Itcheh, Mordechai, Yechiel and their families, my sister Chaneh with her husband Gedalyeh and family.

Chaim Gothelf

[Page 405]

Alter-Leib Kitenkorn

Temeh Wachenheiser (Kitenkorn)

May God receive the innocent blood shed of my parents Chaim-Yoineh and Malkeh-Leah Kitenkorn, father-in-law, and mother-in-law Yosef-Leib and Chayeh Grossman (from Korew), grandparents Hershl and Ruchl Kitenkorn, Itzchak-Meir and Perl-Bineh Koffeh, sister Beileh and her husband Berish Goldstein and children, Freidl and her husband Chaim Eisental and children, Temeh and husband Yakov Wachenheiser, Sheindl, Tzviah, Yehudit, my brothers: Alter-Leib, Hershl, Tzadok, and Itzchak-Meir, my uncle Binyomin Kaffeh his wife Zissl and children, my aunt Esther with husband Israel Feldweber, aunt Golde and husband Yehoshua Granatstein, aunt Sheindl and husband Hillel Wagshal and children.

Esther Grossman-Kitenkorn

Freidle's children (from Opole)

[Page 406]

> Eternal remembrance of my godly parents:
>
> Tevl (died) and Sureh-Goldeh Glazschneider:
>
> Brother Motl, his wife Esther and two children;
>
> Sister, Liebeh and her husband;
>
> Friend Chaveh Glasman who, before her death, proudly declared her Judaism;
>
> Aunt Rikl Wlastawice with five married children and twelve grandchildren;
>
> Uncle Leibish Glazschneider, aunt Chayakeh with their children and grandchildren, perished in the Warsaw ghetto;
>
> Uncle Betsalel, aunt Rivkeh and the children and grandchildren.
>
> **Gedalieh Glazschneider**

[Page 407]

> I weep for all these martyrs who were killed for their religion by the Nazi murderers and their followers.
>
>
>
> **Sureh Wasserstrom**
>
> My father Pinchas Wasserstrom (died 1917)
>
> My mother, Sureh, murdered with her children by the Nazis;
>
> Chaneh, Yerachmiel, Sheindl, Israel, Tzadok, Yosef and Binyomin Wasserstrom and families.
>
> **Shalom (Velvl) Wasserstrom**

[Page 408]

Moishe Weinriber, his wife, Minche-Dvoireh and their children, Ittah, Heneh, and Yakov

We mourn bitterly for our loved ones brutally murdered at the hands of the Nazis.

Their memory will be forever etched in our hearts.

Our father R' Moishe Weinriber, z"l, shot on the way to the train station by the execrable Nazis for refusing to go to the extermination camp; our mother Minche-Dvoireh, z"l, our sisters Itteh, Hennneh, our brother Yakov; our grandfather Beinish Handlesman, our grandmother Etil Handlesman who died; our aunt Perl-Leah, her husband Yehoshua-Tuvieh Friedman and family; our aunt Ruchl, her husband Binyomin Goldstein and their family, z"l.

Aryeh Weinriber, Sureh Fianka (Weinriber) Yosef Weinriber

[Page 409]

Lipeh Weinriber, his wife Geyleh and children Yosl, Itzchak-Isaac, Tobeh-Reizl, Shaul-Zelig and Chayeh-Tilleh

May the Lord avenge the blood of our loved ones, children and infants, savagely killed by the Nazis.

Their image will forever stand before our eyes. Our brother Lipeh Weinriber, z"l, his wife Geyleh and their sons Yosl, Itzchak-Isaac, their daughter Tobeh-Reizl, their son Shaul-Zelig, and daughter Chayeh.

Aryeh Weinriber, Sureh Fianka (Weinriber) Yosef Weinriber

[Page 410]

Hershl and Hentsheh Weberman

With pain and sorrow we remember our unforgettable parents, Aharon-Hersh and Hentsheh Weberman, killed by the Nazi murderers, our sister Chayeh-Sureh and her husband Yosef Glasman and children Chaveh and Yerachmiel—burned alive by the German barbarians.

Beirech and Itteh Weberman (Paris)

[Page 411]

Freideh Goldwasser

In eternal memory our mother, Freideh Goldwasser.

We will always remember our fallen brother, Chaim-Mendl Goldwasser, and his wife, Frumet.

Sister Itteh and Beirech Weberman, brother Shaul Goldwasser, wife and children (Paris)

[Page 412]

Eliezer and Breindl Wasserstrom

In memory of our parents Eliezer and Breindl Wasserstrom; brother Nechemia, his wife Tobeh and children; sister Miriam and husband, Aharon Weinriber and Malkeh and her husband Shaul Firestein.

Shifra Loterstein, Yakov Wasserstrom

Aharon and Miriam Weinriber

Nechemia and Tova Wasserstrom, Shaul and Malkeh Firestein

[Page 413]

Shimon and Dina Eidelstein

In memory of our murdered parents Shimon and Dina Eidelstein; sister Rivkeh and her husband Yudl Schwartz and their children: Gershon, Shaul, Dvoireh, Mechl, and Itteh; sister Chaveh and her husband and three children: the oldest—Dvoireleh and her husband Shmuel Rosenberg and child; sister Sureleh and her husband Simcheh Ettinger and their two sons Dovid'che and Shmuel and little daughter Blimeleh. Brother Moishe-Yankl with his wife and child; brother Yosef Hertz and his wife and children, Dovid and Malkeh; brother Israel and his wife and son. The families: Geddalieh Schwartz, his wife and children Tobah'le and Miriam; Yosef Schwartz and his wife and two children; Yocheved Loterstein and her daughter Miriam; Dvoireh and her husband Yechiel-Moishe Laks and their son Veveh; Moishe Schwartz and his wife and children; Berish Schwartz, Itteh and her husband Mendl Ettinger and two children; Hentche and her husband Nachum Kestelman and their two children; Eliezer Eidelstein, his wife, and son Avrumtche, Henich and Aharon and their wives and children; Freidl Goldwasser, and her son Chaim-Mendl and wife; Chaim Eidelstein and his wife two daughters and one son.

Chayeh Loterstein-Herz
(Argentina)

Yudl and Rivkeh Schwartz and their children:
Gershon, Shaul, Dvoireh, Mechl and Itteh

[Page 414]

I will never forget the noble memory of the Nazi victims:

My mother Chaneh Loterstein (Ettinger),

Oldest sister Esther-Laneh and husband Shmelke Fenshmid,

Their daughters Peseh and Freideh, their sons Mordechai and Moishe,

Second sister Rivkeh and husband Chaim-Mendl, their sons Mattis and Tuvieh,

Sister-in-law Yocheved and her daughter Miriam (Manyeleh);

Uncle Tuvieh Nudelstein, aunt Sureh-Esther and their sons Israel and Hershl;

Uncle Pinchas Kandel and aunt Sima;

Aunt Leah and uncle Aryeh and their children;

Uncle Moishe Ettinger and family;

Uncle Leibl Ettinger and family;

Uncle Yosl Ettinger, aunt Nemi and their children, Sureh, Moishe, Leibl, Laizer;

Aunt Hindeh-Nechama (Loterstein), son Yankl, daughters Sureh and Malkeh;

Cousin Ber Loterstein and wife;

Cousin Ruchl and husband Hersh-Leib Lamberg

Itteh Loterstein (Kerschenblatt), Argentina

[Page 415]

Golde Granatstein (Capa) with daughter Sureleh

My father R' Itcheh Meir, z"l, my mother Perl Bineh, my brother Yerachmiel-Binyomin Capa, his wife Zissl and children;

My sister Golde and her husband Yehoshua Granatstein and children; my sister Sheindl and her husband Hillel and Wegshol; ,p> My sister Esther and her children.

**Your son and your brother will always remember
Moshe Nachshon (Capa)**

My father R' Elchanan Garfinkle, my mother Chayeh-Ruchl, my brother Tzadok, his wife Malkeh and children Zalman, My sister Sureh and her husband Ruben, Fishman and his son Zalman, my sister Yocheved and her husband Shloime Reisfeld.

May they always be remembered!

Your daughter and your sister Rivkeh Nachshon (Garfinkle)

[Page 416]

Motl and Eliyahu Pelz and their two sisters

Velvl and Feige-Malkeh

In memorium: my father Shloime and my mother Sureh Pelz, my sisters Feige-Malkeh and her husband Ze'ev Loterstein, Dvoireh, and Esther. My brother Eliyahu and wife Feige and their son Moishe, my brother Shmuel—the holy and pure martyrs were killed on the road to Belzec by savage murderers October 1942.

I will carry their precious memory with me until my dying day.

To the perpetual memory of my parents Shloime and Sureh Pelz, my brothers Eliyahu, his wife Feige and son Moishe; Mordechai (fell with the partisans); Shmuel. Sisters: Feige-Malkeh and husband Ze'ev Loterstein, Dvoireh Pelz; Esther Pelz.

Moishe Pelz

[Page 417]

Itzchak Kerschenblatt z"l

To the eternal memory of the martyrs—our father: Itzchak Kerschenblatt, mother Beile-Tzirl Kerschenblatt, brother Hersh-Mechl and his family.

Moishe Kerschenblatt
Mordechai ("Martchinek") Kerschenblatt
(Paris)

[Page 418]

Yoineh and Tobeh Kopelman

May they rest in peace the martyrs Yoineh and Feige-Tobeh Kopelman (my parents), my brother Leizer Mandelzweig; his wife Miriam and children; brother Yosef Kopelman, his wife Shifreh and children; sister Dina and husband Itcheh, sister Chayeh and husband Moishe Sheiner, sister Golde and husband Abraham Kestelman and their children.

Hershl Kopelman

May the victims of German murder rest in peace.

My parents Mendl and Eidl-Blimeh Goldstein; my sister Chaveh and husband Yosl Goldiner.

My brothers: Chaim (shoichet) Goldstein and wife Tzirl and childen; Leibl and his wife Ettl Goldstein and children; Dan and wife and children

Kopelman Tcharne

[Page 419]

I will mourn them forever:

My father Shalom Rubinstein, Ben Heshl fell on the way in the first transport to Belzec in his 76th year; my mother Sureh-Beile, died in the year 1941, my sister Chayeh wife of Yekil Rubinstein and her 5 children; (Her husband Yekil Rubinstein died in 1937; my sister Chayeh wife of Zisheh Greenwald and her 4 children (her husband Zisheh Greenwald died in 1931); my brother Menachem Ben Shalom Rubinstein, age 42, his wife Golde and 3 children; my first wife Mirl-Dina, my daughter, age 8, and my son Zvi age 5.

Aharon Rubinstein

[Page 420]

With great sorrow and grief we mourn our parents killed by the Nazis, may their names be erased.

Warshenbroit Simche-Dovid; Chayeh-Tobeh; Perl; Yakov and his wife; Freidl, Itzchak, Chaneh, Avrum.

Tzipora Weinriber (Warshenbroit), Aryeh Weinriber

Malkeh Kerschenblatt

Sureh Zilbering, her child, Chantche's daughter and three girlfriends

To the blessed memory of my parents Chaim and Tzipeh Kerschenblatt, sisters: Chantche and her husband Itzchak Geyer and children; Sureh and husband Dovid Zilbering and children; Freide with her husband Eliyahu Rotenberg and children; Malkeh and husband Eliyahu Rik and children; the brothers Yechiel-Isaac Kerschenblatt with his wife and five children; Avigdor Kerschenblatt.

Esther Zilbering (Kerschenblatt)

[Page 421]

In perpetual sorrow for our deceased parents—Shloime Gershon and Shifra-Leah Fishbein, sister Chayeh and husband Binyomin Kerschenblat; brother Israel Fishbein and Itzchak.

Dvoireh Chapnik (Fishbein)

Shloime Gershon and Shifra-Leah Fishbein, their children Chayeh and Itzchak, and grandchild

Yizkor:

My father: Leibish Laks, mother: Hindeh Laks; brother: Ze'ev (Vevey) Laks; brother Noach Laks; grandfather Meir Laks; grandmother Ruchl Laks; grandfather Chaim Zilberman; grandmother Dvoireh Zilberman; uncle Yechiel-Moishe Laks and family; Itzchak Rosenberg and family; Yosl Kopleman and family, Gershon Ettinger and family; Pinchas Laks, his wife Sureh; Shmuel Laks, his wife Leah and children; Meir Zilberman and family; Shimon Kirshenboim and family; Yerachmiel Zukerman and family; Tzirl Zilberman, Shmuel Zilberman.

Shmuel Laks

[Page 422]

Chaim-Leib Fishbein

Itzchak and Feige-Leah Fishbein, their children Moishe-Velvl Issar and two daughters Ruchl and Dina

Eternal shame for the murderers of my unforgettable parents, Itzchak and Feige-Leah Fishbein; brother Moishe-Velvl, his wife Tobeh and son Isser; brothers Chaim-Leib and Isser; sisters Ruchl and Dina.

Shifra Mardiks

With pain and sorrow I remember those murdered by the Nazis—the godly parents Avrum-Chaim and Ruchl-Leah Kandel, my brother Yakov, his wife Mindl and children, my sisters Necheh, Tzipora, and Tobeh; my brothers Israel-Zalman and Mordechai.

Itteh Frieder (Kandel)

Brother Yakov and Mindl Kandel and their children, brother and sister Mordechai and Necheh Kandel

[Page 423]

Isser and Chaneh Rosenberg, Yakov Gothelf

Eternal glory to the memory of my parents Aharon-Leib and Golde Gothelf, brother Yakov, sister Chaneh and her husband Isser Rosenberg and brother Yerocham (all four fell as partisans).

Reich (Gothelf) Dina

To the noble memory of our brothers and uncles Yudl, Gedalieh, Yosl, Moishe with their wives and children; brother Berish, our sister and aunts Dvoireh Laks, Itteh Ettinger, and Hentsche Kastleman and their husbands and children; our mother and sister Yocheved Loterstein, Miriam Loterstein.

**Gershon Schwartz and Michal Loterstein
(Paris)**

[Page 424]

We will never forget our parents Israel and Sima Zilberman; brothers Shimon, Yehoshua, Avraham, Hersh, Berish, Henech, and sister Feige.

Fradl Ushenker (Zilberman)
Rivkeh Kestelbrenner (Zilberman)

I mourn the tragic death of my mother Tcharneh Kestelbrenner, my sister Manye and family.

Eisenberg (Kestelbrenner) Tziporah

Malkeh Gothelf and her daughter

In deep sorrow I remember my blessed parents—Berish and Malkeh Gothelf.

Zvi Gothelf

I honor the memory of my parents Aharon and Golde, sister Ruchl-Leah, and her husband Melech Rosen and their little daughter Chaneleh.

Goldman Yehoshua-Berish

[Page 425]

To the memory of my mother, my wife who was devoted to her children in life and in death at the hands of the Nazis—Beile Hoffeld age 38, hy"d, and to the memory of the twins Yocheved and Nechama, age 10.

Israel and Yakov Hoffeld

Captain A. Glazschneider

Yizkor!

Our father Noach Glazschneider, sister Yachtche and her husband Mordechai Rik and children, our son captain Aryeh Glazschneider, who fell in the liberation war of the state of Israel.

In loving memory
Chaim and Dvoireh Glazschneider

Yizkor!

My father Noach Glazschneider, died in Israel in 1954, our brothers Israel- Moishe Halberstein and his wife Chaneh-Feige, my sister Yachtche and her husband Mordechai Rik and children.

Yahalom David

I will forever remember my deceased parents—Mordechai and Ruchl Westelschneider, my sisters: Malkeh, Rivkeh, Dvoireh, Feige, Perl, Gnendl, and brothers Hershl and Yudl.

Nathan Westelschneider

[Page 426]

I will always remember you!

My husband Israel Fishbein, my father Aharon-Yosef Nirenberg, my mother Sureh, my sister Chaneh and her husband Moishe Kerschenblatt and children, my brother Moishe Nirenberg.

Eidl Fishbein (Nirenberg)

To the memory of my parents—Nathan and Tzlube-Itteh Zeidenberg, my grandfather Sender Fishbein, my uncles Yechiel, Betsalel, Tzadok, and Shmuel with their families, my aunt Chayeh and her husband Zvi Must; Sheindl and her husband Eliyahu Tzereshnik and children.

Malkeh Skornik

I honor the memory of my brothers: Aharon-Leib Fraberstein, his wife Maleh and children; Nachum Fraberstein and family, Shalom Fraberstein and family.

Freda Stein

My little sister

In eternal memory

In memory of our beloved mother Rivkeh Fishbein, our sister Chaveh, our brothers Dovid and Nechemieh, z"l, who died at the hands of the Germans.

Esther and Yakov Fishbein

[Page 427]

In sorrow I remember the martyr's death of my father, Berish Schwartz, my aunt, the wife of Gershon Scwartz, cousin Israel Eidelstein and his wife and children (transported by the Germans from Paris to Poland and killed there); my grandfather Shloime Schwartz.

Do not forget, do not forgive!

Michal Schwartz

In perpetual sorrow for my parents—Pinchas and Gehle Kandel, brother Israel-Ber and his wife Gitl and 5 children, my sister Tseitl and her husband Kalman Gothelf and three children, brother Yakov and his wife and child, brother Avraham, his wife Sheva and child.

Leibish Kandel

Binyomen and Zissl Capa

My father Yerachmiel-Binyomin, my mother, Zissl. My sisters Mindl, Ruchl, Chaneleh, my brother Israel, all killed at the hands of the Nazis.

I will never forget you!

Yakov Capa

[Page 428]

Dvoireh (Dora) Pelz

We mourn the sudden death of Dvoireh Pelz, the life companion of our board member, Moishe Pelz, who was taken from us forever at the tender age of 32 on the 24th of October, 1955.

Organization of former Markuszowers in Israel

[Page 429]

Markuszowers in Israel

[Page 430]

Board of Markuszow *landsleit*[1] in Israel

(From right to left): Moishe Pelz, Dovid Brenner, Sholem Wasserstrom, Moishe Nachshon (Capa), Hershl Kopelman, Aryeh Weinriber, Ze'ev Bratten

[Page 431]

Very few Jews managed to get to Eretz-Israel in the period between the two world wars. But those who did succeed in coming to the land of our fathers, tried with all their strength, as much as the conditions permitted, to maintain close contact among themselves, and in that way, to remain true to the family atmosphere of the shtetl. The connection was also expressed in reciprocal brotherly aid for those who needed it. There was not a simcha in which a Markuszower in Israel did not invite all his fellow citizens to share in the joy. As individuals and as a group, we all felt close like a family, and did not want to become estranged.

This family framework became too small, however, after the arrival of the survivors of Hitler's hell. The need for an organization was felt because every newcomer presented a problem: how to help him get settled, get a loan, find a place to live, work, and all the rest that a new immigrant requires. So they got down to really talking about creating an organization offering financial aid. But it would take time to realize these tasks. And help was needed immediately. In 1946 a partisan couple from the shtetl arrived and we considered it our holy duty to help them with both the wedding, and with getting them settled into the new land. Good intentions, love of one's fellow man and Markuszow good-heartedness from individuals brought help and encouragement to our *olim*[2]. They were given loans for constructive goals, or given practical suggestions as to how to make their first steps, or given the address of someone from the town, our own people with whom they could rejoice after surviving such horrible years of separation, hope and yearning.

The actual organization of Markuszow *landsleit* in the state of Israel dates from winter 1951, when we got together in the home of

[Page 432]

Markuszowers in Israel at a Yizkor evening

[Page 433]

Mr. Hershl Kopelman in Tel Aviv. We immediately began to talk about concrete matters like: helping the *olim*, memorial services, yizkor book, and connections overseas.

Now, after five years of organizational activity, we can state that all four of our goals were fulfilled.

More than one Markuszower in Israel, of the fifty, could tell of the warmth and help he received from the moment he stepped over the threshold of the state and sought out a landsman. With no relief fund, without special contacts, and limited opportunities the organization tried to deliver a helping hand wherever there was a need. Every year since 1951, on *Isru Chag Pesach*,[3] a memorial service took place in which all the Markuszowers in Israel participated. On these impressive occasions, the unforgettable sorrow for the lives of our loved ones that were cut down is expressed. These Yizkor evenings also brought the opportunity for people to get together and share memories, talk about the present, and form plans for the future.

There was a feeling, however, that memorial service alone would not fulfill the debt of perpetuating their memory, if we did not create a spiritual memorial in the form of a yizkor book. That idea was circulated–and from the beginning of 1953 all the effort and exertion of the board was directed to creating the yizkor book, the true monument to Jewish Markuszow.

The entire organization was converted to a book committee that, together with the editor, had the laborious responsibility to put together material for the book. Three years of constant financial, moral, and physical efforts gave results in the form of the present yizkor book.

Work on this book gave us the opportunity to be in constant contact with our *landsleit* in both Americas, France and Australia. The first financial help for the yizkor book from Markuszowers in Argentina gave us in Israel a push toward wide-ranging efforts to find the necessary sums for such an undertaking.

The issuing of the book did not mean the end of the committee's task. There was a project to publish the book in Hebrew, maintain the beautiful tradition of annual memorial services, caring for and helping the *landsleit* in need, and continuing contact with Markuszowers through the world.

[Page 434]

Markuszowers in Argentina

Translator's Footnotes:

1. People from the same town
2. An immigrant to Israel is called an "*oleh*," one who has "ascended."
3. Ritual on the day after Passover

NAME INDEX

A

Akerman, 78, 80
Aleph, 207
Angluster, 273
Asch, 54, 55, 56, 57, 58, 60
Avram-Ber, 31
Axmann, 191

B

Bachar, 106
Baker, 223
Balagoleh, 39
Banaszek, 179, 180, 204
Baranowski, 210, 211, 270
Barenholtz, 274
Bauman, 175, 273
Beck, 195
Beigelman, 82, 84, 253, 274
Ben-Yekutiel, 8
Berenbaum, 273
Bereza, 142, 145
Bishing, 9
Bleichman, 206, 208
Bleiweiss, 180, 274
Bochan, 141
Boczkowski, 25
Bolek, 170, 172, 207
Borenholz, 299
Bratten, 74, 85, 274, 299, 300, 322
Breinsky, 61, 112, 113, 121, 261, 274
Brenner, 74, 77, 81, 85, 87, 95, 299, 322
Brikenbau, 250
Bronska, 153, 155
Burek, 221, 233, 235, 245
Burka, 234
Burstin, 79

C

Capa, 26, 44, 57, 66, 71, 72, 91, 111, 112, 173, 193, 218, 221, 226, 293, 319, 322
Chaim, 282, 283
Chapnik, 313
Charney, 211
Chil, 207, 208, 209, 210, 211
Cohen, 106, 109

Czebicki, 10
Czepa, 251

D

Deckermacher, 278
Dina, 315
Dinar, 106
Drobner, 209
Drozd, 231, 232, 237, 239, 241, 243, 244
Dudek, 195, 197, 200, 201, 202, 267
Dzedzits, 180

E

Edelstein, 49, 70, 74, 75
Eidelstein, 25, 49, 61, 64, 67, 70, 74, 75, 86, 114, 116, 117, 118, 119, 273, 303, 319
Eisenberg, 163, 225, 273, 316
Eisental, 302
Eliezers, 282
Eliyahi, 28
Ettinger, 30, 38, 50, 58, 59, 70, 75, 76, 78, 102, 103, 116, 121, 127, 141, 154, 156, 161, 170, 195, 197, 200, 201, 204, 209, 223, 226, 227, 233, 249, 253, 264, 267, 287, 308, 309, 313, 315

F

Fajga, 291
Faliks, 283
Fedberg, 82
Feix, 191, 192
Feldberg, 290
Feldweber, 302
Fenshmid, 309
Fianka, 305
Fierstein, 68, 290, 307
Fiertog, 225, 240, 288, 299
Filipek, 233, 235, 236
Fingerhut, 22, 70, 289, 290
Finkelstein, 250
Fishbein, 69, 78, 96, 121, 137, 138, 141, 147, 154, 167, 168, 173, 174, 182, 183, 184, 186, 188, 197, 199, 200, 223, 226, 261, 264, 265, 288, 289, 313, 314, 318
Fishman, 11, 86, 87, 309
Flamenbaum, 290

Fraberstein, 283, 289, 318
Franek, 172, 270
Freidheim, 288
Frieder, 314
Friedmacher, 61
Friedman, 72, 81, 150, 183, 290, 304

G

Garfinkle, 193, 194, 309
Gatz, 261, 262, 264
Geier, 276, 312
Gerondi, 106
Glasman, 74, 80, 81, 82, 222, 225, 226, 275, 299, 303, 305
Glazschneider, 29, 61, 74, 75, 85, 86, 87, 275, 276, 303, 317
Glozsheiner, 193
Gnieczak, 227
Goldberg, 61, 112, 113, 115, 227
Goldiner, 278, 311
Goldman, 277, 316
Goldschlager, 74, 75, 131, 249, 274, 276
Goldstein, 50, 51, 87, 104, 125, 224, 277, 302, 304, 311
Goldwasser, 50, 57, 59, 60, 74, 75, 78, 124, 147, 149, 150, 174, 175, 184, 223, 250, 277, 278, 306, 308
Gothelf, 49, 77, 78, 81, 96, 121, 122, 152, 153, 154, 158, 159, 196, 197, 199, 200, 261, 264, 276, 277, 299, 300, 301, 315, 316, 319
Granastein, 302, 309
Greenboim, 66, 67
Greenwald, 312
Greier, 254, 277, 283
Grinspan, 142, 207, 209
Grivald, 277
Grob, 79
Grossman, 65, 67, 221, 226, 230, 234, 242, 243, 244
Grushchanski, 203
Grzegorz, 211
Gutanow, 134, 158, 174, 185, 225, 226, 235, 247, 263

H

Halbershtat, 56
Halberstein, 317
Handlesman, 304
Hanneman, 209
Hendler, 279

Herschenhorn, 279
Hoffeld, 278, 317
Hoffman, 278
Holtzhendler, 77, 278
Holtzman, 279
Huberman, 189, 278

I

Iberkleid, 121, 180, 219, 226, 272, 273
Idlish, 106, 107
Inzsh, 79

J

Jabotinsky, 65, 67, 68, 69, 70, 123
Janowski, 171
Jastkow, 133, 135, 138, 151, 152, 153, 164, 165, 166, 174, 177, 186

K

Kalfak, 268
Kaller, 14, 15, 35
Kandel, 32, 61, 85, 121, 130, 185, 261, 299, 309, 314, 319
Kapitko, 38, 293
Karliner, 86
Kastleman, 315
Katz, 283
Kenner, 79
Kerschenbaum, 191, 192, 291, 292
Kerschenblatt, 59, 74, 86, 87, 121, 128, 130, 155, 163, 168, 197, 200, 205, 213, 26, 294, 309, 311, 312, 3181
Kesselbrenner, 218, 316
Kestelman, 121, 155, 261, 292, 293, 308, 311
Kirshenboim, 313
Kitenkorn, 63, 102, 242, 293, 302
Kleinman, 293, 294
Knobowitz, 79
Koganovitch, 205
Kolka, 269
Kolkhoz, 221
Kook, 67, 107
Kopelman, 311, 293, 313, 322, 323
Kozak, 121, 128, 131, 152, 175, 179, 204, 260
Krazeh, 293
Kuropatwa, 223, 293

L

Laks, 61, 64, 68, 69, 102, 103, 121, 141, 154, 155, 161, 168, 170, 195, 197, 199, 200, 201, 203, 204, 209, 244, 248, 253, 285, 308, 313, 315
Lamberg, 284, 309
Laterman, 261
Lederman, 285
Lehrer, 31
Lerman, 75, 76
Letterstein, 151
Levi, 76
Liebhober, 50, 53, 61, 63, 64, 66, 67, 102, 112, 113, 114, 116, 223, 284
Lomberg, 86, 87
Loterstein, 54, 55, 58, 59, 60, 86, 87, 111, 121, 146, 153, 196, 200, 225, 226, 227, 233, 247, 258, 259, 284, 307, 308, 309, 310, 315
Loterstein-Herz, 308
Lustman, 285

M

Machornik, 78
Mahler, 6, 9, 10
Maidener, 215
Maltz, 286
Mandelzweig, 286, 310
Mapai, 67, 286
Marchewka, 61, 112
Mardiks, 314
Margalit, 106
Markuszow, 108
Markuszower, 109
Martchinek, 121, 168, 200, 213, 214, 261
Mast, 77, 225, 285
Mastboim, 75
Mayer, 47
Melhendler, 121, 158, 285
Mietek, 207, 211
Migdal, 102, 144, 282
Miller, 79, 286
Mindel, 285, 286
Mittleman, 76, 79
Moczer, 170
Morawski, 209
Morel, 49, 102, 121, 139, 168, 175, 209, 234, 266, 286
Moshkoablit, 286
Mousssafia, 106
Must, 318

Myetek, 170

N

Nachshon, 44, 57, 66, 91, 111, 112, 173, 193, 218, 221, 322
Nadelman, 78
Nechami, 106
Nepert, 251
Nierenberg, 74, 174, 286, 318
Nissenbaum, 286
Nudelstein, 286, 309

O

Opolski, 76, 151
Oshinska, 273

P

Peel, 69, 70
Pelweber, 289
Pelz, 121, 138, 143, 144, 152, 155, 163, 168, 184, 244, 253, 264, 266, 271, 290, 291, 310, 320, 322
Pfefferkorn, 290
Pietrak, 226
Pietrowizer, 25
Plashower, 160
Plashowitzer, 152, 266
Platter, 195, 207
Prachi, 67

R

Rapaport, 26
Rasset, 213
Reich, 79, 122, 261
Reinman, 67
Reis, 296
Reisfeld, 309
Rik, 295, 312, 217
Rivka, 296
Rodak, 177
Roguski, 61, 64, 66, 87, 114, 116, 117, 225, 294
Roizes, 32
Rola-Zymierski, 170, 209, 212, 270
Rosen, 316
Rosenberg, 17, 56, 61, 67, 121, 135, 140, 160, 177, 233, 244, 255, 261, 262, 264, 296, 299, 308, 313, 315
Rosenblit, 145
Rosenstein, 121, 160, 296

Rosenzweig, 158, 296
Rottenberg, 84, 295, 312
Rothstein, 81, 104, 186, 295, 296
Rubinstein, 53, 69, 121, 132, 138, 141, 142, 154, 155, 159, 163, 168, 184, 195, 197, 204, 208, 209, 226, 227, 233, 240, 241, 244, 249, 261, 264, 294, 312

S

Saba, 176, 177, 178, 180, 181
Sabinski, 28
Samokleski, 171
Sandberg, 75, 76
Schatz, 297
Schechtman, 296
Scheiner, 297
Schildkraut, 76, 103, 249, 296
Schneider, 27
Schneidleder, 225, 297
Schtrassen, 250
Schwartz, 49, 53, 56, 59, 61, 67, 69, 233, 258, 261, 297, 308, 315, 319
Shalom, 35
Sheinberg, 56, 57
Sheiner, 311
Shikora, 228, 229, 238, 242, 244, 245
Shoichet, 20, 223, 224
Shomen, 108
Shpender, 106
Shustak, 39
Sikorski, 220
Shornik, 318
Smolak, 153, 260
Sobinski, 28
Soifer, 38, 110
Spichalski, 209
Spivak, 297
Stachura, 182
Stankewicz, 25
Stein, 318
Steinmetz, 79
Stempicki, 25
Stengl, 206
Stockfish, 1, 80

T

Tahori, 67
Tarchitz, 74, 76, 86
Tcharne, 311
Teitelbaum, 96, 121, 138, 159, 233, 261, 283

Tolek, 131, 132, 133, 134, 135, 136, 259, 260, 261, 267
Toliek, 205, 206, 207
Trapper, 266
Trombicka, 231
Tzaig, 291
Tzereshnik, 291, 318
Tzirolnik, 291

U

Ushenker, 316

W

Wachenheiser, 87, 281
Wagshal, 281, 302
Wallach, 92, 282
Warrenheiser, 224
Warshenbroit, 312
Wartacz, 178, 179, 225, 235, 245
Wasilewka, 268
Wasilewska, 268, 270
Wasserman, 279, 283
Wasserstrom, 13, 40, 58, 60, 97, 98, 101, 107, 109, 111, 117, 280, 303, 307, 322
Wassertreger, 33, 34
Weberman, 59, 281, 305, 306
Weiner, 49, 184, 223, 226, 240, 281
Weinrib, 305, 307, 312
Weinriber, 49, 51, 61, 65, 102, 104, 114, 116, 185, 223, 225, 253, 280, 281, 304, 305, 312, 322
Weinstock, 280
Weintzicher, 281
Weisenblum, 281, 282
Weissenberg, 54, 55
Weizman, 53, 281
Westelschneider, 51, 121, 164, 165, 279, 317
Wetzer, 281
Wichter, 49, 74, 77, 78, 79, 81, 82, 83, 86, 102, 121, 152, 279, 280
Wiejek, 239, 240, 241, 242
Wiener, 104, 147
Wlastawice, 303
Wohlstein, 209
Woitek, 197, 199, 200
Wolf, 281

Y

Yahalom, 317

Yaari, 107
Yeager, 136, 140, 141, 169, 195, 197, 200, 207, 208, 261, 262, 264
Yellin, 72
Yuri, 106

Z

Zamoyski, 161
Zang, 191
Zeidenberg, 318
Zelichower, 52, 53
Zemel, 191
Zemsto, 170, 172, 210
Zeznik, 180, 181
Zgodzinski, 151
Zilbering, 215, 282, 312
Zilberman, 145, 218, 220, 265, 282, 313, 316
Zimmerman, 61
Zukerman, 254, 256, 291, 313

www.ingramcontent.com/pod-product-compliance
Lightning Source LLC
Chambersburg PA
CBHW082004150426
42814CB00005BA/224